The
Federalist Papers

The
Federalist Papers

In Modern Language
Indexed for Today's Political Issues

Edited by
Mary E. Webster

Merril Press
BELLEVUE, WASHINGTON

The Federalist Papers

First Edition
Published by Merril Press

Typeset in Times New Roman. Cover design by Northwoods Studio.

Published by Merril Press, P.O. Box 1682, Bellevue, Washington 98009. Additional copies of this book may be ordered from Merril Press at $19.95 each. Phone 425-454-7009.

LIBRARY OF CONGRESS CATALOGING-IN-PUBLICATION DATA

Federalist.
    The Federalist papers : in modern language indexed for today's political issues / edited by Mary E. Webster. — 1st ed.
        p.   cm.
    Includes bibliographical references and index.
    ISBN 0-936783-21-4
    1. Constitutional history—United States—Sources. I. Webster, Mary E.   II. Title.
KF4515.F4   1999c
342.73'029—dc21   99-21880
                                                                CIP

PRINTED IN THE UNITED STATES OF AMERICA

Table of Contents

To my dear friend,
Zak Alder
and to the memory of my parents
Katherine and Gordon Webster

Editor's Preface

The *Federalist Papers* are, as expert Clinton Rossiter once said, "the most important work in political science that has ever been written, or is likely ever to be written, in the United States." Their impact on American life is incalculable.

But in recent years the *Federalist Papers* have increasingly become a study for specialists: historians, legislators and jurists. Unfortunately, few students emerging from modern universities have read them. The average newspaper reader trying to plow through the 85 essays grows impatient with the convoluted 18th-century sentences and elegant Enlightenment flourishes. Yet in these pages lie answers to basic questions we ask about our government every day. Thus, it is high time that the language of these priceless documents was brought up to date.

It is in that spirit that I have edited the *Federalist Papers* into modern language and indexed them to today's political issues. I am not a specialist in history or law, but a writer fascinated by the power of these founding documents and their continued relevance to our daily lives. Aside from credits as a novelist, I found myself with a unique advantage to undertake this task: I am a trained and experienced interpreter for the deaf, certified in American Sign Language. That turned out to be the best preparation to convery simply and exactly what the authors, Alexander Hamilton, James Madison, and John Jay, actually said. I have no political or social axe to grind, no "new reading" of the Papers to offer, and no agenda to fulfill. My intent is simply and purely to translate the Federalist Papers into modern language, preserving the meaning as closely as possible. I am probably the quintessential citizen editor.

This work is not intended as a substitute for reading the originals. It is intended to open the *Federalist Papers* to all reading people today, and to inspire readers to go back to the originals to enjoy them as first written.

The *Papers* were written to encourage ratification of the new United States Constitution to replace the Articles of Confederation. They appeared in New York newpapers between the end of the Constitutional Convention in September, 1787, and New York's vote to ratify the Constitution the following spring. Any encyclopedia can provide a description of what happened there and the details of how the *Papers* came to be written. Scholarly treatises on the text, meanings, problems and misinterpretations are abundant.

To make the *Papers* easier to read, I've broken up long sentences and long paragraphs (numbering the original paragraphs), substituted words more commonly used today, titled each *Paper*, and subtitled each original paragraph. The titles and subtitles create an outline of the *Papers*.

The Constitutional index shows which *Paper* number discusses which clauses within the Constitution.

The subject index gives the *Paper* number and paragraph number of the references (rather than page number). Therefore, any edition of the *Federalist Papers* can be used to look up all references cited in this edition.

The glossary will be a big help for anyone reading an earlier edition of the *Federalist Papers*. And the bibliography features early discussions of the Constitution.

Mary E. Webster
Arlington, Washington

Editor's Notes

- Subheading numbers refer to actual paragraphs within original documents.
- *Italics* and CAPITALIZATIONS same as in the original text.
- Footnotes same as in original text.
- **Bold** added by editor.
- [Bracketed] text added by editor.
- When the word "state" refers to a State within the United States rather than a nation state, I've capitalized the word.
- When the word "constitution" refers to the United States Constitution rather than constitutions generally, I've capitalized the word.
- The phrase, "Constitutional Convention," is capitalized when referring to the convention held in the summer of 1787 that drafted the Constitution.

The Constitution of the United States of America
September 17, 1787

We, the people of the United States, in Order to form a more perfect Union, establish Justice, insure domestic Tranquility, provide for the common defence, promote the general Welfare, and secure the Blessings of Liberty to ourselves and our Posterity, do ordain and establish this

Constitution for the United States of America.

Article One

SECTION 1. All legislative Powers herein granted shall be vested in a Congress of the United States, which shall consist of a Senate and House of Representatives.

5 　SECTION 2. The **House of Representatives** shall be composed of Members chosen every **second Year** by the People of the several States, and the Electors in each State shall have the Qualifications requisite for Electors of the most numerous 10 Branch of the State legislature.

No person shall be a Representative who shall not have attained to the Age of **twenty five** Years, and been **seven Years** a Citizen of the United States, and who shall not, when elected, be an In-15 habitant of that State in which he shall be chosen.

[**Representatives** and **direct Taxes** shall be **apportioned** among the several States which may be included within this Union, according to their respective Numbers, which shall be determined by 20 adding to the whole Number of free Persons, including those bound to Service for a Term of Years, and excluding Indians not taxed, three-fifths of all other persons.]* The actual Enumeration shall be made within three Years after the first Meeting of 25 the Congress of the United States, and within every subsequent Term of ten Years, in such Manner as they shall by Law direct. The number of Representatives shall not exceed one for every thirty Thousand, but each State shall have at Least one Representative; and until such enumeration shall be made, 30 the State of *New Hampshire* shall be entitled to choose three, *Massachusetts* eight, *Rhode Island and Providence Plantations* one, *Connecticut* five, *New York* six, *New Jersey* four, *Pennsylvania* eight, *Delaware* one, *Maryland* six, *Virginia* ten, *North Caro-35 lina* five, *South Carolina* five, and *Georgia* three.

When vacancies happen in the Representation from any State, the Executive Authority thereof shall issue Writs of Election to fill such Vacancies.

The House of Representatives shall chuse their 40 Speaker and other Officers; and shall have the sole Power of **Impeachment.**

*Changed by section 2 of the 14th Amendment

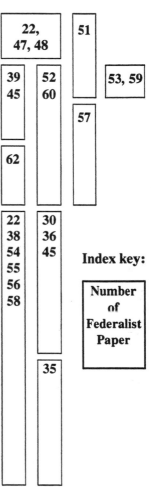

22, 47, 48 | 51

39 45 | 52 60 | 53, 59

57

62

22 38 54 55 56 58 | 30 36 45

Index key:

| Number of Federalist Paper |

35

51, 65, 66, 79

1

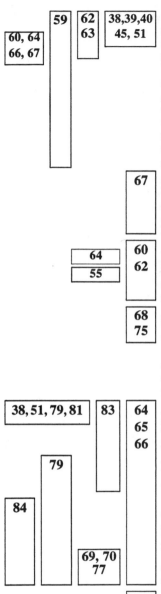

SECTION 3. The **Senate** of the United States shall be composed of **two** Senators from each **State,** [chosen by the legislature thereof,]* for **six years**; and each Senator shall have one vote. 45

Immediately after they shall be assembled in Consequence of the first Election, they shall be divided as equally as may be into three Classes. The Seats of the Senators of the first Class shall be vacated at the Expiration of the second Year, of the second 50 Class, at the Expiration of the fourth Year, and of the third Class, at the Expiration of the sixth Year, so that one third may be chosen every second Year; [and if Vacancies happen by Resignation, or otherwise, during the Recess of the Legislature of any 55 State, the Executive thereof may make temporary Appointments until the next Meeting of the Legislature, which shall then fill such Vacancies.]*

No person shall be a Senator who shall not have attained to the Age of **thirty Years**, and 60 been **nine Years a Citizen** of the United States, and who shall not, when elected, be an **Inhabitant of that State** for which he shall be chosen.

The Vice President of the United States shall be President of the Senate, but shall have no Vote, 65 unless they be equally divided.

The Senate shall choose their other Officers, and also a President *pro tempore,* in the absence of the Vice President, or when he shall exercise the office of President of the United States.   70

The Senate shall have the sole Power to try all **Impeachments**. When sitting for that Purpose, they shall be on Oath or Affirmation. When the President of the United States is tried, the Chief Justice shall preside: And no Person shall be con- 75 victed without the Concurrence of two thirds of the Members present.

Judgment in Cases of **Impeachment** shall not extend further than to removal from Office, and disqualification to hold and enjoy any Office of 80 honor, Trust or Profit under the United States: but the Party convicted shall, nevertheless, be liable and subject to Indictment, Trial, Judgment and Punishment, according to Law.

SECTION 4. The Times, Places and Manner of 85 holding **Elections for Senators and Representatives,** shall be prescribed in each State by the Legislature thereof; but the Congress may at any time by Law make or alter such Regulations, except as to the Places of Chusing Senators.   90

The Congress shall assemble at least once in every Year, and such Meeting shall be [on the first Monday in December,]** unless they shall by Law appoint a different Day.

*Changed by 17th Amendment
**Changed by section 2 of the 20th Amendment

95   SECTION 5. Each House shall be the Judge of the
Elections, Returns and Qualifications of its own Members, and a Majority of each shall constitute a Quorum
to do Business; but a smaller Number may adjourn from
day to day, and may be authorized to compel the Atten-
100 dance of absent Members, in such manner, and under
such Penalties, as each House may provide.

51, 53, 59

Each House may determine the **Rules** of its Proceedings, punish its Members for disorderly
Behaviour, and, with the Concurrence of two thirds,
105 expel a member.

51

Each House shall keep a **Journal** of its Proceedings,
and from time to time publish the same, excepting such
Parts as may in their Judgment require Secrecy; and the
Yeas and Nays of the Members of either House on any
110 question shall, at the desire of one fifth of those Present,
be entered on the Journal.

Neither House, during the Session of Congress,
shall, without the Consent of the other, **adjourn** for
more than three days, nor to any other Place than that
115 in which the two Houses shall be sitting.

SECTION 6. The Senators and Representatives shall
receive a **Compensation** for their Services, to be ascertained by Law, and paid out in the Treasury of the United
States. They shall in all Cases, except Treason, Felony
120 and Breach of the Peace, be privileged from Arrest during their Attendance at the Session of their respective
Houses, and in going to and returning from the same;
and for any Speech or Debate in either House, they
shall not be questioned in any other Place.

125   No Senator or Representative shall, during the Time
for which he was elected, be appointed to any civil Office under the Authority of the United States, which shall
have been created, or the Emoluments whereof shall have
been increased during such time; and no Person hold-
130 ing any Office under the United States, shall be a Member of either House during his Continuance in Office.

51
52
55
76

SECTION 7. All Bills for **raising Revenue** shall originate in the House of Representatives; but the Senate may
propose or concur with Amendments as on other Bills.

66

135   Every Bill which shall have passed the House of
Representatives and the Senate, shall, before it becomes
a Law, be presented to the President of the United
States; If he approve he shall sign it, but if not he shall
return it, with his Objections to that House in which it
140 shall have originated, who shall enter the Objections
at large on their Journal, and proceed to reconsider it.
If after such reconsideration two thirds of that House
shall agree to pass the Bill, it shall be sent, together
with the Objections, to the other House, by which it
145 shall likewise be reconsidered, and if approved by two
thirds of that House, it shall become a Law. But in all
Cases the Votes of both Houses shall be determined by
Yeas and Nays, and the Names of the Persons voting
for and against the Bill shall be entered on the Journal
150 of each House respectively.

73

51
69

		73	51

If any Bill shall not be returned by the President within ten Days (Sundays excepted) after it shall have been presented to him, the Same shall be a Law, in like Manner as if he had signed it, unless the 155 Congress by their Adjournment prevent its Return, in which Case it shall not be a Law.

Every Order, Resolution, or Vote to which the Concurrence of the Senate and 160 House of Representatives may be necessary (except on a question of Adjournment) shall be presented to the President of the United States; and before the same shall take Effect, shall be approved by 165 him, or being disapproved by him, shall be repassed by two thirds of the Senate and House of Representatives, according to the Rules and Limitations prescribed in the Case of a Bill.   170

12 34 36 45   **30**   **31 33 41**   **22, 32 35, 38, 56**

SECTION 8. The Congress shall have Power To lay and collect **Taxes,** Duties, Imposts, and Excises, to pay the Debts and provide for the common **Defence** and general Welfare of the United States; but all 175 Duties, Imposts, and Excises shall be uniform throughout the United States;

23, 26   **22**

To **borrow money** on the credit of the United States;

41

To regulate **Commerce** with foreign 180 Nations and among the several States, and with the Indian Tribes;

42   **41**   **12, 23 45, 56, 69**

To establish an uniform Rule of **Naturalization**, and uniform Laws on the subject of **Bankruptcies** throughout the 185 United States;

32

To **coin Money**, regulate the Value thereof, and of foreign Coin, and fix the Standard of **Weights and Measures**;

69

To provide for the Punishment of 190 **counterfeiting** the Securities and current Coin of the United States;

To establish **Post Offices** and post Roads;

43

To promote the Progress of Science and useful Arts, by securing for limited Times 195 to **Authors** and **Inventors** the exclusive Right to their respective Writings and Discoveries;

81, 82

To constitute **Tribunals** inferior to the supreme Court;   200

42

To define and punish **Piracies** and Felonies committed on the high Seas, and Offenses against the **Law of Nations**;

41, 69

To **declare War**, grant Letters of Marque and Reprisal, and make Rules 205 concerning Captures on Land and Water;

To raise and support Armies, but no Appropriation of Money to that Use shall be for a longer
Term than two Years;

210 To provide and maintain a Navy;
To make Rules for the Government and Regulation of the land and naval Forces;
To provide for calling forth the Militia to execute the Laws of the Union, suppress Insurrec-
215 tions, and repel Invasions;
To provide for organizing, arming, and disciplining the Militia, and for governing such Part
of them as may be employed in the Service of
the United States, reserving to the States respec-
220 tively, the Appointment of the Officers, and the
Authority of training the Militia according to
the discipline prescribed by Congress;
To exercise exclusive Legislation in all Cases
whatsoever, over such District (not exceeding ten
225 Miles square) as may, by Cession of particular
States and the Acceptance of Congress, become
the Seat of the Government of the United States,
and to exercise like Authority over all Places purchased by the Consent of the Legislature of the
230 State in which the Same shall be, for the Erection of Forts, Magazines, Arsenals, dockYards,
and other needful Buildings;—And
To make all Laws which shall be necessary
and proper for carrying into Execution the
235 foregoing Powers, and all other Powers vested by
this Constitution in the Government of the United
States, or in any Department or Officer thereof.
SECTION 9. The Migration or Importation of
such Persons as any of the States now existing
240 shall think proper to admit, shall not be prohibited by the Congress prior to the Year one thousand eight hundred and eight, but a tax or duty
may be imposed on such Importation, not exceeding ten dollars for each Person.
245 The privilege of the Writ of Habeas Corpus shall
not be suspended, unless when in Cases of Rebellion or Invasion the public Safety may require it.
No Bill of Attainder or ex post facto Law shall
be passed.
250 No Capitation, or other direct, Tax shall be laid,
unless in Proportion to the Census or Enumeration hereinbefore directed to be taken.
No Tax or Duty shall be laid on Articles exported from any State.
255 No Preference shall be given by any Regulation of Commerce or Revenue to the Ports of one
State over those of another; nor shall Vessels,
bound to, or from, one State, be obliged to enter,
clear, or pay Duties in another.
260 No Money shall be drawn from the Treasury,
but in Consequence of Appropriations made by
Law; and a regular Statement and Account of

25 26 41 69	22 38	23	24
	29 56		24
32	43		
22, 29 31, 33 44			
42 38			
84	83		
		36	56
12 22	32		

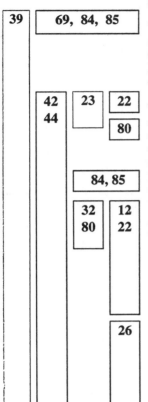

the Receipts and Expenditures of all public Money shall be published from time to time.

No Title of Nobility shall be granted by the 265 United States; And no Person holding any Office of Profit or Trust under them, shall, without the Consent of the Congress, accept of any present, Emolument, Office, or Title, of any kind whatever, from any King, Price, or foreign State. 270

SECTION 10. No State shall enter into any Treaty, Alliance, or Confederation; grant Letters of Marque and Reprisal; coin Money; emit Bills of Credit; make any Thing but gold and silver Coin a Tender in Payment of Debts; pass any Bill 275 of Attainder, ex post facto Law, or Law impairing the Obligation of Contracts, or grant any Title of Nobility.

No State shall, without the Consent of Con- 280 gress, lay any Imposts or Duties on Imports or Exports, except what may be absolutely necessary for executing its inspection Laws: and the net Produce of all Duties and Imposts, laid by any State on Imports or Exports, shall be for the Use 285 of the Treasury of the United States; and all such Laws shall be subject to the Revision and Controul of the Congress.

No State shall, without the Consent of Congress, lay any duty of Tonnage, keep Troops, or 290 Ships of War in time of Peace, enter into any Agreement or Compact with another State or with a foreign Power, or engage in War, unless actually invaded, or in such imminent Danger as will not admit of delay. 295

Article Two

SECTION 1. The executive Power shall be vested 300 in a President of the United States of America. He shall hold his Office during the Term of four Years, and together with the Vice President, chosen for the same Term, be elected as follows:

Each State shall appoint, in such Manner as 305 the Legislature thereof may direct, a Number of Electors, equal to the whole Number of Senators and Representatives to which the State may be entitled in Congress: but no Senator or Representative, or Person holding an Office of Trust or 310 Profit under the United States, shall be appointed an Elector.

[The Electors shall meet in their respective States, and vote by Ballot for two Persons, of whom one at least shall not be an Inhabitant of the same 315 State with themselves. And they shall make a List of all the Persons voted for, and of the Number of Votes for each; which List they shall sign and certify, and transmit sealed to the Seat of the Government of the United States, directed to the 320 President of the Senate.

6

The President of the Senate shall, in the Presence of the Senate and House of Representatives, open all the Certificates, and the Votes shall then be counted. The Person having the greatest Number
325 of Votes shall be the President, if such Number be a Majority of the whole Number of Electors appointed; and if there be more than one who have such Majority, and have an equal Number of Votes, then the House of Representatives shall immediately chuse
330 by Ballot one of them for President; and if no person have a Majority, then from the five highest on the List the said House shall in like manner chuse the President. But in chusing the President, the Votes shall be taken by States, the Representation
335 from each State having one Vote; a quorum for this Purpose shall consist of a Member or Members from two-thirds of the States, and a Majority of all the States shall be necessary to a Choice. In every Case, after the Choice of the President, the Person having
340 the greatest Number of Votes of the Electors shall be the Vice President. But if there should remain two or more who have equal Votes, the Senate shall chuse from them by Ballot the Vice President.]*

The Congress may determine the Time of
345 chusing the Electors, and the Day on which they shall give their Votes; which Day shall be the same throughout the United States.

No person except a natural born Citizen, or a Citizen of the United States at the time of the Adop-
350 tion of this Constitution, shall be eligible to the Office of President; neither shall any Person be eligible to that Office who shall not have attained to the Age of thirty-five Years, and been fourteen Years a Resident within the United States.

355 [In Case of the Removal of the President from Office, or of his Death, Resignation, or Inability to discharge the Powers and Duties of the said Office, the same shall devolve on the Vice President, and the Congress may by Law provide for the Case of
360 Removal, Death, Resignation, or Inability, both of the President and Vice President, declaring what Officer shall then act as President, and such Officer shall act accordingly until the Disability be removed, or a President shall be elected.]**

365 The President shall, at stated Times, receive for his Services, a Compensation, which shall neither be increased nor diminished during the Period for which he shall have been elected, and he shall not receive within that Period any other Emolument
370 from the United States, or any of them.

Before he enter on the execution of his Office, he shall take the following Oath or Affirmation:—

39
60
64
68

66

55

64

73
79

*changed by 12th Amendment
**changed by 25th Amendment

"I do solemnly swear (or affirm) that I will faithfully execute the Office of President of the United States, and will to the best of my Ability preserve, protect, and defend the Constitution of the United States." 375

SECTION 2. The **President** shall be **Commander in Chief** of the Army and Navy of the United States, and of the Militia of the several States, when called into the actual Service of the United States; he may require the Opinion, in writing, of the principal Officer in each of the executive Departments, upon any subject relating to the Duties of their respective Offices, and he shall have Power to Grant Reprieves and **Pardons** for Offenses against the United States, except in Cases of Impeachment. 380 385 390

He shall have Power, by and with the Advice and Consent of the Senate, to make **Treaties**, provided two-thirds of the Senators present concur; and shall nominate, and, by and with the Advice and Consent of the Senate, shall appoint **Ambassadors**, other public Ministers and Consuls, **Judges** of the supreme Court, and all other Officers of the United States, whose Appointments are not herein otherwise provided for, and which shall be established by Law; but the Congress may by Law vest the Appointment of such inferior Officers, as they think proper, in the President alone, in the Courts of Law, or in the Heads of Departments. 395 400 405

The President shall have Power to fill up all Vacancies that may happen during the Recess of the Senate, by granting Commissions which shall expire at the end of their next Session. 410

SECTION 3. He shall from time to time give to the Congress Information of the **State of the Union,** and recommend to their Consideration such Measures as he shall judge necessary and expedient; he may, on extraordinary Occasions, convene both Houses, or either of them, and in Case of Disagreement between them, with Respect to the Time of Adjournment, he may adjourn them to such Time as he shall think proper; he shall receive Ambassadors and other public Ministers; he shall take Care that the Laws be faithfully executed, and shall Commission all the Officers of the United States. 415 420 425

Left-margin reference brackets: 74, 69, 69, 66, 77, 38, 42, 22, 64, 75, 39, 78, 67, 76, 72, 42

SECTION 4. The President, Vice President and all civil Officers of the United States, shall be removed from Office on **Impeachment** for, and Conviction of, Treason, Bribery, or other high Crimes and Misdemeanors.

Article Three

SECTION 1. The judicial Power of the United States, shall be vested in one **supreme Court,** and in such **inferior Courts** as the Congress may from time to time ordain and establish.

The **Judges,** both of the supreme and inferior Courts, shall hold their Offices during good Behaviour, and shall, at stated Times, receive for their Services, a Compensation, which shall not be diminished during their Continuance in Office.

SECTION 2. The judicial Power shall extend to all Cases, in Law and Equity, arising under this Constitution, the Laws of the United States, and Treaties made, or which shall be made, under their authority;—to all Cases affecting Ambassadors, other public Ministers and Consuls;—to all Cases of admiralty and maritime Jurisdiction;—to Controversies to which the United States shall be a Party;—to Controversies between two or more States;—[between a State and Citizens of another State;—]* between Citizens of different States;—between Citizens of the same State claiming Lands under Grants of different States, [and between a State, or the Citizens thereof, and foreign States, Citizens, of Subjects.]*

In all Cases affecting Ambassadors, other public Ministers and Consuls, and those in which a State shall be a Party, the supreme Court shall have original Jurisdiction. In all the other Cases before mentioned, the supreme Court shall have appellate Jurisdiction, both as to Law and Fact, with such Exceptions, and under such Regulations as the Congress shall make.

The Trial of all Crimes, except in Cases of Impeachment, shall be by Jury; and such Trial shall be held in the State where the said Crimes shall have been committed; but when not committed within any State, the Trial shall be at such Place or Places as the Congress may by Law have directed.

SECTION 3. **Treason** against the United States, shall consist only in levying War against them, or in adhering to their enemies, giving them Aid and Comfort. No Person shall be convicted of Treason unless on the Testimony of two Witnesses to the same overt Act, or on Confession in open Court.

The Congress shall have power to declare the Punishment of Treason, but no Attainder of Treason shall work Corruption of Blood, or Forfeiture except during the Life of the Person attained.

*changed by 11th Amendment

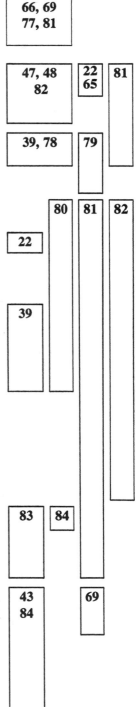

39
66, 69
77, 81

47, 48
82
22
65
81

39, 78
79

80
81
82
22

39

83
84

43
84
69

Article Four

SECTION 1. **Full Faith and Credit** shall be given in each State to the public Acts, Records, and judicial Proceedings of every other State. And the Congress may be general Laws prescribe the Manner in which such Acts, Records and Proceedings shall be proved, and the effect thereof. 485

SECTION 2. The Citizens of each State shall be entitled to all Privileges and Immunities of Citizens in the several States. 490

A Person charged in any State with Treason, Felony, or other Crime, who shall flee from Justice, and be found in another State, shall on Demand of the executive Authority of the State from which he fled, be delivered up, to be removed 495 to the State having Jurisdiction of the Crime.

[No Person held to Service or Labour in one State, under the Laws thereof, escaping into another, shall, in Consequence of any Law or Regulation therein, be discharged from such 500 Service or Labour, but shall be delivered up on Claim of the Party to whom such Service or Labour may be due.]*

SECTION 3. New States may be admitted by the Congress into this Union; but no new State 505 shall be formed or erected within the Jurisdiction of any other State; nor any State be formed by the Junction of two or more States, or parts of States, without the Consent of the Legislatures of the States concerned as well as of the Congress. 510

The Congress shall have Power to dispose of and make all needful Rules and Regulations respecting the **Territory** or other Property belonging to the United States; and nothing in this Constitution shall be so construed as to 515 Prejudice any Claims of the United States, or of any particular State.

SECTION 4. The United States shall **guarantee** to every State in this Union a **Republican Form** of Government, and shall protect each 520 of them against Invasion; and on Application of the Legislature, or of the Executive (when the Legislature cannot be convened) against **domestic Violence.**

Article Five

The Congress, whenever two-thirds of both 525 Houses shall deem it necessary, shall propose **Amendments** to this Constitution, or, on the Application of the Legislatures of two thirds of the several States, shall call a Convention for proposing Amendments, which, in either Case, shall 530 be valid to all Intents and Purposes, as Part of

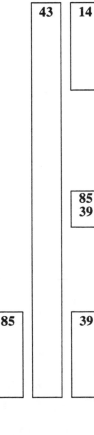

*changed by the 13th Amendment

this Constitution, when ratified by the Legislatures of three-fourths of the several States, or by Conventions in three fourths thereof, as the
535 one or the other Mode of Ratification may be proposed by the Congress; provided that no Amendment which may be made prior to the Year One thousand eight hundred and eight shall in any manner affect the first and fourth Clauses
540 in the Ninth Section of the first Article; and that no State, without its Consent, shall be deprived of its equal Suffrage in the Senate.

Article Six

All Debts contracted and Engagements entered into, before the Adoption of this Consti-
545 tution, shall be as valid against the United States under this Constitution, as under the Confederation

This Constitution, and the Laws of the United States which shall be made in Pursu-
550 ance thereof; and all Treaties made, or which shall be made, under the Authority of the United States, shall be the supreme Law of the Land; and the Judges in every State shall be bound thereby, any Thing in the Constitution or Laws
555 of any State to the Contrary notwithstanding.

The Senators and Representatives before mentioned, and the Members of the several State Legislatures, and all executive and judicial Officers, both of the United States and of
560 the several States, shall be bound by Oath or Affirmation, to support this Constitution; but no religious Test shall ever be required as a Qualification to any Office or public Trust under the United States.

Article Seven

565   The Ratification of the Conventions of nine States, shall be sufficient for the Establishment of this Constitution between the States so ratifying the Same.

Done in Convention by the unanimous Con-
570 sent of the States present the Seventeenth day of September in the Year of our Lord one thousand seven hundred and Eighty seven and of the Independence of the United States of American the Twelfth In Witness whereof We have
575 hereunto subscribed our Names,

G Washington—Presid

and deputy from Virginia
    Attest:
    William Jackson Secretary

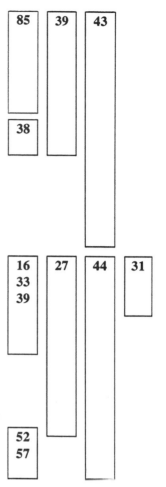

85 39 43
38

16 27 44 31
33
39
52
57

22, 39
40, 43, 85

11

Amendments

Article One

Congress shall make no law respecting an establishment of religion, or prohibiting the free exercise thereof; or abridging the freedom of speech, or of the press; or the right of the people peaceably to assemble, and to petition the Government for a redress of grievances.

Article Two

A well-regulated Militia, being necessary to the security of a free State, the right of the people to keep and bear Arms shall not be infringed.

Article Three

No Soldier shall, in time of peace, be quartered in any house, without the consent of thee Owner, nor in time of war, but in a manner to be prescribed by law.

Article Four

The right of the people to secure in their persons, houses, papers, and effects, against unreasonable searches and seizures, shall not be violated, and no Warrants shall issue, but upon probable cause, supported by Oath or affirmation, and particularly describing the place to be searched, and the persons or things to be seized.

Article Five

No person shall be held to answer for a capital, or otherwise infamous crime, unless on a presentment or indictment of a Grand Jury, except in cases arising in the land or naval forces, or in the Militia, when in actual service in time of War or public danger; nor shall any person be subject for the same offense to be twice put in jeopardy of life or limb; nor shall be compelled in any criminal case to be a witness against himself, nor be deprived of life, liberty, or property, without due process of law; nor shall private property be taken for public use, without just compensation.

Article Six

In all criminal prosecutions, the accused shall enjoy the right to a speedy and public trial, by an impartial jury of the State and district wherein the crime shall have been committed; which district shall have been previously ascertained by law, and to be informed of the nature and cause of the accusation; to be confronted with the witnesses against him; to have compulsory process for obtaining witnesses in his favor, and to have the assistance of counsel for his defence.

Article Seven

In Suits at common law, where the value of controversy shall exceed twenty dollars, the right of trial by jury shall be preserved, and no fact tried by a jury shall be otherwise reexamined in any Court of the United States, than according to the rules of the common law.

Article Eight

Excessive bail shall not be required, nor excessive fines imposed, nor cruel and unusual punishments inflicted.

Article Nine

The enumeration in the Constitution of certain rights shall not be construed to deny or disparage others retained by the people.

Article Ten

The powers not delegated to the United States by the Constitution, nor prohibited by it to the States, are reserved to the States respectively or to the people.

Article Eleven

The judicial power of the United States shall not be construed to extend to any suit in law or equity, commenced or prosecuted against one of the United States by Citizens of another State, or by Citizens or Subjects of any Foreign State.

Article Twelve

The Electors shall meet in their respective states, and vote by ballot for President and Vice President, one of whom, at least, shall not be an inhabitant of the same State with themselves; they shall name in their ballots the person voted for as President, and in distinct ballots the person voted for as Vice-President, and they shall make distinct lists of all persons voted for as President, and of all persons voted for as Vice-

President, and of the number of votes for each, which lists they shall sign and certify, and transmit sealed to the seat of the government of the United States, directed to the President of the Senate;—The President of the Senate shall, in the presence of the Senate and House of Representatives, open all the certificates and the votes shall then be counted;—The person having the greatest number of votes for President, shall be the President, if such number be a majority of the whole number of Electors appointed; and if no person have such majority, then from the persons having the highest numbers not exceeding three on the list of those voted for as President, the House of Representatives shall choose immediately, by ballot, the President. But in choosing the President, the votes shall be taken by states, the representation from each State having one vote; a quorum for this purpose shall consist of a member or members from two-thirds of the states, and a majority of all the states shall be necessary to a choice. And if the House of Representatives shall not choose a President whenever the right of choice shall devolve upon them, before the fourth day of March next following, then the Vice-President shall act as President, as in the case of the death or other constitutional disability of the President—The person having the greatest number of votes as Vice-President, shall be the Vice-President, if such number be a majority of the whole number of Electors appointed, and if no person have a majority, then from the two highest numbers on the list, the Senate shall choose the Vice-President; a quorum for the purpose shall consist of two-thirds of the whole number of Senators, and a majority of the whole number shall be necessary to a choice, But no person constitutionally ineligible to the office of President shall be eligible to that of Vice-President of the United States.

Article Thirteen

Section 1. Neither slavery nor involuntary servitude, except as a punishment for crime whereof the party shall have been duly convicted, shall exist within the United States, or any place subject to their jurisdiction.

Section 2. Congress shall have power to enforce this article by appropriate legislation.

Article Fourteen

Section 1. All persons born or naturalized in the United States, and subject to the jurisdiction thereof, are citizens of the United States and of the State wherein they reside. No State shall make or enforce any law which shall abridge the privileges or immunities of citizens of the United States; nor shall any State deprive any person of life, liberty, or property, without due process of law; nor deny to any person within its jurisdiction the equal protection of the laws.

Section 2. Representatives shall be apportioned among the several States according to their respective numbers, counting the whole number of persons in each State, excluding Indians not taxed. But when the right to vote at any election for the choice of Electors for President and Vice-President of the United States, Representatives in Congress, the executive and judicial officers of a State, or the members of the Legislature thereof, is denied to any of the male inhabitants of such State, being twenty-one years of age, and citizens of the United States, or in any way abridged, except for participation in rebellion, or other crime, the basis of representation therein shall be reduced in the proportion which the number of such male citizens shall bear to the whole number of male citizens twenty-one years of age in such State.

Section 3. No person shall be a Senator or Representative in Congress, or elector of President and Vice-President, or hold any office, civil or military, under the United States, or under any State, who, having previously taken an oath, as a member of Congress, or as an officer of the United States, or as a member of any State Legislature, or as an executive or judicial officer of any State, to support the Constitution of the United States, shall have engaged in insurrection or rebellion against the same, or given aid or comfort to the enemies thereof. But Congress may by a vote of two-thirds of each house, remove such disability.

Section 4. The validity of the public debt of the United States, authorized by law, including debts incurred for payment of pensions and bounties for services in suppressing insurrection or rebellion, shall not be questioned. But neither the United States nor any State shall assume or pay any debt or obligation incurred in aid of insurrection or rebellion against die United States, or any claim for the loss or emancipation of any slave; but all such debts, obligations and claims shall be held illegal and void.

Section 5, The Congress shall have power to enforce, by appropriate legislation, the provisions of this article.

Article Fifteen

Section 1. The right of citizens of the United States to vote shall not be denied or abridged by the United States or by any State on account of race, color, or previous condition of servitude—

Section 2. The Congress shall have power to enforce this article by appropriate legislation.

Article Sixteen

The Congress shall have power to lay and collect taxes on incomes, from whatever source derived, without apportionment among the several States, and without regard to any census enumeration.

Article Seventeen

The Senate of the United States shall be composed of two Senators from each State, elected by the people thereof, for six years; and each Senator shall have one vote. The electors in each State shall have the qualifications requisite for electors of the most numerous branch of the State legislatures.

When vacancies happen in the representation of any State in the Senate, the executive authority of such State shall issue writs of election to fill such vacancies: Provided, That the Legislature of any State may empower the executive thereof to make temporary appointments until the people fill the vacancies by election as the legislature may direct.

This amendment shall not be so construed as to affect the election or term of any Senator chosen before it becomes valid as part of the Constitution.

Article Eighteen

Section 1. After one year from the ratification of this article the manufacture, sale, or transportation of intoxicating liquors within, the importation thereof into, or the exportation thereof from the United States and all territory subject to the jurisdiction thereof for beverage purposes is hereby prohibited.

Section 2. The Congress and the several States shall have concurrent power to enforce this article by appropriate legislation.

Section 3 This article shall be inoperative unless it shall have been ratified as an amendment to the Constitution by the legislatures of the several States, as provided in the Constitution, within seven years from the date of the submission hereof to the States by the Congress.

Article Nineteen

The right of citizens of the United States to vote shall not be denied or abridged by the United States or by any State on account of sex.

Congress shall have power to enforce this article by appropriate legislation.

Article Twenty

Section 1. The terms of the President and Vice-President shall end at noon on the 20th day of January, and the terms of Senators and Representatives at noon on the 3d day of January, of the years in which such terms would have ended if this article had not been ratified; and the terms of their successors shall then begin.

Section 2. The Congress shall assemble at least once in every year, and such meeting shall begin at noon on the 3d day of January, unless they shall by law appoint a different day.

Section 3. If, at the time fixed for the beginning of the term of the President, the President elect shall have died, the Vice

President elect shall become President. If a President shall not have been chosen before the time fixed for the beginning of his term, or if the President elect shall have failed to qualify, then the Vice President elect shall act as President until a President shall have qualified; and the Congress may by law provide for the case wherein neither a President elect nor a Vice-President elect shall have qualified, declaring who shall then act as President, or the manner in which one who is to act shall be selected, and such person shall act accordingly until a President or Vice-President shall have qualified.

Section 4. The Congress may by law provide for the case of the death of any of the persons from whom the House of Representatives may choose a President whenever the right of choice shall have devolved upon them, and for the case of the death of any of the persons from whom the Senate may choose a Vice-President whenever the right of choice shall have devolved upon them.

Section 5. Sections 1 and 2 shall take effect on the 15th day of October following the ratification of this article.

Section 6. This article shall be inoperative unless it shall have been ratified as an amendment to the Constitution by the legislatures of three-fourths of the several States within seven years from the date of its submission.

Article Twenty-one

Section 1 The eighteenth article of amendment to the Constitution of the United States is hereby repealed.

Section 2 The transportation or importation into any State, Territory, or possession of the United States for delivery or use therein of intoxicating liquors, in violation of the laws thereof, is hereby prohibited.

Section 3 This article shall be inoperative unless it shall have been ratified as an amendment to the Constitution by conventions in the several States, as provided in the Constitution, within seven years from the date of the submission hereof to the States by the Congress.

Article Twenty-two

Section 1. No person shall be elected to the office of the President more than twice, and no person who has held the office of President, or acted as President, for more than two years of a term to which some other person was elected President shall be elected to the office of the President more than once. But this Article shall not apply to any person holding the office of President when this Article was proposed by the Congress, and shall not prevent any person who may be holding the office of President, or acting as President, during the term within which this Article becomes operative from holding the office of President or acting as President dung the remainder of such term.

Section 2. This article shall be inoperative unless it shall have been ratified as an amendment to the Constitution by the legislatures of three-fourths of the several States within seven years from the date of its submission to the States by the Congress.

Article Twenty-three

Section 1. The District constituting the seat of Government of the United States shall appoint in such manner as the Congress may direct:

A number of electors of President and Vice-President equal to the whole number of Senators and Representatives in Congress to which the District would be entitled if it were a State, but in no event more than the least populous State; they shall be in addition to those appointed by the States, but they shall be considered, for the purposes of the election of President and Vice President, to be electors appointed by a State; and they shall meet in the District and perform such duties as provided by the twelfth article of amendment.

Section 2. The Congress shall have power to enforce this article by appropriate legislation.

Article Twenty-four

Section 1. The right of citizens of the United States to vote in any primary or other election for President or Vice-President, for electors for President or Vice-President, or for Senator or Representative in Congress, shall not be denied or abridged by the United States or any State by reason of failure to pay any poll tax or other tax.

Section 2. The Congress shall have power to enforce this article by appropriate legislation.

Article Twenty-five

Section 1. In case of the removal of the President from office or of his death or resignation, the Vice President shall become President.

Section 2. Whenever there is a vacancy in the office of the Vice President, the President shall nominate a Vice President who shall take office upon confirmation by a majority vote of both Houses of Congress.

Section 3. Whenever the President transmits to the President pro tempore of the Senate and the Speaker of the House of Representatives his written declaration that he is unable to discharge the powers and duties of his office, and until he transmits to them a written declaration to the contrary, such powers and duties shall be discharged by the Vice President as Acting President.

Section 4. Whenever the Vice President and a majority of either the principal officers of the executive departments or of such other body as Congress may by law provide, transmit to the President pro tempore of the Senate and the Speaker of the House of Representatives their written declaration that the President is unable to discharge the powers and duties of his office, the Vice President shall immediately assume the powers and duties of the office as Acting President.

Thereafter, when the President transmits to the President pro tempore of the Senate and the Speaker of the House of Representatives his written declaration that no inability exists, he shall resume the powers and duties of his office unless the Vice President and a majority of either the principal officers of the executive department or of such other body as Congress may by law provide, transmit within four days to the President pro temp ore of the Senate and the Speaker of the House of Representatives their written declaration that the President is unable to discharge the powers and duties of his office. Thereupon Congress shall decide the issue, assembling within forty-eight hours for that purpose if not in session. If the Congress, within twenty-one days after receipt of the latter written declaration, or, if Congress is not in session, within twenty-one days after Congress is required to assemble, determines by two-thirds vote of both Houses that the President is unable to discharge the powers and duties of his office, the Vice President shall continue to discharge the same as Acting President; otherwise, the President shall resume the powers and duties of his office.

Article Twenty-six

Section 1. The right of citizens of the United States, who are eighteen years of age or older, to vote shall not be denied or abridged by the United States or by any State on account of age.

Section 2. The Congress shall have power to enforce this article by appropriate legislation.

Number 1

Call to Citizens to Study New Constitution

Having experienced the undeniable inefficiency of the existing federal government, you are asked to study and consider adopting a new Constitution for the United States of America.

The importance of this deliberation can not be overstated. The very existence of our country hangs in the balance, as does the safety and welfare of its people, communities, and states. We are called to decide the fate of a nation that is, in many respects, the most interesting in the world.

It has been often said that the people of this country will decide the important question of whether societies can establish a good government by careful thought and choice. Or whether people are forever destined to be governed only by accident and force. If this is true, the answer depends on our response to the current crisis. And the wrong decision deserves to be considered a misfortune for all of mankind.

Variety of Interests Influence Debate

2 Conscientious patriots understand the weighty importance of deciding whether to adopt the new Constitution. Knowing their decision will affect all human societies raises their anxiety.

It would be wonderful if we based our decision only on the best interests of our society, unbiased by less noble interests unconnected with the public good. Although we may ardently wish this, it can't be seriously expected. The Constitution offered for consideration affects too many special interests and changes too many local institutions not to expect discussions on subjects other than its merits. Views, passions and prejudices unrelated to discovering the truth and meaning of the document are expected.

Opposition From Politicians

3 Politicians will present some of the most formidable obstacles to the new Constitution. Some will resist any change that might diminish the power and benefits of their current State offices. The perverted ambition of others will see potential self-aggrandizement within a country in disarray. Or will flatter themselves into believing they can rise to a higher level of power within an alliance of several States than within a union under one government.

Moderation Urged

4 However, I don't plan to dwell on observations of this nature. It would be presumptuous for me to indiscriminately declare person's opposition due to self-interest or ambitious views merely because their situation might subject them to suspicion. Candidly, we admit even politicians may be motivated by upright intentions. And, undoubtedly, much of the opposition will spring from blameless, if not valid, motivations. Preconceived jealousies and fears will lead arguments astray into honest errors in thinking.

Indeed, so many powerful reasons can create a false bias that there are often wise and good men arguing on both the wrong and right side of society's most important questions.

This reality should furnish a lesson of moderation to anyone who thinks they are always in the right in any controversy.

A further reason for caution—we are not always sure that people who advocate the truth are influenced by purer principles than their antagonists. Ambition, avarice, personal animosity, party opposition, and many other motives no more laudable than these, operate as well on those who support, as those who oppose, the right side of a question.

Moderation is important. Nothing is more repugnant than the intolerant spirit that has, at all times, characterized political parties. In politics, as in religion, it's absurd to aim at making proselytes by fire and sword. Heresies in either can rarely be cured by persecution.

Constitution Called Thief of Liberty

5 Despite these arguments, a torrent of angry and malignant passions will be let loose about this subject, as in all former cases of great national debate. To judge from the conduct of the opponents of the new Constitution, we will conclude that they hope to show evidence of the justness of their opinions and increase the number of their converts by the loudness of their rhetoric and the bitterness of their denunciations.

Those who argue with enlightened zeal for the energy and efficiency of government will be demonized as being fond of despotic power and hostile to liberty. When supporters profess that the rights of the people must be scrupulously protected, it will be characterized as insincere, a blatant bid for popularity at the expense of the public good.

It will be forgotten that dangers to the rights of people most commonly spring from the head rather than the heart, that the noble enthusiasm of liberty is apt to be infected with narrow-minded bigotry and distrust.

It will also be forgotten that a vital government is essential to secure liberty. Sound judgment shows these can never be separated. And dangerous ambition more often lurks behind the specious mask of zeal for the rights of the people than under the zeal for a firm and efficient government. History teaches us that of the men who have overturned the liberties of republics, most began their career by proclaiming their devotion to the people. They gain position by arousing people's prejudices and end as tyrants.

My Support of New Constitution

6 As I wrote the above I've tried, my fellow citizens, to put you on guard against all attempts, from whatever quarter, to influence you. Your decision on the new Constitution, of the highest importance to your welfare, should result from the evidence of truth.

I'm sure you have noticed that I am not unfriendly to the new Constitution. Yes, my countrymen, I admit that after having given it attentive consideration, I believe it is in your interest to adopt it. I am convinced that this is the safest course for your liberty, your dignity, and your happiness.

I don't pretend to have reservations I don't feel. I won't amuse you with an appearance of deliberation when I have decided. I frankly acknowledge to you my convictions, and I will freely lay before you the reasons on which they are founded. The consciousness of good intentions disdains ambiguity.

The new Constitution has my full and unambiguous support. I shall not, however, dwell on professions of my faith in it. And my motives must remain in my heart.

My arguments will be offered in the spirit of presenting the truth. They will be open to all and may be judged by all.

Discussion of Constitutional Issues

7   I propose, in a series of papers, to discuss the following interesting particulars:

The usefulness of a successful federal government to the UNION.

The insufficiency of the present Confederation to preserve the UNION.

The necessity of a federal government at least as energetic as the one proposed in the Constitution to attain this objective.

The conformity of the proposed Constitution to the true principles of republican government.

Its analogy to the New York constitution.

And the additional security its adoption will afford to the preservation of the republican form of government, to liberty, and to property.

As this discussion progresses, I will endeavor to give satisfactory answers to objections that arise and may claim your attention.

Opponents:
Thirteen States Too Big

8   Arguments proving the utility of the UNION may be thought superfluous. The importance of the UNION may be seen as deeply engraved on the hearts of the people in every State, with no adversaries. But the fact is, we already hear it whispered among those who oppose the new Constitution that thirteen States are too many for any general system. They argue that we must break into several separate confederacies.*

This doctrine will, in all probability, be gradually propagated until it has enough votes to approve it. To those who take an enlarged view of the subject, nothing is more evident than that the alternative to adoption of the new Constitution is dismemberment of the Union.

Therefore, it will be useful to examine the advantages of the Union, and the probable dangers and certain evils to which every State will be exposed from its dissolution. Accordingly, this will constitute the subject of my next editorial.

PUBLIUS

_____

* The same idea, tracing the arguments to their consequences, is held out in several recent publications against the new Constitution.

Number 2

Government, Constitution, United America

When the people of America realize the importance of the question they're called upon to decide, their responsibility to make a serious, comprehensive study of it will be evident. The decision and its consequences will prove to be the most important that has ever engaged their attention.

People Empower Government

2 Government is an indispensable necessity. It is equally undeniable that, whatever its form, the people must cede some of their natural rights to the government to vest it with requisite powers. Therefore, it's worth considering what will best serve the interest of the people of America, one nation, under one federal government, or should Americans divide themselves into separate confederacies, giving the central government of each the same kind of powers as placed in one national government?

Recent Calls to Disunite

3 Until recently, it's been unanimously agreed that the prosperity of the people of America depends on their staying firmly united. The wishes, prayers, and efforts of our best and wisest citizens have been constantly directed to that objective.

But some politicians now say that looking for safety and happiness in a union is wrong. They insist that we should seek division of the States into distinct confederacies, or sovereign nations.

This new doctrine may appear extraordinary, but it has advocates, even some people previously opposed to it. It doesn't matter what arguments induced these people to change their opinions. But it certainly would not be wise for citizens to adopt these new political tenets without being fully convinced that they are founded in truth and sound policy.

America is Geographically United

4 I find pleasure in observing that independent America isn't composed of detached, distant territories. Instead, the destiny of our western sons of liberty is one connected, fertile, wide-spreading country.

God blessed it with a variety of soils, watered with innumerable streams, for the delight and accommodation of it inhabitants. As if to bind it together, navigable water forms a kind of chain around its borders. And the most noble rivers in the world form convenient highways for easy communication and transportation of commodities.

Americans Culturally United

5 I often note with equal pleasure that God gave this one connected country to one united people—a people descended from the same language, professing the same religion, attached to the same principles of government, very similar in manners and customs. They fought side by side through a long and bloody war, establishing liberty and independence.

One Country, People

6 This country and this people seem to have been made for each other. It appears like this inheritance was designed by God for a band of brethren united by the strongest ties. They should never split into a number of unsocial, jealous, and alien sovereignties.

States Have Acted As Nation

7 Until recently, everyone—all classes of men among us—agreed that we should remain united.

We have acted as one people. Each individual citizen everywhere enjoys the same national rights, privileges, and protection. As a nation we have made peace and war. As a nation we have formed alliances and made treaties, and entered into compacts with foreign states.

Government Hastily Formed

8 Very early, the people instituted a federal government to preserve and perpetuate the strong sense of value and blessings of union. They formed it almost as soon as they had political existence, at a time when their homes were in flames, and citizens were bleeding. However, hostility and desolation left little room for the calm and mature reflections that must precede the formation of a wise and well-balanced government for free people.

Therefore, it's not strange that a government formed at such a time has since been found greatly deficient and inadequate to serve the purpose intended.

Union and Liberty

9 Being intelligent, the people recognized and regretted the government's defects. They were both attached to the union and enamored with liberty. They observed that the union was in immediate danger, a danger that would eventually jeopardize liberty.

Being persuaded that both—the union and personal liberty—could only be secure in a national government, more wisely framed, they convened the recent convention in Philadelphia to consider the important subject.

Constitutional Convention

10 The men gathered at the convention possessed the confidence of the people. Many had become highly distinguished by their patriotism, virtue, and wisdom during a time that tried the minds and hearts of men.

The convention undertook the arduous task. During a time of peace, with minds unoccupied by other subjects, they spent many months in cool, uninterrupted, daily consultation.

Finally, without being awed by power or influenced by any passion except love for their country, they unanimously recommended to the people their plan—the proposed Constitution.

Discussion Will Not Always Center on Nation's Best Interest

11 Admittedly, this plan is only *recommended*, not imposed. Remember, it is neither recommended for *blind* approval nor *blind* rejection. Rather, it is submitted for the sedate, candid consideration that the magnitude and importance of the subject demands, and that it certainly should receive.

But, as has already been said, a thoughtful examination is more to be wished than expected. Experience on a former occasion teaches us not to be too optimistic.

Let's remember what happened in 1774. The people of America felt, correctly, that they were in imminent danger. They formed the Congress of 1774. It recommended certain measures that later proved prophetically wise. However, the immediate reaction by the press was pamphlets and weekly papers against those very measures.

Relentless calls to reject the advice of that patriotic Congress came from many quarters. Many officers of the government obeyed the dictates of personal interest. Other people predicted mistaken consequences, or were unduly influenced by former attachments, or saw it as a threat to ambitions that did not correspond with the public good.

Although men were deceived and deluded, the great majority of the people reasoned and decided judiciously. Reflecting back, they are happy they did so.

Public Rationally Evaluated 1774 Congressional Recommendations

12 The people concluded that the 1774 Congress was composed of many wise and experienced men. That they had brought with them, from the different parts of the country, a wide variety of useful information. That as they discussed the true interests of their country, they acquired very accurate knowledge of the subject. That each delegate was committed to public liberty and prosperity. And, therefore, it was both their inclination and their duty to recommend, after mature deliberation, only measures thought prudent and advisable.

Framers of Constitution

13 The people relied on the judgment and integrity of the 1774 Congress, taking its advice despite efforts to deter them. If the people felt confidence in the men of that Congress, few of whom were well known, they now have a greater reason to respect the judgment and advice of the recent convention. Some of the most distinguished members of the 1774 Congress, who have since proved their patriotism and abilities, and have grown old acquiring political information, carried to this year's Constitutional Convention their accumulated knowledge and experience.

Remaining One Nation Imperative

14 Every Congress, including the recent Constitutional Convention, has joined with the people in thinking that the prosperity of America depends on its Union. To preserve and perpetuate the Union was the objective of the people in forming a convention and the Constitution the convention has advised them to adopt.

With what propriety, therefore, or what are the real motives behind, current attempts to depreciate the importance of the Union? Why is it suggested that three or four confederacies would be better than one?

I believe people have always thought right on this subject. Their universal and uniform attachment to the cause of the Union is based on great and weighty reasons, which I will endeavor to develop and explain in some ensuing papers.

Those who promote the idea of substituting a number of separate confederacies for the convention's plan [the Constitution] know that the rejection of that plan would put the continuance of the Union in utmost jeopardy.

I sincerely wish that every good citizen realizes that, if the Union is dissolved, America will have reason to exclaim, in the words of the poet: "FAREWELL! A LONG FAREWELL TO ALL MY GREATNESS.'

                                        PUBLIUS

Number 3

National Union Provides Safety Against Foreign Danger

People of any country (if, like Americans, they are intelligent and well informed) seldom hold and keep erroneous beliefs about their best interests for many years. This explains why Americans feel that remaining firmly united under one federal government, vested with sufficient powers for all national purposes, is important.

Reasons for Unity Valid

2 The more I seriously consider and investigate the reasons for this opinion, the more I'm convinced they are valid and conclusive.

Safety: Society's First Objective

3 A wise and free people must focus their attention on many objectives. First is *safety*. The concept of *safety* relates to a wide variety of circumstances and ideas, giving great latitude to people who wish to define it precisely and totally.

Safety Against Hostilities

4 At this time, I will discuss safety as it relates to the preservation of peace and tranquility against dangers from *foreign arms and influence* and *similar* dangers arising from domestic causes.

The first of these is danger from foreign nations. And it will be discussed first. We'll examine whether the people are right and a Union, under an efficient national government, gives the best security devised against *hostilities* from abroad.

Union Helps Preserve Peace

5 The number of wars in the world is always proportionate to the number and severity of causes, whether *real* or *imagined*, which *provoke* or *invite* them. If this is true, it becomes useful to ask whether a *United America* will find as many *just* causes of war as a *disunited* America. If it seems that United America will find fewer reasons, it follows that the Union tends to preserve a state of peace with other nations.

Current Relationships With Nations

6 *Just* causes of war generally arise from violations of treaties or direct violence, attack or invasion. America already has treaties with at least six foreign nations. All, except Prussia, are maritime and able to annoy and injure us. We have extensive commerce with Portugal, Spain, and Britain. The latter two also have neighboring territory.

Foreign Laws Must Be Obeyed

7 It is vital to American peace that she observes the laws of foreign nations. For several reasons, it is evident that this will be more perfectly and punctually done by one national government than by either thirteen separate States or by three or four distinct confederacies.

Highest Qualified Men Govern Union

8 When an efficient national government is established, usually the best men in the country will be appointed to manage it and will consent to serve. A town or county can place men in State assemblies, senates, courts, or executive departments. However, to recommend men to offices in the national government a wider reputation for talents and qualifications will be necessary. The public will choose from the widest field, never lacking qualified persons, as has happened in some States.

Hence, the administration, political counsels, and judicial decisions of the national government will be more wise, systematical, and judicious than those of individual States. Consequently, a Union will be *safer* with respect to other nations, as well as *safer* with respect to us.

National Treaties, Policies

9   Under the national government, treaties, and laws of nations, will always be detailed and executed in the same manner. However, thirteen States, or three or four confederacies, adjudicating the same points and questions, will not always be consistent. Different, independent governments, appointing courts and judges, would have different local laws and interests influencing them. Therefore, the convention's wisdom in committing such questions to the jurisdiction of courts appointed by and responsible to one national government cannot be too much commended.

Temptations: Local Officials

10   The people governing one or two States may be tempted to swerve from trustworthiness and justice by the prospect of an immediate advantage or loss. Those localized temptations would have little or no influence on the national government, preserving good faith and justice. The peace treaty with Britain is a good case in point.

Temptations: National Officials

11   Temptations commonly result from circumstances specific to an individual State and may affect a great number of its inhabitants. The governing party may not always be able, if willing, to prevent the planned injustice or punish the aggressors.

Not being affected by local circumstances, nation officials will be neither induced to commit wrong themselves nor avoid prevention or punishing its commission by others.

Union: Fewer Treaty Violations

12   Since intentional or accidental violations of treaties and laws of nations provide *just* cause for war, they are less likely to happen under one general government than several lesser ones. Therefore, one national government most favors the *safety* of the people.

Unlawful Violence Against Nations

13, 14   It seems equally clear to me that one good national government also provides the greatest security against just causes of war stemming from direct, unlawful violence because it is usually caused by passions and interest of one or two States, rather than the whole Union.

For example, not a single Indian war started because of aggressions of the present federal government. But several instances of Indian hostilities were provoked by improper conduct of individual States. Those States were either unable or unwilling to restrain or punish offenses leading to the slaughter of many innocent inhabitants.

Foreign Hostilities in Border States

15   Some States border Spanish and British territories. Only bordering States, because of a sudden irritation or sense of injury, would be likely to use violence to excite war with these nations. Nothing can so effectively obviate that danger as a national government, whose wisdom and prudence will not be swayed by regional passions.

Federal Government Settles Hostilities

16 Not only will a national government find fewer just causes for war, it will have more power to accommodate and settle them amicably. It will be more temperate and cool, and in that respect, as well as others, it will have a better capacity to act advisedly than the offending State.

The pride of States, as well as men, naturally disposes them to justify all their actions and opposes their acknowledging, correcting or repairing their errors and offenses. Not affected by this pride, the national government will proceed with moderation and candor to consider and decide on the proper means to extricate them from threatening difficulties.

Apologies from Strong Nations Accepted

17 Besides, it is well known that explanations and compensations from a strong united nation are often accepted as satisfactory, when they would be rejected as unsatisfactory if offered by a State or confederacy of little power.

France Wouldn't Humiliate Spain or Britain

18 In 1685, the state of Genoa offended Louis XIV. He demanded they send their chief magistrate, accompanied by four senators, to *France* to ask his pardon and receive his terms. They were forced to obey for the sake of peace. Would he, on any occasion, either demanded, or received, like humiliation from Spain, Britain or any other *powerful* nation?

PUBLIUS

Number 4

Strong Union Provides Strong Defense

My last paper gave several reasons why a union would better secure the safety of the people against the danger exposed by *just* causes of war given by other nations. Besides supplying fewer causes for grievances, difficulties would be more easily settled by a national government than either the State governments or the proposed small confederacies.

Feigned Motives Start Wars

2 The safety of the people of America not only depends on their not giving other nations *just* causes for war but, also, on their not putting themselves in situations that *invite* hostility. It need not be observed that both *pretended* and just causes of war exist.

Variety of Motives Start Wars

3 Although a disgraceful fact of human nature, nations, in general, will make war whenever they have a prospect of getting anything from it. In fact, absolute monarchs often make war when their nations get nothing from it.

Motives, clear only to the monarch, often lead him to start wars not sanctified by justice or the interests of his people. These motives include: a thirst for military glory, revenge for personal affronts, ambition, and private compacts to aggrandize or support particular families or partisans. These, and a variety of other motives that affect only the mind of the monarch, lead him to start wars not sanctified by justice or the interests of his people. And they deserve our attention.

But other motives affect nations, as often as kings. And some of them grow out of situations and circumstances like ours.

Commerce Source of Rivalry

4 France and Britain are fishery rivals. We can supply their markets cheaper than they can themselves, despite their efforts to prevent it with bounties on their own and duties on foreign fish

Cargo Transport

5 We are rivals with them and most other European nations in navigation and cargo transport. We're lying to ourselves if we think they'll rejoice to see ours flourish. Since an increase in our transportation industry diminishes theirs, it's in their interest to restrain our trade rather than promote it.

Direct Imports

6 Our trade with China and India interferes with several nations. We now directly import commodities we used to purchase through, what was essentially, a monopoly.

North American Commerce

7 The growth of our commerce in our own vessels can't give pleasure to any nation with territories on or near this continent. Our productions are cheap and excellent. Our convenient location gives our enterprising merchants and navigators more advantages in those territories than consistent with the wishes or policies of European sovereigns.

Europe Controls Our Rivers

8 Spain thinks it is convenient to shut the Mississippi against us on one side. Britain excludes us from the Saint Lawrence on the other. And neither permits the other waterways between them and us to become the means of mutual intercourse and traffic.

Our Success Will Spawn Jealousies

9 From these and similar considerations that, if it was practical, could be listed and explained, it's easy to see that jealousies and uneasiness may gradually slide into the minds and cabinets of other nations. We can't expect them to regard our advancement in union and power, land and sea, with an eye of indifference and composure.

Healthy Defense Discourages War

10 Americans know these circumstances may lead to war. As will other reasons, not currently obvious. Whenever such inducements find opportunity, pretenses to justify them will not be wanting. Therefore, union and a good national government is necessary to defensively repress and discourage war instead of *inviting* it. The best defense depends on the government, the arms, and the resources of the country.

All Americans Want to be Safe

11 The safety of the whole is the interest of the whole. It cannot be provided for without government, either one or many.

In this context, is one good government more competent than any other number?

Defensive Advantages Of Union

12 One government can use the talents and experience of the ablest men, wherever in the Union they may be found. It can move on uniform policy principles. It can harmonize, assimilate, and protect the parts, extending the benefits of its foresight and precautions to each.

In drafting treaties, one government will regard both the interest of the whole and the specific interests of the parts of the whole. It can use the resources and power of the whole to defend a particular part more easily and expeditiously than state governments or separate confederacies that lack the unity of system.

The militia can be under one discipline with officers in a proper line of subordination to the Chief Executive [President], making it a consolidated corps, that is more efficient than thirteen, or three or four distinct independent forces.

Example: Great Britain

13 What would the militia of Britain be if the English militia obeyed the government of England, if the Scot militia obeyed the government of Scotland, and if the Welsh militia obeyed the government of Wales? If invaded, would those three governments (if they agreed at all) be able to operate against the enemy as effectively as the single government of Great Britain would?

Strength of Britain's National Navy

14 The fleets of Britain have been praised. In time, if we are wise, the fleets of America may gain attention. But if Britain's one national government hadn't regulated navigation, making it a nursery for seamen—if one national government hadn't used national means and materials for forming fleets—their prowess and thunder would never have been celebrated.

Let England have its navigation and fleet—let Scotland have its navigation and fleet—let Wales have its navigation and fleet—let Ireland have its navigation and fleet—let those four constituent parts of the British empire be under four independent governments and it is easy to perceive how soon they would each dwindle into comparative insignificance.

Divided America More Vulnerable

15 Apply these facts to our case. Divide America into thirteen or, if you please, three or four independent confederacies. What armies could they raise and pay? What fleets could they hope to have? If one was attacked, would the others fly to its aid, spend blood and money in its defense?

Or would foreign powers flatter and seduce the separate confederacies into neutrality with specious promises of peace until they fear threatening their tranquility and safety for the sake of their neighbors—neighbors they may already envy?

Although unwise, such conduct is natural. The history of Greece and other countries abounds with examples. And under similar circumstance it probably would happen again.

Union: Better Defense Decisions

16 Let's say neighboring States are willing to help an invaded State or confederacy. How, when, and what shall determine proportionate aid of men and money? Who will command the allied armies? Who will settle terms of peace? If disputes arise, who will umpire them and compel acquiescence? Various difficulties and inconveniences would be part of the situation.

But one government, watching over the general and common interests, directing the powers and resources of the whole, would be free from these tricky questions and conduce far more safety of the people.

Strong National Structure Creates Strong Defense

17 Whatever our situation—one national government or several confederacies—foreign nations will know and will act towards us accordingly. If they see our national government is efficient and well administered, our trade prudently regulated, our militia organized and disciplined, our resources and finances discreetly managed, our credit reestablished, our people free, contented and united, they will be more disposed to cultivate our friendship than provoke our resentment.

On the other hand, if they find our government ineffectual (each State doing right or wrong, as its ruler finds convenient) or split into three or four independent, and probably discordant, republics or confederacies—one inclining to Britain, another to France, a third to Spain, and perhaps played off each other by the three—what a poor, pitiful figure America will be in their eyes! She'd become a target for not only their contempt, but also their outrage. How soon our dear-bought experience will proclaim that when a people or family divide, it never fails to be against themselves.

PUBLIUS

Number 5

Greatest Threat to American Confederacies: Each Other

Queen Anne, in her letter of 1 July 1706 to the Scot Parliament, made some observations on the importance of the *Union*, then forming between England and Scotland, that merit our attention. I will present one or two extracts from it:

"An entire and perfect union will be the solid foundation of lasting peace: It will secure your religion, liberty, and property; remove the animosities amongst yourselves, and the jealousies and differences betwixt our two kingdoms. It must increase your strength, riches and trade; and by this union the whole island, being joined in affection and free from all apprehensions of different interest, will be *enabled to resist all its enemies. . .*"

"We most earnestly recommend to you calmness and unanimity in this great and weighty affair, that the union may be brought to a happy conclusion, being the only *effectual* way to secure our present and future happiness, and disappoint the designs of our and your enemies, who will doubtless, on this occasion, *use their utmost endeavors to prevent or delay this union.*"

Weak Nation Invites Foreign Danger

2 The previous paper noted that weakness and divisions at home would invite dangers from abroad. Nothing will more secure us from them than union, strength, and good government. This subject is copious and cannot easily be exhausted.

Great Britain Before Unification

3 We are acquainted with the history of Great Britain. It gives us many useful lessons. We may profit by their experience without paying the price it cost them.

Although it seems obvious to common sense that the people of such an island should be only one nation, for ages they were divided into three, three nations almost constantly embroiled in quarrels and wars with one another. Despite their mutual interests in dealing with the continental European nations, policies, practices and jealousies kept them perpetually inflamed. For years they were far more inconvenient and troublesome than useful and assisting to each other.

Separation Promotes Disputes

4 Would not the same thing happen if the people of America divide themselves into three or four nations? Would not similar jealousies arise and be cherished?

Instead of being "joined in affection" and free from worry about different "interests," envy and jealousy would soon extinguish confidence and affection. Instead of the general interests of all America, the specific, limited interests of each confederacy would be the only objectives of their policy and pursuits. Hence, like most other *bordering* nations, they would always be either involved in disputes and war, or live with the constant fear of them.

Confederacies Won't Remain Equal

5 The most devoted advocates for three or four confederacies cannot reasonably assume they would remain equal in strength, even if it was possible to form them so at first. What human plan can guarantee the equality will continue? Besides local circumstances, which tend to increase power in one part and impede its progress in another, superior policy and good management would probably distinguish one government above the rest. This would destroy the relatively equal strength. It cannot be presumed the same degree of good policy, prudence, and foresight would be uniform among these confederacies for very many years.

Distrust Between Confederacies

6 Whenever and however it might happen, and it would happen, at the moment when one of these nations or confederacies rise on the scale of political importance above her neighbors, her neighbors would behold her with envy and fear. Because of these passions they would listen to, if not promote, anything that promised to diminish her importance. Jealousy and fear would also restrain them from actions that might advance or even to secure her prosperity. It wouldn't take long for her to discern these unfriendly dispositions. She would soon begin to lose confidence in her neighbors and feel a disposition equally unfavorable to them.

Distrust naturally creates distrust. Nothing changes goodwill and kind conduct more speedily than jealousies and imputations, whether expressed or implied.

Northern Would Grow Stronger Than Southern Confederacies

7 The North is generally the region of strength. Many local circumstances render it probable that, in a relatively short period, the most Northern of the proposed confederacies would be unquestionably more formidable than any of the others. As soon as this became evident, the more southern parts

29

of America would have the same ideas and feelings about the northern States as the southern parts of Europe felt towards the *Northern Hive*. Nor does it appear rash to suppose that northerners might be tempted to gather honey in the blooming fields and milder air of their luxurious and more delicate southern neighbors.

Confederacies Become Enemies

8 The history of similar divisions and confederacies has abundant examples that several American confederacies would not become neighbors. They would neither love nor trust one another but, on the contrary, they would be prey to discord, jealousy, and mutual injuries. In short, they would place us in the exact situation some nations wish to see us, that is, *formidable only to each other*.

No American Confederacies' Alliance

9 Knowing this, it appears those gentlemen who expect alliances, offensive and defensive, might be formed between these confederacies, that they would unite arms and resources to keep them in a formidable state of defense against foreign enemies, are greatly mistaken.

Commerce Creates Foreign Alliances

10 Britain and Spain were formerly divided into independent states. When did they ever combine in alliance or unite their forces against a foreign enemy?

The proposed American confederacies will be *distinct nations*. Each would have commerce with foreigners regulated by distinct treaties. And since their products and commodities are different, and targeted for differ-

ent markets, the treaties would be essentially different.

Different commercial concerns create different interests and, of course, different degrees of political attachments with different foreign nations. The *Southern* confederacy might be at war with a nation that the *Northern* confederacy would be desirous of preserving peace and friendship. Therefore, an alliance so contrary to their immediate interest would not be easy to form, nor, if formed, easily observed and fulfilled.

Dangers From Other Confederacies

11 No. It is far more probable that in America, as in Europe, neighboring nations, with opposite interests and unfriendly passions, would frequently take different sides.

Considering our distance from Europe, it would be more natural for confederacies to fear danger from one another than from distant nations. Therefore, each would guard against the others with the aid of foreign alliances, rather than guard against foreign dangers with alliances between themselves.

And let us not forget how much easier it is to receive foreign fleets into our ports and foreign armies into out country than it is to persuade or compel them to depart. How many conquests did the Romans and others make under the guise of allies? What changes did they make in the governments they pretended to protect?

Would Independent Confederacies Secure Us From Foreign Invasions?

12 Let candid men judge, then, whether the division of America into a number of independent sovereignties would tend to secure us against the hostilities and improper interference of foreign nations.   PUBLIUS

Number 6

Hostilities Between Separated States, Several Confederacies

The last three papers enumerated the dangers from foreign nations to which we'd be exposed by a state of disunion. Now I'll delineate dangers of a different, and perhaps more alarming, kind—those that will flow from dissension between States and from domestic factions and convulsions. Although previously mentioned, they deserve a fuller investigation.

Disunited States Would Be Enemies

2   Only a man lost in Utopian speculations would think that if the States are totally disunited or only united in partial confederacies, the subdivisions would not have frequent, violent contests with each other. To presume that there would be few motives for such contests would require forgetting that men are ambitious, vindictive, and rapacious. To expect continued harmony between a number of individual, unconnected sovereignties in the same neighborhood would be to disregard the uniform course of human events, and the accumulated experience of the ages.

Reasons for War

3   The causes of hostility among nations are innumerable.

Some operate almost constantly on the collective bodies of society. Reasons include the love of power, the desire for preeminence and dominion, the jealousy of power, or the desire for equality and safety.

Other causes have a more indirect, but equally operative, influence. Such are the rivalries and competitions between commercial nations.

Still other reasons, no fewer than the former, originate entirely from private passions—attachments, hatreds, interests, hopes, fears—of leaders in the community. Whether favorites of a king or of people, men have too often abused their positions of public trust by using the pretext of public good to sacrifice the national tranquility for personal advantage or gratification.

Reasons Pericles Began Wars

4   Reacting to a prostitute's resentment, the celebrated Pericles [Athens, born c. 500 BC, died 429 BC] attacked, vanquished, and destroyed the city of the *Samnians*, costing his countrymen much blood and treasure.[1]

The same man started the famous and fatal *Peloponnesian* war—which eventually led to the ruin of the Athenian commonwealth—for one or more reasons: to assuage a private pique against the *Megarensians*,[2] another nation of Greece, to avoid prosecution as a coconspirator in the theft of a statue of Phidias,[3] to get rid of accusations of using state funds to purchase popularity.[4]

Example: Ambition Led to War

5   The ambitious Cardinal Wolsey, prime minister to Henry VIII, aspired to become pope and hoped to succeed through the influence of Emperor Charles V. To secure the favor of this powerful monarch, he pushed England into war with France, contrary to policy, hazarding the safety and independence of England as well as Europe. Wolsey was both an instrument

31

and a dupe in Emperor Charles V's intrigues as he attempted to become universal monarch.

Example: Women Stirred Up Strife

6   The influence on contemporary European policy, ferments, and pacification of Madame de Maintenon's bigotry, the Duchess of Marlborough's petulance, and the cabals of Madame de Pompadour has often been discussed and is generally known.

Example: Personal Motives Start Wars

7   Multiple examples of the affect of personal motivations on national events, either foreign or domestic, would be a waste of time. Those who have even a superficial acquaintance with history will remember a variety of examples. And those who know a little bit about human nature will need no examples to form their opinion of its reality or prevalence.

However, a reference to a recent event illustrating the general principle may be appropriate. If Shays had not been a *desperate debtor*, it's doubtful Massachusetts would have been plunged into a civil war.

Claim Commerce Brings Peace

8   In spite of the concurring testimony of experience, some visionaries, or designing men, make the paradoxical claim that the dismembered and alienated States will exist in perpetual peace. They say republics are inherently pacific.

They contend commerce softens men, extinguishing the inflammable temperament that has so often kindled wars. They claim commercial republics, like ours, will not want to waste themselves in ruinous conflicts with each other, that they will be governed by mutual interest and will cultivate a spirit of peaceful relations.

Commercial Motives Start Wars

9   We may ask these political prophets, isn't it in the interest of all nations to cultivate a benevolent and philosophic spirit? If this is in their true interest, have they in fact pursued it?

To the contrary, don't momentary passions and immediate interests have a more active and imperious control over human conduct than considerations of policy, utility, or justice? Have republics been less addicted to war than monarchies? Aren't the former administered by *men* as well as the latter?

Do not aversions, predilections, rivalship, and desires of unjust acquisitions affect nations as well as kings? Are not popular assemblies frequently subject to the impulses of rage, resentment, jealousy, avarice, and other violent propensities?

Isn't it well known that republics governed by a few trusted individuals are liable to be colored by the passions of those individuals? Has commerce ever done anything more than change the objects of war? Is not the love of wealth as domineering a passion as power or glory?

Haven't as many wars started from commercial motives, since that has become the prevailing system of nations, as were before started by the desire for territory or dominion? Hasn't commerce often given new incentives? Let experience, the least

---

[1] Aspasia, vide *Life of Pericles.*
[2] *Ibid.*
[3] *Ibid.*
[4] *Ibid.* Phidias, with Pericles, was supposed to have stolen some public gold for the embellishment of the statue of Minerva.

fallible guide to human behavior, answer these inquiries.

Wars: Commercial Republics

10 Sparta, Athens, Rome, and Carthage were all republics. Athens and Carthage were commercial republics. Yet they engaged in war, offensive and defensive, as often as the neighboring monarchies. Sparta was little more than an army camp. And Rome was never sated of carnage and conquest.

Republics of Carthage, Rome

11 Carthage, a commercial republic, was the aggressor in the war that ended in her destruction. Hannibal carried her arms into the heart of Italy, to the gates of Rome [217 BC]. Then Scipio [of Rome] overthrew the territories of Carthage and conquered the commonwealth [201 BC].

League of Cambray
Defeated Venice

12 In later times, Venice figured in more than one war of ambition until it became a target of other Italian states. Finally, Pope Julius II founded the League of Cambray (including the Emperor, King of France, King of Aragon, and most of the Italian princes and states) that gave a deadly blow to the power and pride of this haughty republic [c. 1509].

Holland's Role in European Wars

13 The provinces of Holland, until overwhelmed by debt and taxes, led and participated in European wars. They had furious contests with England for dominion of the sea. And they were among the most persevering and implacable of Louis XIV's opponents.

Great Britain

14 For ages, Britain's predominant pursuit has been commerce. And one branch of the national legislature is composed of representatives of the people. Nevertheless, few nations have engaged in more wars, frequently initiated by the people.

Representatives Caused British Wars

15 Britain has been involved in, if I may say so, almost as many popular as royal wars. On various occasions, the nation's representatives have dragged their monarchs into war or, contrary to the monarch's desires and, sometimes, the real interests of the state, continued a war.

In the long European struggle between *Austria* and *Bourbon*, the English antipathies against the French and the ambition, or rather the avarice, of the Duke of Marlborough, protracted the war well beyond sound policy and the opposition of the royal court.

Wars with Commercial Motives

16 The wars of these last two nations have been greatly influenced by commercial considerations, either to protect or increase trade and navigation advantages. And sometimes even the more culpable desire of sharing in the commerce of other nations without their consent.

Britain, Spain Commerce War

17 The last war but two between Britain and Spain sprang from the British merchants attempting to prosecute an illicit trade with the Spanish Main. These unjustifiable practices produced severity on the part of the Spaniards towards the subjects of Great Britain that were not justifiable, because they exceeded the bounds of just retaliation and were inhuman and cruel. Many of the English who were taken on the Spanish coast were sent to dig in the mines of Potosi. And as resentment progresses, after a while, the innocent were confused with the guilty in indiscriminate punishment.

The complaints of English merchants kindled a violent flame that spread throughout the nation, then through the House of Commons, and from that body to the ministry. Letters of reprisal were granted and war ensued. Consequently, all the alliances formed only 20 years before, with sanguine expectations of the most beneficial fruits, were overthrown.

Can't Expect Peace Among Separated States

18 From this summary of situations similar to our own, why should we confidently expect peace and cordiality between members of the present confederacy if the States separate? Haven't we seen the fallacy and extravagance of idle theories promising an exemption from the imperfections, weaknesses, and evils incident to every type of society?

Isn't it time to awake from the deceitful dream of a golden age? We must adopt the practical maxim for our political conduct that we, as well as the other inhabitants of the globe, are a long way from the happy empire of perfect wisdom and perfect virtue.

Many Excuses for Conflicts

19 Let the extreme depression over our national dignity, let the inconveniences felt everywhere from a lax and ill government, let the revolt within North Carolina, the late menacing disturbances in Pennsylvania, and the actual insurrections and rebellions in Massachusetts, declare—!

One Republic Remedies Interstate Conflict

20 Generally, mankind behaves quite differently than predicted by those endeavoring to lull asleep our fears of discord and hostility if the States disunite. A sort of political axiom, founded on historical observation, is that nearness makes nations natural enemies.

An intelligent writer expresses himself on this subject: "NEIGHBORING NATIONS (says he) are naturally enemies of each other, unless their common weakness forces them to league in a CONFEDERATE REPUBLIC, and their constitution prevents the differences that neighborhood occasions, extinguishing that secret jealousy that disposes all states to aggrandize themselves at the expense of their neighbors."[5]

This passage both points out the EVIL and suggests the REMEDY.

PUBLIUS

---

[5] Vide *Principes des Negociations*, par l'Abbe de Mably.

Number 7

Potential Reasons for Wars Between Disunited States

It is sometimes condescendingly asked, if the States were disunited, what reasons would they have to make war on each other? It would be a full answer to say, precisely the same reasons that have, at different times, deluged in blood all the nations in the world.

However, unfortunately for us, there is a more specific answer to the question. We can think of reasons for differences between us. Even under the restraints of a federal constitution, we have felt their effect. We can deduce the consequences of removing those restraints.

Territorial Disputes

2   Territorial disputes are always a fertile source of hostility among nations. Perhaps this is the reason for the greatest number of wars that have desolated the earth. This cause would exist among us in full force.

Vast tracts of territory within the boundaries of the United States remain unsettled. Several States still have discordant and undecided claims. If the Union was dissolved, all the States would have similar claims.

Rights to lands not granted at the time of the Revolution, crown lands, remain the subject of serious and animated discussion. The States that controlled their colonial governments claim them as property. Other States contend the rights to that land, which had been granted by the crown, devolved at the founding of the Union. They say this is especially true of the Western territory that was either actually owned by the crown or was under the king of Great Britain's jurisdiction because the Indians who lived on it had been conquered.

Great Britain relinquished this land in the peace treaty. Some claim this territory was an acquisition to the Confederacy by compact with a foreign power. Hoping for an amicable termination of the dispute, Congress prudently prevailed upon States to cede it to the United States for the benefit of the whole. A dismemberment of the Confederacy, however, would revive this dispute and create others on the same subject.

At present, a large part of the vacant Western territory is, by cession if not anterior right, the common property of the Union. If the Union ended, States that had ceded the property as a federal compromise would probably reclaim the lands. The other States would insist on a proportion, arguing that the territory was acquired or secured by joint efforts of the Confederacy.

Even if, contrary to probability, all the States agreed to share in this common territory, the question of proper apportionment would remain. Different principles would be set up by different States with differing interests. They might not easily be persuaded to make an amicable agreement.

Dispute over Wyoming Territory

3   Therefore, the Western territory provides a theatre for hostile pretensions without any common judge to interpose between the contending parties. History shows we have good ground to fear that the sword would sometimes be used as the arbiter of their differences.

The dispute between Connecticut and Pennsylvania over Wyoming land reminds us not to expect easy answers to such differences. Under the Articles of Confederation, the parties appealed to a federal court for the decision. The court decided in favor of Pennsylvania. But Connecticut was dissatisfied until, by negotiation, an equivalent was found for her perceived loss.

I don't intend to suggest misconduct by Connecticut. She sincerely believed herself injured by the decision and States, like individuals, acquiesce with great reluctance in determinations to their disadvantage.

Dispute over District of Vermont

4   Those watching the controversy between New York and the district of Vermont can vouch for the opposition from even States not a part of the claim. The peace of the confederacy might have been in danger if New York had attempted to assert its rights by force.

Two primary motives prompted opposition from States that were not part of the claim: (1) jealousy of New York's future power and (2) land grants made to individuals in neighboring States by the government of Vermont.

States who brought claims contrary to New York's (New Hampshire, Massachusetts, Connecticut) seemed more interested in dismembering New York than establishing their own pretensions. New Jersey and Rhode Island discovered a zeal for Vermont's independence; and Maryland agreed until alarmed by the appearance of a connection between Canada and that State. These small States worried about New York's growing greatness. Reviewing these actions shows some causes that would likely embroil the States with each other, if it would be their unfortunate destiny to become disunited.

Commercial Disputes

5   Commerce offers another fruitful source of contention. The States in less favorable circumstances would want to share in the advantages of their more fortunate neighbors.

Each State, or separate confederacy, would pursue a commercial policy peculiar to itself, creating distinctions, preferences, exclusions and discontent. Since the earliest settlement of the country, commerce has been based on equal privileges. The change would sharpen discontent.

We should be ready to name the injuries that were caused, in reality, *by justifiable acts of independent sovereignties regarding their distinct interests.*

The spirit of enterprise characterizing the commercial part of America uses every occasion to improve itself. This unbridled spirit probably won't respect trade regulations designed to secure exclusive benefits for the citizens of a specific State. The infractions of regulations on one side, and the efforts to prevent and repel them on the other, would naturally lead to outrages, then reprisals, then wars.

Example: New York's Import Duties

6   Some States would have opportunities to make others involuntarily subservient through commercial regulations. The situation of New York, Connecticut, and New Jersey gives an example of this.

In need of revenue, New York put duties on imports. As consumers of the same products, the citizens of these two exporting States pay a large part of these duties. New York would not voluntarily forego this advantage. Her citizens wouldn't consent to a rebate to the citizens of those neighboring States. And it would be impossible to segregate the customers in the New York market.

How long would Connecticut and New Jersey submit to taxation for the exclusive benefit of New York? How long would New Yorkers be permitted to enjoy the advantage of a metropolis that its neighbors find oppressive? Could we preserve New York with the weight of Connecticut on one side and the cooperating pressure of New Jersey on the other? Temerity alone would allow an affirmative answer to these questions.

Disputes Over National Debt

7   The Union's public debt would cause further collision between the separate States or confederacies. First the apportionment, then the progressive extinguishment, would produce ill humor and animosity.

How could a satisfactory rule of apportionment be possible? Scarcely any proposal is free from real objections. As usual, opposing parties would exaggerate them.

Already, the States have dissimilar views on the general principle of discharging public debt. Some of them, either not impressed with the importance of national credit or because their citizens have little, if any, interest in the question, feel an indifference or repugnance to paying the domestic debt. They would be inclined to magnify the difficulties of a distribution.

Other States have an additional complication. Their citizens' total public credit is greater than their State's proportion of the national debt. They would demand an equitable and effective provision.

The procrastination of debtor States would create resentments in creditor States. Real differences of opinion and manufactured excuses would delay the settlement of an apportion rule.

The citizens of the States would clamor. Foreign powers would demand satisfaction. And the peace of the States would be in double jeopardy from external invasion and internal strife.

Debt: Hostilities Between States

8   Suppose an apportionment rule was made. Some States would still find it harder to bear than others. Naturally, the suffers would seek mitigation of the burden.

Just as naturally, others would be disinclined to any revision that might increase their own encumbrances. Their refusal would supply a pretext for complaining States to withhold their contributions. The noncompliance of these States would be ground for bitter discussion and altercation.

Even if the rule adopted was equal in principle, some States would be delinquent because of a real deficiency of resources, financial mismanagement, accidental governmental mismanagement, and the reluctance of men to postpone immediate wants by using money to pay debts.

Delinquencies, from whatever causes, produce complaints, recriminations, and quarrels. Perhaps nothing disturbs the tranquility of nations more than their being bound to mutual financial obligations that don't yield an equal, coincident benefit. It is as true as it is trite that men differ over nothing so readily as the payment of money.

Disputes Over Citizens' Contracts

9   Another probable source of hostility is laws in violation of private contracts, when they injure citizens of a State. We have seen too many instances of State codes being disgraced. We can not expect a more liberal and equitable spirit in the State legislatures if they are unrestrained by checks.

We've seen Connecticut disposed to retaliate against Rhode Island as a consequence of offenses perpetrated by the Rhode Island legislature. We can reasonably assume that under other circumstances, a war, not of *parchment* but of the sword, would punish atrocious breaches of moral obligation and social justice.

Dangers of State Alliances with Foreign Nations

10 Preceding papers sufficiently unfolded the probability of alliances between States, or confederacies, and different foreign nations, and the effects of such alliances on the peace of the whole. They've shown that, if America is not connected at all or only by the feeble tie of a league, foreign alliances will gradually entangle it in all the pernicious labyrinths of European politics and wars. And the destructive contentions of the parts would be likely to become prey to the artifices and machinations of nations equally the enemies of them all. *Divide et impera** must be the motto of every nation that either hates or fears us.

PUBLIUS

* Divide and command.

Number 8

Disunited States Threat to Each Other

Let us assume the States were disunited, or in alliances formed from the wreck of the Union. They would face the same vicissitudes of peace and war, friendship and enmity, experienced by all neighboring nations not united under one government. Let us study some of the consequences in concise detail.

Strong Defense Reduces Wars

2 During the first period of their separate existences, war between the American States would cause more distress than in countries with long military establishments. Although they damage liberty and economy, the presence of disciplined armies in Europe make sudden conquests impractical, and prevent the rapid devastation that foreshadowed war before their introduction.

Fortifications also delay conquests. The nations of Europe are encircled by fortified places that mutually obstruct invasions. To gain admittance into an enemy's country, invasion resources are wasted on campaigns against two or three frontier garrisons.

Similar impediments occur at every step, exhausting the strength and delaying the progress of an invader. Formerly, an invading army penetrated into the heart of a neighboring country almost as quickly as news of its approach reached its rulers. Now, a comparatively small force of disciplined defensive troops in outposts impedes, finally frustrating, larger invasions.

The history of war in Europe no longer includes whole nations subdued and empires overturned. Instead, towns are taken and returned, battles decide nothing, retreats are more beneficial than victories. There is much effort and little acquisition.

Disunited States: Conquests, Ruin

3 In this country, the opposite would happen. Jealousy would postpone military spending as long as possible. The lack of fortifications, leaving State frontiers open to one another, would facilitate inroads. With little difficulty, populous States would overrun less populous neighbors. Conquests would be easily made but difficult to retain. Therefore, war would be desultory and predatory. PLUNDER and devastation march behind irregular troops. The primary result of our military exploits would be calamities on individuals.

Tradeoff Between Liberty, Safety

4 This is not an exaggeration. Though, I confess, the situation would soon change.

Safety from external danger is the most powerful motivator of national conduct. After a time, even the ardent love of liberty will diminish under its dictates. War's violent destruction of life and property, and the vigilance under a continuous state of danger, will compel even those nations most attached to liberty to resort, for repose and security, to institutions that tend to destroy their civil and political rights. To be safer, they will risk being less free.

Increases Military Defense, Executive Authority

5 I'm referring to STANDING ARMIES and the appendages of military establishments. The new Constitution has no prohibition of a standing army; therefore, by inference they may exist under it.[1]

This inference is, at best, problematical and uncertain. However, it can be argued that standing armies are the inevitable result of the dissolution of the Union. Frequent wars and constant fear require and produce a state of constant military preparedness.

First, the weaker States, or confederacies, would need standing armies to make themselves equal with their stronger neighbors. They would

endeavor to supplement their smaller population and fewer resources with a more effective system of defense, including disciplined troops and fortifications. At the same time, their executive arm of government would need to be strengthened and, in doing so, their constitutions would evolve towards a monarchy. It is the nature of war to increase the executive at the expense of the legislative authority.

States Deteriorate Into Despotism

6 Those States or confederacies who do the above would soon be superior to their neighbors. Small States with less natural strength but vigorous governments and disciplined armies, often triumph over larger States or States with greater natural strength but lacking these advantages.

Neither the pride nor safety of more important States, or confederacies, would permit them to submit to this mortifying and adventitious superiority for long. They would quickly use similar military means to reinstate their lost preeminence. Thus, in a little time, the same engines of despotism that are the scourge of the Old World will be established in every part of this country. This is the natural course of things. Our reasonings will be just in proportion as follow this model.

Natural Course of Human Societies

7 These are not vague inferences drawn from speculative defects in a Constitution that derives its power from a people, their representatives, or delegates. Rather, they are solid conclusions drawn from the natural progression of human affairs.

Commercial Nation Needs Professional Army

8 It may be asked why standing armies did not spring up out of the fre-

---

[1] This will be fully examined in its proper place and be shown to be a natural precaution, and a much better one than found in any constitution heretofore framed in America, most of which contain no guard at all on this subject.

quent conflicts in the ancient republics of Greece. Different answers, equally satisfactory, may be given to this question.

First, Greece was essentially a nation of soldiers. Today, people industriously pursue profits, devoting their efforts to improvements in agriculture and commerce. Capitalism is incompatible with a nation of soldiers.

The growth of revenue, multiplied by increases of gold, silver, industry, and the modern science of finance, along with the habits of nations, have produced an entire revolution in the system of war. Professional, disciplined armies, separate from the body of citizens, have become the companions of frequent hostility.

Small, Unintrusive Peacetime Army

9 Also, military establishments in a country seldom exposed to military invasions are quite different than those in a nation often subject to, and always fearing, them. Rulers of the former, even if so inclined, won't have any excuse to keep armies as numerous as is necessary in the latter situation.

In countries not exposed to military invasions, armies are rarely, if ever, activated for interior defense. The people are in no danger of being broken by military subordination. Laws are rarely relaxed because of military emergencies. The civil state remains vigorous, neither corrupted nor confounded by the principles or propensities of a military state. The smallness of the army makes the community's natural strength an over match for it.

Since the citizens neither look to the military for protection nor submit to its oppressions, they neither love nor fear soldiers. The citizens view soldiers as a necessary evil and are ready to resist any attempt to curtail their civil rights.

Executive Use of Military

10 Under these circumstances, the executive branch of government may use the army to suppress a small faction, an occasional mob or insurrection, but it won't be able to enforce encroachments against the united efforts of the great body of the people.

Large Military Decreases Civil Rights

11 In a country faced with perpetual menacings, the opposite happens. The government must always be prepared to repel it. It needs armies large enough for instant defense. The continual necessity for their services proportionately enhances the importance of the soldier and degrades the condition of the citizen. The military state becomes elevated above the civil.

The inhabitants of territories, often the theater of war, are unavoidably subjected to frequent infringements on their rights, which weakens their sense of those rights. By degrees, the people begin to consider soldiers not only as their protectors but as their superiors. The transition to seeing them as masters is neither remote nor difficult. Once it has happened, however, it's difficult to get the people to make a bold or effectual resistance to usurpations supported by the military power.

Britain Doesn't Need Large Army

12 Great Britain is seldom exposed to internal invasions. An insular situation and a powerful navy, guarding it against foreign invasion, supersede the necessity of having a large army within the kingdom. A force that can hold invaders at bay until the militia can be raised, is all that is necessary. Neither national policy nor public opinion has tolerated more domestic troops. It has been a long time since an internal war has produced the enumerated consequences.

To a great degree, Britain being an island has helped preserve the liberty that it enjoys until this day, in spite of prevalent venality and corruption. If Britain was on the continent, she would need home military establishments as extensive as those of the other great European powers. She, like them, would probably be a victim of the absolute power of a single man.

It is possible, but not easy, that the island may be enslaved from other causes, but not from the prowess of an army as small as that usually kept within Britain.

United, States Insulated from Danger

13 If we're wise enough to preserve the Union, usually we may enjoy the advantage of an insulated situation for a long time. Europe is a great distance from us. Her colonies in our vicinity will probably continue having such disproportionate strength to ours that they'll be unable to be a dangerous annoyance. Therefore, extensive military establishments will be unnecessary for our security.

But if we become disunited, with the parts either separated or thrown together in two or three confederacies, in a short time we would be in the predicament of the continental powers of Europe—our liberties would be at risk because of the armies needed to defend ourselves against the ambition and jealousy of each other.

No Constitution, Dangers Will Be Real

14 This concern is not superficial or futile, but solid and weighty. It deserves the most serious and mature consideration of every judicious and honest man of whatever party.

If such men will pause and meditate dispassionately on the importance of this interesting idea, if they will contemplate it and trace it to all its consequences, they will give up trivial objections to a Constitution that, if rejected, would probably end the Union. The airy phantoms that flit before the distempered imaginations of some of its adversaries would quickly be replaced by more substantial forms of dangers: real, certain, and formidable.

PUBLIUS

Number 9

Constitution Refines "Confederate Republic" Form

A firm Union will act as a barrier against domestic strife and insurrection, preserving the peace and liberty of the States.

Reading the history of the petty republics of Greece and Italy produces sensations of horror and disgust at the continuous agitation. A rapid succession of revolutions perpetually oscillated them between the extremes of tyranny and anarchy. The occasional calms serve only as short-lived contrasts to the furious storms to follow. We view intervals of felicity with some regret because we know they will be quickly replaced by the tempestuous waves of sedition and party rage. Momentary rays of glory break through the gloom, dazzling us with a transient and fleeting brilliancy. At the same time, their history admonishes us to lament political vices that pervert the direction and tarnish the luster of bright talents so justly celebrated.

"Ordered Society Can't Be Free"

2   From the disfiguring disorders of the republics of Greece and Italy, the advocates of despotism argue against both the republican form of government and the principles of civil liberty. They declare an ordered society incompatible with all free governments. And they indulge in malicious exultation over its supporters.

Happily for mankind, astounding governmental structures formed on the foundation of liberty have, in a few glorious instances, refuted their gloomy sophisms. And, I trust, that America will be the broad and solid foundation of other edifices, no less magnificent, that will become equally permanent monuments to their errors.

Improvement in Republic Form

3   The histories of the republican governments of Greece and Italy undeniably represent their experience. But if a more perfectly crafted republican-based structure was impossible, the enlightened friends of liberty would have abandoned the cause of that form of government as indefensible.

However, like most sciences, the science of politics has greatly improved. The effectiveness of various principles, ones either not known or imperfectly known to the ancients, is now understood. This includes: a fixed procedure for distribution of power into distinct branches, the introduction of legislative balances and checks, the institution of courts with judges holding their offices during good behavior, and legislative representation by deputies elected by the people. These are new discoveries or have progressed toward perfection in modern times. By these powerful means, the excellancies of republican government may be retained with its imperfections lessened or avoided.

I offer another improvement to the popular systems of civil government. Adding it may seem odd, since it's been used as an objection to the new Constitution. I'm referring to the ENLARGEMENT of the ORBIT within which the systems will revolve, either in respect to the dimensions of a single State or to the consolidation of several smaller States into one great confederacy. The latter is the object of immediate consideration. An examination of the principle as applied to a single State will be useful and will be done in another place.

"Republic Requires Small Territory"

4   The utility of a Confederacy to suppress internal faction, guarding the tranquillity of states, as well as increasing their external force and security, isn't a new idea. Different countries in different ages have practiced it and have received the approval of political scholars. The opponents of the proposed Constitution have unremittingly cited and circulated Montesquieu's observations that a republican government requires a small territory. But they seem uninformed of sentiments expressed by that great man in another part of his work. Nor do they call attention to the consequences of the principle they support with ready acquiescence.

Size Smaller Than Most States

5   When Montesquieu recommends a small area for republics, he's referring to dimensions much smaller than almost every one of our States. Neither Virginia, Massachusetts, Pennsylvania, New York, North Carolina, nor Georgia can be compared with the models he described. Therefore, if we were to take his ideas on this point as unquestionably true, we would have to either take refuge in the arms of monarchy or split ourselves into an infinity of little, jealous, clashing, tumultuous commonwealths, the wretched nurseries of unceasing discord and the miserable objects of universal pity or contempt.

Some opponents of the Constitution seem aware of this dilemma. They've even been bold enough to hint that dividing the large States is desirable. Such an infatuated, desperate, self-serving policy might provide a multitude of political offices for men not qualified to hold positions beyond the narrow circles of personal intrigue. But it could never promote the greatness or happiness of the people of America.

Theory Relates to Size of States

6 As already mentioned, the principle itself will be examined at another place. It's sufficient to say here that Montesquieu's theory would only dictate a reduction of the SIZE of the largest MEMBERS of the Union. And it does not argue against them being joined under one confederate government. And this is the true question in the present discussion.

Montesquieu: Confederate Republic

7 Montesquieu is so far from opposing a Union of the States that he explicitly regards a CONFEDERATE REPUBLIC as suitable, reconciling the advantages of monarchy with republicanism.

Advantages of Republic, Monarchy

8 In the *Sprit of Laws*, book ix, he says mankind very probably would have constantly lived under the government of a single person if a constitution had not been contrived that has all the internal advantages of a republic together with the external force of a monarchy, that is, a CONFEDERATE REPUBLIC.

States Combine into Larger Republic

9, 10 In this form of government, he continues, several smaller *states* agree to become members of a large *one*. It is like an assemblage of societies to make a new one that is able to grow by adding new associations until it is powerful enough to provide security for the united body. This kind of republic can withstand external force and internal corruption, preventing all inconveniences.

Help to Stop Usurpers

11 He explains that if one man attempted usurping supreme authority, he wouldn't have equal influence in all the confederate states. If he had too great an influence over one, it would alarm the rest. If he subdued a part, the rest would be free to oppose and overpower him with forces independent of those he usurped.

Confederacy of Republics Stable

12, 13 A popular insurrection in one state would be quelled by the others. If abuses creep into one part, he argues, it is reformed by those that remain sound. The state may be destroyed on one side and not on the other. The confederacy might be dissolved and the states preserve their sovereignty. Since it is a government composed of small republics, it has internal happiness. And it has the advantage of a large monarchy in external situations.

Union Represses Domestic Faction

14 I have paraphrased Montesquieu's writing at such length because they are arguments in favor of the Union and they remove false impressions made when other parts of his work is quoted out of context. This part of his writing also speaks to the point of this paper, the tendency of the Union to repress domestic faction and insurrection.

Confederacy vs. Consolidation

15 A distinction, more subtle than accurate, has been raised between a *confederacy* and a *consolidation* of States. The essential characteristic of the confederacy is the restriction of its authority to the members in their collective capacities, without reaching the individuals of whom they are composed [legislation for states]. It is contended that the national council should not be concerned with any object of internal administration. Equality of suffrage between members has also been insisted on as an important feature of a confederate government.

These are largely arbitrary positions, neither supported by principle nor precedent. Governments of this kind generally seem to be marked with these distinctions and it's easy to assume they are an inherent part of their nature. But there have been such extensive exceptions to the practice, no absolute rule on the subject can be concluded

On the other hand, this investigation will clearly show that wherever the principle argued for by the opposition has prevailed, it caused incurable disorder and imbecility in the government.

States Retain Some Sovereignty

16 The definition of a *confederate republic* is "an assemblage of societies," or an association of two or more states into one state. The extent, modifications, and objects of federal authority are discretionary. As long as the separate organization of members isn't abolished, constitutionally existing for local purposes, and even if it is in subordination to the general authority of the union, it will be, in fact and in theory, an association of states, or a confederacy.

The proposed Constitution, rather than implying an abolition of the State governments, makes them constituent parts of the national sovereignty with direct representation in the Senate. It leaves in their possession certain exclusive and very important portions of sovereign power. This corresponds with the idea of a federal government.

Constitution Refines Form

17 In the Lycian confederacy with 23 CITIES or republics, the largest had *three* votes in the COMMON COUNCIL, the middle had *two*, and the smallest *one*. The COMMON COUNCIL appointed all judges and executives of the respective CITIES. This was certainly the most invasive interference in their internal administration; if anything seems exclusively appropriate to local jurisdictions, it is the appointment of their own officers. Yet Montesquieu says, "Were I to give a model of an excellent Confederate Republic, it would be that of Lycia."

Thus we realize that the distinctions insisted upon in the Constitution were not within the contemplation of this enlightened civilian and we shall be led to conclude that they are the novel refinements of an erroneous theory.

PUBLIUS

Number 10

Large Republic: Best Control of Effects of Faction

The important tendency of a well-constructed Union to break and control the violence of faction deserves careful examination. The propensity for this dangerous vice alarms every friend of popular governments. Therefore, they will appreciate any plan providing a cure that doesn't violate the principles of liberty he so values.

Public councils rift with instability, injustice, and confusion are the mortal diseases that have killed popular governments everywhere. The adversaries of liberty continue to use this excuse for their most specious declamations.

The American State constitutions make valuable improvements on the popular governing models, both ancient and modern, that cannot be too much admired. But claiming they effectually obviate the danger as was wished and expected would be an unwarranted partiality.

Our most considerate and virtuous citizens, equally friends of public and private faith, and public and personal liberty, complain our governments are too unstable. They say the public good is disregarded in the conflicts of rival parties. Too often, measures are decided by the superior force of an interested and overbearing majority rather than the rules of justice and the rights of the minority party.

We may fervently wish these complaints had no foundation, but the evidence shows they are in some degree true.

A candid review shows that some of our distresses have been erroneously blamed on the operation of our governments. However, other causes, alone, will not account for many of our heaviest misfortunes. Specifically, the prevailing and increasing distrust of public engagements and alarm for private rights echoed from one end of the continent to the other. These must be largely, if not totally, the effects of distrusting the injustice that a factious spirit has tainted our public administrations.

Faction Defined: Group Acts Against Community Interests

2   By a faction, I mean a group of citizens, either a majority or minority, united and actuated by some common passion or interest adverse to the rights of other citizens or to the aggregate interests of the community.

Faction Cure: Remove Causes or Control Effect

3   There are two methods of curing the mischiefs of faction: remove its causes or control its effects.

Remove Causes: Destroy Liberty or Equalize Passions

4   There are also two methods of removing the causes: destroy the liberty essential for it to exist or give every citizen the same opinions, passions, and interests.

Destroy Liberty: Worse Than Factions

5   The first remedy is far worse than the disease. Liberty is to faction what air is to fire. Without the nourishment of liberty, faction instantly dies. But abolishing liberty, an essential of political life, because it nourishes faction is as silly as the wish to annihilate air, an essential of animal life, because it gives fire its destructive energy.

Equal Passions: Impossible

6   The second cure is an impractical as the first is unwise. As long as man's reasoning remains fallible and he's free to use it, different opinions will be formed. As long as a connection between reasoning and self-love exists, opinions and passions will influence each other. Especially, passions will sway opinions.

Property rights originate from the people. But the diversity in men's abilities is an insurmountable obstacle to equality of acquisitions. Protection of these abilities is government's primary function. Because government protects different and unequal abilities to acquire property, the people end up owning properties of varying value and kind. This diversity of property ownership divides society into groups with different interests and concerns.

Faction: Inherent in Human Nature

7   Therefore, faction is part of the very nature of man. We see different degrees of it in different circumstances. Differing opinions on religion and government in both theory and practice, the various ambitions of leaders, human passions, and diversity of interests have, at various times, divided mankind into parties and inflamed animosity, making them more apt to oppress each other than cooperate for their common good.

Mankind's propensity toward mutual animosities make even frivolous and insubstantial differences a sufficient excuse to kindle unfriendly passions and excite violent conflicts.

But the most common and durable source of factions is the unequal distribution of property. Those who have property and those who are without property always have different interests. Likewise, creditors and debtors.

From necessity, civilized nations develop property owners, manufacturers, merchants, bankers and many less defined occupations creating different classes with different sentiments and views. The regulation of these various and conflicting interests is the principal task of modern legislation. Therefore, factions are a part of the ordinary operations of government.

Legislators: Both Advocates, Parties to Causes

8   No man is allowed to be a judge in his own cause because his interest would certainly bias his judgement and probably corrupt his integrity.

For even greater reasons, a group of men are unfit to be both judges and litigants at the same time. Yet the most important legislative acts are basically judicial determinations, not about the rights of individuals, but about the rights of large bodies of citizens. And the different classes of legislators are but advocates and parties to the causes they determine.

Does a proposed law concern private debts? Creditors are parties on one side; debtors on the others. Justice ought to hold the balance between them. Yet the parties are, and must be, themselves the judges. The most numerous party or, in other words, the most powerful **faction** must be expected to prevail.

Should domestic manufacturers be encouraged, and how much, by restrictions on foreign manufacturers? Landowners would answer differently than manufacturers. Neither would probably use justice and the public good as sole motivators.

The apportionment of taxes on different types of property would seem to require the most exact impartiality. Yet there is, perhaps, no legislative act with greater opportunity and temptation for the predominant party to trample on the rules of justice. With every dollar they overburden the minority party, they save a dollar in their own pockets.

All Private Interests Never Ignored

9   It is naïve to say that enlightened statesmen will adjust the clashing interests, making them all subservient to the public good. Enlightened statesmen will not always be at the helm. Besides, to make such an adjustment indirect and remote effects must be considered. And they will rarely prevail over the immediate interest one party may have in disregarding the rights of another or the good of the whole.

Effect Must Be Controlled

10   The obvious inference is that the *causes* of faction cannot be removed and relief can only be sought in the means of controlling its *effects*.

Majority Faction: Downside of Popular Government

11   If a faction isn't a majority, relief comes from the republican principle that enables the majority to defeat sinister views by vote. The minority faction may clog the government systems and convulse society, but under the Constitution it can't execute and mask its violence.

When a faction is a majority, popular government enables it to sacrifice public good and the rights of other citizens to their passions and interests.

To secure the public good and private rights against the danger of such a faction and, at the same time, preserve the spirit and form of popular government, is the objective of our discussion. Let me add that our most fervent desire is to rescue popular government from the disgrace of shameful conduct under which it has so long labored and recommend it be appraised and adopted by mankind.

Prevent Majority Faction's Passions Or Actions

12   How is this objective obtainable? Evidently, by only one of two ways. Either the negative passions and interests in a majority faction must be prevented or that faction must be rendered unable to effect schemes of oppression.

If the desire and opportunity coincide, neither moral nor religious motives can be relied on as adequate control. Moral values don't control the injustice and violence of individuals and their efficacy decreases proportionately to the number of people involved. In other words, the effectiveness of moral values decreases as their need increases.

Pure Democracy Magnifies Violent Effects of Faction

13   It may be concluded from this view of the subject that pure democracy, by which I mean a society of citizens who assemble and administer the government in person, won't cure the harm caused by faction. In a pure democratic government, a common passion or interest will, almost always, be felt by a majority of the whole. There is nothing to check the inducement to sacrifice the weaker party or obnoxious individual.

Therefore, such democracies are always spectacles of turbulence and contention. They are incompatible with personal security or property rights. Their lives are as short as their deaths, violent. Political theorists who support this type of government erroneously suppose that after people are reduced to perfect political equality, their possessions, their opinions, and their passions will also be equal.

Republic vs. Pure Democracy

14 A republic, by which I mean a government with a representation plan, suggests a different expectation and promises the cure we are seeking. Let's examine the points it varies from pure democracy and we will understand both the nature of the cure and the efficacy it derives from the Union.

Representatives, Larger Area

15 The two great points of difference between a democracy and a republic are: first, in a republic, a small number of governmental delegates are elected by the rest of the citizens; secondly, a republic can be composed of a greater number of citizens over a larger country.

Representatives: Guard Public Good

16 The first difference, representation, refines and enlarges public views by passing them through the chosen body of citizens. The representatives' wisdom may discern the true interest of their country and their patriotism and love of justice will make it less likely to sacrifice it to temporary or partial considerations. Under this system, the public voice, as pronounced by the representatives of the people, may be more in line with the public good than if all the people gathered and spoke for themselves.

On the other hand, the effect may be inverted. Men with local preju-dices or sinister designs may, by intrigue, corruption, or other means, be voted into office, then betray the interests of the people.

The question becomes whether small or extensive republics elect better guardians of the public good. For two obvious reasons, extensive republics do.

Large Nation: Qualified People

17 In the first place, no matter how small the republic may be, there must be enough representatives to guard against the plots of a few. However, in a large republic the number must be limited to guard against the confusion of a multitude. Hence, the number of representatives in the two cases are not in the same proportion to their constituents, with the larger proportion in the small republic. If the proportion of qualified people is the same in a large as a small republic, the large republic will present greater options and, consequently, result in a greater probability of a fit choice.

Large Republic: More Qualified Men

18 Since each representative is chosen by a greater number of citizens in a large than a small republic, it will be more difficult for unworthy candidates to successfully win through election fraud. And with wide voter freedom, elections will more likely center on men who possess the most attractive merit and the most diffusive and established character.

Representative/Constituent Ratio

19 It must be confessed that, as in most things, inconveniences will be found. Too large a number of electors (voters) leaves the representative too little acquainted with all their local circumstances and lesser issues. Reducing the electorate too much renders the representative unduly attached and unfit to comprehend and pursue great and national issues. The federal Constitution forms a happy combination in this respect. The great and aggregate issues are referred to the national government, local issues referred to State legislatures.

Large Area: Conspiracy Harder

20 The second difference between a pure democracy and a republic is that a republic can encompass a greater number of citizens and larger territory than a democracy. This circumstance makes factious combinations difficult.

The smaller the society, the fewer the distinct parties and interests, and the more frequently they will be a majority. The smaller the number of individuals composing a majority and the smaller area they inhabit, the more easily will they combine and execute their plans of oppression.

Expanding the size adds a greater variety of parties and interests. It becomes less probable that a majority of the whole will have a common motive to invade the rights of other citizens. Even if a common motive exists, it will be more difficult for those holding it to discover their combined strength and act in unison with each other.

Besides other impediments, when a consciousness of unjust or dishonorable purposes exists, communication is limited by distrust in proportion to the number whose concurrence is necessary.

Union Controls Effects of Faction

21 Hence, it clearly appears that the same advantage a republic has over a democracy, controlling the effects of faction, is enjoyed by a large over a small republic, and enjoyed by the Union over the States composing it. Is the advantage the result of substituting enlightened, virtuous representatives who are above local prejudices and schemes of injustice? It won't be denied that Union representatives will most likely possess these requisite endowments. Is it the greater security afforded by a greater variety of parties, so one party can't outnumber and oppress the rest? Does the increased variety of parties within the Union increase this security? Is a large republic safer because it has more obstacles to the accomplishment of the secret wishes of an unjust majority? Again, the large size of the Union gives it the most obvious advantage.

Factious Passions: Effect on Union

22 Factious leaders may kindle a flame within their specific States, while not able to spread a general conflagration through the other States. A religious sect may degenerate into a political faction in a part of the Confederacy. But the variety of sects dispersed over the entire country secures the national councils against danger from that source. A rage for paper money, for an abolition of debts, for an equal division of property, or for any other improper or wicked project, will be less apt to pervade the whole body of the Union than a specific member of it, just like a malady is more likely to taint a specific county or district than an entire States.

Positive Effects of Size, Structure of Government

23 In the size and proper structure of the Union, therefore, we see a republican remedy for the most common diseases of republican government. And according to the degree of pleasure and pride we feel in being a republic, we will cherish and support the character of Federalists. PUBLIUS

Number 11

Benefits of Strong Union to American Commerce

Few people doubt that the Union is important to American commerce. Most men knowledgeable about the subject generally agree. This applies to both trade with foreign countries and each other.

European Policies
Restrain Our Trade

2 The adventurous spirit of America's commercial character already worries several of Europe's maritime powers. They seem apprehensive of our intruding on their shipping trade, which is the support and foundation of their naval strength. Nations with colonies in America worry about our country's capabilities. They foresee the possible threats to their American territories from a Union with the power and resources to create a powerful marine.

Impressions like these will foster divisions among us and, as far as possible, deprive us of an ACTIVE COMMERCE in our own ships. This would fulfill their threefold goal: preventing our interference in their navigation, monopolizing the profits of our trade, and clipping the wings by which we might soar to dangerous greatness.

If it wasn't an impractical exercise, the European policy of restraining our commerce could be traced back to the cabinets of European ministers.

Unified Commerce Regulations

3 If we remain united, we can counteract policies unfriendly to our prosperity in a variety of ways.

Prohibitory regulations throughout the States may force foreign countries to bid against each other for the privilege of our markets. This conclusion won't seem fanciful to people who appreciate the importance of a market of three million people—with a rapidly growing population dedicated to agriculture, and likely to remain so—to any manufacturing nation. This nation's trade and navigation would be dramatically different if it could use its own ships rather than be forced to use the ships of another country to indirectly convey its products to and from America.

For instance, suppose the American government could exclude Great Britain (with whom we presently have no commerce treaty) from all our ports. How would this effect her politics? Could we successfully negotiate valuable and extensive commercial privileges in that kingdom?

In the past, these questions received plausible, but not solid or satisfactory, answers. Some said prohibitions on our part would not change the British system because her trade with us would continue through the Dutch, who would buy and transport British goods to be sold in our markets. But losing the advantage of being her own carrier would seriously injure British navigation. Would not the Dutch intercept the primary profits as compensation for their agency and risk? Wouldn't paying for freight considerably reduce Britain's profit? Wouldn't the British circuitous supply line encourage competition among other nations, increasing the price of British commodities in our markets and transferring to other nations the management of this branch of British commerce?

Britain Would Change Policies

4 A mature consideration of the ideas suggested by these questions highlight Britain's disadvantages in such a situation. After adding to this argument the established British habit of American trade and the importance of the West India Islands, Britain would relax her present system, letting us enjoy the privileges of the island markets and substantially benefiting our trade.

Navy Will Effect Commerce

5 An established federal navy would further influence the conduct of European commerce towards us. If the Union continued under an efficient government, in the near future it would undoubtedly have the power to create a navy. It might not vie with great maritime powers but it could change a struggle if it allied with either side of a conflict. Our ships would be especially influential in West Indian operations. A few ships, reinforcing either side, could decide the fate of a campaign that had halted trade important to many people. In this respect, our position is a commanding one.

If we add to the prosecution of military operations in the West Indies the usefulness of supplies from this country, we'd gain an advantageous position to bargain for commercial privileges. Our friendship and our neutrality would be valuable. By keeping the Union, we may hope to become the arbiter of Europe in America, influencing the balance of European competitions in this part of the world as our interests dictate.

Disunited We'll Be Weak, Easy Prey

6 But if we disunite, the rivalries between our separate parts will produce a stalemate, frustrating all our great natural advantages. Our insignificant commerce would fall prey to the wanton intermeddling of warring nations. They would have nothing to fear from us. With few scruples, they'll plunder our property as often as it falls in their way. Neutrality rights are respected only when defended by adequate power. A despicably weak nation forfeits even the privilege of being neutral.

Strong Government Aids Commerce

7 A vigorous national government dedicating its strengths and resources to a common interest would deflect all European alliances attempting to restrain our growth. Since a single national government makes success impractical, it removes the motive for such alliances. Moral and physical necessity would create an active commerce, extensive navigation, and a flourishing marine. We could defy the ploys of little politicians to control or vary the irresistible and unchangeable course of nature.

If States Disunite, Europe Will Dominate Our Commerce

8 But if we were disunited, European coalitions might exist and operate with success. Powerful maritime nations, responding to our universal impotence, would dictate the conditions of our political existence.

They have a common interest in being our carriers and preventing our becoming theirs. They'd probably ally to embarrass our navigation, destroying it and confining us to PASSIVE COMMERCE. We would be compelled to accept the first price for our commodities and see the profits of our trade snatched from us to enrich our enemies and persecutors. The unequaled spirit of enterprise and genius of American merchants and navigators, in itself an inexhaustible mine of national wealth, would be stifled and lost, poverty and disgrace would spread across a country that, with wisdom, might make herself the admiration and envy of the world.

If States Disunite, Europe Controls Our Waterways

9 The American Union has some very important trade rights—I refer to the fisheries, the navigation of Western lakes and the Mississippi. The dissolution of the Union would make room for delicate questions about the future of these rights. The more powerful foreign partners, no doubt, would change them to their advantage.

Spain's attitude towards the Mississippi needs no comment.

France and Britain view our fisheries as important to their navigation. Of course, they wouldn't long remain indifferent to our mastery of this valuable branch of traffic, by which we are able to undersell those nations in their own markets. What would be more natural than that they ban such dangerous competitors?

Commerce Improves Navigation

10 This is an important branch of trade. In different degrees and with an extension of mercantile capital, all navigating States would probably advantageously participate. As the United States improves its navigation, it will become a universal resource. It is indispensable to establishing a navy.

Vast Resource For U.S. Navy

11 A NAVY. Union will contribute to this great national objective in various ways. Every institution grows and flourishes in proportion to the quantity and extent of the means concentrated towards its formation and support.

A United States navy, using the resources of all, is a far more attainable objective than a navy of any single State or partial confederacy. Indeed, different areas of confederate America possess the various resources needed for this essential establishment. The southernmost States furnish an abundance of certain naval stores—tar, pitch, and turpentine. Their wood for the construction of ships is more solid and lasting. The longer duration of naval ships chiefly constructed of Southern wood would be particularly important to naval strength and the national economy. Some Southern and Middle States yield plenty of high quality iron. The Northern States will supply most of the seamen.

The necessity of naval protection to external or maritime commerce doesn't require elucidation any more than the importance of maritime commerce to the prosperity of a navy.

Union Promotes Commerce

12 Unrestrained commerce between the States will advance the trade of each through exchange of their respective products, supplying reciprocal wants at home and exportation to foreign markets. In every area, the veins of commerce will be replenished from the free circulation of commodities.

The diversity of State products will increase the range of commercial enterprise. When the staple of one fails from a bad harvest or unproductive crop, it can call to its aid the staple of another.

Both the variety and value of products for exportation contributes to an active foreign commerce. Trade competitions and market fluctuations mean foreign commerce can be conducted on better terms with a large number of materials of a given value than a small number of the same value. Specific articles may be in great demand at certain periods and unsalable at others. But if there were a variety of articles, rarely would they all be unsalable so merchant operations would be less susceptible to obstruction or stagnation.

The speculative trader will immediately understand the validity of these observations and acknowledge that the aggregate of United States commerce would be much more favorable than that of the thirteen States without union or with partial unions.

Disunity Creates
Commercial Barriers

13 Some may argue that whether the States are united or disunited, interstate commerce would achieve the same ends. But commerce would be fettered, interrupted, and narrowed for many reasons, as listed in these papers. A unity of commercial and political interests can only be achieved through a unity of government.

Union Eliminates
European Domination

14 There are other striking and animating point of views. But they lead to speculations about the future and involve topics not proper for a newspaper discussion. I will briefly observe that our situation and interests encourage us to aim for a position of dominance in American affairs.

The world may be politically and geographically divided into four parts, each with a distinct set of interests. Unhappily for the other three, Europe, using arms and negotiations, by force and fraud, has, to varying degrees, extended her dominion over them all. Africa, Asia and America have successively felt her domination. Her long superiority has tempted her to crown herself Mistress of the World, considering the rest of mankind as created for her benefit.

Men who are admired as profound philosophers have, in direct terms, attributed to Europe's inhabitants physical superiority. And they have gravely asserted that all animals, including the human species, degenerate in America. Even dogs cease to bark after having breathed our atmosphere for awhile.*

For too long, facts have supported these European pretensions. It is up to us to vindicate the honor of the human race and teach that assuming brother moderation.

As a Union, we will be able to do it. Disunion will add another victim to Europe's triumphants.

Let Americans refuse to be the instruments of European greatness! Let the thirteen States, bound together in a strict and indissoluble Union, erect one great American system with the superiority to control all transatlantic force or influence, able to dictate the terms of the connection between the old and the new world.

PUBLIUS

---

* *Recherches philosophiques sur les Americans.*

Number 12

Union Promotes Revenue

The effects of Union on the commercial prosperity of the States have been sufficiently delineated. The subject of this inquiry is its tendency to promote revenue interests.

Commerce Increases Nation's Wealth

2 All enlightened statesmen acknowledge that commerce is the most productive source of national wealth. Therefore, it's become a primary political concern.

The introduction and circulation of precious metals, those darling objects of human avarice and enterprise, will multiply the means of gratification. This will invigorate the channels of industry, making them flow with greater activity and copiousness. The industrious merchant, the laborious farmer, the active mechanic, and the industrious manufacturer—all orders of men look forward with eager expectation and growing alacrity to this pleasing reward for their toils.

Experience has silenced the former rivalry between agriculture and commerce. Their interests are intimately blended and interwoven. Various countries have discovered that as commerce flourishes, land values rise. And what else could happen? Commerce procures a freer movement for the products of the earth. It stimulates the cultivation of land. Commerce is the most powerful instrument in increasing the quantity of money in a state. Commerce is the faithful handmaid of labor and industry, in every way. Therefore, how could commerce fail to augment agriculture, the prolific parent of the majority of commercial products?

It's astonishing that so simple a truth ever had an adversary. It is one of many proofs of how a spirit of ill-formed jealousy or dependence on theoretical abstraction can lead men astray from the plainest truths of reason and conviction.

Money Turnover Increases Tax Revenue

3 A country's ability to pay taxes is related, to a great degree, to the quantity and turnover of money in circulation. Commerce contributes to both these objectives. This renders the payment of taxes easier and facilitates the requisite supplies to the treasury.

The German Emperor's realm is fertile, cultivated and populous. Much of it enjoys mild, luxuriant climates. Some parts of it contain the best gold and silver mines in Europe. But the failure to foster commerce has severely limited the monarch's revenues. Several times he's been compelled to borrow money from other nations to preserve his essential interests. And he is unable, using the strength of his own resources, to sustain a long or continued war.

New Tax Laws Don't Increase Tax Revenue

4 But this is not the only way that Union will encourage revenue. The Union's influence will appear more immediate and decisive in other ways. From the state of the country, the people's habits, and our experience, raising very considerable sums by direct taxation is impractical.

Tax laws have been multiplied in vain. New methods to enforce collection have been tried in vain. The public expectation has been uniformly disappointed. And the States' treasuries have remained empty.

The nature of popular government promotes a popular system of administration. A languid and mutilated state of trade results in a real scarcity of money. Combined, these have defeated every experiment for extensive collections. And the different legislatures have learned the folly of attempting them.

Britain: Tax Commerce

5 This circumstance won't surprise anyone acquainted with what happens in other countries. In Britain, an opulent nation, direct taxes from superior wealth is much more tolerable. And the vigor of the government makes it much more practical than in America. Yet, by far the greatest part of her national revenue is derived from indirect taxes, imposts and excises. Import duties form a large part of this latter description.

Commerce Source of Tax Revenue

6 Clearly, America must depend chiefly on revenue from such duties for a long time. Excises must be confined within a narrow compass because the character of the people won't tolerate the inquisitive and peremptory spirit of excise laws. On the other hand, farmers will reluctantly pay even very limited taxes on their houses and lands. Personal property is too precarious and invisible an asset to tax in any way than by the imperceptible agency of taxes on consumption.

Union Increases Tax Revenues

7 If these remarks have any basis, we must adopt the system best able to improve and extend our valuable resources. Without a doubt, a general Union is that system. As this helps commerce, State revenues from that source will increase. A Union simplifies regulations and makes collecting duties more efficient. The rate of duties would be consistent, and the government would increase the rate without prejudice to trade.

Illicit Trade Lowers State Revenues

8 Many circumstances conspire to make illicit trade easy and insure frequent evasions of the commercial regulations of each State, including the relative situation of the States, the intersecting rivers, the bays, the ease of communication in every direction, the affinity of language and manners, and similar commercial habits.

Separate States or confederacies would be forced to keep their duties low to avoid the temptations of illicit trade. For a long time, the temper of our governments would not permit those rigorous precautions used by European nations to guard the land and water avenues into their respective countries. Even there, avarice leads to adventurous strategies around the obstacles.

French Armies Slowed Smuggling

9 In France, an army of patrols (as they are called) secures their commercial regulations against the inroads of the dealers in contraband trade. Mr. Neckar computes the number of these patrols at more than twenty thousand. This shows the immense difficulty in preventing that type of traffic in areas of inland communication. And it throws a strong light on the disadvantages in collecting duties this country would encounter if the disunion of the States placed it in a situation resembling that of France with respect to her neighbors. The arbitrary and vexatious powers with which the patrols are necessarily armed would be intolerable in a free country.

Coast Protected from Contraband

10 However, since the principal part of our commerce transactions are only on ONE SIDE—the ATLANTIC COAST—if all the States were under one government, there would be only one side to guard. Vessels laden with valuable cargoes arriving directly from foreign countries would rarely choose to hazard themselves to the complicated and critical perils attendant to attempts to unladen prior to their coming into port.

They would dread dangers of the coast and detection, both before and after arriving at their final destination. Only normal vigilance would be needed to prevent substantial tax evasion. At a small expense, a few armed vessels, judiciously stationed at our port entrances, could serve as sentinels of the laws. And since the national government is interested in providing against violations everywhere, the cooperation with each State would tend to render them effectual.

In this respect, too, the Union would preserve the natural advantage that would be lost if the States separated. The United States lie a great distance from Europe and all other places with extensive foreign trade connections. Separation would reduce international shipping time to a few hours or overnight, as between France and Britain, eliminating our natural prodigious security against direct contraband with foreign countries. Circuitous contraband to one State through another would be both easy and safe. The difference between direct importation and indirect, through a neighboring State in small parcels as time and opportunity presents as determined through the ease of inland communication, must be obvious to every man of discernment.

Increase Consumption Tax

11 It is evident that one national government could extend duties on imports further than practical to separate States or partial confederacies and at much less expense. Until now, I believe these duties in any State have not averaged more than 3%. In France they are estimated to be 15% and in Britain the proportion is still greater.

Nothing would hinder this country from tripling the present amount. Alcohol alone, under federal regulation, might furnish considerable revenue. Based on the importation into New York, the whole quantity imported into the United States may be estimated at four million gallons. A shilling per gallon would produce 200,000 pounds. Alcohol would easily bear this rate of duty. However, if the tax diminished the consumption of alcohol, such a consequence is equally favorable, favorable to agriculture, the economy, the morals, and the health of society. There is, perhaps, nothing so much a subject of national extravagance as these spirits.

Commerce Tax

12 What will be the consequence if we are not able to fully use this resource? A nation cannot long exist without revenues. Destitute of this essential support, it must resign its independence and sink into the degraded condition of a province. No government would choose this extremity.

Therefore, revenue is necessary. In this country, if it isn't drawn from commerce, it must oppressively fall upon land. It has already been mentioned that the people are largely opposed to internal taxation. With agriculture almost the sole employment in the States, there are so few objects proper for excise taxes, collections would be limited. As said before, because personal assets are difficult to trace, large tax contributions can only be achieved through consumption taxes. In populous cities, individuals would probably be oppressed into paying personal taxes, with little benefit going to the State. Outside these cities, assets, for the most part, escape the eye and hand of the tax gatherer.

Nevertheless, resources must be gathered in some fashion to pay the expenses of the State. When they can't be obtained from any other source, the principal weight of public burden must be carried by landowners.

On the other hand, unless all sources of revenue are open when needed for government finances, the community won't have the money to remain respectable and secure. So we won't even have the consolation of a full treasury to atone for the oppression of citizens employed in the cultivation of the soil. Public and private distress will be equal, and will unite in deploring the foolishness of those counsels that led to disunion.

PUBLIUS

Constitutional References:

Article 1, section 8	175-177	lay and collect taxes
Article 1, section 8	180-182	regulate commerce
Article 1, section 9	253-254	no tax on State exports
Article 1, section 9	255-259	no commercial preference for any State
Article 1, section 10	280-288	no State shall tax imports or exports

---

Number 13

One National Government Cheaper Than Several Confederacies

While discussing revenue, economy of scale may be considered. Money saved in one area may be applied to another, and less money need be drawn from the pockets of the people. If the States are united under one government, only one national governmental structure will need to be supported. If they are divided into several confederacies, there will be that many national bureaucracies, each as extensive as one national government bureaucracy.

Separating the States into thirteen unconnected sovereignties is too extravagant and too filled with danger to have many advocates. The men who speculate on the dismemberment of the empire generally suggest three confederacies: one consisting of the four Northern, another of the four Middle, and a third of the five Southern States. A greater number is improbable.

As described, each confederacy would be larger than Great Britain. No intelligent man can suggest such a confederacy can be properly regulated by a government smaller than the one proposed by the Constitutional Convention. When the dimensions of a State attain a certain size, it requires the same governmental energy and administration as much larger territories.

This can't be proven because no rule exists to measure the momentum of civil power necessary to govern any given number of individuals. But we can consider the concept as follows: each proposed confederacy is approximately the size of the British island, which contains about eight million people. When we consider the size of governmental authority required to direct the passions of so large a society towards the public good, we can suppose the same size power would suffice for a much larger population. Properly organized and exerted, civil power can diffuse its force to a very great extent. By a judicious arrangement of subordinate institutions, it can, in a manner, reproduce itself in every part of a great empire.

Each Confederacy Would Need Large Government

2 Each individual confederation of States would require a government no smaller than the one proposed. If we consider geography and commerce, including the habits and prejudices of the different States, we'll conclude that if disunited, they will most naturally league themselves under two governments.

The four Eastern States (New Hampshire, Massachusetts, Connecticut, Rhode Island), linked through national sympathy, would certainly be expected to unite. New York, situated as she is, would never be unwise enough to expose a feeble, unsupported flank to the weight of the confederacy. There are other obvious reasons that would facilitate her ac-

cession to it. New Jersey is too small to think of being a frontier in opposition to this still more powerful combination. And there doesn't appear to be any obstacles to her admission into it. Even Pennsylvania would have strong inducements to join the Northern league. Her active foreign commerce, based on her own navigation, coincides with the opinions and dispositions of her citizens.

For various reasons, the Southern States may not be much interested in the encouragement of navigation. They may prefer a system allowing all nations to be carriers as well as purchasers of their commodities.

Pennsylvania may not choose to undermine her interests in a connection so adverse to her policy. No matter what happens, she will be a frontier. She may deem it safest to have her exposed side turned towards the weaker power of the Southern Confederacy, rather than towards the stronger Northern power. This would give her the best chance to avoid being the Flanders of America.

Whatever Pennsylvania decides, if the Northern Confederacy includes New Jersey, there is no likelihood of more than one confederacy to the south of that State.

Easier For Thirteen States to Support Government

3 Nothing is more evident than that the thirteen States will be able to support a national government better than one half, or one third, or any number less than the whole. This fact must have great weight in preventing the objection to the proposed plan that is based on its expense. This objection, when we take a closer look at it, will appear in every light to stand on mistaken ground.

Separate Confederacies Creates Many Problems

4 There are considerations in addition to having several civil bureaucracies. People must be employed to guard the inland confederacies against the inevitable illicit trade. Military establishments would be the unavoidable result from jealousies and conflicts between the divided States. We would also discover that a separation would injure the economy, tranquility, commerce, revenue, and liberty of every part.

PUBLIUS

Number 14

Republican Unique, Best for American People

We have seen that we need a Union:
> as our **bulwark against foreign danger** [Numbers 3, 4, 5],
> as **conservator of peace among ourselves** [Numbers 5. 6. 7. 8],
> as **guardian of our commerce** [Number 11] and other common interests,
> as the **only substitute for those military establishments** that have subverted the liberties of the Old World [Number 8].

The **diseases of faction** have proved fatal to other popular governments and alarming symptoms of them have already appeared in our own. We have seen that a Union is the proper antidote. [Number 10].

The only objection left to discuss is based on the **large geographic area** the Union embraces. A few observations on this subject are proper. Adversaries of the new Constitution are using the current prejudice regarding the practicality of republican administration in order to invent problems because they endeavor in vain to find solid objections.

Democracy Must Be Small

2 The illogical argument that a republic must be limited to a small district has been discussed and refuted in a preceding paper [Number 9]. The argument seems to arise from confusing a republic with a democracy, applying to a republic theories drawn from the nature of a democracy.

The distinction between these systems was previously discussed [Number 10]. In a democracy, the people meet and administer the government in person. In a republic, representatives and agents assemble and administer it. Consequently, a democracy will be confined to a small area. But a republic may be extended over a large region.

Monarchy vs. Democracy or Republic

3 To this unintentional error may be added the artifice of some celebrated authors whose writings have influenced modern public opinions. They were subjects of monarchies, absolute or limited. They stress the advantages or rationalize the evils of monarchies by comparing them to the vice and defects of a republic. Then, to prove their points, they cite the turbulent democracies of ancient Greece and modern Italy.

The confusion of the two names makes it easy to transfer to a "republic" the observations applicable only to a "democracy." One observation is that a republic can only be established among a small number of people, living within a small territory.

Popular Governments— Democracies

4 The fallacy may not have been noticed because most popular governments of antiquity were democracies. Even modern Europe, to which we owe the great principle of representation, has no example of a completely popular and republican government.

If Europe discovered the system that concentrates the objectives on the largest political body and directs its force as the public good requires, America can claim using the discovery as the basis of extensive republics. That any citizen wishes to deprive her the additional credit of displaying the full efficacy of establishing the comprehensive system now under consideration is lamentable.

Democracy Limits Area, Population

5 A democracy has a natural geographic limit—the distance from the central point that permits the most remote citizens to assemble as often as public functions demand. The population of a democracy is limited to the number that can join those functions.

The natural limit of a republic is the distance from the center that barely allows representatives to meet as often as necessary for the administration of public affairs.

Does the United States exceed this distance? The Atlantic coast is the longest side of the Union. During the last thirteen years, representatives of the States have been almost continually assembled. The attendance records of members from the most distant States have been no worse than those from the States in the neighborhood of Congress.

Potential Geographic Area of Union

6 To form a more precise estimate on this interesting subject, let's use the actual dimensions of the Union. According to the peace treaty, the eastern boundary is the Atlantic, the southern is the latitude of 31 degrees, the western is the Mississippi, and the northern is an irregular line running between 42 degrees and 45 degrees. The southern share of Lake Erie lies below that latitude.

The distance between 31 degrees and 45 degrees is 973 miles, between 31 degrees and 42 degrees is 764½ miles. The average, therefore, is 868¾ miles. The average distance between the Atlantic and the Mississippi probably doesn't exceed 750 miles.

Comparing this to the size of several European countries seems to demonstrate the practicality of the republican system. Our territory is not much larger than Germany, where representatives of the whole empire continually assemble, or than Poland, where before the recent dismemberment another national assembly was the center of supreme power. Passing by France and Spain, although Great Britain is smaller, representatives from the northern extremity of the island travel as far to their national council as required of those from the most remote parts of the Union.

Other Advantages of Republic

7 Favorable as this view of the subject may be, more observations will place it in a still better light.

Federal Government: Defined, Limited Jurisdiction

8 First, remember that the federal government is not charged with the whole power of making and administering laws. Its defined jurisdiction is limited to specific objectives of the whole republic. The subordinate [State and local] governments will retain their authority to care for all other concerns.

If the convention proposed abolishing the State governments, adversaries would have some ground for objection. In fact, if they were abolished, self-preservation would compel the national government to reinstate them in their proper jurisdiction.

Constitution: Union, Adding States

9 Second, the federal constitution's immediate objectives are securing the union of the thirteen original States, which we know is practical, and adding other States, which we cannot doubt to be equally practical. The arrangements necessary for territory on our northwestern frontier must be left to those whose further discoveries and experience will render them more equal to the task.

Commerce, Communication Will Improve

10 Third, new improvements will facilitate commerce throughout the Union. Roads will be shortened and better maintained. Traveler accommodations will multiply and improve. Interior navigation on our eastern side will extend throughout, or nearly throughout, the thirteen States. Communication between the Western and Atlantic districts and different parts within each will become easier by the numerous canals with which the beneficence of nature has intersected our country and engineers find easy to connect and complete.

Frontier Benefits from Union's Defense

11 A fourth and still more important consideration is safety. Almost every State will be, on one side or other, a frontier. This will induce some sacrifices for the sake of general protection. States that lie at the greatest distance from the heart of the Union and may partake in fewer ordinary benefits are, at the same time, immediately contiguous to foreign nations. On some occasions, they will have the greatest need for the Union's strength and resources.

It may be inconvenient for Georgia, or the States forming our western or northeastern borders, to send representatives to the seat of government. However, it would be much more than inconvenient for them to struggle alone against an invading enemy, or even carry the full expense of defensive precautions dictated by being in the neighborhood of continual danger. So, if they derive less benefit from the Union in some respects than less distant States, they will derive greater benefit from it in other respects. Thus, the proper equilibrium will be maintained throughout.

American Spirit Unique in History

12 I submit to you, my fellow citizens, these considerations with full confidence that the good sense that has so often marked your past decisions will allow you to objectively evaluate them. I am confident you will never automatically allow predictions of catastrophe, however formidable in appearance or fashionable the error on which they may be founded, drive you into the gloomy despair the advocates for disunion would lead you.

Do not listen to the unnatural voice telling you that the people of America, knit together as they are by so many cords of affection, can no longer live together as members of the same family. That they can not continue to be mutual guardians of their mutual happiness. That they can no longer be fellow-citizens of one great, respectable, and flourishing empire.

Do not listen to the voice petulantly telling you that the form of government recommended for your adoption is a novelty in the political world. That it has no place in even the wildest political theories. That it rashly attempts what is impossible to accomplish.

No, my countrymen, shut your ears against this unhallowed language. Shut your hearts against the poison it conveys. The kindred blood flowing in the veins of American citizens, the mingled blood shed in defense of their sacred rights, consecrate their Union and excite horror at the idea of their becoming aliens, rivals, enemies.

And if new concepts are to be shunned, believe me, the most alarming ideas, the most wild of all projects, the most rash of all actions is that of rending us into pieces in order to preserve our liberties and promote our happiness.

Why is the experiment of an extended republic to be rejected merely because it is a new concept? Is it not the glory of the American people that while they study and respect opinions of former times and other nations,

they do not suffer from blind veneration for antiquity, for custom, or for names, allowing them to overrule the suggestions of their own good sense, the knowledge of their own situation, and the lessons of their own experience?

Posterity will be indebted to the American spirit for having and showing the world numerous innovations in favor of private rights and public happiness. If the leaders of the Revolution had not taken unprecedented steps, establishing a unique model of government, the people of the United States might currently be numbered among the melancholy victims of misguided councils, laboring under the weight of some form of government that has crushed the liberties of the rest of mankind.

Happily for America. Happily, we trust, for the whole human race, they pursued a new and more noble course. They accomplished a revolution that has no parallel in the annals of human society. They tailored fabrics of governments that have no pattern on the face of the globe. They formed the design of a great Confederacy, which it is incumbent on their successors to improve and perpetuate. If their works have imperfections, we wonder at the fewness of them.

If they erred most in the structure of the Union [Articles of Confederation], this was their most difficult work. Your Constitutional Convention has made a new model. And it is that act on which you are now to deliberate and decide.

PUBLIUS

Constitutional reference:
Article 4, section 3   504-510   adding States

Number 15

Confederation Near Total Collapse

In the preceding papers I have endeavored, my fellow citizens, to clearly and convincingly show you how our remaining united is important to your political safety and happiness. I've exposed the dangers of permitting the sacred knot binding the American people together to be severed or dissolved by ambition or avarice, by jealousy or misrepresentation.

I next propose to discuss truths based on facts and arguments that, until now, have remained unnoticed. If this road sometimes seems tedious or irksome, remember that you are seeking information about the most momentous subject that can engage the attention of a free people. The countryside through which you must travel is vast. And mazes of sophistry have unnecessarily increased the difficulties of the journey. My goal is to simplify the issues without sacrificing thoroughness.

Current Confederacy Can't Preserve Union

2 Following my discussion plan, the next point for examination is the "insufficiency of the present Confederation to the preservation of the Union."

Some people may ask why this needs proof when both opponents and supporters of the new Constitution agree it's true, that material imperfections exist in our national system and something needs to be done to rescue us from impending anarchy.

This opinion is supported by facts, not speculation. These facts force themselves upon the sensibility of the people. Even those people whose mis-taken policies have made our current precarious situation even worse reluctantly confess to the defects in the organization of our federal government. Intelligent friends of the Union have been pointing out, and regretting, these defects for a long time.

Nation Faces Total Humiliation

3 We may have reached almost the last stage of national humiliation. We experience nearly everything that can wound the pride or degrade the character of an independent nation.

Do we have commitments that should be honored? These are constantly and unblushingly violated. Do we owe debts to foreigners and our own citizens, contracted during imminent peril to our political existence? The debts remain with no plan or provision for their discharge.

Does a foreign power still occupy territories that, by express stipulations, should have been surrendered a long time ago? They remain, against our best interests and our rights. Are we in a condition to repel an aggressor? We have neither neither troops, nor treasury, nor government.* Are we even in a condition to protest with dignity? The just imputations on our own faith, in respect to the same treaty, should first be removed.

Are we entitled by nature and treaty to navigate the Mississippi? Spain excludes us from it. Is public credit an indispensable resource in time of public danger? We seem to have given up, deciding it's impos-

---

* "I mean for the Union."

sible. Is commerce important to our national wealth? Ours is at the lowest point of deterioration.

Is respectability in the eyes of foreign powers a safeguard against foreign encroachments? Our government is so weak that they need not negotiate with us. Our ambassadors abroad merely imitate representatives of a sovereign nation.

Is a dramatic, unnatural decrease in land value a symptom of national distress? In most parts of the country, the price of improved land is much lower than can be accounted for by the quantity of wasteland on the market. It can only be fully explained by an alarmingly prevalent lack of private and public confidence that has depreciated property of every kind.

Is private credit the friend and supporter of industry? Consumer credit is at its lowest. This is more the result of insecurity than scarcity of money.

To shorten the list of particulars, because it gives neither pleasure nor instruction, it can be asked: what indication of national disorder, poverty, and insignificance could befall a community, so specially blessed with natural advantages as we are, that does not form a part of the dark catalogue of our public misfortunes?

People Responsible Oppose Constitution

4 We have been brought to this sad situation by maxims and councils of the very people who now oppose the proposed Constitution. Not content with leading us to the brink of a precipice, they now seem resolved to plunge us into the abyss.

Here, my countrymen, impelled by every motive influential on enlight-ened people, let us make a firm stand for our safety, our tranquillity, our dignity, our reputation. Let us break the fatal charm that has too long seduced us from the paths of felicity and prosperity.

Amendments Can't Correct Flaws

5 As previously observed, obvious facts have produced general agreement to the abstract proposition that there are material defects in our national system. But the usefulness of this concession by old adversaries of the federal system is destroyed by their strenuous opposition to a remedy based on the only principles that give it a chance of success. While admitting the United States government is destitute of energy, they fight against giving it those powers necessary to supply that energy.

They still seem to have repugnant and irreconcilable, mutually exclusive goals. They want augmentation of federal authority without a diminution of State authority. They want a sovereign Union with completely independent members. They still seem to cherish blind devotion to the political monster of an *imperium in imperio*.

The principal defects of the Confederation must be listed, to show that the evils we experience are not the result of minor imperfections but fundamental structural flaws that cannot be amended but must be completely rebuilt.

Problem: Legislation For States

6 The existing Confederation's great and fundamental defect is the principle of LEGISLATION for STATES in their COLLECTIVE CAPACITIES rather than for the INDIVIDUALS living in the States.

Although this principle doesn't apply to all the powers delegated to the Union, it pervades those on which the effectiveness of the rest depends. Except for the rule of apportionment, the

United States has indefinite discretion to requisition men and money. But it has no authority to raise either directly from individual citizens of America. Therefore, in theory their resolutions are constitutionally binding on members of the Union. But in practice they are merely recommendations that the States observe or disregard at their option.

Principle Ruined Confederation

7   This shows the capriciousness of the human mind that, after all the warnings on the subject, some men still object to the new Constitution because it deviates from the principle [legislation for states] that ruined the old. A principle, in short, that must substitute the violence of the sword to the mild influence of the magistracy.

Treaties: Limited Effectiveness

8   The idea of a league or alliance between independent nations for purposes defined in a treaty that precisely regulates details of time, place, circumstance, and quantity is not absurd or impractical, a treaty that leaves nothing to future discretion, and with its execution depending on the good faith of the parties.

Compacts of this kind exist among all civilized nations, subject to the vicissitudes of peace and war, observance and nonobservance, as the interests or passions of the signature nations dictate. In the early part of this century, these compacts were very popular in Europe, with politicians hoping for benefits that were never realized. Trying to establish an equilibrium of power and peace in Europe, all negotiation resources were exhausted, and triple and quadruple alliances were formed. But they were scarcely formed before they were broken, showing how little dependence should be placed on treaties with no sanctions except obligations of good faith and signed on impulse, fulfilling an immediate interest or passion, while ignoring considerations of peace and justice.

States as Nations: Both Allies, Enemies

9   If the States in this country decide to abandon the federal DISCRETIONARY SUPERINTENDENCE and become separate nations, then form alliances in a manner similar to Europe, it would be ruinous, as previously detailed. But it would have the merit of being consistent. However, without a confederate government, offensive and defensive alliances would make us alternately friends then enemies of each other, as dictated by jealousies and rivalries, and nourished by intrigues of foreign nations.

Federal Authority Over Citizens

10   But if we are unwilling to be in this dangerous situation, if we stay with the plan of a national government or, in other words, a superintending power under the direction of a common council, we must decide to incorporate into that plan ingredients that differentiate between a league and a government. We must extend the authority of the Union to the citizens— the only proper objects of government.

Courts or Armies Enforce Laws

11   Having a government implies it has the power to make laws. A law needs a sanction. Or, in other words, a punishment or penalty for disobedience. If no penalty is tied to disobedience, resolutions that pretend to be laws will, in reality, amount to nothing more than advice or recommendations.

A penalty, whatever it might be, can be only inflicted in two ways: by the courts or by military force—by COERCION of the magistracy or by CO-ERCION of arms. The first can apply only to individual people; the last must be employed against politic groups, communities, or states.

Of course, courts have no way to directly enforce laws. Sentences may be pronounced against violators. But sentences can only be executed by the sword. If the authority is confined to an alliance between collective bodies, every breach of the law must involve a state of war, with punishment by the military the only instrument of civil obedience. Such a situation doesn't deserve to be called a government. Nor would any prudent man choose to depend on it for his happiness.

Government: Controls Passions

12 We were once told that States wouldn't violate federal regulations, that a feeling of common interest would control the conduct of the respective members, producing full compliance with all the constitutional requisitions.

Today, this sounds ludicrous; current pronouncements from the same people will sound just as wild after we receive more lessons from that best oracle of wisdom, experience. It betrayed an ignorance of the actual motivator of human behavior and contradicted the original reason for establishing civil power.

Why has government been instituted at all? Because the passions of men won't conform to the dictates of reason and justice without constraint. Do groups of men act with more virtue or greater disinterest than individuals? Observers of human behavior infer the opposite; and this inference is founded on obvious reasons. An individual worries more about his reputation than that of his group, because blame for the detestable action of a group is divided among a number of people. A spirit of faction often poisons the deliberations of bodies of men, pushing the group into improper and excessive behavior that would embarrass the individuals.

Sovereignties Hate Outside Control

13 In addition, by its very nature, sovereign power hates control and looks with an evil eye on all external attempts to restrain it or direct its operations. Because of this, when lesser sovereignties are united in political associations by a common interest, there will be a perpetual tendency for the smaller units to fly off from the common center.

This tendency can be easily understood. Its origin is the love of power. Power controlled or restrained is almost always the enemy of that power doing the controlling. This simple proposition shows that administrators of individual members of an alliance will not be always ready, with perfect good humor and unbiased by the public's well being, to execute the decrees of the general authority. So predicts the psychology of human nature.

Allies Can't Be Forced to Comply

14 Therefore, if the resolutions of an alliance cannot be implemented without the intervention of individual administrations, they probably won't be implemented at all. The rulers of the member states, whether they have a constitutional right to do it or not, will try to judge the necessity of the resolution itself. They will consider whether complying with the resolution conforms to their immediate interests, and the conveniences or inconveniences its adoption would cause. All this scrutiny will be done without knowing the national situation or the reasons for the resolution, an essential for an informed decision. And local objectives will also influence the decision.

Every member of the alliance will repeat this process. The execution of plans drafted by the alliance will always fluctuate, depending on the ill-informed and prejudiced opinions of the individual parts.

Those familiar with popular assemblies know harmonious resolutions on important issues are difficult to achieve even without pressure from external circumstances. They will quickly agree it is impossible to induce a number of assemblies, deliberating at a distance from each other, at different times, with different impressions, to cooperate by having the same views and pursuits.

States Not Supporting Confederation

15 In our case under the Confederation, the thirteen distinct sovereignties must agree to the execution of every important measure proposed by the Union. What happened was expected.

The measures have not been executed. State delinquencies have matured and grown until they have clogged and stopped the wheels of the national government.

Congress barely has the means to keep some kind of administration until the States can agree on a substantial substitute for the present shadow of a federal government.

This desperate situation didn't happen overnight. The causes discussed here first produced unequal degrees of compliance with the Union's requisitions. The greater deficiencies of some States furnished a temptation to the complying, least delinquent States, who wondered why they should pay proportionately more than others embarked on the same political voyage. Why they should bear more than their proper share of the common burden. Human selfishness could not withstand these suggestions. Even speculative men, who can foresee remote consequences, would not hesitate to combat these arguments. Each State, yielding to persuasion and immediate convenience, has successively withdrawn its support. Now the frail and tottering edifice seems ready to fall on our heads and crush us beneath its ruins.

PUBLIUS

Number 16

Legislation for States; Replace with Laws for Individuals

The principle of **legislation for States** or communities is detrimental to all confederate governments. Our experiment has shown this. And it was also proven by governments we know about in the past. The negative effects of legislation for States are in exact proportion to its prevalence in those systems.

A confirmation from history is worthy of examination. Of the confederacies remembered from antiquity,

67

the Lycian and Achaean leagues appear to have been most free from the restraints of the principle of legislation for States. They deserve, and have liberally received, the approval of political writers.

Force Compliance with Military

2 This objectionable principle may truly and emphatically be called the parent of anarchy. Delinquencies by Union members (States) are its natural and necessary offspring. When they happen, the only constitutional remedy is force. And the immediate consequence of using force is a civil war.

Disunited States => Civil War

3 Whether our government would even be capable of enforcement remains to be seen. If the national government doesn't have a standing army, it might be incapable of employing force. If it could use force, it would amount to a war between parts of the Confederacy over league infractions. The strongest force would prevail, whether it consisted of supporters or resisters of the national authority.

A delinquency would rarely be confined to a single member. If more than one neglected their duty, they probably would unite for common defense.

Independent of this sympathy motive, if a large, influential state is delinquent, it would often win over some non-delinquent neighbors to its cause. Specious arguments of the danger to liberty would easily be contrived. Plausible excuses for deficiencies would be invented to increase apprehensions, inflame passions, and conciliate the good-will of some States not in violation or omission of their duty.

This could happen when a large State is delinquent because of the ambitious premeditation of rulers who want all external control on their plans for personal aggrandizement removed. Presumably, they would tamper beforehand with the leaders of adjacent States.

If other States didn't become allies, foreign powers would be asked for aid. They would often encourage dissensions within the Confederacy because if it is firmly united, they will have much to fear.

Once the sword is drawn, men's passions observe no moderation. If the Union used force against delinquent States, wounded pride and irritated resentment would push those States to any extreme necessary to avenge the affront or to avoid the disgrace of submission. The first war of this kind would probably end in the dissolution of the Union.

More States Will Be Delinquent

4 The Confederacy would suffer a violent death. Currently we are close to experiencing a more natural death, if the federal system isn't quickly and substantially renovated.

Considering our history, complying States would rarely support the Union's authority by engaging in a war against non-complying States. They would often prefer pursuing the milder course of putting themselves on equal footing with the delinquent members, imitating their example and making their common guilt become their common security. Our experience has shown this in full light.

In fact, it would be very difficult to determine when force should properly be used. When a State's monetary contribution is delinquent,, it would often be impossible to decide if this was because they didn't want to pay or were unable to pay. The latter excuse would always be available. And the deception must be very flagrant to justify the harsh expedient of forced compulsion.

It's easy to see that every time this problem occurred, factious views, partiality, and oppression by the majority in the national council would be common.

Enforcing with Army

5　Obviously the States shouldn't want a national Constitution that has to be enforced by a standing army ready to execute ordinary governmental decrees. Yet this is the alternative to a Constitution extending its operations to individuals. If practical at all, such a scheme would instantly degenerate into military despotism.

But it is, in every way, impractical. Union resources won't be large enough to maintain an army capable of confining the larger States within the limits of their duty. The Union won't have the money to even form such an army. When you look at the current strength and population of several of the large States, then look forward even half a century, you'll dismiss any scheme aimed at regulating State movements by laws that have to be enforced by coercion. Such a project is but a little less fanciful then the monster-taming spirit attributed to the fabulous heroes and demigods of antiquity.

Legislation Enforced By Military

6　Even in confederacies composed of members smaller than many of our States, the principle of legislation for sovereign States, supported by military coercion, has never been effectual. It has only been employed against the weaker members. And in most cases, it produced bloody wars, with half of the confederacy fighting the other half.

Citizen Laws; Judiciary Enforces

7　If a federal government able to regulate common concerns and pre-serve tranquility could be constructed, an intelligent mind must clearly see that the objectives committed to its care must be based on the reverse of the principle supported by the opponents of the proposed Constitution. It must carry its authority to the persons of the citizens. It must not need inter-mediate legislatures. It must be em-powered to use the ordinary judiciary to execute its own resolutions. National authority must manifest through the courts of justice.

The government of the Union, like that of each State, must be able to address itself directly to the hopes and fears of individuals and attract support from the passions with the strongest influence on the human heart. In short, it must have the means and the right to resort to the same methods of executing the powers entrusted to it as possessed and exercised by State governments.

States Block Union's Laws

8　An objection to this reasoning could be raised: if any State becomes disloyal to the Union's authority, it could still obstruct the execution of the Union's laws, bringing up the same issue of using force.

Passive vs Active Resistance

9　This objection will not seem plausible when we point out the essential difference between NON-COMPLIANCE, and DIRECT and ACTIVE RESISTANCE.

If State legislatures must approve every measure of the Union, they only need to NOT ACT or to ACT EVASIVELY to defeat the measure. This neglect of duty might be disguised under bogus unsubstantial provisions so the people won't be alarmed about the Constitution's safety. State leaders might even excuse their surreptitious evasions of it on the grounds of some temporary convenience, exemption, or advantage.

Need Conspiracy to Block Laws

10 But if the implementation of national laws doesn't require the intervention of State legislatures, if they apply immediately to citizens, then a State government couldn't block them without an open and violent exertion of unconstitutional power. No omissions or evasions would suffice. They would be forced to act and, therefore, leave no doubt that they had encroached on national rights.

This action would always be hazardous with a constitution able to defend itself and enlightened citizens who can distinguish between legal authority and illegal usurpation of authority.

Blocking a national law would require both a factious majority in the State legislature, and the concurrence of the courts and the citizens. If judges were not conspiring with the legislature, they would pronounce the resolutions contrary to the supreme law of the land, unconstitutional, and void. If the people didn't concur, as the natural guardians of the Constitution, they would support the national government, giving it the heavier weight in the contest.

State leaders would not attempt this with levity or rashness because of the danger to them, except when the federal government uses its authority tyrannically.

All Laws Enforced Same Way

11 If opposition to the national government arises from the disorderly conduct of rebellious individuals, it could be overcome by the same method used daily against the same evil under the State governments. The judiciary, being ministers of the law of the land, would be as ready to guard national as local regulations from the inroads of private licentiousness.

The federal government could command more resources to suppress the smaller commotions and insurrections that sometimes disquiet society, the intrigues or ill humor of a small faction, than would be in the power of any single State.

And as to those deadly feuds that sometimes spread a conflagration through a whole nation or a large part of it, those caused by either a weighty discontent of the government or by the spread of a violent popular paroxysm, they do not fall within any ordinary rules of calculation. When they happen, they commonly amount to revolutions and dismemberments of empire. No form of government can always either avoid or control them. It is vain to hope to guard against events too mighty for human foresight or precaution. It would be idle to object to a government because it could not perform impossibilities.

PUBLIUS

Constitutional reference:
Article 6 lines 548-555   Constitution, laws, treaties,supreme law of the land

---

Number 17

Authority Over Individual Citizens:
National Government Usurp State Authority?

A different objection than addressed in my last paper may also be argued against the principle of legislation for the individual citizens of America: that it would tend to make the national government too powerful. The Union might assume authority more properly left with the States for local purposes.

Even allowing for the greatest love of power, I confess I am at a loss to discover what might tempt national government administrators to divest the States of their authorities. The regulation of State domestic police appears to me to hold few allurements to ambition.

Commerce, finance, negotiation, and war seem to cover all the objects attractive to people with a passion for power. And all these powers should be vested in the national government.

The administration of private justice between citizens of the same State, the supervision of agriculture, and concerns of a similar nature are properly provided for by local legislation and can never be desirable worries of a national government. Therefore, it's improbable that federal politicians would usurp these powers, because the attempt would be as troublesome as it would be trifling. Possession of these powers would contribute nothing to the dignity, importance, and splendor of the national government.

Encroachment by States

2 But let's say, for argument's sake, that mere wantonness and lust for domination would be enough to want control over State issues. Still, it can be safely said that the congress of national representatives or, in other words, the people of all the States, would control the indulgence of so extravagant an appetite.

It will always be far easier for State government to encroach upon the national authorities, than for the national government to encroach on State authorities. The proof of this conclusion is based on the greater degree of influence that the State governments will generally have over the people, if they administer their affairs with honesty and prudence. Therefore, all federal constitutions are inherently and intrinsically weak. They must be carefully structured to give them all the force compatible with the principles of liberty.

States More Influential

3 Local governments have more influence because of the diffusive construction of the national government and, more importantly, from the type of issues State administrations address.

Nearness Promotes Affection

4, 5 It's a fact of human nature that affections are weak in proportion to distance or diffusiveness of the object. Man is more attached to his family than his neighborhood, to his neighborhood than the community at large. People of a State feel a stronger bias towards their local governments than towards the government of the Union, unless this basic fact of human nature is destroyed by a much better administration of the latter.

This strong propensity of the human heart would find powerful inducements in the issues of State regulation.

Local Governments: Small Vital Issues

6 A variety of minutia will fall under the supervision of local governments. They will form many rivulets of influence through every part of society. Itemizing them would involve too much tedious and uninteresting detail to compensate for its instructive value.

Judiciary Gives States Power

7 The authority of State governments has one transcendent advantage that, by itself, puts the matter in a clear and satisfactory light. I am referring to the administration of criminal and civil justice. This is the most powerful, most universal, and most attractive source of popular obedience and attachment. It is the immediate, visible guardian of life and property, with its benefits and its terrors constantly before the public eye. It regulates the personal interests and everyday concerns of individuals. More than anything else, this influences the people's affection, esteem, and reverence towards the government.

This great unifying authority will almost totally diffuse itself through local governments. Without any other influence, this power over their citizens will make the States, at all times, a complete counterbalance and, frequently, dangerous rivals to the power of the Union.

National Focus: Esoteric Issues

8 On the other hand, the national government's functions are not as easily observed by the majority of the citi-zens. The benefits derived from it will chiefly be watched and perceived by speculative men. Since they relate to more general interests, they will be less in touch with the feelings of people at home and, proportionately, less likely to inspire obligation and active attachment.

Historical Proof

9 There are abundant examples in all historical federal constitutions and all others similar to them.

European Feudal Period

10 Although the ancient feudal systems were not, strictly speaking, confederacies, they had similarities. There was a common head, chieftain or sovereign, whose authority extended over the whole nation. A number of subordinate vassals, barons or lords supervised large portions of land allotted to them. And numerous *inferior* vassals or retainers occupied and cultivated that land out of loyalty or obedience to the persons who held it. Each supervising vassal was a kind of sovereign within his particular territory.

This situation created constant opposition to the national sovereign's authority and frequent wars between the great barons or chief feudatories themselves. The nation was usually too weak to preserve the public peace or protect the people against the oppressions of their immediate lords. Historians emphatically categorize this European era as a time of feudal anarchy.

Barons More Power than King

11 When the sovereign was vigorous, with a warlike temper and superior abilities, he acquired personal influence fulfilling, for a time, the role of authority. But in general, the power of the barons triumphed over that of the prince. And in many instances, the

sovereign's rule was entirely thrown off and the great fiefs were erected into independent principalities or States.

In those instances where the monarch finally prevailed over his vassals, he was successful primarily because of the tyranny of the barons over their dependents. The barons, or nobles, were both enemies of the sovereign and oppressors of the common people. They were dreaded and detested by both. Eventually, mutual danger and mutual interest created a union between the monarch and the common people that was fatal to the power of the aristocracy. If the nobles had preserved the fidelity and devotion of the common people through clemency and justice, the contests between the barons and the prince would have almost always ended in their favor, with subversion of the royal authority.

Clans More Power than King

12 This assertion isn't based in speculation or conjecture. Scotland will furnish an example. Early on, the spirit of clanship was introduced into that kingdom, uniting the nobles and their dependents by ties equivalent to those within an extended family. This made the aristocracy more powerful than the monarch, until the incorporation with England subdued its fierce and ungovernable spirit with the civility already established in England.

States like Feudal Barons

13 The separate, State government in a confederacy may be compared with the feudal barons. With this advantage, for reasons explained, they will generally possess the confidence and goodwill of the people.

With such important support, they will effectually oppose all encroachments of the national government. It's a good idea that they will not be able to counteract the national government's legitimate and necessary authority.

The points of similarity include the rivalry of power and the CONCENTRATION of large portions of the community strength into particular DEPOSITS. In one case, the feudal barons, as individuals, held the power. In the other case, the State, as a political body, holds it.

Historical Confederacies

14 A concise review of events in confederate governments will further illustrate this important doctrine. Inattention to history has been the great source of our political mistakes and allowed jealousy to point us in the wrong direction. This will be the subject of some ensuing papers.

PUBLIUS

Number 18

Weaknesses that Doomed Ancient Greek Confederacies

The most important ancient confederacy was the association of Greek republics under the Amphi-tyonic federal council. Historical accounts present very instructive analogies to our present Confederation of the American States.

Council's Powers, Duties

2   The individual Greek city-states remained independent, sovereign states with representatives (Amphictyons) and equal votes in the federal council. The council had the authority to propose and resolve whatever it judged necessary for the common welfare of Greece: to declare and wage war, to be the last court of appeals in controversies between states, to fine the aggressing party, to employ the force of the confederacy against the disobedient, to admit new members.

The federal council was the guardian of religion and the immense riches of the temple of Delphos, where it had jurisdiction in controversies between inhabitants and those who came to consult the oracle.

To promote the efficacy of federal powers, council members took an oath to defend and protect the united cities, punish violators of this oath, and inflict vengeance on sacrilegious despoilers of the temple.

In Theory: Council's Power Enough

3   In theory, these powers seem sufficient. In several ways, they exceed the powers enumerated in the Articles of Confederation. For example, superstitions strengthened the Amphictyon federal government. They could use coercion against disobedient cities. And they pledged to exert this authority on necessary occasions.

In Reality, Not Enough Power

4   Nevertheless, reality was very different than the theory. The powers, like those of our Congress, were administered by deputies appointed by the member city-states as political units. Hence the weakness, disorders and, finally, the destruction of the confederacy.

The more powerful cities, instead of being in awe and subordination, tyrannized the rest. Demosthenes [b.-384 d.-322] writes that Athens was the arbiter of Greece for 73 years [c.- 477 to - 404]. Sparta next governed it for 29 years. After the battle of Leuctra [-371], Thebes ruled.

Strong States Tyrannized Weak

5   Greek historian Plutarch (b. 47 d. 120) wrote that the representatives of the strongest cities often threatened and corrupted those of the weaker and judgment favored the most powerful party.

Wars Didn't Unite City-States

6   Even during dangerous wars with Persia (- 490 to - 449) and Macedon (-330), the member States never acted as a unit and were, more or less, eternally the dupes or hirelings of the common enemy. The intervals between foreign wars were filed with domestic vicissitudes, convulsions, and carnage.

Athenian Self-Interest

7   After the war with Persia, Sparta demanded some cities be expelled from the confederacy for being unfaithful.

However, the Athenians decided they would lose more partisans than Sparta, giving the latter a majority in public. So, Athens opposed and defeated the attempt.

This piece of history proves the inefficiency of the confederacy. Ambition and jealousy motivated its most powerful members. The rest were degraded, becoming dependent. In theory, the smaller members were entitled to equal pride and majesty; in fact, they became satellites of the larger members.

Weak Federal Government; Most Danger from Other States

8 Abbe' Milot says that if the Greeks had been as wise as they were courageous, experience would have taught them the necessity of a closer union. And they would have used the peace following their success against Persia for reforms.

Instead of following this obvious coarse, Athens and Sparta, inflated by victories and glory, became rivals and then enemies. They then inflicted more mischief against each other than they had suffered from Persia. Their mutual jealousies, fears, hatreds, and injuries ended in the famous Peloponnesian war (Athens vs. Sparta, - 431 to -404), which ended in the ruin and slavery of Athens, who had begun it.

Internal, External Problems

9 When a weak government is not at war, it is constantly agitated by internal dissensions that always bring fresh calamities from abroad.

After the Phocians plowed up consecrated ground at the temple of Apollo, the Amphictyonic council fined the sacrilegious offenders. The Phocians, aided by Athens and Sparta, refused to submit to the decree.

On the other side, the Thebans, with some other cities, supported the Amphictyons' authority to avenge the violated god.

Enter as Ally; Stay as Conqueror

Philip of Macedon (-343) was invited to help the Thebans. However, he'd secretly started the feud, so he gladly seized the opportunity to execute his plans against the liberties of Greece. By his intrigues and bribes, he won over the popular leaders of several cities. Their influence and votes gained his admission into the Amphictyonic council. And by his intrigues and his arms, Philip made himself master of the confederacy. [Philip defeated the Greeks in −339.]

Stronger Government Might Have Repelled Invaders

10 Such were the consequences of the fallacious principle on which Greece was founded. A judicious observer of her fate says that if Greece had been united by a stricter confederation and fought to stay unified, she never would have worn the chains of Macedon. And she might have been a barrier to Rome.

Achaean League

11 The Achaean league, another society of Grecian republics, supplies valuable instruction.

Better Organization

12 This union was far more intimate and organized more wisely than the preceding one. Although not exempt from a similar catastrophe, it did not equally deserve it.

Division of Authorities

13 The **cities** in the league retained their municipal jurisdiction, appointed their own officers, and were perfectly equal.

They were represented in the **senate** that had the sole and exclusive rights of: peace and war, sending and receiving ambassadors, entering into treaties and alliances, appointing a chief magistrate or praetor.

The **praetor** commanded their armies and, with the advice and consent of ten senators, administered the government during the senate recess and shared in its deliberations when assembled. Their primitive constitution called for two administrative praetors but in practice one was preferred.

All City-States had Same Laws

14 It appears the cities had all the same laws and customs, the same weights and measures, and the same money. But it's uncertain whether this was a federal decree. The only mandate was that cities have the same laws and usages.

As a member of the Amphictyonic confederacy, Sparta fully exercised her government and her legislation. However, when Sparta became part of the Achaean league, her ancient laws and institutions were abolished and those of the Achaeans adopted. This shows the material difference between the two systems.

If Knew More, We'd Learn Much

15 It is too bad that a better historical record of these interesting political systems doesn't exist. If their internal structure could be studied, we would probably learn more about the science of federal government than by any of the similar experiments with which we are acquainted.

Achaean Government More Just

16 Historians who study Achaean affairs agree on one fact. Both after Aratus renovated the league and before its dissolution by Macedon, its government was infinitely more

moderate and just and its citizens were less than those in any solitary city exercising all the power of a sovereignty.

In his observations on Greece, Abbe' Mably says that the popular government, so tempestuous elsewhere, caused no disorders in the members of the Achaean republic, *because it was tempered by the general authority and laws of the confederacy.*

Faction Caused Problems

17 However, we shouldn't hastily conclude that faction did not agitate particular cities, or that subordination and harmony reigned. The contrary is shown in the vicissitudes and fate of the republic.

Allies Became Conquerors

18 During the Amphictyonic confederacy, the less important cities of the Achaeans were minor characters in the theater of Greece. When the Achaean cities fell to Macedon, the policy of Philip II and his son, Alexander the Great, saved Greece. Their successors followed a different policy. Each city had separate interests and the union was dissolved. Some fell under the tyranny of Macedonian garrisons; others fell to usurpers within Greece.

Before long, shame and oppression awakened their love of liberty. A few cities reunited. Others followed their example as opportunities to cut off their tyrants were found. Soon the league embraced almost the whole Peloponnesus. Macedon saw its progress but internal dissensions hindered her from stopping it.

All Greece caught the enthusiasm and seemed ready to unite in one confederacy until jealousy and envy in Sparta and Athens, over the rising glory of the Achaeans, threw a fatal wrench into the enterprise. The dread of

Macedonian power induced the league to court an alliance with the kings of Egypt and Syria who, as successors of Alexander, were rivals of the Macedonian king.

Ambition led Cleomenes, king of Sparta, to make an unprovoked attack on the Achaeans [- 236]. As an enemy of Macedon, Cleomenes got the Egyptian and Syrian princes to breach their engagements with the league. The Achaeans were reduced to the dilemma of submitting to Cleomenes or requesting the aid of Macedon, its former oppressor.

The Achaeans chose the aid of Macedon, who often enjoyed meddling in Greek's affairs. A Macedonian army quickly appeared and took possession of Sparta. Cleomenes was vanquished to Egypt. But the Achaeans soon learned that a victorious and powerful ally is often just another name for a master. All their abject compliances earned them only a toleration of their laws.

The tyrannies of Philip, on the throne of Macedon, provoked new alliances among the Greeks. The Achaeans were weakened by internal dissensions and by the revolt of one of its members, Messene, but they joined the Aetolians and Athenians in opposition. However, they were unequal to the undertaking and once more had to resort to the dangerous expedient of help from foreign arms. The Romans were invited and eagerly accepted. Philip was conquered. Macedon was subdued.

A new crisis ensued to the league. The Roman fostered dissensions broke out among its members. Popular leaders became mercenary instruments for manipulating their countrymen. To nourish discord and disorder, the Romans proclaimed universal liberty* throughout Greece, much to the astonishment of those who trusted their sincerity. With the same insidious views, they reduced members from the league by appealing to their pride, highlighting the violation it committed on their sovereignty. Because of these tactics, this union, the last hope of Greece and the last hope of ancient liberty, was torn into pieces. Such imbecility and distraction reigned that the Roman army easily completed the ruin that their intrigues had begun. The Achaeans were cut to pieces and Achaia loaded with chains under which it groans at this hour.

Federal Government Tends Towards Anarchy, Not Tyranny

19 I do not think an outline of this important portion of history is superfluous. It teaches several lessons. And, as a supplement to the outlines of the Achaean constitution, it emphatically illustrates the tendency of federal bodies more towards anarchy among the members than to tyranny in the head.   PUBLIUS

---

* This was but another name more specious for the independence of the members on the federal head.

Number 19

Current Confederacies—German, Polish, Swiss

The examples of ancient confederacies cited in my last paper have not exhausted the sources of instruction on the subject. Some existing institutions, founded on a similar principle, merit particular consideration. The first is the Germanic body.

History of Germany

2 In the early ages of Christianity, seven distinct nations occupied Germany with no common chief. After conquering the Gauls, the Franks established the kingdom named for them. [c. 418]

In the ninth century, its warlike monarch, Charlemagne, carried his victorious arms in every direction. Germany became part of his vast dominions. On the dismemberment under his sons, Germany became a separate, independent empire.

Charlemagne and his immediate descendants possessed both power and the dignity of imperial power. But the principal vassals, whose lands became hereditary and who composed the national assembly, which Charlemagne had not abolished, gradually threw off the yoke and moved towards sovereign jurisdiction and independence. The imperial sovereignty was unable to restrain such powerful dependents or preserve the unity and tranquility of the empire. Furious private wars, accompanied by every type of calamity, raged between different princes and states.

Unable to maintain public order, the imperial authority declined by degrees until anarchy agitated during the long interval between the death of the last emperor of the German province of Swabia and the first emperor of Austria.

In the eleventh century the emperors held full sovereignty; in the fifteenth, they were only symbols and decorations of power.

Structure Federal Authority

3 The feudal system had many important features of a confederacy. The federal system that constitutes the German empire grew from it.

An assembly, the diet, representing the component members of the confederacy, holds its legislative power. The emperor, who is the executive magistrate, has veto power over the decrees of the assembly. The two judiciary tribunals, the imperial chamber and the aulic council, have supreme jurisdiction in controversies concerning the empire or among its members.

Legislative Authorities

4 The assembly has general legislating power for the empire, making war and peace, contracting alliances, assessing quotas for troops and money, constructing fortresses, regulating coins, admitting new members, and punishing disobedient members by removing sovereign rights and forfeiture of possessions.

Member State Restrictions

Members of the confederacy are expressly restricted from entering into compacts prejudicial to the empire, imposing tolls and duties on interstate commerce without the consent of the emperor and assembly, altering the value of money, doing injustice to one another, or giving assistance or retreat to disturbers of the public peace. And violators of these restrictions are subject to the above stated punishment.

Judiciary

Members of the diet, as such, are to be judged by the emperor and the assembly, and as private citizens by the aulic council and imperial chamber.

Emperor: Duties, Rights

5 The emperor has numerous prerogatives. The most important are: an exclusive right to propose legislation to the assembly, veto its resolutions, name ambassadors, confer dignities and titles, fill vacant electorates, found universities, grant privileges not injurious to the states of the empire, receive and apply public revenues, and generally watch over the public safety.

In certain cases, the electors form a council to the emperor. As emperor, he possesses no territory within the empire nor receives any revenue for his support. But his revenue and dominions, in other qualities, constitute him one of the most powerful princes in Europe.

Sovereign Members

6 This set of constitutional powers of the representatives and head of this confederacy suggests that it must be an exception to the general character of similar systems. Nothing could be further from the reality. The fundamental principle on which it rests—that the empire is a community of sovereigns, that the assembly represents sovereigns, and that the laws are addressed to sovereigns—renders the empire a nerveless body. It couldn't regulate its members or secure against external dangers. Unceasing fermentations agitated its bowels.

Battles, Invasions, Misery

7 The history of Germany is a history of wars. Wars between the emperor and the princess and states. Wars among the princes and states. Its history includes the licentiousness of the strong and oppression of the weak. Foreign invasions and intrigues. Requisitions of money and men are largely disregarded and enforcement attempts have been either aborted or accompanied by slaughter of the innocent with the guilty. It's a history of general imbecility, confusion, and misery.

Constant Civil War

8 In the sixteenth century, the emperor, supported by part of the empire, fought other princes and states. The emperor had to flee from one conflict after nearly being made prisoner by the Elector of Saxony. The late king of Prussia fought his imperial sovereign more than once, usually defeating him.

Controversies and wars among members were so common that German annals are crowded with bloody descriptions.

Before the peace of Westphalia (1648), thirty years of war desolated Germany. The emperor with one half the empire opposed Sweden and the other half. Foreign powers finally negotiated and dictated the peace. Peace treaty articles became a fundamental part of the German constitution.

Crises, Internal Conflict

9 If the nation happens to unite in self-defense during an emergency, its situation is still deplorable. Military preparations must be preceded by so many tedious assembly discussions—inflamed by jealousies, pride, separate views, and clashing pretensions of sovereign bodies—that enemy troops are in the field before the assembly settles the military counter-strategy. And the enemy is retiring into winter quarters before federal troops are prepared to fight.

Army Inadequate, Underpaid

10 The small body of national troops judged necessary in peacetime is poorly maintained, badly paid, infected with local prejudices, and supported by irregular and disproportionate contributions to the treasury.

Districts, Constant Civil War

11 Because maintaining order and dispensing justice among sovereign subjects was impossible, the empire was divided into nine or ten circles or districts. They had interior organization and were authorized to use the military to enforce laws against delinquent and disobedient members.

This experiment fully demonstrates the radical vice of the constitution. Each circle is the miniature picture of the deformities of this political monster. They either fail to execute their commissions or do it with all the devastation and carnage of civil war. Sometimes whole circles default, increasing the mischief they were established to remedy.

Internal Military Coercion

12 We may judge the use of military coercion from an example presented by Thuanus. In Donawerth, a free and imperial city within the Swabian circle, the Abbe de St. Croix enjoyed certain reserved immunities. While exercising them on some public occasions, the people of the city committed outrages on him. In consequence, the city was put under the ban of the empire.

The director of another district, the Duke of Bavaria, obtained an appointment to enforce it. He arrived in the city with 10,000 troops to forcefully revive and move on an antiquated claim that the city had been stolen from his ancestors' territory. He took possession of it in his own name, disarmed and punished the inhabitants, and reannexed the city to his domain.

Weakness Promotes Status Quo

13 What has kept this disjointed machine from completely falling apart? The answer is obvious: most members are weak and unwilling to expose themselves to the mercy of the formidable foreign powers around them. The emperor derives vast weight and influence from his own hereditary properties, so he wants to preserve a system that is tied with his family pride and makes him the first prince of Europe.

These circumstances support a feeble and precarious Union. The nature of sovereignty includes a repellent quality, which time strengthens, preventing any reform by consolidation.

Even if this obstacle could be surmounted, neighboring powers would not allow a revolution because it would give the empire the force and preeminence to which it is entitled. Foreign nations are interested in any changes made to the German constitution and, on various occasions, their policy of perpetuating its anarchy has been evident.

Poland: Sovereigns

14 There are more examples. Poland, a government over local sovereigns, might be noticed. It gives striking proof of the calamities flowing from institutions that are equally unfit for self-government and self-defense. Poland has long been at the mercy of its powerful neighbors who recently, and graciously, disburdened it of one-third of its people and territories.

Swiss States Not Confederacy

15 The connection between the Swiss states can scarcely be called a confederacy, even though it is sometimes cited as an example of the stability of such institutions.

No Common Sovereignty

16 They have no common treasury, no common armies even in war, no common coin, no common judicatory, nor any other common mark of sovereignty

League's Unifying Features

17 They are kept together by their geographic location, their individual weakness and insignificance, the fear of powerful neighbors (one formerly ruled them), by the few contentions among the basically homogeneous manners, by their joint interest in their dependent possessions, by mutual aid for suppressing insurrections and rebellions, and by some regular and permanent provision for solving disputes among the states.

To settle disputes, each party involved chooses four judges from neutral states who, in case of disagreement, choose an umpire. Under the oath of impartiality, this tribunal pronounces a definitive sentence that all the states are bound to enforce. This regulation's effectiveness may be estimated by a clause in their treaty of 1683 with Victor Amadeus of Savoy. In it, he is obliged to interpose as mediator in disputes between states and employ force, if necessary, against the disobedient party.

Problems Easily Severed League

18 Comparing their case to the United States confirms our opinion. However effective the union may be in ordinary cases, as soon as severe differences appeared, it failed. In three instances, religious controversies have kindled violent and bloody contests that severed the league.

The Protestant and Catholic states established separate assemblies where the most important concerns are adjusted, leaving the general assembly little business other than to take care of common bailages.

Opposing Foreign Alliances

19 The consequence of that separation merits attention. It produced opposite alliances with foreign powers. Berne, the head of the Protestant association, is allied with the United Provinces. Luzerne, head of the Catholic association, with France.

PUBLIUS

Number 20

United Netherlands: Failure of Legislation for States

The United Netherlands is an interesting confederacy of aristocracies, yet it confirms the lessons derived from others we have reviewed.

Equal States, Independent Cities

2 The United Netherlands has seven equal sovereign provinces. Each province is composed of equal, independent cities. In all important issues, both the provinces and the cities must be unanimous.

States-General: Terms Vary

3 The sovereignty of the union is represented by the States-General, consisting usually of about 50 deputies appointed by the provinces. They hold their seats, some for life and some for one, three, or six years. From two provinces, their appointment continues at the state's pleasure.

Authorities of States-General

4   The States-General can enter into treaties and alliances, make war and peace, raise armies and equip fleets, determine quotas and quotes, and demand contributions. In each case, however, unanimity and the sanction of their constituents are requisite.

They have authority to appoint and receive ambassadors, execute treaties and alliances already formed, provide for collection of duties on imports and exports, regulate the mint with a saving to the provincial rights, and govern the dependent territories as sovereigns.

Without general consent, the provinces are restrained from entering into foreign treaties and establishing duties injurious to others or higher than that charged their own subjects.

A council of state and a chamber of accounts, with five colleges of admiralty, aid and fortify the federal administration.

National Executive

5   The stadholder (executive magistrate of the United Provinces of the Netherlands) is a hereditary prince. His principal weight and influence derive from his independent title, his family connections with some of the chief potentates of Europe, and, most of all, his being stadholder (viceroy, governor) in several provinces in addition to the union.

As a provincial stadholder, he appoints town magistrates under certain regulations, executes provincial decrees, presides when he pleases in the provincial tribunals, and has throughout the power of pardon.

Stadholder: Authorities

6   As stadholder of the union, he has considerable prerogatives.

Political Executive

7   In his political capacity, he settles disputes between provinces when other methods fail, assists at the deliberations of the States-General and their particular conferences, meets with foreign ambassadors, and keeps agents for his particular affairs at foreign courts.

Military Commander

8   In his military capacity, he commands the federal troops, provides for posts and garrisons in fortified towns, and confers military ranks.

Naval Admiral-General

9   In his marine capacity, he is admiral-general. He directs everything relative to naval forces and affairs, presides in the admiralties in person or by proxy, appoints lieutenant-admirals and other offices, and establishes councils of war, whose decisions are not executed until he approves them.

Salary; Standing Army

10   His revenue, exclusive of his private income, amounts to 300,000 florins. The standing army he commands has about 40,000 men.

Theory Only; Reality, Chaos

11   This is the nature of the celebrated Belgic confederacy as spelled out on paper. How has it functioned in reality? Imbecility in the government. Discord among provinces. Foreign influence and indignities. Precarious existence in peace and the calamities accompanying war.

Hatred Keeps Country Whole

12   Long ago Grotius said nothing but the hatred of his countrymen to the house

of Austria kept them from being ruined by the vices of their constitution.

Jealousy Among Provinces

13 Another respectable writer says the union has enough authority in the States-General to secure harmony, but jealousy in each province renders reality very different from theory.

Inland Provinces Can't Pay Taxes

14 Another says the constitution obliges each province to levy contributions. But this article never could, and probably never will, be executed because inland provinces, which have little commerce, cannot pay an equal quota.

Military Extracts Tax Quotas

15 In practice, the articles of the constitution relating to contribution are waived. The consenting provinces are obliged to furnish their quota without waiting for the others, then obtain reimbursement from the others anyway they can. The great wealth and influence of Holland enable her to do both.
16 More than once, deficiencies were ultimately collected at bayonet point. Although practical, this is a dreadful solution in a confederacy where one member is stronger than the rest and several are too small to offer any resistance. And this solution is utterly impractical in a confederacy composed of several members of equal strength, resources, and defenses.

Ministers Overstep Authority

17 Former foreign minister Sir William Temple says foreign ministers avoid matters taken *ad referendum* by tampering with the provinces and cities. In 1726, the treaty of Hanover was delayed this way for a year. Similar instances are numerous and notorious.

Congress Oversteps Authority

18 In critical emergencies, the States-General are often compelled to overstep their constitutional bounds. In 1688, they concluded a treaty themselves at the risk of their heads. In 1648, the treaty of Westphalia, formalizing their independence, concluded without the consent of Zealand. Even as recently as the last peace treaty with Great Britain, the constitutional principle of unanimity was ignored.

Weak Constitution => Tyranny

A weak constitution must end in dissolution either from a deficiency in power or the usurpation of powers necessary for the public safety. Whether the usurpation, when once begun, will stop at a healthy point or go forward to a dangerous extreme, depends on the circumstances at the time. Tyranny more frequently grows out of the assumptions of power needed in an emergency by a defective constitution, than out of the full exercise of the largest constitutional authorities.

Ruler Holds Confederacy Together

19 Despite the calamities produced by the stadholdership, it has been assumed that without his influence in individual provinces, the causes of anarchy manifest in the confederacy would have dissolved it long ago.

The Abbe Mably says under such a government, the Union could not have survived without a motivator from within the provinces, capable of quickening their tardiness and compelling them to the same way of thinking. This motivator is the stadholdership.

Sir William Temple said that during vacancies in the stadholdership, Holland, with her riches and authority, drew others into dependence, supplying the role.

Other Nations Influence

20 Other circumstances have also controlled the tendency to anarchy and dissolution. The surrounding foreign powers make union absolute necessity. At the same time, their intrigues nourish the constitutional vices, keeping the republic to some degree always at their mercy.

Can't Agree How to Fix

21 True patriots have long bewailed the fatal tendency of these vices and have convened four *extraordinary assemblies* for the special purpose of finding a remedy. But even with their enthusiasm, they have found it impossible to *unite the public councils* in reforming the known, acknowledged, fatal evils or the existing constitution.

Let us pause for one moment, my fellow citizens, over this melancholy and monitory lesson of history. Let's shed a tear for the calamities brought on mankind by their adverse opinions and selfish passions. Then let our combined praise of gratitude for the auspicious amity distinguishing our political counsels rise to Heaven.

Federal Tax Plan Failed

22 A design establishing a general tax administered by the federal government was also conceived. It had adversaries and also failed.

Crises May Form Stronger Union

23 This unhappy people seem to currently suffer from popular convulsions, dissentions among states, and foreign invasion, crises that will determine their destiny. The eyes of all nations are fixed on the awful spectacle.

Humanity's first wish is that this severe trial will create a governmental revolution that will strengthen their union, making it the parent of tranquillity, freedom, and happiness. Our next wish is that the speed with which our country secures these blessings will comfort them after the catastrophe of their own.

Fatal Flaw: Government Governing Government

24 I don't apologize for dwelling so long on the study of these federal precedents. Experience is the oracle of truth. When its lessons are unambiguous, they should be regarded as absolutely conclusive.

The important truth that experience unequivocally pronounces in this present case is that just as a sovereignty over sovereigns, a government over governments, a legislation for communities— as distinguished from a government over individuals—is illogical in theory, in practice it subverts order and ends civility by substituting *violence* in place of *law*, or the destructive *coercion* of the *sword* in place of the mild and solitary *coercion* of the *magistracy*.

PUBLIUS

Number 21

Defects of United States Articles of Confederation

Having summarized the roots and fates of other confederate governments in the last three papers, I will now proceed to enumerate the most important and disappointing defects in our system. To decide a safe and satisfactory remedy, we absolutely must become well acquainted with the extent and malignity of the disease.

No Power to Enforce Federal Laws

2 An obvious defect of the existing Constitution is the total lack of SANCTION to its laws. Currently, the United States has no power to demand obedience or punish disobedience to their resolutions either by fines, by suspension or divestiture of privileges, or by any other constitutional mode. The federal government is not expressly given the authority to use force against delinquent members.

If we say that, from the nature of the social compact between the States, the right to enforce federal resolutions exists, the assumption is contrary to the wording in the *States' rights* clause, Article Two, Articles of Confederation: "that each State shall retain every power, jurisdiction, and right, not *expressly* delegated to the United States in Congress assembled."

To suppose this federal right does not exist seems absurd. But we are faced with the dilemma of either accepting this preposterous supposition, or violating or explaining away the provision in Article Two.

Recently, the lack of a States' rights clause in the new Constitution has been the subject of severe criticism, opponents arguing that this will cause it to fail. However, if we are unwilling to weaken the force of this praised provision, the United States will become the extraordinary spectacle of a government without even the shadow of constitutional power to enforce the execution of its own laws. From the historical examples cited, the America Confederacy appears different in this area from every similar federation. It will become a unique, new phenomenon in the political world.

No Federal/State Guaranty

3 The lack of a mutual guaranty of the State governments is another major imperfection in the federal plan. The Articles say nothing on this subject. To suggest the guaranty exists simply because it's useful would be an even more flagrant departure from the above quoted clause than to imply a tacit power of coercion. The consequences of not having a guaranty may endanger the Union, but it isn't as dangerous to its existence as the lack of a constitutional sanction to its laws.

Can't Defend State Constitutions

4 Without a guaranty, the Union cannot assist in repelling domestic dangers that may threaten State constitutions. Usurpation may arise and trample upon liberties in each State, while the national government could legally do nothing more than watch its encroachments with indignation and regret. A successful faction may erect a tyranny on the ruins of order and law, while the Union could not constitutionally help the friends and supporters of the government.

Concrete evidence of this danger is the recent tempestuous situation that Massachusetts barely survived. Who can say what might have happened if the malcontents had been led by a Caesar or by a Cromwell? Who can predict the effect of despotism, if established in Massachusetts, on the liberties of New Hampshire, Rhode Island, Connecticut, or New York?

Mutual Guaranty

5 Some people, influenced by exaggerated State pride, object to a federal government guaranty. They say it would involve an objectionably aggressive and undesired interference in the internal concerns of States.

They would deprive us of important advantages expected from union because they misunderstand the provision. It could not impede reforming State constitutions by a majority of the people in a legal and peaceful mode. This right would remain undiminished. The guaranty could only operate when violence was used to force changes.

Too many checks cannot be provided against calamities of this kind. The peace of society and the stability of government depend absolutely on the efficacy of precautions in this area.

People Hold Authority

When the people hold the whole power of the government, fewer pretenses to use violence to remedy partial or occasional distempers will appear. In a popular or representative government, the natural cure for poor administration is changing men. A national authority guaranty would as often be leveled against the usurpations of rulers as against the ferments and outrages of faction and sedition in the community.

Taxation by State Quotas

6 Regulating State contributions to the national treasury by QUOTAS is another fundamental error in the Confederation. It has already been pointed out that the national financial needs haven't been met during this trial period, with plenty of examples. Now I will address it as it relates to equality among the States.

People who study the circumstances that produce and constitute national wealth must agree that no common standard or barometer exists to measure the degrees of it. Neither land values nor population numbers, both proposed as the rule for State contributions, are just representations.

For example, if we compare the wealth of the United Netherlands with that of Russia, Germany, or even France with their land value and aggregate population, we immediately discover no comparison between the proportion of either of these and the relative wealth of those nations. The United Netherlands has the higher wealth; the three other nations have immense land and much larger populations.

The same analysis between several American States would furnish a similar result. Contrast Virginia with North Carolina, Pennsylvania with Connecticut, or Maryland with New Jersey and we will be convinced that the respective revenue abilities of those States bear little or no analogy to their comparative stock in lands or comparative population. A similar process between counties in the same State illustrates the same thing. Any man acquainted with New York State will not doubt that the active wealth of King's County is in much greater proportion than that of Montgomery if either total land value or total number of people is used as a criterion.

Measuring Wealth

7 A nation's wealth depends on an infinite variety of causes. Situation, soil, climate, type of productions, nature of government, genius of the citizens, the amount of information they possess, the state of commerce, arts, industry—these circumstances, and many more too complex, minute, or adventitious to quantify, create differences in the relative opulence and riches of different countries.

There clearly can be no common measure of national wealth and, of course, no general or stationary measurement to determine a State's ability to pay taxes. Therefore, trying to regulate State contributions to the confederacy by any such rule cannot fail to be glaringly unequal and extremely oppressive.

Quotas, States Unequal

8 If a way of enforcing compliance with federal requisitions could be devised, the inequality between States' wealth, alone, would be sufficient to eventually destroy the American Union. Suffering States would soon refuse to remain associated on a principle that so unequally distributes public burdens and is calculated to impoverish and oppress citizens of some States while citizens of others are scarcely conscious of the small proportion of the weight they are required to sustain. However, this evil is inseparable from the principle of quotas and requisitions.

National Government Taxes

9 The only method of avoiding this inconvenience is by authorizing the national government to raise its own revenue in its own way.

Imposts, excises and, in general, all duties on articles of consumption may be compared to a fluid that will, in time, find its level with the means of paying them. Each citizen's contribution will be, to a degree, his own option, regulated by attention to his resources. The rich may be extravagant. The poor can be frugal. And private oppression may be avoided by a judicious selection of objects proper for such taxes. If inequalities arise in some States from duties on particular objects, these will probably be counterbalances by proportional inequalities in other States from duties on other objects. In time, an equilibrium, as far as it is attainable in so complicated a subject, will be established everywhere. Or, if inequalities continue to exist, they will not be in so great a degree, so uniform, or so odious in appearance as those that would spring from quotas.

Limited Tax Revenue Limits Federal Authority

10 The advantage of taxes on articles of consumption is that their nature contains a security against excess. They prescribe their own limit. And it cannot be exceeded without defeating the end proposed, increasing government's revenue.

Excessive Taxes Decrease Revenue

When applied to taxation policy, the saying is as true as true as it is witty that, "in political arithmetic, 2 and 2 do not always make 4." If duties are too high, they lessen consumption, collection is eluded, and the product to the treasury is less than when taxes are confined within proper and moderate bounds. This forms a complete barrier against any significant oppression of citizens by taxes of this kind. And it naturally limits the power of the imposing authority.

Indirect vs. Direct Federal Taxes

11 This kind of imposition is usually called indirect taxes. For a long time, this must be the chief way of raising revenue in this country.

Direct taxes principally relate to land and buildings and may be appropriate for the rule of apportionment. Either the land value or the number of people may serve as a standard. The states of agriculture and population density of a country are considered co-related. For the purpose intended, numbers are usually preferred because of their simplicity and certainty.

In every country, land valuation is a herculean task. In a country imperfectly settled and constantly being improved, the difficulties make it more impractical. In all situations, the expense of an accurate valuation is a formidable objection.

Direct taxes, by their nature, have no limits to the discretion of the government. Therefore the establishment of a fixed rule, compatible with its purpose, may have fewer inconveniences than to leave that discretion unbound.

PUBLIUS

Articles of Confederation references:

Article 2	States' rights clause
Article 8	federal taxation by quotas

Number 22

Defects in Articles of Confederation

In addition to the defects in the existing federal system already discussed, others, just as important, make it completely unfit to administer the affairs of the Union.

No Federal Regulation of Commerce

2 One is the lack of power to regulate commerce. We have discussed the importance of this power. For this reason, as well as common knowledge on the subject, little needs to be said here.

Even the most superficial view shows no area of trade or finance that more strongly demands federal authority than regulation of commerce. The absence of that authority has barred the formation of beneficial treaties with foreign powers. Occasionally, disputes between the States have arisen. No nation aware of our political association would be unwise enough to enter into stipulations that cede privileges to the United States, because they know arrangements made with the Union may, at any time, be violated by its members. Besides, they enjoy every advantage they desire in our markets without granting us any in return except what is momentarily convenient.

So, it isn't a big surprise that when Mr. Jenkinson introduced a bill in the British House of Commons for temporarily regulating intercourse between our two countries, he declared that similar provisions in former bills had answered every need of Great Britain's commerce and they should continue their plan until it appeared the American government was likely or not to acquire greater consistency.[1]

---

[1] As nearly as I can recollect, this was the sense of his speech on introducing the bill.

Foreign Commerce Authority

3 Several States have endeavored, through separate prohibitions, restrictions, and exclusions, to influence the conduct of Great Britain. But without the consistency of a uniform federal authority, clashing and dissimilar State views frustrate every experiment and will continue to do so as long as obstacles to uniform measures continue to exist.

Interstate Commerce Laws

4 Contrary to the true spirit of the Union, interfering and unneighborly regulations of some States have given other States good cause for umbrage and complaints. It is feared that, if these policies are not restrained by a national control, they will multiply and extend, becoming both serious sources of animosity and injurious impediments to commerce between different parts of the Confederacy.

"The commerce of the German empire is in continual trammels from the multiplicity of the duties which the several princes and states exact upon the merchandises passing through their territories, by means of which the fine streams and navigable rivers with which Germany is so happily watered are rendered almost useless."[2]

This description may not ever be strictly applicable to us, yet we may reasonably expect, from gradually conflicting State regulations, that eventually citizens will treat other citizens in no better light than foreigners and aliens.

Requisitions to Raise Armies

5 By the most obvious interpretation of the Articles of Confederation, the power of raising armies is limited to requisitioning quotas of men from the States. During the recent war, this policy created many obstructions to a vigorous and economical system of defense.

Competition between States became a kind of auction for men. To furnish their required quotas, States outbid each other until bounties grew to an enormous and insupportable size. Hoping to receive a larger inducement, men who wanted to serve procrastinated their enlistment, postponing military service for considerable periods.

The result? Scant and short enlistments at an unparalleled expense during critical emergencies. Continual fluctuations in troops ruined their discipline. The public safety frequently was threatened by the perilous crisis of a disbanded army. Additionally, the occasional forced enlistment only worked because the enthusiasm for liberty induced people to endure them.

Unfair, States Not Compensated

6 This method of raising troops is both unfriendly to the economy and an unequal distribution of the burden. The States near the heart of the war, influenced by self-preservation, tried to furnish their quotas, even exceeding their abilities. States more distant from danger were, for the most part, as remiss in their exertions as the others were diligent.

In this case, unlike disproportionate monetary contributions, States have no hope of a final liquidation. States that didn't pay their proportions of money might, at least, be charged with their deficiencies. But it would be impossible to supply delinquent deficiencies of men.

However, delinquent States probably won't make compensation for their pecuniary failures. Whether it is applied to men or money, the system of

---

[2] Encyclopaedia, article "Empire."

quotas is, in every view, a system of imbecility in the Union and of inequality and injustice among the members.

States' Equal Suffrage, Problems

7   The right of equal suffrage among the States is another difficulty in the Confederation. Every rule of proportion and fair representation conspires to condemn the principle that gives Rhode Island equal power with Massachusetts or Connecticut or New York. That gives Delaware an equal voice in national deliberations as Pennsylvania or Virginia or North Carolina. This contradicts the fundamental maxim of republican government, which is, the will of the majority should prevail.

Sophistry may reply that sovereigns are equal and a majority of the votes of States will be a majority of confederate America. But this kind of logical sleight of hand will never counteract the plain dictates of justice and common sense. It may happen that a majority of States is a small minority of people of America.[3]

And two-thirds of the people of America could not long be persuaded, based on artificial distinctions and syllogistic subtleties, to allow their interests to be managed by the one third. After a while, the larger States would revolt against the idea of living under the law of the smaller. Giving up their political majority rights would be not only contrary to the love of power but even a sacrifice of equality. It is neither rational to expect the first, nor just to require the last.

The safety and welfare of the smaller States depends on union. They should readily renounce a pretension that, if not relinquished, would prove fatal to that union.

2/3 States Doesn't Assure Majority

8   It may be proposed that not seven but nine States, two-thirds of the whole number, must consent to the most important resolutions. The inference is that nine States would always include a majority of the Union. But this doesn't change the impropriety of an equal vote between States of unequal dimensions and populations. Besides, it is possible to have nine States that together have less than a majority of the people. And it is constitutionally possible that these nine may win the vote.[4]

Further, a bare majority may decide significant issues. Other matters for which doubts exist could evolve into the first magnitude of importance if the vote of seven States were a sufficiency. Additionally, the number of States will probably increase and there is no provision for a proportional augmentation of the ratio of votes.

2/3 Majority = Minority Control

9   But this is not all. What may at first be seen as a remedy, is, in reality, a poison. Giving a minority a negative over the majority (the consequence of requiring more than a majority for a decision), tends to subordinate the feelings of the greater number to those of the lesser.

Because a few States have been absent, Congress has frequently been in the situation of the Polish assembly where a single VOTE has been sufficient

---

[3] New Hampshire, Rhode Island, New Jersey, Delaware, Georgia, South Carolina and Maryland are a majority of the whole number of States but they do not contain one third of the people.

[4] Add New York and Connecticut to the foregoing seven and they will be less than a majority.

to stop all business. A sixtieth part of the union, which is about the size of Delaware and Rhode Island, has several times barred the operation of Congress.

In practice, this refinement has the reverse effect of what is expected from the theory. The necessity of unanimity in public bodies, or something approaching it, was based on the supposition that it would contribute to security. But in reality, it embarrasses the administration, destroys the government's energy, substituting the pleasure, caprice, or artifices of an insignificant, turbulent, or corrupt junta to the regular deliberations and decisions of a respectable majority.

In national emergencies, when the goodness or badness, the weakness or strength of government is of the greatest importance, action is commonly necessary. Public business must, one way or another, go forward. If a stubborn minority controls the opinion of a majority about the best way of conducting business, to get something done, the majority must conform to the views of the minority; thus, the smaller number will overrule the greater and set a tone to the national proceedings. The reality will include tedious delays, continual negotiation and intrigue, and contemptible compromise of the public good.

In such a system, it is good when compromises are possible. But some occasions won't permit accommodation, leaving legislative solutions injuriously suspended or fatally defeated. The inability to obtain the necessary number of concurring votes often maintains a state of governmental inaction. The situation creates weakness, sometimes bordering on anarchy.

Corruption Easier

10 It's easy to see that this principle provides greater opportunity for both foreign corruption and domestic faction than having a majority decide, even though the opposite has been assumed. This mistake arises from not carefully considering the consequences from obstruction of governmental progress on certain critical issues.

While it's true that when the constitution requires the concurrence of a large number to pass any national act, we may be satisfied that nothing improper will be likely *to be done*. But we forget how much good may be prevented and ill produced because doing what may be necessary is hindered, keeping affairs in the same unfavorable positions.

Simple Majority More Difficult to Corrupt

11 For instance, suppose we were allies with one foreign nation against another. Suppose our situation demanded peace but the interest or ambition of our ally promoted war, possibly justifying our making separate terms. In this situation, it would be easier for our ally to use bribes and intrigues to tie the hands of our government from making peace if a vote of two-thirds were required rather than a simple majority. In the first case, a smaller number [34%] would need to be corrupted; in the latter, a greater number [51%].

By the same principle, a foreign power at war with us could perplex our councils and embarrass our exertions.

Commercially we may suffer similar inconveniences. We might have a commerce treaty with a nation, who could easily prevent our forming a connection with her trade competitor, even though such a connection would be beneficial to us.

Republics, Foreign Corruption

12 These kinds of evils are not imaginary. A weak side to republics, among their many advantages, is that they allow easy access to foreign corruption. Although a monarch often sacrifices his subjects to his ambition, his personal interest in both the government and the external glory of his nation make it difficult for a foreign power to make a bribe large enough to sacrifice his state. So the world has seen few examples of this type of royal prostitution, even though there have been abundant examples of every other kind.

Foreign Corruption of Republics

13 In a republic, people are elected from and by their fellow-citizens to stations of great pre-eminence and power. They may be offered adequate compensations to betray their trust that only the most virtuous can resist. Others may find that their personal interest over-rides their obligations to duty.

Hence, history furnishes us with many mortifying examples of foreign corruption in republican governments. The amount this contributed to the ruin of ancient commonwealths already has been delineated.

It is well known that the emissaries of neighboring kingdoms have, at various times, purchased the deputies of the United Provinces. If my memory serves me right, the Earl of Chesterfield wrote his court, suggesting that his success in an important negotiation depended on his getting a major's pay for one of those deputies.

In Sweden, the parties were alternately bought by France and England in such an open, notorious manner that it excited universal disgust in the nation. It was a principal cause for the most lim-ited monarch in Europe to become one of the most uncontrolled within a single day without tumult, violence, or opposition.

Lack of Federal Supreme Court

14 The crowning defect of the Confederation is the lack of a judiciary power. Laws are pointless without courts to interpret and define their true meaning and operation.

To have any force at all, treaties of the United States must be considered as part of the law of the land. Their effect on individuals must, like all other laws, be ascertained by judicial decisions. To produce uniformity in these decisions, as a last resort they should be submitted to one SUPREME TRIBUNAL. This tribunal should be instituted under the same authority that forms the treaties themselves. Both ingredients are indispensable.

If each State has a court of final jurisdiction, there may be as many different final decisions on an issue as there are courts. Men hold endless diversities in opinions. We often see not only different courts, but judges of the same court, differing from each other. Confusion is the unavoidable result of contradictory decisions of a number of independent judiciaries. To avoid this, all nations have established one court of last resort, paramount to the rest and authorized to settle a uniform rule of civil justice.

State Courts Don't Always Agree

15 This is more necessary when a government's structure is such that the laws of the whole are in danger of being contravened by the laws of the parts. In this case, if State or regional tribunals possess the right of ultimate jurisdiction, besides producing the contradictions expected from different opinions, there will be much to fear from bias of local views and prejudices and from the interference of local regulations. A fear that previsions of local laws may be preferred to those of the federal laws is reasonable. Men in office naturally defer towards the authority to which they owe their official existence.

13 Courts of Final Jurisdiction

16 Under the present Constitution, the treaties of the United States are liable for the infractions of thirteen different legislatures, with many different courts of final jurisdiction, acting under the authority of those legislatures. Thus the faith, reputation, and peace of the whole Union are continually at the mercy of the prejudices, passions, and interests of every member. Is it possible that foreign nations can either respect or trust such a government? How long will Americans entrust their honor, happiness, and safety to so precarious a foundation?

Amendments Won't Cure Flaws

17 In this review of the Confederation, I confined myself to exhibiting the most material defects, passing over the details of those imperfections that make its intended power largely impotent. By this time, all men of reflection, who are able to divest themselves of preconceived opinions, must realize that it is a system so radically vicious and unsound that it cannot be cured by amendments. It requires an entire change in its important features and characters.

One Congress: Dangerous

18 The organization of Congress is utterly incapable of exercising the powers that need to be deposited in the Union. A single assembly may be the proper receptacle for the slender, or

rather fettered, authorities currently delegated to the federal government. But it is inconsistent with all the principles of good government to entrust it with additional powers that, even moderate and rational adversaries of the proposed Constitution admit, should reside in the United States.

If the new Constitution is not adopted and if the Union could withstand the ambitious aims of men who may indulge in magnificent schemes of personal aggrandizement from its dissolution, we would probably end up conferring supplementary powers upon Congress, as now constituted. Then either the "machine" will disintegrate from its intrinsic feebleness in spite of our ill-judged efforts to prop it up or, by successive injections of force and energy as necessary, we well eventually accumulate in a single body all the prerogatives of sovereignty, laying on our posterity one of the most utterly detestable forms of government humans have ever contrived. Thus we would create that very tyranny that adversaries of the new Constitution either are, or pretend to be, solicitous to avert.

People Didn't Ratify Articles

19 The fact that the PEOPLE never ratified the existing federal system adds to its infirmities. Its only foundation is the consent of the legislatures, which has exposed it to frequent and probing questions about the validity of its powers. These have given birth to the outrageous doctrine of the right of legislative repeal. It is rationalized that since it was ratified by the State, the same authority can repeal it. However gross the heresy that a *party* to a *compact* has a right to revoke that *compact*, the doctrine itself has respectable advocates.

Questions of this nature prove the necessity of laying the foundation of our national government deeper than in the mere sanction of delegated authority.

The American empire should rest on the solid basis of THE CONSENT OF THE PEOPLE. The streams of national power should flow immediately from that pure, original fountain of all legitimate authority.   PUBLIUS

Constitutional references:

Article 1, Section 8	171-173	taxes, duties, imposts, excises
Article 1, Section 8	175-177	taxes uniform throughout U.S.
Article 1, Section 8	233-237	make "necessary and proper" laws
Article 1, Section 9	253-254	no export tax
Article 1, Section 9	255-257	no commercial preference among States
Article 1, Section 9	257-259	no State duties: to other States
Article 1, Section 10	280-288	no State duties on imports, exports
Article 1, Section 8	207-212	military: raise, support, regulate
Article 1, Section 2	16-35	apportionment of Representatives
Article 2, Section 2	392-395	treaties
Article 1, Section 10	271-272	treaties, no State can make
Article 1, Section 1	1-4	Congress, two houses
Article 3, Section 1	434-435	Supreme Court
Article 3. Section 2	446	Supreme Court, treaties
Article 7	565-568	ratification of Constitution

Number 23

Federal Responsibilities, Powers, Organization

Our examination now focuses on the necessity of an energetic Constitution to preserve the Union.

2   Our inquiry divides itself naturally into four topics:
1. The objectives of the federal government.
2. The quantity of power necessary to fulfill its purposes.
3. The persons who should control that power.
4. The organization of the federal government.

3   The principal purposes of union are:
1. The common defense of the members.
2. The preservation of public peace against both internal convulsions and external attacks
3. Regulating commerce with other nations and between the States.
4. Supervising our political, commercial intercourse with foreign countries.

Powers Essential for Defense

4   The authorities essential to common defense are: to raise armies, build and equip fleets, prescribe rules to maintain both, direct their operations, and provide their support.

These powers should exist without limitation, *because it's impossible to foresee the extent and variety of national emergencies, or the size and type of force that may be necessary to solve them.*

An infinite number of circumstances endanger the safety of a nation. For this reason, constitutional limits on the power to protect it are unwise. This power should equal the strength of all possible circumstances. And it should be under the direction of the same councils that preside over the common defense.

Defense: Unlimited Authority

5   To a rational, unprejudiced mind, this truth carries its own evidence. It may be obscured, but argument or reasoning cannot make it plainer. It rests on axioms as simple as they are universal. The *means* ought to be pro-portionate to the *end*; the persons charged with attaining the *end* ought to possess the *means* for attaining it.

Direct, Support National Army

6   The first question is whether a federal government should be entrusted with the care of the common defense. Once decided in the affirmative, it follows that the government needs the power required to execute that trust. And unless circumstances effecting public safety can be reduced to within certain determinable limits, authority to provide for the defense and protection of the community can not be limited. Any matter essential to its efficacy should not be limited; that is, any matter essential to the *formation, direction,* or *support* of the NATIONAL FORCES.

Defense: States Requisitioned

7   Despite the present Confederation's defects, the framers apparently recognized this principle, even though they made no adequate provisions for its implementation. Congress has unlimited discretion to requisition men and money, govern the army and navy, and direct their operations. Since requisitions by Congress are constitutionally binding on the States, who are obligated to furnish the required supplies, it was evidently intended that the United States command whatever resources they judged necessary for the "common defense and general welfare." It was presumed that States, being aware of their best interests and duty to the Union, would punctually respond to federal requisitions.

Union: Authority Over Citizens

8 However, experience has demonstrated that this expectation was ill founded and illusory. I imagine the observations in the last paper convinced impartial, discerning people that an entire change in the first principles of the system is absolutely necessary. If we are earnest about giving the Union energy and duration, we must abandon the vain project of legislating upon States in their collective capacities and extend federal laws to individual citizens. We must discard the fallacious scheme of quotas and requisitions as equally impractical and unjust.

The Union should have the full power to levy troops, build and equip fleets, and raise the revenues required to form and support an army and navy in the same way as other governments.

Power to Fulfill Responsibilities

9 If the circumstances of our country demand a compound or confederate government instead of a simple, single government, then the essential remaining determination is what the RESPONSIBILITIES of the different parts and branches of power will be, delegating to each ample authority to fulfill the responsibilities committed to its charge.

Shall the Union be constituted the guardian of the common safety? Are fleets, armies and revenues necessary for this purpose? The government of the Union must be empowered to pass all laws and regulations in relation to them.

The same must be true for commerce and every other matter to which its jurisdiction is permitted to extend.

Is the administration of justice between citizens of the same State properly the jurisdiction of local government? They must possess the authority for this and every other responsibility allotted to them.

Not to confer the degree of power needed to obtain each end would violate the most obvious rules of prudence and propriety and would improvidently trust the great interests of the nation to disabled hands.

Federal Duty, Needs Authority

10 Who would make more suitable provisions for public defense than the body charged with guarding public safety? At the center of information, it will best understand the extent and urgency of threats. Representing the WHOLE, it will be deeply interested in the preservation of every part. It will accept the responsibility of necessary actions. And with the extension of its authority throughout the States, it can establish uniform plans to secure the common safety.

Isn't there an obvious inconsistency in giving the federal government the responsibility of general defense, but leaving the *effective* power of providing for it with the State governments? Isn't lack of cooperation the inevitable consequence of such a system? Will not weakness, disorder, and unequal distribution of the burden and calamities of war, and an unnecessary and intolerable increase of expense, naturally and inevitably accompany it? Didn't we have unambiguous experience of these effects during the revolution we have just achieved?

Powers = Federal Goals

11 As we candidly seek the truth, every view of the subject serves to convince us that it is both unwise and dangerous to deny the federal government full authority over those objects entrusted to its management. The people must be vigilant in seeing that it is modeled in a manner so that it is safely vested with the necessary powers. If any plan is, or may be, offered for our consideration that, after a dispassionate inspection, doesn't answer this description, it should be rejected.

A government formed under a constitution that makes it unfit to be entrusted with all the powers a free people *ought to delegate to any government* would be an unsafe and improper depository of the NATIONAL INTERESTS. Wherever these interests can properly be confided, the coinciding powers can safely accompany them. This is the conclusion drawn from a careful examination of the subject.

Adversaries of the Constitution would have seemed more sincere if they had confined their arguments to showing that the internal structure of the proposed government is unworthy of the people's confidence. They shouldn't have wandered into trivial and pointless rhetoric about the extent of the powers.

The POWERS are not too extensive for the OBJECTS of federal administration; or, in other words, for the management of our NATIONAL INTERESTS. Nor can any satisfactory argument be made showing it has excess powers. If there are, as insinuated by some writers on the other side, then the difficulty stems from the nature of government. If the extent of the country will not permit us to form a government in which such ample powers can safely be reposed, then we should downsize our ideas and simply form the more practical separate confederacies.

The absurdity of entrusting the national interests to a government without the authority to properly and efficiently manage them is obvious. Let's not try to reconcile contradictions, but firmly embrace a rational alternative.

Energetic Government

12 I trust, however, that one general system cannot be proven impractical. I don't think any significant argument has shown this. And I also flatter myself that the ideas presented in these papers have shown the reverse as clearly as is humanly possible. In all events, it must be evident that the size of the country is the strongest argument in favor of an energetic government. No other could preserve the Union of so large an empire.

If we embrace the arguments of those opposing the proposed Constitution as our political creed, we will verify the gloomy predictions of the impracticality of a national system spread across the entire area of the present Confederacy.

PUBLIUS

Constitutional references:

Article 1, section 8	174	provide for common defense
Article 1, section 8	180-182	regulate commerce
Article 1, section 8	207-210	raise and support armies, navy
Article 1, section 8	211-219	militia
Article 1, section 10	271-273	no State international commitments

Number 24

Standing Armies During Times of Peace

Only one specific objection has been raised to giving the federal government the power to create and direct the national armed forces. If I understand the objection correctly, it is that the Constitution contains no provision against the existence of standing armies in time of peace. I shall now endeavor to show that this objection rests on weak and insubstantial foundations.

Objection to Standing Armies

2 The objection is vague and generalized, supported by nothing but loud assertions without logical argument or a base in theoretical opinions. The objection contradicts the general feelings in America and the practice of other free nations, as expressed in their constitutions. Remember that the objection stems from the apparent need to restrain the LEGISLATURE from establishing national military bases, a principle rejected under all but one or two State constitutions.

Armies Not Mandatory

3 A stranger to our politics, who reads current newspapers without studying the proposed Constitution, would be led to one of two conclusions: either the Constitution says that standing armies should be kept up in time of peace or it vests in the EXECUTIVE the whole power of raising troops without subjecting his decision, in any way, to legislative control.

Only Legislature Raises Army

4 After studying the Constitution, he would be surprised to discover that neither the one nor the other was true.

The *legislature*, not the *executive*, has the power to raise armies. The legislature will consist of periodically elected representatives of the people.

Instead of a provision favorable to standing armies, he'd find an important limitation to even the legislature discretion in this area. A clause forbids the appropriation of money to support an army for any period longer than two years. This precaution becomes security against keeping troops when unnecessary.

Do States Ban Armies in Peace?

5 Disappointed by his first assumption, my hypothetical person might pursue his conjectures a little further. Naturally he would think that there must be some colorful pretext for the vehement and pathetic declamations. He might assume Americans are so jealous of their liberties that all preceding established constitutional models contain precise and rigid precautions on this point and that its omission in the new Constitution has given birth to all this apprehension and clamor.

States Allow Peacetime Armies

6 If this assumption leads him to review the State constitutions, he would be disappointed to find that only *two* of them prohibit standing armies in peacetime. The other eleven are either silent on the subject or expressly allow the legislature to authorize their existence.[1]

---

[1] This is taken from the printed collection of State constitutions. Pennsylvania and North Carolina are the two that contain the interdiction in these words: "As standing armies in time of peace are dangerous to liberty, THEY OUGHT NOT to be kept up." This is, in truth, rather a CAUTION than a PROHI-

Do Articles Ban Peacetime Armies?

7　However, he would continue to believe that there must be some plausible foundation for the cry raised on this subject. As long as any source of information remained unexplored, he would never assume that the outcry is only an experiment on the public's credulity, either dictated to deliberately deceive or by an over flowing zeal too excessive to be honest. He would expect to eventually find a solution to the enigma.

Next he would probably assume the precautions he was searching for were in the Articles of Confederation. No doubt, he would say to himself, the existing Confederation must contain explicit provisions against military establishments in peacetime. And that a departure from this model has caused the discontent that is influencing these political champions.

No Prohibition

8　After a careful and critical study of the Articles of Confederation, his astonishment would increase. And he would become indignant that instead of containing the prohibition he expected, the Articles jealously restrict the

---

BITION. New Hampshire, Massachusetts, Delaware, and Maryland have, in each of their bills of rights, a clause to this effect: "Standing armies are dangerous to liberty, and ought not to be raised or kept up WITHOUT THE CONSENT OF THE LEGISLATURE," which is a formal admission of the authority of the LEGISLATURE. New York has no bills of rights, and her constitution says not a word about the matter. No bills of rights appear annexed to the constitutions of the other States, except the foregoing, and their constitutions are equally silent. I am told, however, that one or two States have bills of rights that do not appear in this collection and those also recognize the legislative authority in this respect.

authority of State legislatures on this subject but do not impose a single restraint on the United States.

If he was a sensible, rational man, he would start regarding the clamors as dishonest artifices of a sinister, unprincipled opposition to a plan that should at least receive a fair and candid examination from all sincere lovers of their country! Why else, he would ask, would the authors of the objections so harshly criticize a part of the Constitution that seems to reflect the general feelings of America as seen in its different forms of government? It even has a new, powerful guard not seen in any of the State constitutions.

If he was a calm, dispassionate man, he would sigh at the frailty of human nature and lament that, in a matter so important to the happiness of millions, the true merits of the question is entangled by unfriendly expedients to an impartial and right determination. Even such a man could hardly help but remark that the objections appear intended to mislead the people by alarming their passions rather than convince them with arguments addressed to their reason.

Ban Wouldn't Be Observed

9　But however unacceptable the argument against a standing army may be, even by precedents among ourselves, it could be helpful to study its intrinsic merits. A close examination shows restraining legislative discretion in respect to military establishments in peacetime would be an improper imposition, and if imposed because society demands it, it probably would not be observed.

Dangers: Europe, Indians

10　Although a wide ocean separates the United States from Europe, circumstances warn us against being over-confident of our security. British settlements are growing and stretching to our rear. Spanish settlements are on the other side and extend to meet the British settlements. This situation and the vicinity of the West India Islands, belonging to these two powers, create, in respect to us, a common interest. The savage tribes on our Western frontier should be regarded as our natural enemies and their natural allies because they have the most to fear from us and the most to hope from them.

Improvements in navigation have so facilitated communication that many distant nations seem more like neighbors. Britain and Spain are maritime powers in Europe. A future agreement between them seems probable.

The family compacts between France and Spain are becoming more distant every day. Politicians, with good reason, consider blood ties feeble and precarious links in the political chain.

These combined circumstances warn us not to be over confident, believing we are entirely out of the reach of danger.

Protection Needed on Borders

11 Since before the Revolution, small garrisons on our Western frontier have been necessary. No one doubts that they will continue being indispensable, if only for protection against the ravages and plundering of the Indians. Occasionally, these garrisons must be supplemented by either the militia or by permanent corps in the pay of the government.

Using militia members is impractical. And even if it was practical, it would be dangerous. The militia would not long, if at all, submit to being dragged from their occupations and

families to perform the most disagreeable duty in times of peace. Even if they could be prevailed upon or compelled, the increased expense of frequent service rotation and individuals' loss of labor on industrious pursuits would form conclusive objections to the scheme. It would be as burdensome and injurious to the public as it would be to private citizens.

A permanent corps paid by the government amounts to a standing army in peacetime–a small one, indeed, but no less real for being small.

This simple view of the subject clearly shows the impropriety of a constitutional prohibition of a standing army and the necessity of leaving the matter to the discretion and prudence of the legislature.

Future Border Needs Will Increase

12 As our strength increases, it is probable—no, it may be certain—Britain and Spain will augment their military establishments in our neighborhood. If we are unwilling to be exposed—naked and defenseless—to their encroachments, it will be expedient to increase our frontier garrison as the need to protect our Western settlements increases. Some military posts will service large districts of territory and facilitate future invasions of the remainder. Some posts will also be important to the trade with the Indian nations.

Can any man think it would be wise to leave such posts vulnerable to seizure by one or the other of two neighboring and formidable powers? This would be against all normal maxims of prudence and policy.

Navy Replace Some Garrisons

13 If we expect to be commercial, or even secure on our Atlantic side, as soon as possible we must form a navy. Dockyards and arsenals will need to be defended by fortifications and, probably, garrisons. When a nation becomes powerful enough to protect its dockyards by its sea fleets, garrisons for that purpose are not necessary. But where naval establishments are in their infancy, moderate garrisons will, in all likelihood, be found an indispensable security against destructive attacks on arsenals and dockyards, and sometimes the fleet itself.

PUBLIUS

Constitutional references:
Article 1, Sect 8 207-209 legislature raises, supports armies; 2-year appropriations
Article 1, Sect 8 216-222 provision for militia

Number 25

Defense: Federal, Not State, Responsibility

It may be argued that State governments, under the direction of the Union, should provide the objectives listed in the preceding paper. But this would invert the primary principle of our political association, transferring the responsibility for common defense from the federal government to the States—a situation oppressive to some States, dangerous to all, and harmful to the Confederacy.

Defense Not State Duty

2 The territories of Britain, Spain, and the Indian nations do not border on particular States but encircle the Union from Maine to Georgia. The danger, to differing degrees, is common. In like manner, the means of guarding against it should be the responsibility of common councils and a common treasury.

Some States are more directly exposed. New York is in this group. If the States had to make separate provisions, New York would sustain the whole burden of her immediate safety and, ultimately, the protection of her neighbors. This would be neither equitable for New York nor safe for other States.

Various inconveniences would accompany such a system. The States who need to support military establishments would be neither willing nor able to bear the burden of competent provisions for a long time to come. Therefore, the security of all would be subject to the stinginess, lack of foresight, or inability of one State.

On the other hand, if the resources of such a State became abundant and extensive, its military spending would increase proportionately. Then the other States would be alarmed that the whole military force of the Union would be in the hands of two or three of the most powerful States. They would want to take counter measures, and justifications could easily be contrived.

In this situation, military establishments, nourished by mutual jealousy, would probably swell beyond their natural or proper size. Created and controlled by separate States, they would become the instruments of abridgment or demolition of the national authority.

State Military a Danger to Liberty

3 Reasons have been given as to why State governments are natural rivals with the Union. The foundation is the love of power. And in any dispute between the federal government and one of its States, people will be more apt to unite with their local government. If you add to this advantage State supported military forces, there would be a strong temptation and a great facility to challenge and, finally, subvert the constitutional authority of the Union.

The liberty of the people would be less safe under these circumstances than if national forces are in the hands of the national government. If an army is a dangerous weapon of power, it is better to be controlled by the targets of envy than the least likely targets of jealousy. History proves that people are in the most danger when the capability of injuring their rights is in the possession of those who they least suspect.

State Military Would Be Dangerous

4 The framers of the existing Confederation, fully aware that States with separate military forces are a danger to the Union, expressly prohibited them from having either ships or troops, unless with Congressional consent. The truth is, the existence of both a federal government and State sponsored armies are as incompatible with each other as the debts due to the federal treasury and the system of quotas and requisitions.

Peace Military Ban Unenforceable

5 Improper restraints on the discretion of the national legislature will manifest in additional ways. As mentioned, the objection is to ban standing armies in time of peace. But we have not been informed how far the prohibition should extend. Will it ban raising armies as well as to *keeping them up* in time of tranquility?

If the prohibition is limited to keeping them up, it isn't specific and will not fulfill the purpose intended. Once armies are raised, what does the constitution mean by "keeping them up"? What time frame will constitute a violation? A week, a month, a year?

Or may they continue as long as the danger that occasioned their being raised continues? This would admit that they can be kept up *in time of peace,* against threats or impending danger, a deviation from the literal meaning of the prohibition and introduces an extensive latitude of discretion. Who will judge that the danger continues? This must undoubtedly be decided by the national government. To provide against a possible danger, the national government can first raise troops, then keep them as long as the peace or safety of the community was in any degree of jeopardy. It is easy to see that such a latitude of discretion would give ample room for eluding the force of the provision.

Excuses to Fortify Military

6 The supposed utility of a provision against peacetime armies can only be based on the assumption, or at least the possibility, that the executive and legislative could conspire in a usurpation scheme. However, if they did conspire, it would be easy to fabricate pretenses of approaching danger! Indian hostilities, instigated by Spain or Britain, would always be an available excuse. Or a foreign power could be provoked to produce the desired threatening appearance, then appeased again by timely concessions. If such a conspiracy happened and seemed likely to succeed, the army could be raised—

using any pretext—and applied to the usurpation scheme.

Army Ban, Union Defenseless

7 If, to avoid this consequence, the prohibition is extended to the raising of armies in time of peace, the United States would be in the most extraordinary situation the world has yet seen—a nation incapacitated by its Constitution to prepare for its defense before it was actually invaded.

Since formal declarations of war have fallen into disuse, an enemy would have to be physically within our territories before the government could begin drafting men for the protection of the state. We must receive the blow before we can even prepare to return it. A national policy of anticipating and preparing to meet a danger, could not be done, because it is contrary to the genuine maxims of a free government. Therefore, we would expose our property and liberty to the mercy of foreign invaders, our weakness inviting them to seize the naked and defenseless prey because we were afraid that rulers—elected by us and ruling according to our will—might endanger our liberty by abusing the means necessary for its preservation.

Militia Insufficient National Defense

8 Here, I expect, we'll be told that the country's militia is its natural bulwark and will always be equal to the national defense. The substance of this doctrine nearly lost us our independence. It cost the United States millions that could have been saved.

The facts from our recent experience forbid our being duped into reliance on this suggestion. The steady operations of war against a regular and disciplined army can only be successfully conducted by a force of the same

kind. Economic considerations, no less than considerations of stability and vigor, confirm this.

The American militia's valor on numerous occasions during the recent war erected eternal monuments to their fame, but the bravest of them know that they could not have established the liberty of their country alone, however great and valuable they were. Like most things, war is a science to be acquired and perfected by diligence, perseverance, time, and practice.

Peacetime Military in States

9 Since they are contrary to the natural experience of human affairs, all distorted policies defeat themselves. Pennsylvania affords a current example. Its Bill of Rights declares that standing armies are dangerous to liberty and should not be kept up in peacetime. Nevertheless, during this time of profound peace, Pennsylvania has used disorders in one or two counties as an excuse to raise a body of troops and, in all probability, will keep them up as long as there is any appearance of danger to the public peace.

The conduct of Massachusetts affords a lesson on the same subject, though on different ground. That State (without waiting for Congressional sanction, as the Articles of the Confederation require) raised troops to quell a domestic insurrection and still keeps a corps to prevent a revival of the spirit of revolt. The Massachusetts constitution has no obstacle to this but it still is instructive of cases likely to occur under our government—as well as under those of other nations—which will sometimes make a military force essential to the security of society in peacetime. Therefore, it is improper to control legislative discretion in this respect.

It also teaches us, as applied to the United States, how little the rights of a feeble government are likely to be respected, even by its own constituents. Additionally, it teaches us that the struggle between written provisions and public necessity is very unequal.

Ignoring Laws Weakens Government

10 It was a fundamental maxim of the ancient Lacedaemonian commonwealth that the post of admiral should not be conferred twice on the same person. After the Peloponnesian confederates suffered a severe defeat at sea from the Athenians, they demanded that Lysander, previously a successful admiral, command the combined fleets. The Lacedaemonians, to gratify their allies and yet preserve the semblance of an adherence to their ancient institutions, resorted to the flimsy subterfuge of giving Lysander the power of an admiral under the nominal title of vice-admirals.

This example is selected from a multitude that could be cited to confirm the truth already illustrated by domestic examples, the truth that nations basically ignore rules and maxims that, in their very nature, run counter to the necessities of society.

Wise politicians will be cautious about fettering the government with restrictions that cannot be observed. They know that every breach of the fundamental laws, though dictated by necessity, impairs that sacred reverence that rulers ought to maintain towards the constitution of their country. And it forms a precedent for other breaches where the same plea of necessity does not exist at all or is less urgent and palpable.

PUBLIUS

Articles of Confederation:
Article 8   State supported military
Article 6   military

Constitutional reference:
Article 1, section 8   207-222   army, navy, militia

Number 26

Legislative Military Authority

One can hardly expect that during a popular revolution men would stop at the proper boundary between POWER and PRIVILEGE. That is, the balance between a strong government and secure private rights.

Our present inconveniences result from a failure on this delicate and important point. In our future attempts to correct and improve our system, we must be careful and not repeat this error. Otherwise, we may go from one unrealistically utopian plan to another. We may try change after change. But will probably never make any material change for the better.

Balancing Liberty, Public Safety

2 Limiting legislative authority to provide for the national defense is one of those refinements that originate from a zeal for liberty and is more ardent than enlightened.

So far, there hasn't been widespread support for limiting the legislature's power to authorize armed forces. Since the concept first appeared, only Pennsylvania and North Carolina have implemented it to any degree. The other States refuse to even consider it, wisely judging that confidence must be placed somewhere. The very act of delegating power implies this necessity. It is better to hazard the abuse of that confidence than embarrass the government and endanger the public safety with impractical restrictions on the legislative authority. In this respect, the opponents of the proposed Constitution oppose the view held by a majority of Americans.

Instead of learning from experience how to safely correct extreme imbalances in our system, the opponents seem determined to lead us into others still more dangerous and extravagant. As if the government's structure was too powerful or rigid, they promote doctrines designed to depress or relax it, using methods already rejected or condemned. We may safely say without fear of denunciation that, if the principles they repeatedly support became popular creed, they would make the people of this country utterly unfit for any type of government whatever.

But there is no need to fear that danger. The citizens of America are too intelligent to be persuaded into anarchy. Unless I'm really out of touch, experience has produced in the public mind a deep and solemn conviction that greater government energy is essential to the welfare and prosperity of the community.

Origin of No Military During Peace

3 This might be the place to discuss the origin and progress of the idea of excluding military establishments during peacetime. Some may speculate that it arises from the historical nature and tendencies of such institutions. But as an American sentiment, it can be directly traced back to England, the country of origin of most Americans.

England Decreased Military

4 For a long time after the Norman Conquest [1066], the English monarch's authority was almost unlimited. Gradually, liberty made inroads into the monarch's power, first by barons and later by the people, until the majority of the monarch's formidable pretensions became extinct. Finally, after the revolution in 1688, which elevated Prince William of Orange to the throne of Great Britain, English liberty was completely triumphant.

As an extension of the crown's power to make war, Charles II [1661-1685] kept a body of 5,000 troops during peacetime. James II [1685-1688] increased the number to 30,000, paid out of his civil list. To abolish so dangerous an authority, after the revolution it became an article of the Bill of Rights that "the raising or keeping a standing army within the Kingdom in time of peace, *unless with the consent of Parliament,* was against the law."

Powers = Possible Emergencies

5 Although the pulse of liberty was at its highest peak in that kingdom, the only security against the danger of standing armies thought required was the prohibition against the executive magistrate to raise and keep them.

The revolutionary patriots were too temperate, too well informed to restrain legislative discretion. They were aware that a certain number of troops were indispensable. No precise limits could be set to national emergencies. A power equal to every possible scenario must exist somewhere in the government. They gave the discretion to use that power to the judgment of the legislature. By giving the legislature this power, they had arrived at the ultimate point of precaution reconcilable with the safety of the community.

States: Legislatures Raise Military

6 The people of America derived from the same source an hereditary impression of the danger to liberty from standing armies in peacetime. The revolution heightened the public sensibility to the security of popular rights. In some instances, our zeal went further than is practical. The attempt of two States to restrict legislative authority over military establishments are examples.

The principles that taught us to be jealous of an hereditary monarch's power were, by an injudicious overreaction, extended to the people's representatives in their popular assemblies. Even some States that didn't adopt this error have unnecessary declarations that standing armies are not to be kept up in peacetime WITHOUT THE CONSENT OF THE LEGISLATURE.

I call them unnecessary because the reason for a similar provision in the English Bill of Rights is not applicable to any of the State constitutions. Under those constitutions, the power of raising armies only resides in the legislatures. So, it was superfluous, if not absurd, to declare that the matter should not be done without the consent of a body, which alone had the power of doing it. Accord-

ingly, other constitutions, including New York's, have been justly celebrated both in Europe and America as the best forms of government established in this country and have total silence on the subject.

No State Prohibits Peace Military

7 Remarkably, even in the constitution of the two States that seem to have intended to prohibit military establishments in time of peace, the mode of expression is more cautionary than prohibitory. It says they *ought not* be kept up, not that armies *shall not be* kept up in time of peace. This ambiguity seems to be the result of a conflict between jealousy and conviction, between totally excluding them and the belief that an absolute exclusion would be unwise and unsafe.

Precaution Ignored If Need Arises

8 Can it be doubted that when a situation arises requiring a departure, the legislature will interpret the clause as a mere admonition and yield to the necessities, or supposed necessities, of the State? Let the Pennsylvania example, already mentioned, decide. What then (it may be asked) is the use of such a provision if it ceases to operate the moment there is an inclination to disregard it?

State Restrictions vs. Constitution

9 Let us compare the efficacy between the provision alluded to [i.e., ban on all peacetime federal military] and that contained in the new Constitution, restraining military appropriations to a two-year period. The former, by aiming at too much, is calculated to effect nothing; the latter, by steering clear of an imprudent extreme and being perfectly compatible with a proper provision for emergencies, will provide a powerful remedy.

Politicians, States
Guard Against Abuse

10 With this provision, at least once in every two years the legislature of the United States will be *obliged* to deliberate on the propriety of keeping a military force, come to a new decision, and declare their position by a formal, public vote. Even if they were incautious enough to want to give the executive branch permanent funds for the support of an army, they are not *at liberty* to do so.

A partisan spirit, in different degrees, must be expected to infect all political bodies. Some people in the national legislature will find fault with the measures and incriminate the views of the majority. The provision for support of a military force will always be a favorite topic to denounce. As often as the question arises, public attention will be roused and attracted to the subject by the opposition party. If the majority party really wants to exceed the proper limits, the community will be warned of the danger and have an opportunity to take measures to guard against it.

People other than representatives in the national legislature will also join the debate. State legislatures will always be not only vigilant but suspicious and jealous guardians of citizens' rights against encroachments from the federal government. They will constantly be attuned to the conduct of the national rulers and ready, if anything improper appears, to sound the alarm to the people. State legislatures will not only be the VOICE but, if necessary, the ARM of the people's discontent.

Subversion Requires Collusion

11 Schemes to subvert the liberties of a great community require time to mature before execution. An army large enough to seriously menace those liberties could only be formed by progressive augmentations. This suggests not merely a temporary collusion between the legislature and executive but a continued conspiracy over a period of time.

Is such a combination probable at all? Would its perseverance through a succession of new representatives, produced by biennial elections to the national legislature, be probable? Can we presume that every man seated in the national Senate or House of Representatives would instantly become a traitor to his constituents and his country? Would not one man be discerning enough to detect so atrocious a conspiracy, or bold, or honest enough to tell his constituents of their danger?

If such presumptions are possible, there should be an immediate end to all delegated authority. The people should resolve to take back the powers already given the government and divide themselves into as many States as there are counties so they can manage their own concerns in person.

Military Expansion Noticed

12 Even if such suppositions could be reasonably made, concealing the design for any duration would be impractical. The intentions would be telegraphed by the reality of a fast growing army during peacetime. What excuse could be given for such vast augmentation of the military force? People could not be deceived for long; destruction of the project and its sponsors would quickly follow the discovery.

Need Reasons to Build Military

13 Some say the provision limiting military appropriations to the period of two years would be ineffectual because once the Executive possessed a large enough force to awe the people into submission, the force would also be large enough to no longer need to depend on legislative acts for supplies.

But the question recurs, what pretense could the President use to build a force of that magnitude in peacetime? If it was created in response to some domestic insurrection or foreign war, then it is not a situation within the principles of the objection because the objection is against the power of keeping up troops in peacetime. Few people will be so visionary as to seriously contend that military forces should not be raised to quell a rebellion or resist an invasion. If defense of the community makes it necessary to have an army large enough to threaten its liberty, this is one of those calamities that can't be prevented or cured. No form of government can provide against this. It might even result from a simple league offensive or defensive, if it's ever necessary for the confederates or allies to form an army for common defense.

Military Expansion
If States Disunite

14 But it is an evil infinitely less likely to happen to us if united than disunited. It isn't easy to imagine dangers formidable enough to attack the whole nation, demanding a force large enough to place our liberties in the least jeopardy, especially when we remember that the militia should always be counted on as a valuable and powerful auxiliary. But in a state of disunion (as has been fully shown in another place)[see disunited States], the contrary of this supposition would become not only probable, but almost unavoidable.

PUBLIUS

Constitutional references:
Article 1, Section 8   174   Congress provides for common defense
Article 1, Section 8   207-222   military authority, militia
Article 1, Section 10   289-295   no State troops, ships

Articles of Confederation:
Article 6   peacetime army
Article 6   militia

Number 27

Federal Constitutional Authority Over Individual Citizens
Military Not Needed to Enforce Federal Laws

The argument, in various forms, has been made that the proposed Constitution cannot operate without the aid of a military force to execute its laws. However, like most things alleged by the opposition, it rests on a general assertion, unsupported by any foundation of precise, intelligible reasons.

As I understand the opposition's reasoning, it is based on the assumption that people dislike the use of federal authority in any internal matter. Putting aside exceptions caused by inaccuracy or inexplicitness of the distinction between internal and external, let us look into the grounds for this assumption.

Unless we presume that the federal government will be administered worse than State governments, there's no reason to presume ill-will, disaffection, or opposition by the people. I believe that, as a general rule, their confidence in and obedience to a government will be proportionate to the goodness or badness of its administration.

Admittedly, there are exceptions to this rule. But the exceptions depend so entirely on accidental causes, they cannot be considered to have any relation to the intrinsic merits or demerits of a constitution. Constitutions can only be judged by general principles and maxims.

Quality of Federal Administration

2 These papers suggest reasons why the national government under the proposed Constitution will probably be better administered than the State governments. The principal reason is that the larger area will give voters greater options and choices.

The elected State legislators will appoint the members of the national Senate Senators will generally be selected with care and judgment. This method promises great knowledge and information in the national Senate. Members will be less apt to be tainted by faction. And they will be further from the reach of those occasional ill-humors, temporary prejudices and propensities that, in smaller societies, frequently contaminate the public councils, produce injustice and oppression, and engender schemes that gratify a momentary inclination or desire, but end in general distress, dissatisfaction, and disgust.

When we direct a critical eye on the interior structure of the edifice we are invited to erect, several additional and important reasons will strengthen this position. For now, it is sufficient to say that until satisfactory reasons are given to justify the opinion that the federal government administration will be odious or contemptible to the people, there is no reason to suppose that federal laws will meet with any greater obstruction from the people or will need any additional method of enforcement than State laws.

State Factions More Successful Than Federal

3 The hope of immunity is a strong incitement to sedition. The dread of punishment provides a proportionately strong discouragement. If it has adequate power, will not the national government, using the collective resources of the whole Confederacy, be more likely repress *tendencies toward sedition* and inspire the *dread of punishment*, than a single State with only the resources within itself?

A turbulent faction in a State may think it can make deals with friends in the State government. But it won't be so foolish as to imagine itself a match for the combined efforts of the Union. If this conclusion is reasonable, there is less possibility of opposition to federal authority from dangerous coalitions of individuals that to the authority of a single State.

Federal Government Will Seem Normal

4 I will hazard an observation that is no less true because to some people it may appear new. The attachment and respect of the community towards the national authority will increase as the federal government becomes more involved in ordinary governmental operations. Citizens will grow accustomed to the common occurrences of political life as it becomes a familiar part of their daily lives and touches the most sensible chords of the human heart.

Man is a creature of habit. A thing that rarely strikes his senses will usually have only a little influence on his mind. A remote government can hardly be expected to be of large interest to the people. By inference, the authority of the Union and the affections of the citizens towards it will be strengthened, not weakened, as it effects matters of internal concern.

At the same time, the union will have proportionately fewer reasons to use force as citizens become more familiar with its functions. The more it circulates through those channels and currents of mankind's natural passions, the less it will need the aid of violent and perilous expedients.

Legislation for States Dangerous

5 In any event, one thing must be evident. The proposed governmental structure would be less likely to need to use force than the type of government promoted by its opponents. Its authority would only operate on the States in their political or collective capacities. It has been shown that such a confederacy has no sanction for its laws but force. Frequent delinquencies by members naturally result from the very structure of the government. And as often as they happen, they can only be redressed, if at all, by war and violence.

Constitution: Courts Enforce Laws

6 The new Constitution, by extending the federal government's authority to the individual citizens of the States, allows the government to use State courts to execute its laws. This will give the federal government the same advantage for securing obedience to its authority that is now enjoyed by the government of each State. In addition, public opinion will be influenced by the important fact that the State has the power to call on the resources of the whole Union for assistance and support.

It merits particular attention, at this time, to note that the laws of the Union, as to the *enumerated* and *legitimate* objects of its jurisdiction, will will become the SUPREME LAW of the land. All officers—legislative, executive, and judicial—in each State, will be bound by the sanctity of an oath. Thus the legislatures, courts, and executives of the States will be incorporated into the operations of the national government *as far as its just and constitutional authority ex-*

tends and will be rendered auxiliary to the enforcement of its laws.*

Any man who reflects on the consequences of this situation, will understand that there is good reason to expect regular and peaceable executions of the laws of the Union, if its powers are administered with a common share of prudence.

If we arbitrarily suppose the contrary, we may deduce any inferences

* The sophistry employed to show this will tend to destruct State governments will, in its proper place, be fully detected.

we please from the supposition. An injudicious exercise of the authority of even the very best government can provoke and precipitate the people into the wildest excesses. But even if the adversaries of the proposed Constitution presume that the national rulers would be indifferent to the motives of public good or the obligations of duty, I would still ask: How could the interests of ambition or the views of encroachment be promoted by such conduct?

PUBLIUS

Constitutional references:

Article 6 548-555   Constitution supreme law of the land
Article 6 556-561   governmental officers bound by oath

Number 28

National Force Will Sometimes Be Used Against Citizens

It cannot be denied that sometimes the national government may need to use force. Our own experience corroborates the lessons taught by the examples of other nations.

Emergencies sometimes arise in all societies, however constituted. Revolts and rebellions are, unhappily, diseases as inseparable from the political body as tumors and rashes from the natural body.

The idea of governing at all times solely by the force of law (which, we have been told, is the only admissible principle of republican government) has no place but in the daydreams of those political pundits who intellectually disdain the warnings of experience.

Local Force for Local Danger

2   Should such emergencies happen under the national government, there could be no remedy but force. The type

of force used must be proportionate to the extent of the mischief.

If it is a slight commotion in a small part of a State, the militia from other parts of the State would adequately suppress it. And the natural presumption is that they would be ready to do their duty. An insurrection, whatever its immediate cause, eventually endangers all government. Respect for public peace, if not the rights of the Union, would engage citizens who are not involved to oppose the insurgents. And if the national government is found conducive to the prosperity and happiness of the people, it would be irrational to believe that the people would not support it.

More than Militia Might Be Needed

3   If, on the contrary, the insurrection spread throughout a whole State or a majority of it, employing a differ-

ent kind of force might become unavoidable. It appears that Massachusetts found it necessary to raise troops for repressing the disorders within the State. Pennsylvania, fearing commotions from some of her citizens, thought it proper to do the same thing.

Suppose the State of New York decided to reestablish lost jurisdiction over the inhabitants of Vermont, could she have hoped for success from the efforts of the militia alone? Would she not have been compelled to raise and maintain a more regular force for the execution of her design?

If State governments need a force other than the militia in cases of this extraordinary nature, why should the possibility that the national government might need one during similar emergencies be an objection to the national government's existence? Isn't it surprising that men who declare an attachment to the Union in the abstract should urge, as an objection to the proposed Constitution, what applies tenfold to the plan they support? And what, in truth, is an inevitable consequence of a large civil society? Who would not prefer the use of force to the unceasing agitation and frequent revolutions that are the continual scourges of petty republics?

Confederacies Sometimes Need Force

4   Let's look at this in a different way. Suppose that instead of one general system, two, three, or even four American confederacies were formed. Wouldn't the operations of these confederacies be exposed to the same casualties? When these happened, wouldn't the confederacies use the same methods for upholding their authority that are objected to in a government for all the States?

Continuing this supposition, would the militia be more ready or able to support the confederate authority than in the case of one general union? After consideration, all candid, intelligent men must acknowledge that the objection is equally applicable to either case. Whether we have one government for all the States, or different governments for different parcels of them, or if there should be as many unconnected governments as there are States, sometimes a force other than the militia may be necessary to preserve the peace of the community and maintain the lawful authority against violent invasions of them that amount to insurrections and rebellions.

People Control Government/Military

5   People who require a more decisive provision against military establishments in peacetime need to be reminded that the whole power of the proposed government will be in the hands of the representatives of the people. In civil society, this is the essential, and only effective, security for the rights and privileges of the people.*

Blocking Usurpation in 1 State Hard

6   If the elected representatives of the people betray their constituents, the only resource left is self-defense, the most important right in every positive form of government. It may be used against the usurpations of national rulers with infinitely better expectation of success than against rulers of an individual State.

If the rulers of a single State become usurpers, the different subdivisions of districts don't have distinct governments able to defend the people. The citizens must rush tumultuously without plan, without system, without resource except in their courage and

---

* Its full efficacy will be examined later.

despair. Because they are cloaked in legal authority, the usurpers can too often crush the opposition in embryo. The smaller the territory, the more difficult it will be for the people to organize a systematic plan of opposition and the easier it will be to defeat their efforts. Intelligence of their preparation and movements would be speedily obtained. The military force, under the command of the usurpers, can rapidly deploy against the district where the opposition has begun. In this situation, only lucky coincidences will insure the success of the popular resistance.

Obstacles to Usurpation, Tyranny

7 The obstacles to usurpation and the ability to resist increase with the increased size of the state, provided the citizens understand their rights and want to defend them. The natural strength of the people in a large community, in proportion to the artificial strength of the government, is greater than in a small and, of course, more competent to struggle with the attempts of the government to establish a tyranny.

In a confederacy the people are, without exaggerating, entirely the masters of their own fate. Since power is almost always the rival of power, the national government will always stand ready to check the usurpations of the State governments. And the States will be in the same position towards the national government.

Whichever side [State or national government] the people support will infallibly be the stronger. If their rights are invaded by either, they can use the other as the instrument of redress. How wise the people will be to cherish the Union, preserving to themselves an advantage that can never be too highly prized!

States Protect Citizen's Liberty

8 It may be safely said as an axiom in our political system that the State governments will, in all situations, provide complete security against invasions of liberty by the national authority.

Usurpation projects cannot be masked under pretenses likely to escape the notice of the people's representatives, as of the people at large. The legislatures will have better sources of information. They can discover the danger in its infancy. Since they possess the structure of civil power and the confidence of the people, they can immediately adopt a plan of opposition using the combined resources of the community. They can easily communicate with each other in the different States and unite their common forces for the protection of their common liberty.

Armed Force against Government

9 The large size of the country is further security. We have already experienced its benefits in protecting against the attacks of a foreign power. It would have precisely the same effect against the enterprises of ambitious rulers in the national councils.

If the federal army quelled the resistance of one State, distant States would raise fresh forces. The advantages obtained by the usurpers in one place would be abandoned to subdue the opposition in others. The moment the area reduced to submission was left to itself, it would renew its efforts, reviving its resistance.

State Forces Better Than National

10 We must remember that the military force is regulated by the resources of the country. For a long time to come, maintaining a large army will be impossible. As our ability to enlarge the military increases, so will the proportionate population and strength of the community. Therefore, when will the federal government be able to raise and maintain an army capable of erecting a despotism over the great body of the people of an immense empire, who are, through the medium of their State governments, able to defend themselves, with the swiftness, regularity, and organization of independent nations?

The apprehension may be considered as a disease, for which there can be found no cure in the resources of argument and reasoning.

PUBLIUS

Number 29

Militia Not Threat to Liberty

The power of regulating the militia and commanding it in times of insurrection and invasion is a natural part of superintending the common defense and watching over the internal peace of the Confederacy.

National Control: Uniformity

2   It requires no skill in the science of war to know that when called into service for the public defense, uniformity in the organization and discipline of the militia creates the most beneficial effects. It could discharge its duties with mutual intelligence and concert—always an advantage in an army. It would quickly acquire military proficiency.

This uniformity can only be accomplished by national regulation of the militia. Therefore, the Constitution properly proposes to empower the Union "to provide for organizing, arming, and disciplining the militia, and for governing such part of them as may be employed in the service of the United States, *reserving to the States respectively the appointment of the officers, and the authority of training the militia according to the discipline prescribed by Congress.*"

Less Need for Standing Army

3   Of the reasons for opposing the Constitution, none have been less expected or more untenable than the attack of this provision.

If a well-regulated militia is the most natural defense of a free country, it certainly should be regulated and at the disposal of the authority that the Constitution makes the guardian of national security.

If the standing armies endanger liberty, then when the non-military body committed to protect the country, the national government, has authority over the militia, it takes away the inducements and pretexts, as far as possible, for the unfriendly institutions of standing armies. If the federal government can command the militia in emergencies when civil authorities need military support, it won't use the army. If it can't use the militia, it will be obliged to resort to the army. Making an army unnecessary is a more certain method of preventing its existence than a thousand prohibitions on paper.

No Ban of Posse Comitatus

4   To discredit the power to use the militia to execute the laws of the Union,

114

opponents say the Constitution has no provision for calling out the POSSE COMITATUS to assist the chief executive in his duty. From this, it has been inferred that military force is the only alternative.

Objections have been strikingly incoherent, sometimes even from the same people. They don't inspire a very favorable opinion of the sincerity or fairness of their authors. The same people tell us with one breath that the federal government's power will be despotic and unlimited, then next say it doesn't even have the authority to call out the POSSE COMITATUS. Fortunately, the latter is as much short of the truth as the former exceeds it.

Since the government has the right to pass all laws *necessary and proper* to execute its declared powers, it is absurd to doubt that it has the authority to require citizens to assist officers entrusted with the execution of those laws. This is just as absurd as believing that a right to enact laws necessary and proper for the imposition and collection of taxes would include changing the rules of descent and alienating landed property. Or as absurd as abolishing trial by jury in cases relating to it.

Clearly, supposing there is no power to require the aid of the POSSE COMITATUS is implausible. Therefore, the conclusion drawn from it, its application to the authority of the federal government over the militia, is as uncandid as it is illogical. Why infer that force is intended to be the sole instrument of authority, merely because there is a power to use it when necessary? What motives could induce sensible men to reason in this manner? How can we prevent a conflict between charity and judgement?

Illogical Fear of Militia

5 In a curious twist of republican jealousy, we are even taught to fear the militia itself, if it is in the hands of the federal government. It is said that select corps of the young and ardent may be formed, then become subservient to the views of arbitrary power.

How the national government will regulate the militia is impossible to be foreseen. But I wouldn't view the subject in the same way as people who object to a select corps as dangerous. If the Constitution was ratified and I delivered my sentiments on the subject of a militia establishment to a member of the federal legislature from my State, I would essentially say:

Lost Productivity

6 "Trying to discipline all the militia of the United States is as impossible as it would be injurious. Being an expert in military movements requires time and practice. A day, or even a week, isn't sufficient to attain it. To oblige all the farmers, and every class of citizen, to go through military exercises as often as necessary to acquire the degree of perfection that would give them the character of a well regulated militia, would be a real grievance to the people and a serious public inconvenience and loss. It would annually deduct from the productive labor of the country an amount that, calculating from the present number of people, would not be much less than the whole expense of the civil governments of all the States.

"To attempt something so injurious to labor and industry would be unwise. And if it was tried, it couldn't succeed, because it wouldn't be endured long. With respect to the people at large, little more can be attempted than to have them properly armed and equipped. And in order that this is not neglected, it will be necessary to assemble them once or twice every year.

Militia Security against Standing Army

7 "Although the idea of disciplining the whole nation must be abandoned as mischievous or impractical, yet it is very important that as soon as possible a well-formed plan to establish a militia should be adopted. The government should form a moderate number of select corps, using principles that will fit them for service in case of need. With a well-defined plan, it will be possible to have an excellent body of trained militia ready whenever the defense of the States requires it. This will not only lessen the call for military establishments, but if circumstances should ever force the government to form an army of any size, that army can never be a formidable threat to the liberties of the people while there is a large body of citizens who are little, if at all, inferior to them in discipline and the use of arms, who stand ready to defend their own rights and those of their fellow citizens. This appears to me the only substitute that can be devised for a standing army, and the best security against, if it should exist."

I See Safety; Critics See Danger

8 Thus I reason differently on the same subject than the adversaries of the proposed Constitution. I deduce arguments of safety from the very sources that they represent as fraught with danger and perdition. But how the national legislature may reason on the point is something that neither they nor I can foresee.

How Can Militia Endanger Liberty?

9 There is something so far-fetched and extravagant in the idea that the militia will endanger liberty, one is at a loss whether to treat it with gravity or ridicule. Should it be considered cleverly constructed paradoxes of rhetoricians, as a disingenuous artifice to instill prejudices at any price, or as the serious offsprings of political fanaticism?

Where, in the name of common sense, are our fears to end if we can't trust our sons, our brothers, our neighbors, our fellow citizens? What shadow of danger can there be from men who are daily mingling with the rest of their countrymen, and who join with them in the same feelings, sentiments, habits, and interests?

What can reasonably cause apprehension from the Union having the power to prescribe militia regulations and command its services when necessary, when the States have the *sole and exclusive appointment of the officers*? If it was possible to seriously worry about a militia under the federal government, having the officers appointed by the States should extinguish it as once. This circumstance will guarantee that the States have the greatest influence over the militia.

Constitution Distorted into Monster

10 In reading many of the publications against the Constitution, a man might imagine he is perusing some ill-written tale or romance that, instead of having natural and agreeable images, exhibits nothing but frightful and distorted shapes—

Gorgons, hydras, and chimeras dire;

discoloring and disfiguring whatever it represents, transforming everything it touches into a monster.

Outrageous Uses of Militia Imagined

11 A sample of this is the exaggerated and improbable suggestions in respect to the power of calling for the services of the militia. That the New Hampshire militia is to be marched to Georgia, Georgia to New Hampshire, New York to Kentucky, and Kentucky to Lake Champlain. The debts due to the French and Dutch are to be paid in militiamen instead of louis d'ors and ducats.

At one moment, there will be a large army to lay prostrate the liberties of the people. At another moment, the militia of Virginia are to be dragged from their homes 500 or 600 miles to tame the republican rebels of Massachusetts, and that of Massachusetts is to be transported an equal distance to subdue the refractory haughtiness of the aristocratic Virginians.

Do the people who rave to this extent imagine that their eloquence can convince the people of America that any conceits or absurdities are infallible truths?

Tyrannical Use of Militia Illogical

12 If an army is going to be used as the engine of despotism, why is a militia needed? If there was no army, where would the militia, irritated by being called upon to undertake a distant and hopeless expedition to rivet chains of slavery on some of their countrymen, direct their course but to the seat of the tyrants who had so foolishly and wickedly begun the project, to crush them in their imagined entrenchment? Do rulers begin by exciting the detestation of the very instruments of their intended usurpations? Do they usually start their career by wanton, disgusting acts of power, calculated to answer no end, but will draw upon themselves universal hatred?

Is this sort of supposition the sober admonition of discerning patriots to a discerning people? Or is it the inflammatory ravings of incendiaries or distempered enthusiasts?

Even if we suppose that the national rulers were actuated by the most ungovernable ambition, it is impossible to believe they would employ such preposterous means to accomplish their designs.

Militia Used for Insurrections, Invasions

13 In times of insurrection or invasion, it would be natural and proper that the militia of a neighboring State should be marched into another to resist a common enemy or to guard the republic against the violence of faction or sedition. The first frequently happened during the course of the recent war and this mutual security is, indeed, a principal goal of our political association. If the power to do this is under the direction of the Union, there will be no danger of a supine, listless inattention to the dangers of a neighbor until its near approach had added the incitements of self-preservation to the too feeble impulse of duty and sympathy.

PUBLIUS

Published in newspapers as Number 35, then changed to Number 29 in the first edition of 1788.

Constitution reference:

Article 1, section 8	213-222	militia
Article 1, section 8	233-237	make necessary and proper laws

Number 30

Taxation: Revenue Source to Support National Government

It has been said that the federal government should have the power to support the national army. This includes the expenses of recruiting troops, building and equipping fleets, and all expenses connected with military operations.

However, the Union must be empowered to raise revenue for other reasons as well. It must support national civil employees, pay current and future national debts, and make appropriate disbursements from the national treasury. Therefore, the government must have some sort of power of taxation.

Need for Adequate Revenue

2   Money, properly, is vital to the government. It sustains its life and enables it to perform its most essential functions. Therefore, the complete power to procure a regular and adequate supply of revenue, as far as community resources will permit, is an indispensable ingredient in every constitution.

One of two evils will ensue from a deficiency of money—either the people will be continually plundered, as a substitute for a legitimate method of supplying the public wants, or the government will sink into a fatal atrophy and, in a short time, perish.

Inability to Tax => Pillaging or Decay

3   Although the sovereign of the Ottoman [Turkish] empire is absolute master of the lives and fortunes of his subjects, he has no right to impose a new tax. As a consequence, the bashaws [province governors] pillage the people without mercy, squeezing from them the money the emperor needs to satisfy his own needs and those of the state.

From a similar cause, the American Union has gradually dwindled into a state of decay, approaching annihilation. The people's happiness in both countries would be promoted by the proper authority to provide the revenue for pubic necessities.

State Requisitions => Bad Situation

4   The present Confederation, feeble as it is, intended to give the United States unlimited power to provide for the financial needs of the Union. But operating under an erroneous principle, it has been done in such a way as to entirely frustrate the intention.

As has been stated, the Articles of Confederation authorize Congress to determine and call for any sums of money necessary, in their judgment, to the service of the United States. If their requisitions conform to the rule of apportionment, they are constitutional obligations of the States. The States have no right to question the propriety of the demand. The States' only discretion is in devising the ways and means of furnishing the sums demanded.

Though this is strictly the case, though the assumption of such a right would be an infringement of the Articles of the Union, and though it may have seldom or never been avowedly claimed, it has been constantly exercised in practice and will continue to be so long as the revenues of the Confederacy remain dependent on the intermediate agency of its members. Every man knowledgeable about our public affairs knows the consequences of this system, which have been amply detailed in different parts of these papers. This is the chief reason we have been reduced to a situation that supplies mortification to ourselves and triumph to our enemies.

Remedy: Directly Raise Revenues

5 The remedy for this situation is to change the system that has produced it, change the fallacious and delusive system of quotas and requisitions. What substitute can be imagined for this *ignis fatuus* in finance but to permit the national government to raise its own revenues by the ordinary methods of taxation, as authorized in every well-ordered constitution of civil government? Clever men can plausibly declaim on any subject, but no human ingenuity can point out any other way to rescue us from the inconveniences and embarrassments resulting from limited supplies in the public treasury.

Opponents: Tax Only Imports

6 The more intelligent adversaries of the new Constitution admit the force of this reasoning. But they qualify their admission by distinguishing between what they call *internal* and *external* taxation. They reserve the former to State governments, the latter, which are duties on imported articles, they declare themselves willing to concede to the federal government.

Power Proportionate to Objective

This distinction, however, violates the maxim of good sense and sound policy. Every POWER ought to be in proportion to its OBJECT. The limitation would still leave the federal government in a kind of tutelage to the State governments, inconsistent with every idea of strength or efficiency.

Who can pretend that commercial imports are, or would be, by themselves, equal to the present and future revenue requirements of the Union? Considering what must be included in any plan to extinguish the existing foreign and domestic debt for it to be approved by any man who believes in the importance of public justice and public credit, in addition to the federal agencies that everyone acknowledge as necessary, we could not reasonably flatter ourselves that import duties alone, even the most optimistic estimate, would even suffice for present necessities.

Government's future necessities cannot be calculated or limited. And under the principle, mentioned several times, it must have the equally unconfined power to make provision for them.

I believe history proves that *in the usual progress of things, the necessities of a nation, in every stage of its existence, will be found at least equal to its resources.*

Banning Internal Tax => Union Weak

7 Saying that deficiencies will be made up by State requisitions exposes an inherent flaw in the system of using import taxes, alone, for federal revenue. This argument acknowledges that deficiencies will occur so it cannot be depended upon, yet it depends on it for all revenue needed beyond a certain limit. Those aware of the vices and deformities of using State requisitions, either from experience or reading these papers, must feel invincible repugnancy towards the idea of trusting the national interests, in any way, to its operation. Whenever used, it will inevitably enfeeble the Union, sowing seeds of discord and conflict between the federal government and the States, and between the States themselves.

Can we expect that deficiencies will be covered any better than the wants of the Union have been up until now? It should be remembered that if less is required from the States, they will have proportionately less means to answer the demand. If it was true the deficiencies could be provided for by requisition on the States, one must conclude that at some known point in the economy of national affairs it would be safe to stop and say: this is the limit of where public happiness will be promoted by supplying the wants of government and everything beyond this point is unworthy of our care or anxiety.

How can a government, half supplied and always in need, provide for the security, advance the prosperity, or support the reputation of the commonwealth? How can it ever possess either energy or stability, dignity or credit, confidence at home or respectability abroad? How can its administration be anything else than a succession of expedients temporizing, impotent, disgraceful? How will it avoid frequent sacrifices of commitments to immediate necessity? How can it undertake or execute any liberal or enlarged plans for pubic good?

War Funding Nearly Impossible

8   Let's examine the effects of this situation during our very first war. We will presume, for argument's sake, that import duties cover the cost of both debt payments and the peacetime federal government. Then, under this circumstance, a war breaks out. How would the government probably act in such an emergency?

Taught by experience that State requisitions can't be depended on, without the authority to get fresh resources and motivated by national danger, would not the federal government be driven to the expedient of diverting funds already appropriated from their proper objects to the defense of the States?

During a modern war, even the wealthiest nations need large loans. For a country as poor as ours, loans are absolute necessities. But who would lend to a government that has demonstrated it has no reliable method of raising repayment funds. The loans it could get would be the same that loan sharks commonly lend to bankrupt and fraudulent debtors—with a sparing hand and at enormous premiums.

Internal Taxes: Emergencies Met

9   Because the country has few resources, some people might fear that allocated funds will be diverted during such a crisis, even if the national government has the unrestrained power of taxation. But two considerations will quiet these apprehensions: (1) during a crisis we are sure the full resources of the community will be brought into activity for the benefit of the Union and (2) any deficiencies, without difficulty, can be supplied by loans.

Internal Taxes Protect Union's Credit

10   If the national government had the authority to raise money through new taxes, it would be able to borrow as much as its necessities might require. Both Americans and foreigners could confidently lend to it. But to depend on a government that must, itself, depend on thirteen other governments for the means to fulfill its contracts—once this situation is clearly understood— would require a degree of credulity rarely seen in the pecuniary transactions of mankind and unreconcilable with the usual sharp-sightedness of avarice.

Taxation Issue Needs Attention

11 This discussion may seem unimportant to men who envision a poetic, utopian America. But to those who believe we are likely to experience our share of the vicissitudes and calamities that have fallen to other nations, they appear entitled to serious attention. Such men must see the actual situation of their country with painful solicitude and deprecate the evils that ambition or revenge, too easily, inflict upon it.

PUBLIUS

Articles of Confederation

Article 8   assessment, payment of taxes to confederate government

Constitutional references:

Article 1, Section 2   16-27   apportionment for direct taxes
Article 1, Section 2   171-179   taxes, duties, imposts

Number 31

Federal Taxation Authority Won't Usurp State Powers

In a serious discussion on any subject, there are certain basic truths, or first principles, on which all subsequent reasonings must depend. These basic truths contain obvious internal evidence that verifies their truth. People to whom the truth is not obvious must have defective perception or be influenced by some strong interest, passions, or prejudice.

Geometry maxims are of this nature: "the whole is greater than any of its parts; things equal to the same are equal to one another; two straight lines cannot enclose a space; all right angles are equal to each other."

Ethics and politics also have basic maxims: Every effect has a cause. The means ought to be proportional to the end. Every power ought to be commensurate with its objective. There should be no limitation of a power meant to fulfill a purpose that can't be limited.

Other truths in ethics and politics are, if not axioms, such direct inferences and so obvious—such common sense—they challenge a sound and unbiased mind to concur with an irresistible degree of force and conviction.

Theorems May Conflict with Common Sense

2 Although provable, not all geometry theorems conform with common sense. But geometry is not a subject that stirs up the passions of the human heart. Therefore, people not only accept simple geometric theorems, but even those abstruse paradoxes that, even though they may appear able to be proved through demonstration, vary with the natural conceptions that the mind, without the aid of philosophy, would be led to entertain upon the subject.

For example, mathematicians agree on the INFINITE DIVISIBILITY of matter. In other words, the INFINITE divisibility of a FINITE thing, down to even the minutest atom. Yet this is no more comprehensible to common sense than religious mysteries that non-believers have worked so hard to debunk.

Objective Morals, Ethics Exist

3 But in the behavioral and social sciences of morals and politics, men are far less easily convinced. To a certain degree, this is right and useful. Caution and investigation are necessary armor against error and deception. But this intractableness may be carried too far, deteriorating into obstinacy, perverseness, or disingenuity.

Although we can't pretend that moral and political principles are as objective as those of mathematics, they are far more objective than, to judge from the conduct of men, we might suppose. The obscurity usually exists in the passions and prejudices of the reasoner, not in the subject. Too often, men do not consult their own common sense. Rather, they yield to some unfavorable bias, entangling themselves in words and confounding themselves in subtleties.

Biased Opposition to Taxation

4 How else can we explain (if we assume that the critics are sincere and men of discernment) the position against the Union needing the general power of taxation?

Although previously discussed, it won't hurt to summarize the positions here, as an introduction to an examination of objections. They are, basically, as follows:

Power Must Equal Responsibility

5 A government should have every power required to fully accomplish the objectives committed to its care and completely execute its responsibilities, free from every control except a regard for the public good and the will of the people.

National Defense Can't Be Limited

6 The government has a duty to supervise the national defense and se-cure the public peace against foreign or domestic violence.

Only two things can limit the governmental power of providing for casualties and dangers: the needs of the nation and the resources of the community.

Revenue to Fulfill Responsibilities

7 Since revenue is essential for answering the national needs, the government must also have the power to procure revenue to provide for those exigencies.

State Quotas Hasn't Worked

8 Theory and practice have shown that the power of procuring revenue from the States doesn't work. The federal government must have the unqualified power of ordinary taxation.

Opposition to Union Tax

9 These basic truths seem to validate the proposition that the national government needs the general power of taxation, and that no additional arguments or illustrations are required. But we find, in fact, that rather than accepting their legitimacy, opponents of the proposed Constitution argue most ardently and zealously against this part of the plan. Therefore, it may be a good idea to analyze their arguments.

Union May Usurp State Tax Authority

10 The opponents seem to be saying: "Just because the financial needs of the Union may not be limited, doesn't mean its power to tax ought to be unlimited. Local government requires revenue as much as the Union; and the former are at least of equal importance to the people's happiness as the latter. Therefore, State governments should be as able to collect the revenue for supplying their wants as the national government possesses the same ability in respect to the wants of the Union. But if the *national government* has an indefinite power to tax, in time it would probably deprive the *States* of the means of providing for their own necessities. It would subject the States entirely to the mercy of the national legislature.

"As the laws of the Union will become the supreme law of the land, as it will have the power to pass all the laws that may be NECESSARY to execute the duties proposed for it, the national government might, at any time, abolish State taxes on the pretense that they interfere with its own. It might allege this is necessary to give efficacy to the national revenues. So all tax resources might, by degrees, become a federal monopoly, to the entire exclusion and destruction of the State governments."

"Federal Usurpation" Poor Argument

11 This reasoning sometimes seems based on the supposition that the national government will usurp State powers.

At other times, the reasoning seems to be a deduction of what will happen as a result of the constitutional operation of the national government's intended powers.

Only the latter has any pretensions to fairness. The moment we launch into conjectures about the usurpations of the federal government, we fall into an unfathomable abyss, out of the reach of all reasoning. Imagination may wander until it gets lost in the labyrinths of an enchanted castle, with no idea how to extricate itself from the perplexities into which it has so rashly ventured. No matter how the powers of the Union may be limited or modified, it's easy to imagine an endless train of possible dangers. And by in-

dulging in excesses of jealousy and timidity, we may bring ourselves to a state of absolute skepticism and irresolution.

I repeat here what I've said before, that all arguments based on the danger of usurpation of power ought to refer to the composition and structure of government, not to the nature or extent of its powers. The State governments, by their original constitutions, are invested with complete sovereignty. What is our security against State usurpation? Their structure formation and the dependence of State administrators on the people. If after an impartial examination, the proposed construction of the federal government is found to have the same type of security, all apprehensions on the score of usurpation ought to be discarded.

States Might Encroach On Union

12 Remember that States encroaching on the rights of the Union is as probable as the Union encroaching on the rights of the State governments. The winning side in such a conflict depends on what means the contending parties employ towards insuring success. Because in republics strength is always on the side of the people and there are weighty reasons to believe that the State governments will usually possess the most influence over them, it is natural to conclude that such contests will probably end to the disadvantage of the Union. There is greater probability of encroachments by the States on the federal government, than by the federal government on the States.

However, these conjectures are extremely vague and fallible. By far the safest course is to lay them aside and confine our full attention to the nature and extent of the powers as they are delineated in the Constitution. Everything beyond this must be left to the prudence and firmness of the people. They hold the scales and, it is hoped, they will always take care to preserve the constitutional equilib-rium between the federal and the State governments. On this ground, which is clearly how it should be judged, the objections to an indefinite power of taxation in the United States can be anticipated and countered.

PUBLIUS

Constitutional reference:

Article 1, Section 8	171-175	federal government's taxation power
Article 6	548-552	supreme law of land
Article 1, Section 8	233-237	pass necessary laws

Number 32

Union Tax Authority Doesn't Limit State Authority

I believe that giving the Union power to control levies of money would not create the dangerous consequences feared by the State governments. I·am persuaded that the people's good sense, the extreme hazard of provoking the resentments of the State governments, and a conviction that the utility and necessity of local administrations for local purposes, would be a complete barrier against the oppressive use of such a power.

However, I admit there are just reasons for the States to possess an independent and uncontrollable authority to raise their own revenues to supply their wants. By making this concession, I affirm that (with the sole exception of duties on imports and exports) they would, under the Constitution, retain that authority in the most absolute and unqualified sense. A national government attempt to abridge their exercise of it would be a violent assumption of power, unwarranted by any article or clause of the Constitution.

Only 3 Exceptions to States Sovereignty

2   An entire consolidation of the States into one national sovereignty would imply an entire subordination of the parts. And any powers kept by the States would be completely dependent on the general will.

But since the Constitution is only a partial union or consolidation, the State governments would clearly retain all the rights of sovereignty they had before and are not, by the Constitution, *exclusively* delegated to the United States.

This exclusive delegation, or transfer, of State sovereignty to the Union would only exist in three cases: (1) where the Constitution expressly grants exclusive authority to the Union; (2) where it grants a specific authority to the Union and prohibits the States from exercising the same authority: (3) and where it grants an authority to the Union, to which similar authority in the

States would be absolutely and totally *contradictory* and *repugnant*.

This last case is different from another that might appear to resemble it, but that would, in fact, be essentially different. I mean where the exercise of a concurrent jurisdiction might produce occasional interference in the *policy* of an administration branch, but would not imply any direct contradiction of repugnancy in point of constitutional authority.

These three cases of exclusive jurisdiction in the federal government may be exemplified by the following instances:

1. The next-to-the-last clause of article one, section eight, provides that Congress will exercise *"exclusive legislation"* over the area appropriated as the seat of government. This answers the first case.

2. The first clause of article one, section eight empowers Congress *"to lay and collect taxes, duties, imposts, and excises;"* and the second clause of article one, section ten declares that, *"no State shall*, without the consent of Congress, *lay any imposts or duties on imports or exports*, except for the purpose of executing its inspection laws."

Therefore, the Union would have exclusive power to lay duties on imports and exports, with the specific exception mentioned. But this power is abridged by another clause that declares that no tax or duty shall be laid on articles exported from any State. This qualification limits it to *duties on imports*. This answers the second case.

3. The third will be found in the clause that declares the Congress shall have power "to establish a UNIFORM RULE of naturalization throughout the United States." This must be exclusive because if each State had power to prescribe a DISTINCT RULE, there could not be a UNIFORM RULE.

Opposition Arguments Illogical

3 The question currently under consideration may resemble the latter, but is widely different. I refer to the power to impose taxes on all articles other than exports and imports. This, I contend, is clearly a concurrent and coequal authority in both the United States and the individual States.

The pertinent clause does not give the Union *exclusive* power. No independent clause or sentence prohibits States from exercising it. This is far from being the case. A plain, conclusive argument to the contrary is deduced from the State ban on laying duties on imports and exports. This restriction implies that, without the specific restriction, the States would possess the power it excludes. And it also implies that, as to all other taxes, the authority of the States remain undiminished.

Concluding anything else from the restriction clause would be both unnecessary and dangerous. It would be unnecessary because if the Union's power to charge duties implied the exclusion of the States, the specific restriction would not be needed. It would be dangerous because it leads directly to the conclusion mentioned. Therefore, if the reasoning of the objectors is just, it was not what the authors intended, meaning—that the States, in all cases not restricted, would have a concurrent power of taxation with the Union.

The restriction in question amounts to what lawyers call a NEGATIVE PREGNANT—that is, a *negation* of one thing and an *affirmation* of another—a negation of State authority to impose taxes on imports and exports and an affirmation of their authority to impost them on all other articles. It would be mere sophistry to argue that it was meant to exclude States *absolutely* from duties and allows them to lay others *subject to the control* of the national legislature.

The restraining, or prohibitory, clause only says that States shall not, *without the consent of Congress,* lay such duties. If we are to understand this in the sense last mentioned, the Constitution would need a formal provision to support a very absurd conclusion: that the States, *with the consent* of the national legislature, might tax imports and exports, and tax every other article, *unless controlled* by the same body.

If this is the intention, why not leave it to what is alleged to be the natural operation of the original clause, that is, conferring a general power of taxation on the Union? It is evident that this could not have been the intention and will not bear this interpretation.

Union, States May Tax Same Objects

4   The supposition of incompatibility between the States' and the Union's power of taxation, that it automatically excludes the States' power to tax, cannot be supported. Indeed, perhaps a State tax on a particular article will make it *inexpedient* for the Union to tax the same ar-

ticle. But it doesn't imply a further tax is unconstitutional.

The size of the tax, the expediency or inexpediency of an increase on either side, are questions of prudence, but there is no direct contradiction of power involved. The specific policies of the national and the State systems of finance might now and then not exactly coincide and might require reciprocal forbearances. An inconvenience in the exercise of powers does not imply a constitutional repugnancy that extinguishes a preexisting right of sovereignty.

Tax Clause: Constitutional Interpretation

5   The necessity of joint jurisdiction in certain cases results from dividing sovereign power. The rule that all authorities, except those the States explicitly relinquished to the Union, remain fully with the States, is not a theoretical consequence of that division. Rather, it is the clear meaning of the proposed Constitution. In spite of the affirmative grants of general authority, we find that in cases where it was deemed improper that the same authorities should reside in the States, the Constitution has negative clauses prohibiting the exercise of them by the States.

Article one, section ten consists altogether of such provisions. This clearly indicates the sense of the convention and furnishes a rule of interpretation out of the body of the act, which justifies the position I've advanced and refutes every hypothesis to the contrary.

PUBLIUS

Constitutional references:

Article 1, section 8	223-227	national capital
Article 1, section 8	171-173	Congress taxes imports and exports
Article 1, section 9	265-270	State prohibitions
Article 1, section 10	271-295	State prohibitions
Article 1, section 9	253-254	no taxes on State exports
Article 1, section 8	183-184	naturalization rule

Number 33

Union's Power to Tax: "Necessary and Proper," "Supreme Law of the Land"

The last argument against the Constitution's taxation provisions rests on the following clause. The Constitution authorizes the national legislature "to make all laws which shall be *necessary* and *proper* for carrying into execution the foregoing *powers*, and all other powers vested by this Constitution in the government of the United States, or in any department or officer thereof." and "the Constitution and the laws of the United States which shall be made *in pursuance thereof* and all treaties made, or which shall be made, under the authority of the United States, shall be the *supreme law* of the land; . . . anything in the constitution or laws of any State to the contrary notwithstanding."

Federal Power Implies Power to make Federal Laws

2 These two clauses have been the source of much vehement denunciation and petulant declarations against the Constitution. Through exaggeration and misrepresentation opponents have said that they will destroy local governments and exterminate liberties. They are seen as a hideous monster with devouring jaws that will spare no one—not sex or age, high or low, sacred or profane.

Yet after all this clamor, and as strange as it may seem to people who haven't thought about it, the constitutional operation of the proposed government would be precisely the same if the clauses were removed or if they were repeated in every article. They only declare a truth. The act of con-

stituting a federal government and vesting it with specified powers implies the necessity of these clauses. This is so obvious that even moderate people can't help getting upset over the copious railings against this part of the plan.

Legislature = Power to Make Laws

3 Doesn't power mean having the ability to do a thing? What is the ability to do a thing but the power to employ the *means* necessary to execute it? What is a LEGISLATIVE power but the power to make LAWS? How is LEGISLATIVE power executed but by LAWS? What is the power of laying and collecting taxes but a *legislative power*, that is, a power to *make laws* about taxes? What are the proper means of executing such a power but *necessary* and *proper* laws?

Federal Taxation Requires Tax Laws

4 This simple train of thought furnishes us with a test to judge the true nature of the controversial clause. It leads us to this obvious truth: the power to lay and collect taxes includes all laws *necessary* and *proper* for the execution of that power.

The unfortunate, much slandered clause in question declares the same truth—that is, that the national legislature, which already has the power to lay and collect taxes, might, in the execution of that power, pass all laws *necessary* and *proper* to carry it out.

I'm using the taxation example because it is our current subject and because taxation is the most important authority proposed to be conferred on the Union. But the same process will lead to the same conclusion about every power declared in the Constitution. And it is *expressly* to execute these powers that the "sweeping clause," as it has been frequently called, authorizes the national legislature to pass all *necessary* and *proper* laws.

If there is anything objectionable, it must be looked for in the specific powers upon which this general declaration is based. The declaration itself, though it may be accused of being redundant, is at least perfectly harmless.

Clause Affirms Federal Authority

5   But SUSPICIOUS people may ask, then why was it written? The answer: it must have been added to guard against frivolous refinements by people who might want to limit and evade the legitimate authorities of the Union. The convention probably foresaw the danger most threatening to our political welfare and the principal aim of these papers to inculcate against, that the State governments will eventually sap the foundations of the Union. Therefore, the convention might have thought it necessary, on such an important point, to leave nothing to interpretation.

Whatever the inducement, the wisdom of the precaution is evident from the cry being raised against it. In fact, this cry shows us that some people question the great and essential truth, the reason that this provision has been included.

Laws Judged Against Constitution

6   But it may be again asked, who judges whether laws passed for executing the powers of the Union are necessary and proper?

I answer, first, that this question would be asked about the powers themselves even without the declaratory clause. In the second place, the national government, like every other government, must judge the proper exercise of its powers, as must its constituents.

If the federal government should overreach the just bounds of its authority, making tyrannical use of its powers, the people, who created it, must appeal to the standard they have formed and correct the injury done to the Constitution as needs may suggest and prudence justify. The constitutional propriety of a law must always be determined by the nature of the powers upon which it is founded.

Suppose, by some forced interpretations of its authority (that, indeed, cannot easily be imagined), the federal legislature attempts to vary the law of descent in any State. Would not such an attempt clearly exceed its jurisdiction and infringe upon the authority of the State?

Suppose, again, that the federal government tries to abolish a State's property tax, using the excuse that it interferes with federal revenues. Isn't it equally evident that this would be an invasion of the concurrent tax jurisdiction that the constitution clearly supposes to exist in the State governments? If there ever is a doubt in this area, it will result from people who, in their imprudent zeal, fueled by their animosity to the convention's plan, have tried to envelope the Constitution in a fog calculated to obscure the plainest and simplest truths.

By Definition, National Law Supreme

7   It is said that the laws of the Union are to be the *supreme law* of the land. But what inference can be drawn from this? What would the laws of the Union

amount to if they were not supreme? Clearly, they would amount to nothing. A LAW, by definition, includes supremacy. A law is a rule that those to whom it is prescribed are bound to observe. This results from every political association.

If individuals form a governed society, the laws of that society must be the supreme regulator of their conduct. If a number of political societies combine into a larger political society, the laws enacted by the latter, in accordance with its constitutional powers, must necessarily be supreme over those societies and the individuals in them. Otherwise it would be a mere treaty, which is dependent on the good faith of the parties, and not a government, which is only another word for POLITICAL POWER AND SUPREMACY.

But it doesn't follow from this doctrine that acts of the larger society that are *not among* its constitutional powers, acts that invade the authority of smaller societies, will become the supreme law of the land. These will be acts of usurpation and deserve to be treated as such.

Hence we see that the clause that declares the supremacy of the laws of the Union, like the earlier one, only repeats a truth that flows necessarily from the institution of a federal government. It will not, I presume, have escaped observation that it *expressly* confines this supremacy to laws made *pursuant to the Constitution.* I mention this merely as an example of caution by the convention since the limitation would have been understood even if it had not been expressed.

State, Federal Taxation

8 Therefore, although a United States tax law would be supreme in its nature and couldn't be legally opposed or controlled, a law abolishing or preventing collection of State taxes (unless on imports and exports), would not be the supreme law of the land. It would be a usurpation of power not granted by the Constitution.

As far as an improper collection of taxes on the same object might tend to render the collection difficult or precarious, this would be a mutual inconvenience—not arising from a superiority or defect of power on either side, but form an injudicious exercise of power by one or the other, in a manner equally disadvantageous to both. It is to be hoped and presumed, however, that mutual interest would dictate cooperation to avoid any material inconvenience.

The proposed Constitution infers that individual States can keep an independent, uncontrollable authority to raise revenue by every kind of taxation, except duties on imports and exports, to the extent of their need. The next paper shows that this CONCURRENT JURISDICTION in the realm of taxation was the only admissible substitute for an entire subordination, in respect to this power, of the State authority to that of the Union.

PUBLIUS

Constitutional references:

Article 1, Section 8	233-237	Congress empowered to make laws
Article 6	548-555	United States Constitution/laws/treaties supreme law of land
Article 1, Section 8	171-175	Congress empowered to tax

Number 34

Union, States Concurrent Taxation Jurisdiction

I flatter myself that it was clearly shown in my last paper that the States, under the proposed Constitution, would have COEQUAL authority with the Union in respect to revenue, except as to duties on imports. Since this leaves the greatest part of the community resources to the States, there is no reason to say that the States won't possess abundant taxation methods to supply their own wants, independent of external control. When we discuss the small share of the public expenses for which the State government will be responsible, it will be clear that the field is sufficiently wide.

If Something Exists, Reject Arguments That It Can't Exist

2   To argue, using abstract principles, that this shared authority cannot exist, argues supposition and theory against fact and reality. However clearly arguments show that something *ought not to exist*, they should be completely rejected when evidence proves that it does exist.

For example, in the Roman republic, legislative authority resided in two different political bodies. These were not houses of the same legislature, but different and independent legislatures with opposite interests: the patrician in one and the plebian in the other. Many arguments may have been made to prove the unfitness of two such seemingly contradictory authorities, with each having the power to *annul* or *repeal* the acts of the other. But a Roman would have been regarded as insane if he attempted to disprove their existence.

Of course, I'm referring to the COMITTA CENTURIATA and the CONITTA TRIBUIA. In the former, in which the people voted by centuries [citizen-voters met specific property qualifications], the patrician interest was superior. In the latter, population numbers prevailed, so the plebeian interest predominated. Yet these two legislatures coexisted for ages and the Roman republic attained the utmost height of human greatness.

Coequal Authority

3   The case under consideration holds no such contradiction as the Roman example. No power on either side can annul the acts of the other. Additionally, there is little reason to worry about any inconvenience because, in a short time, the States' needs will naturally reduce themselves within a *very narrow compass*. In the interim, the United States will probably not tax the objects that States would be inclined to tax.

Union Revenue Needs Unlimited

4   To judge the true merits of this question, we must look at what will require federal revenue and what will require State revenue. The former is unlimited and the latter is restricted within very moderate bounds.

In pursuing this inquiry, we must remember to look forward into the remote future. Constitutions of civil government are not framed to meet existing needs; they combine existing needs with the probably future needs, according to the natural and tried course of human affairs. Nothing, therefore, is more deceptive than to infer, from an estimate of immediate necessities, the extent of power it is proper to lodge in the national government. The national government should have a CAPACITY to provide for future contingencies as they may happen. Since these are boundless in their nature, it is impossible to safely limit that capacity. Perhaps a sufficiently accurate computation could determine the revenue needed to discharge the existing obligations of the Union, and maintain those establishments which, for some time to come, would suffice in time of peace.

But would it be wise or extreme folly to stop at this point, leaving the government entrusted with the care of the national defense and absolutely incapable of providing for the protection of the community against future invasions of the public peace by foreign war or domestic convulsions?

If, on the contrary, we should exceed this point, where can we stop, short of an indefinite power to provide for emergencies as they arise?

Though it is easy to say that it is possible to calculate what revenue might be needed against probable danger, we can safely challenge those who make the assertion to bring forward their data. It would be found as vague and uncertain as any data produced to establish the duration of the world.

Observations about the prospect of internal attacks deserve no weight, although even those cannot be satisfactorily calculated. But if we are to be a commercial people, part of our policy must include being able to one day defend that commerce. The support of a navy and naval wars will involve contingencies that baffle all efforts of political arithmetic.

Revenue Always Needed for Defense

5   Even if we agree to try the novel and absurd political experiment of tying the hands of government from offensive war founded upon reasons of State, we certainly ought not disable it from guarding the community against the ambition or enmity of other nations. For some time a cloud has been handing over Europe. If it should break into a storm, who can insure that as it progresses a part of its fury would not be spent on us? No reasonable man would hastily pronounce us entirely out of its reach.

Or if the current combustible materials should dissipate without coming to maturity or if a flame is kindled without extending to us, what security can we have that our tranquility will remain undisturbed from another cause or quarter? Let us remember that peace or war will not always be left to our option. However moderate or unambitious we may be, we can't count on the moderation or hope to extinguish the ambition of others.

Who could have imagined at the conclusion of the last war that France and Britain, wearied and exhausted, would so soon look with hostility on each other? Judging from history, we must conclude that the fiery and destructive passions of war reign in the human breast with much more powerful sway than the mild and beneficent sentiments of peace. Modeling our political systems on speculations of lasting tranquility is to calculate on the weaker springs of the human character.

Defense Largest Expense

6   What are the chief sources of expense in every government? What caused the European nations to accumulate enormous and oppressive debts? Wars and rebellions. Supporting insti-

tutions are necessary to guard against these two most mortal diseases of society.

The expenses from institutions needed by domestic police, to support the legislative, executive, and judicial branches with their different appendages, and the encouragement of agriculture and manufactures (in other words, almost all state expenditures), are insignificant compared with national defense expenses.

England: Defense vs. Executive

7   In the kingdom of Great Britain, only one-fifteenth part of the nation's annual income goes towards providing for the ostentatious apparatus of the monarchy. The other fourteen-fifteenths pays the interest on debts contracted during wars and to maintain fleets and armies.

Someone could observe that the expenses incurred from supporting the ambitious enterprises and vainglorious pursuits of a monarchy are not a proper standard to judge what revenues a republic might need. In response, it could be said that there should be as big a disproportion between the profusion and extravagance of maintaining a domestic monarch's administration in a wealthy kingdom, and the frugality and economy of maintaining the modest simplicity of the executive branch of republican government. If we balance a proper deduction from one side against what ought to be deducted from the other, the proportion may still stand.

Union vs. States Revenue Needs

8   But let us focus on the large debt we contracted in a single war. When we calculate our share of future disturbances of the peace of nations, we well instantly perceive, without the aid of any elaborate illustration, that there must always be an immense disproportion between federal and State expenditures. Several States are encumbered with excessive debts because of the war. But if the proposed system is adopted, this cannot happen again. After these debts are discharged, State governments will only need revenue to support their respective civil lists. If we add all contingencies, the total amount needed in every State ought to fall considerably short of 200,000 pounds.

Future Revenue Needs Unlimitable

9   In framing a government for both posterity and ourselves, we ought to calculate the expense of permanent provisions. If this is a sound principle, the State governments will need an annual sum of about 200,000 pounds. At the same time, the Union's requirements can not be limited, even in imagination.

From this view of the subject, what logic can maintain that local governments should perpetually command an EXCLUSIVE source of revenue for any sum beyond 200,000 pounds? To extend State power further, in *exclusion* of the Union's authority, would take the resources of the community our of the hands that need them for the public welfare, to put them into other hands that have no just or proper use for them.

Current State Debts > Future Needs

10   Suppose the convention had proceeded on the principle of distributing revenue sources between the Union and its members in *proportion* to their comparative needs. What fund for the States could have been selected that

would not have been too much or too little—too little for their present, too much for their future wants?

Separating external and internal taxes would leave to the States roughly two thirds of the community resources to defray a tenth to a twentieth part of its expenses, and the Union, one third of the resources of the community to defray from nine tenths to nineteen twentieths of its expenses.

If we leave this boundary and give the States an exclusive power of taxing houses and lands, there would still be a great disproportion between the *means* and the *end,* with the possession of one third of the community resources to supply, at most, one tenth of its wants.

If any fund equal to and not greater than State needs could have been selected and appropriated, it would have been inadequate to the discharge of existing debts, leaving them dependent on the Union for a provision for this purpose.

Constitutional reference:

Article 1, Section 8   171-177   federal taxation authority; provide for common defense

Solution: Concurrent Tax Jurisdiction

11 The preceding train of thought will justify the position that "a CONCURRENT JURISDICTION in the article of taxation was the only admissible substitute for an entire subordination, in respect to this branch of power, of State authority to that of the Union."

Separating objects of taxation would have amounted to sacrificing the great INTERESTS of the Union to the power of the individual States. The convention thought the concurrent jurisdiction preferable to that subordination. And it is evident that it has at least the merit of reconciling an indefinite constitutional power of taxation in the federal government with an adequate and independent power in the States to provide for their own necessities. A few other points about this important subject of taxation deserve further consideration.

PUBLIUS

Number 35

Representatives Should Understand Effects of Tax Policy

Before we proceed to examine any other objections to the Union having an indefinite power of taxation, I will make one general remark: If the national government is restricted as to what objects it may tax, it would put an undue proportion of public burden on those objects. Two evils would spring from this source: the oppression of specific parts of industry and an unequal tax burden among States as well as among the citizens within a State.

High Taxes Create Severe Problems

2 Some people argue that the federal taxation power should be confined to duties on imports. Because it would have no other resources under this policy, the government would frequently be tempted to increase these duties to an injurious excess. Some people imagine duties can never be too high, alleging that the higher they go, the more they will tend to discourage extravagant consumption, producing a

favorable balance of trade and promoting domestic manufactures.

But all extremes cause harm. Exorbitant duties on imported articles would increase smuggling, which hurts the fair trader and eventually decreases tax revenue. Exorbitant duties tend to give people who manufacture goods within the country a premature market monopoly, able to charge higher prices than in an open market. These duties sometimes force industry out of its more natural channels into less advantageous areas.

And in the last place, they oppress the merchant and, sometimes, exhaust his profits and eat into his capital. The cost of the duty is often divided between the seller and the buyer. It is not always possible to raise the price of a commodity in exact proportion to every additional tax on it. The merchant, especially in a country with small commercial capital, often must keep prices down to promote sales.

High Duties
Effect States Differently

3   The maxim that the consumer pays the tax duties is more often true than the reverse of the proposition. Therefore, it is more equitable that the duties on imports should go into a common stock rather than be used exclusively by the importing States. But it is not fair that duties should form the only national fund.

When duties are paid by the merchant, they become an additional tax on the importing State, whose citizens, as consumers, pay the duties. They would produce an inequality among the States that would increase as duties increased.

Confining national revenues to import duties would produce another

inequality, between the manufacturing and the non-manufacturing States. The States that can supply most of their own wants by their own manufacturers will not consume so great a proportion (in numbers or wealth) of imported articles as States not in the same favorable situation. They would not, therefore, contribute to the public treasury in a ratio to their abilities. Excises would be necessary to increase their contribution, targeting specific kinds of manufacturers.

Citizens of New York who fight for limiting the Union to external taxation may not be aware of how important the subject is to their State. New York is an importing State and, because of the disproportion between her population and territory, is not likely to soon become a manufacturing State, to any great extent. She would, of course, suffer in a double light from restraining the jurisdiction of the Union to commercial taxes.

Increase Taxes ≠ Increase Revenue

4   These observations warn of increasing import duties to an injurious extreme. As mentioned in another paper, the desire to collect tax revenue should be a sufficient guard against such an extreme. And it would be, as long as other resources were available. But if other taxation avenues were closed, HOPE, stimulated by necessity, would beget experiments. Rigorous precautions and additional penalties would increase tax revenues, but only until people had enough time to contrive ways to elude the new taxes. The higher tax revenues at first would probably inspire false impressions, requiring a long course of subsequent experience to correct. Necessity, especially in politics, often occasions false hopes, false reasoning, and a system of measures correspondingly erroneous.

But even if excess is not a consequence of limiting the federal power of taxation, the inequalities delineated earlier would still exist, though from other causes and not in the same degree.

Let us now return to the examination of objections.

Critics: Too Few Representatives

5 One frequent objection is that there are not enough members of the House of Representatives to represent all different classes of citizens, the interests and feelings of every part of the community, and to produce a sympathy between the representative body and its constituents. This is a very specious and seducing argument. It is calculated to lay hold of the prejudices of those to whom it is addressed. But when we carefully study it, we'll see it is composed of nothing but fair-sounding words. It is both impractical and unnecessary to accomplish the goal it supposedly supports.

I reserve for another place the discussion about whether there is a sufficient number of members in the representative body.

I will examine it here as it relates to the subject of this paper.

Mechanics, Manufacturers will Elect Merchants

6 The idea that every class of people will be represented by people in each class is a Utopian fantasy. Unless the Constitution expressly says that each different occupation should send one or more members, it will never happen.

Mechanics and manufacturers will be inclined, with few exceptions, to give their votes to merchants rather than persons in their own professions or trades. Those discerning citizens

understand that the mechanic and manufacturing arts furnish the materials of mercantile enterprise and industry. Many of them are immediately connected with the operations of commerce. They know that the merchant is their natural patron and friend. And they are aware that, however great the confidence they may feel in their own good sense, their interests can be more effectually promoted by the merchant than by themselves. They know that their life habits haven't given them those acquired endowments, without which, in a deliberative assembly, the greatest natural abilities are, for the most part, useless. The merchants' influence, weight, and superior acquirements render them more equal to a contest with any spirit unfriendly to the manufacturing and trading interests that might become a part of public councils. These considerations, and many others, prove what experience confirms, that artisans and manufacturers will commonly vote for merchants or the people who merchants recommend. Therefore, merchants are the natural representatives of all these classes of the community.

Many Elect Learned Professionals

7 With regard to the learned professions, little need be said. They truly form no distinct interest in society. According to their situation and talents, they will be indiscriminately the objects of the confidence and choice of each other and of other parts of the community.

Property Owners' Common Interests

8 Lastly, the landed interest. This group, in a political view and particularly in relation to taxes, I believe are perfectly united, from the wealthiest landlord down to the poorest tenant.

No property tax will not affect the proprietor of millions of acres as well as the proprietor of a single acre. Every landholder, therefore, will have a common interest to keep the taxes on land as low as possible. And common interests is always the surest bond of sympathy.

But even if we could imagine a distinction of interest between the opulent landholder and the middling farmer, why would we conclude that the first would stand a better chance of being elected to the national legislature than the last? If we take facts as our guide and look into the New York senate and assembly, we'll find that moderate proprietors of land prevail in both. This is no less the case in the senate, which has a smaller number than the assembly. Where voters' qualifications are the same, whether they have to choose a small or large number, their votes will go to men in whom they have the most confidence, whether they happen to have large fortunes, moderate property, or no property at all.

Representatives' Knowledge

9 It is said that every class of citizen should have some member of their class in the representative body, so that their feelings and interests are better understood and attended to. But we have seen that this will never happen under any arrangement that leaves the votes of the people free. Where this is the case, the representative body, with too few exceptions to have any influence on the spirit of the government, will be composed of landlords, merchants, and men of the learned professions.

Why is there a fear that the interest and feelings of the different classes of citizens won't be understood by these three descriptions of men?

Will not the landlord know and feel whatever will promote or insure the interest of landed property? And will he not, from his own interest in property, be sufficiently prone to resist every attempt to prejudice or encumber it?

Will not the merchant understand and cultivate, as far as may be proper, the interests of the mechanic and manufacturing arts, to which his commerce is so nearly allied?

Will not the man of the learned profession feel neutrality towards the rivalships between different branches of industry, be an impartial arbiter between them, ready to promote either, as it should appear to him conducive to the general interests of the society?

Elected Officials Inform Themselves

10 If we take into the account the momentary tempers or dispositions that may prevail in particular parts of society, to which wise administrators will never be inattentive, is the man who needs extensive inquiry and information a less competent judge of their nature, extent, and foundation than someone who has never traveled beyond his circles of neighbors and acquaintances? Isn't it natural that a candidate, who depends on the votes of his fellow citizens to continue his public job, will inform himself of their dispositions and inclinations, and be willing to allow a proper degree of influence on his conduct? This dependence on the citizens, and his necessity of binding himself and his posterity by the laws he approves, create strong cords of sympathy between the representative and the constituent.

Knowledge Needed for Tax Policy

11 No part of governmental administration requires more extensive information or thorough knowledge of political economic principles as taxation. The man who best understands these principles will be least likely to resort to oppressive taxes or sacrifice any particular group of citizens to the procurement of revenue.

It might be demonstrated that the most productive system of obtaining governmental revenue will always be the least burdensome. In order to judiciously tax, the person with the power to tax should be acquainted with the general characteristics, habits, and modes of thinking of the people at large and resources of the country. This is what can be reasonably be meant by a knowledge of the interests and feelings of the people. Any other interpretation of the proposition has either no meaning or an absurd one. And in that sense, let every thinking citizen judge for himself who has the required qualification.

PUBLIUS

Constitutional references:
Article 1, Section 8   171-173   federal taxation
Article 1, Section 2   27-35   number of representatives

Number 36

Internal Taxation by Federal Government

The observations of the previous paper show that through the natural operation of the different interests within the community, the representatives, whether more or less numerous, will consist almost entirely of property owners, merchants, and members of the learned professions, who will truly represent all those different interests and views.

If someone disagrees, pointing out that local legislatures have other descriptions of men, I admit that there are exceptions to the rule, but not in sufficient number to influence the general complexion or character of the government. There are strong minds in every walk who will rise above the disadvantages of their situation, commanding the tribute due to their merit, not only from the classes to which they belong, but from society in general.

The door ought to be equally open to all. To the credit of human nature, I believe we will see examples of such vigorous plants flourishing in the soil of federal, as well as, State legislatures. But having this occasionally happen, doesn't make the reasoning, based on the general course of things, less conclusive.

**Representatives: Merchants,
Property Owners, Academicians**

2 Several views of the subject all lead to the same conclusion. Specifically, it might be asked, what great affinity or relationship exists between the carpenter and blacksmith, the linen manufacturer and stocking-weaver, than between the merchant and any of them? Everyone knows that great rivalships between different branches of the mechanic or manufacturing arts arise as often as between any of the departments of labor and industry. So, unless the representative body was bigger than consistent with having regular, wise deliberations, it seems impossible that the spirit of the objection we've been considering will ever be realized in practice.

But I refuse to dwell any longer on a matter that has, until now, worn too loose a garb to allow an accurate inspection of its real shape or tendency.

Representatives Have Local Info

3   Another more precise objection claims our attention. It has been asserted that a national power of internal taxation can never be exercised successfully, not just because there isn't a sufficient knowledge of local circumstances, as from an interference between the revenue laws of the Union and specific States.

The supposition of a lack of proper knowledge seems entirely destitute of foundation. If a State legislature has a question about one of the counties, how is knowledge of local details acquired? No doubt from citizens of the county. Cannot similar knowledge be obtained by the national legislature from the representatives of each State? And isn't it presumed that the men generally sent to Congress will possess the necessary degree of intelligence to be able to communicate that information?

Does knowledge of local circumstances, as applied to taxation, mean being topographically familiar with every mountain, river, stream, highway, and by-path in each State? No. It means a general acquaintance with its situation and resources, the state of its agriculture, commerce, manufacturers, the nature of its products and consumption, the different degrees and kinds of wealth, property, and industry.

Small Councils Prepare Tax Plans

4   Nations in general, even the more popular type governments, usually commit financial administration to single men or boards composed of a few people who digest and prepare taxation plans. These are then passed into laws by the authority of the sovereign or legislature.

Statesmen Select Objects Taxed

5   Inquisitive, enlightened statesmen are believed, everywhere, best qualified to make a judicious selection of the proper objects of taxation. As far as the sense of mankind can have weight in the question, this is a clear indication of the type of knowledge of local circumstances required for the purpose of taxation.

Indirect, Excise Taxes

6   The general category of internal taxes may be subdivided into *direct* and *indirect* taxes. Though the objection is made to both, the reasoning of it seems confined to direct taxes.

It is hard to conceive of the difficulties feared from indirect taxes, that is, duties and excises on articles of consumption. Knowledge about them must either be that suggested by the nature of the article itself or can be procured from any well-informed man, especially of the mercantile class. The circumstances distinguishing an article's situation in one State from that in another must be few, simple, and easy to comprehend. The principle point would be to avoid those articles already taxed by a State. The revenue system of each could be determined from the respective codes of law and the State representatives.

Direct, Property Taxes

7 The objection appears to have, at first sight, more foundation when applied to real property, houses, or land. But even in this view, it will not bear close examination.

Land taxes are commonly laid in one of two modes, either by *actual* valuations, permanent or periodical, or by *occasional* assessments, according to the best judgment and discretion of officers whose duty it is to make them. In either case, knowledge of local details is only needed in the EXECUTION of the duty, which will be carried out by commissioners or assessors, elected by the people or appointed by the government for the purpose. All the law can do is prescribe the manner the persons will be elected or appointed, fix their numbers and qualifications, and draw the general outline of their powers and duties.

What, in all this, cannot be as well performed by the national legislature as by a State legislature? Either can only regulate the general principles. As already observed, local details must be referred to those who execute the plan.

May Use State Collection System

8 But there is a simple point of view that puts this matter into a satisfactory light. The national legislature can make use of the *system of each State within that State*. Each State's method of laying and collecting this type of tax can be adopted and employed by the federal government.

Taxes Uniform Throughout Nation

9 Remember, the proportion of these taxes is not left to the discretion of the national legislature, but is to be determined by each State's population, as described in Article one, Section two. An actual census will furnish the rule, a circumstance effectually shutting the door to partiality or oppression. The abuse of the taxation power seems to have been carefully provided against. In addition to the precaution just mentioned, there is a provision that "all duties, imposts, and excises shall be UNIFORM throughout the United States."

State Requisitions Still Possible

10 Different speakers and writers on the side of the Constitution properly remind us that if the experiment of internal taxation by the Union is really inconvenient, the federal government may stop using it and use State requisitions instead.

As an answer to this, it has been triumphantly asked, why not just omit the ambiguous power and rely on the latter resource?

Two solid answers may be given. First, if the power can be conveniently exercised, it is preferable because it will be more effective. And it is impossible to prove in theory, or by any way other than experiment, that it cannot be advantageously exercised. Indeed, the contrary appears most probable.

Second, the existence of such a power in the Constitution will have a strong influence in giving efficacy to requisitions. When the States know that the Union can apply directly to the people without their agency, it will be a powerful motive for exertion on their part.

Federal, States Tax Different Objects

11 As to Union revenue laws interfering with State laws, we have seen that there can be no clashing or contradictions of authority. Therefore, legally, the laws cannot interfere with each other. However, interference between the policies of their different systems does happen. An effective solution will be to mutually abstain from those objects that either side may have had first recourse to. As neither can *control* the other, each will have an obvious and sensible interest in this reciprocal forbearance. And where these is an immediate common interest, we may safely count upon its operation. When the current State debts are paid off and their expenses become limited within their natural compass, the possibility of interference will almost vanish. A small land-tax will fulfill State needs, becoming their most simple and fit resource.

Fears about Internal Taxation

12 Many specters have been raised out of this power of internal taxation to make the people apprehensive. Double sets of revenue officers, a duplication of their burdens by double taxation, and the frightful forms of odious, oppressive poll-taxes have been played off with all the ingenious dexterity of political legerdemain.

Double Sets of Revenue Officers

13 As to the first point, there are two cases when there is no room for double sets of officers. The first is when the Union has exclusive right to impose the tax, for instance, duties on imports. The other, when the object to be taxed hasn't fallen under a State regulation or provision.

In other cases, the United States probably will either totally abstain from the objects taxed for local purposes or will use State officers and State regulations for collecting the additional tax. This will save collection expense and best avoid any occasion of disgust to the State governments and the people.

Anyway, these are practical solutions to avoid such inconveniences. Nothing more can be required than to demonstrate that the predicted evils do not necessarily result from the plan.

State Influences Federal

14 As to any argument about a possible system of influence, it is sufficient to say that it shouldn't be presumed. However, there is a more precise answer. If such a spirit should infest the councils of the Union, the most certain road to accomplish its aim would be to employ State officers as much as possible, attaching them to the Union through their compensation. This would turn the tide of State influence into the channels of the national government, instead of making federal influence flow in an opposite and adverse current.

But all suppositions of this kind are invidious and should be banished from the consideration of the great question before the people. They serve no other end than to cast a mist over the truth.

Federal or State, Total Taxes Same

15 The answer to the double taxation suggestion is plain. The wants of the Union are to be supplied in one way or another. If fulfilled under the authority of the federal government, they will not be done by the State government. The quantity of taxes paid by the community must be the same in either case.

If the federal government supplies the provision, it can use commercial taxes, the most convenient source of revenue. This revenue source can be prudently improved to a much greater extent under federal than State regulation, making more inconvenient methods less necessary.

There is a further advantage. If there is any real difficulty in the exercise of the power of internal taxation, the federal government will be disposed to take greater care in the choice and arrangement of the means. It will naturally tend to make a fixed policy in the national administration, making the rich pay as much as is practical to the public treasury, diminishing the necessity of impositions that might create dissatisfaction in the poorer and most numerous classes of society. It is a happy circumstance when the government's interest in self-preservation coincides with a proper distribution of public burdens, and tends to guard the least wealthy part of the community from oppression!

Poll Taxes Bad,
But May Be Needed

16 As to poll-taxes, without scruple I confess my strong disapproval of them. And although they have prevailed from an early period in those States* that have uniformly been the most tenacious of their rights, I would lament to see them introduced into practice under the national government.

But does it follow that just because there is a power to lay them that they will actually be laid? Every State in the Union has the power to impose taxes of this kind. Yet in several of them, they are unknown in practice. Are the State governments to be stigmatized as tyrannies because they possess this power? If they are not, how can a similar power justify such a charge against the national government, or even be urged as an obstacle to the adoption of the Constitution?

As unfriendly as I am to this type of taxes, I still feel a thorough conviction that the power of having recourse to it ought to exist in the federal gov-

ernment. Nations have emergencies in which expedients that ordinarily should be forborne become essential to the public well being. Because emergencies are possible, the government should always have the option of making use of them.

The real scarcity of objects in this country that may be considered as productive sources of revenue is a reason itself for not limiting the discretion of the national councils in this respect. And since I know of nothing to exempt this part of the globe from the common calamities that have befallen other parts of it, I acknowledge my aversion to everything that disarms the government of a single weapon that in any possible contingency might be usefully employed for the general defense and security.

Essential Powers
of Federal Government

17 I have gone through an examination of the powers proposed to be vested in the United States that relate to the energy of government and endeavored to answer the principal objections to them. I have passed over minor authorities that are either too inconsiderable to have been thought worthy of the hostilities of the opponents of the Constitution or too manifestly proper to be controversial.

Judicial power might have been investigated under this topic. But its organization and the extent of its authority is more advantageously considered together. Because of this, I refer it to the next of branch of our inquires.

PUBLIUS

* The New England States.

Constitutional references:

Article 1, Section 8	171-175	congressional power to tax
Article 1, Section 8	175-177	taxes uniform throughout U.S.
Article 1, Section 9	250-252	direct tax proportionate to census
Article 1, Section 9	253-254	no tax on articles exported from States
Article 1, Section 2	16-27	proportionate direct taxes

Number 37

Difficulties Faced by Constitutional Convention

We have reviewed the defects of the existing Confederation and showed that they cannot be corrected by a government with less energy than the one now being considered. And we have looked at several important principles of the new Constitution.

But the ultimate object of these papers is to determine clearly and fully the merits of this Constitution and the expediency of adopting it. We should now take a critical and thorough survey of the Constitution drafted by the convention—examining all its sides, comparing all its parts, and calculating its probable effects.

So that this task may be executed under impressions conducive to a just and fair result, candor suggests that some reflections must be made.

Papers' Target Audience: People Objectively Evaluating Constitution

2   It is unfortunate, but a part of human nature, that public policy is rarely investigated with the spirit of moderation that is essential to judge whether it has the tendency to advance or obstruct the public good. And on the occasions when it is most important, objectivity is more apt to be diminished than promoted.

To people who have thought about this subject, it shouldn't be surprising that the Constitution excites dispositions unfriendly to a fair discussion and objective judgment of its merits. It recommends many important changes and innovations that may be viewed in many lights and relations, touching many passions and interests on both sides of the issues.

It is obvious from what they have written that some people scanned the proposed Constitution not with just a predisposition to censure, but with a predetermination to condemn.

The language of other people betrays an opposite predetermination or bias, which makes their opinions of little moment in the question.

By giving equal weight to the opinions of both people predetermined to condemn the new Constitution and people predetermine to praise it, however, I don't want to insinuate that there may not be a material difference in the purity of their intentions. Since our situation is universally admitted to be critical and something must be done for our relief, we could honestly say that the patron writing favorably may have taken his bias from the weight of these considerations, as well as from considerations of a sinister nature. On the other hand, the predetermined adversary can be guided by no venial motive whatever.

The intentions of the first may be upright while also being culpable. The views of the last cannot be upright, and must be culpable.

But the truth is, these papers are not addressed to people in either category. They solicit the attention of people who add to their sincere zeal for the happiness of their country the ability to objectively judge the way to promote it.

Constitution Not Faultless

3   These people will examine the Constitution not only without a disposition to focus on or magnify faults, but the good sense to not have expected a

faultless plan. Nor will they barely make allowances for the errors that may be chargeable on the fallibility to which the convention, as a body of men, were liable. They will keep in mind that they, themselves, are only men and should not assume an infallibility as they judge the fallible opinions of others.

Drafting Good Constitution Difficult

4 Besides these inducements to candor, they will quickly perceive and make allowances for the difficulties inherent in the nature of the convention's work.

Precedents Show Errors to Avoid

5 The novelty of the undertaking immediately strikes us. These papers show that the existing Confederation is founded on fallacious principles. Consequently, we must change both the foundation and the superstructure resting on it.

It has been shown that other confederacies, which could have been consulted as precedents, are impaired by the same erroneous principles. They furnish only beacons that warn which course to shun without pointing to which should be pursued. In this situation, the convention could only avoid the errors suggested by the experience of other countries, as well as our own, and provide a convenient way through amendments of rectifying the convention's errors, as future experience may expose them.

Balance Stable Government, Liberty

6 Among the difficulties encountered by the convention must have been the very important one of combining the required stability and energy in a government with the inviolable attention due liberty and the republican form. Without substantially accomplishing this, both their objective and the public's expectation would have been very imperfectly fulfilled. Yet no one who is unwilling to betray his ignorance of the subject, will deny that it could not be easily accomplished.

Energy in government is essential to secure against external and internal danger and to the prompt salutary execution of the laws that are a part of good government.

Stability in government is essential to national character with its advantages, as well as the repose and confidence it gives the people, one of the chief blessings of civil society. Irregular and mutable legislation is not so much evil in itself as it is odious to the people. Since the people of this country are enlightened as to the nature and interested in the effects of good government, it may be said with confidence that they will never be satisfied until some remedy is applied to the vicissitudes and uncertainties that characterize the State administrations.

However, when comparing stability and energy with the vital principles of liberty, we must see the difficulty of combining them in their proper proportions.

Inherently, republican liberty seems to demand on the one side that all power should be derived from the people and those entrusted with it should be kept in dependence on the people by a short duration of their appointments. And, even during this short period, the trust should be placed not in a few, but a number of hands.

Stability, on the other hand, requires that officials continue in office for a longer time.

Frequent elections create a frequent change in men. A frequent change of men creates a frequent change of policies. However, energy in government requires both duration of power and the execution of it by a single hand.

Did Convention Achieve Balance?

7 Whether the convention succeeded in this part of their work will become clearer after a more accurate view. From this cursory view, it clearly appears to have been an arduous task.

State vs. Federal Authority

8 Determining the proper line between the authority of the federal and State governments was no less difficult a task. Each person will understand this difficulty to the degree that he has spent time contemplating and discriminating between objects extensive and complicated in their nature.

The abilities of the mind, itself, have never been classified and precisely defined, despite all the efforts of the most acute, metaphysical philosophers. The mental activities of sense, perception, judgment, desire, volition, memory, and imagination are separated by such delicate shades and minute gradations that their boundaries have eluded the most subtle investigations and continue to be a fertile source of intelligent, systemic inquires and controversy.

The boundaries within the great kingdom of nature and, more importantly, between the various genuses and species, afford another illustration of the same important truth. The most sagacious and laborious naturalists have not yet succeeded in tracing, with certainty, the line separating vegetable life from the neighboring region of unorganized, non-organic matter, or what marks the termination of the former and the commencement of the animal empire. An even greater obscurity lies in the distinct characteristics by which the objects in each category of nature have been arranged and sorted.

Politics Inexact Science

9 In nature, objective delineations do exist. They are unclear only because of our inability to make perfect observations.

When studying the institutions of man, obscurity arises from both the subject itself and the imperfections of the humans who contemplate it. We must see the necessity of further moderating our expectations and hopes for the efforts of human sagacity. Experience shows that political science hasn't been able to discriminate and define, with sufficient certainty, its three great provinces—the legislative, executive, and judiciary—or even the privileges and powers of the different legislative branches. Daily, questions appear that prove the obscurity of these subjects and puzzle the greatest political science experts.

Ideas Clear, Words Ambiguous

10 The experience of the ages and the continuing studies by the most enlightened legislators and jurists have been equally unsuccessful in delineating the objectives and limits of different codes of laws and different tribunals of justice.

The precise extent of common law, statute law, maritime law, ecclesiastical law, corporate law, and local laws and customs, still isn't clearly defined in Great Britain, where accuracy in such subjects has been more industriously pursued than in any other part of the world. The jurisdiction of Great Britain's general and local courts, law, equity, admiralty, etc., is a source of frequent and intricate discussions, denoting the indeterminate limits by which they are respectively circumscribed.

All new laws, although written with the greatest technical skill and passed after the fullest, most mature deliberation, are considered as more or less obscure and equivocal until their meaning is ascertained by a series of particular discussions and adjudications.

Besides the obscurity arising from the complexity of the subjects and the imperfection of the human faculties, the medium [i.e. words, sentences, language] used to convey men's conceptions adds a fresh embarrassment.

Words are used to express ideas. Clear expression, therefore, requires not only distinctly formed ideas, but they must be expressed by words distinctly and exclusively appropriate for those ideas. But no language is so copious as to supply words and phrases for every complex idea. Nor are the words so precise as not to include many equivocal words that denote several ideas.

Hence, it happens that however accurately subjects may be discriminated within themselves and however accurately the discrimination is, the definition may be rendered inaccurate by the inaccuracy of the terms. And this unavoidable inaccuracy must be, more or less, according to the complexity and novelty of the objects defined.

When the Almighty himself condescends to address mankind in their own language, his meaning, luminous as it must be, is rendered dim and doubtful by the cloudy medium through which it is communicated.

Sources of Ambiguity

11 Here, then, are three sources of vague and incorrect definitions: (1) indistinctness of the subject, (2) imperfection of the organ of conception, and (3) inadequateness of the vehicle of ideas.

Any one of these will produce a degree of obscurity. The constitutional convention, in delineating the boundary between the federal and State jurisdictions, must have experienced the full effect of them all.

States: Conflicting Demands

12 Added to these difficulties were the conflicting demands of the larger and smaller States. We can suppose that larger States argued to have power equivalent to their superior wealth and importance. The smaller States argued, no less tenaciously, for continued equality. We may suppose that neither side would entirely yield to the other and, consequently, the struggle could be terminated only by compromise.

It is extremely probable, also, that after the ratio of representation had been adjusted, the compromise must have produced a fresh struggle between the same parties, each wanting to organize government and distribute its powers, increasing the importance of branches so that they respectively obtained the greatest share of influence.

Features in the Constitution warrant each of these suppositions. And so far as either of them is well founded, it shows that the convention must have been compelled to sacrifice theoretical perfection to the force of extraneous considerations.

States: Other Conflicting Interests

13 Nor could it have been only the large and small States in opposition to each other on various points. States with different local positions and policies must have created additional difficulties.

Every State is divided into different districts and its citizens into different classes giving birth to competing interests and local jealousies. The different parts of the United States are also distinguished from each other by a variety of circumstances, producing a similar effect on a larger scale.

Although this variety of interests, for reasons explained in an earlier paper, may have a healthy influence on the administration of the government once it is formed, everyone must be aware of the conflicting influences that must have been experienced during the task of forming it.

Drafting Constitution

14 Would it be surprising that the pressure of these difficulties forced the convention into deviations from the artificial structure and regular symmetry that an abstract view of the subject might lead an ingenious theorist to bestow on a Constitution planned in his closet or in his imagination?

The real wonder is that so many difficulties were surmounted and surmounted with a unanimity almost as unprecedented as it must have been unexpected. Any man of candor must reflect on this circumstance with astonishment. Any man of pious reflection must perceive in it a finger of that Almighty hand that has so frequently and signally extended to our relief in the critical stages of the revolution.

Opinions Sacrificed for Public Good

15 In a previous paper, we mentioned that the United Netherlands repeatedly and unsuccessfully tried to reform the ruinous and notorious vices of their constitution. [Number 20]

The history of almost all the great councils called to reconcile discordant opinions, assuage mutual jealousies, and adjust respective interests, is a history of factions, contentions, and disappointments. They are dark and degraded pictures, displaying the infirmities and depravities of the human character. The few scattered instances of cooperation only serve as exceptions to caution us about the general truth. Their luster darkens the gloom of the adverse prospect to which they are contrasted.

When considering the causes from which these exceptions result and applying them to our situation, we are led to two important conclusions. First, the convention must have enjoyed, to a very singular degree, an exemption from the pestilential influence of party animosities—the disease most incident to deliberative bodies and most apt to contaminate their proceedings.

The second conclusion is that all the delegations composing the convention were either satisfactorily accommodated by the final act or were induced to accede to it because they felt a deep conviction of the necessity of sacrificing private opinions and partial interests to the public good, and by the fear of seeing this necessity diminished by delays or by new experiments.

                                    PUBLIUS

Number 38

Ancient Republics Structured by Individuals

Objections to Constitution: Wide Variety, Little Agreement

Of every government established with deliberation and consent reported by ancient history, none were framed by an assembly of men, but by some individual citizen of preeminent wisdom and proven integrity.

Authors of Ancient Republics

2 Minos founded the primitive government of Crete. Zaleucus founded Locrians. Theseus, then Draco and Solon, instituted the government of Athens. Lycurgus was the lawgiver of Sparta.

The foundation of the original Roman government was laid by Romulus. The work was completed by two of his elective successors, Numa and Tulius Hostilius. Brutus abolished royalty, substituting a reform that he said was prepared by Tulius Hostilius. It obtained the assent and ratification of the senate and people.

The same applied to confederate governments, too. Amphictyon, we are told, was the author of that which bore his name. The Achaean league received its first birth from Achaeus and its second from Aratus.

Some Governmental Architects Authorized by Citizens

3 To what degree these lawgivers were responsible for their respective governments, or how much legitimate authority they had from the people, cannot be verified in every instance. In some, however, the proceeding was strictly regular.

The people of Athens apparently entrusted Draco with unlimited power to reform its government and laws. And Plutarch says Solon was given, by the universal vote of his fellow-citizens, the absolute power of remodeling the constitution.

The proceedings under Lycurgus of Sparta were less regular. The advocates for regular reform, rather than seeking revolution through the intervention of a deliberative body of citizens, turned their eyes towards the single efforts of that celebrated patriot and sage.

Protection of Liberty vs. Reforms

4 How did it happen that a people as jealous of their liberty as the Greeks abandoned the rules of caution and placed their destiny in the hands of a single citizen?

To protect their liberty, the citizens of Athens demanded that a minimum of ten generals command an army. And they felt the illustrious merit of a fellow-citizen was a danger to their liberties. So why did they place their fortunes and their posterity in the hands of one illustrious citizen rather than a selected group of citizens from whose common deliberation more wisdom, as well as safety, might have been expected?

We must assume that the fears of discord and disunion exceeded the apprehension of treachery or incapacity in a single individual. Additionally, history shows the difficulties these celebrated reformers confronted and the expedients necessary to put their reforms into effect.

Solon, who apparently authored a compromise policy, confessed he had not given his countrymen the government best suited to their happiness, but most tolerable to their prejudices. And Lycurgus, more true to his objective, mixed some violence with the authority of superstition, then voluntarily renounced his country, then his life, to secure his final success.

If these lessons teach us, on the one hand, to admire America's improvement on the ancient mode of preparing and establishing a constitutional government, they also admonish us, on the other hand, about the hazards and difficulties inherent to such experiments and the great imprudence of unnecessarily multiplying them.

U.S. Constitution Unique

5   Is it unreasonable to suggest that the errors that may be in the new Constitution have resulted from a lack of historical experience on this complicated and difficult subject, rather than from a lack of accuracy or care in researching the subject? And consequently, the errors will not be found until actual trial points them out?

Both logical reasoning and our experience with the Articles of Confederation render these conjectures probable. Remember that of all the numerous objections and amendments suggested by States during the ratification process [Articles of Confederation], not one alluded to the great and radical error that actual trial uncovered. And if we leave out the observations made by New Jersey, made because of her local situation not through keen foresight, it may be asked whether any single suggestion was important enough to justify a revision of the system.

Nevertheless, there is abundant reason to believe that, although the objections were immaterial, some States would have adhered to them with a very dangerous inflexibility if their zeal for their opinions and interests had not been stifled by the more powerful sentiment of self-preservation. Although the enemy remained at our gates or, rather, in the very bowels of our country, remember that one State refused her concurrence for several years. Her pliancy, in the end, was the result of the fear of being charged with protracting the public calamities and endangering the outcome of the war. Every candid reader will make the proper reflections on these important facts.

Medical Allegory

6   Let's study the case of a person who grows sicker daily until he decides that he cannot postpone an efficacious remedy without extreme danger. After coolly evaluating his situation and the reputations of different physicians, he selects and calls in those who he judges most capable of administering relief and best entitled to his confidence. The physicians arrive. The patient is carefully examined. The doctors consult. They unanimously agree that the symptoms are critical but that the case, with proper and timely care, is far from being desperate and may even result in an improvement of his health. They also unanimously agree on the prescribed remedy that will produce this happy effect.

The prescription is no sooner made known, however, than a number of persons interpose and, without denying the reality or danger of the disorder, tell the patient that the prescription will poison him and forbid him, under pain of certain death, to make use of it. Might not the patient reasonably demand, before he followed this second advice, that they should at least agree among themselves on some other remedy to be substituted? And if he found them differing as much from one another as from his first doctors, would he not act prudently in trying the experiment unanimously recommended by the first physicians, rather than listen to the people who neither deny the necessity of a speedy remedy nor agree in proposing one?

Criticisms: Irreconcilable Variety

7 This patient mirrors America's current situation. She realizes her malady. She has obtained unanimous advice from men of her own deliberate choice. Then others warn her against following this advice under the pain of fatal consequences.

Do the new monitors deny the reality of the danger? No.

Do they deny the necessity of some speedy and powerful remedy? No.

Are they agreed, do any <u>two</u> of them agree on what is wrong with the proposed remedy or the proper substitution? Let them speak for themselves: One tells us the proposed Constitution should be rejected because it's **not a confederation of the States, but a government over individuals.**

Another admits it should be a government over individuals to a certain extent, but **not to the extent proposed.**

A third doesn't object to the government over individuals, even to the extent proposed, but wants a **bill of rights.**

A fourth concurs in the absolute necessity of a bill of rights but contend that it should be declaratory, not of the personal rights of individuals, but the **rights reserved to the States** in their political capacity.

A fifth believe that a bill of rights of any sort would be superfluous and misplace, and that the constitution wouldn't be criticized but for the fatal power of **regulating the times and places of election.**

An objector from a large State exclaims loudly against the unreasonable **equality** of representation in the **Senate.** An objector from a small State is equally loud against the dangerous **inequality** in the **House of Representatives.**

This quarter is alarmed with the **amazing expense** arising from the number of persons who are to administer the new government. From another quarter, and sometimes from the same quarter on another occasion, the cry is that Congress will only be a shadow of a representation and that the government would be far **less objectionable if** the number and the **expense were doubled.**

A patriot in a State that doesn't import or export discerns insuperable objections against the power of **direct taxation.** The patriotic adversary in a State of great exports and imports is not less dissatisfied that the whole burden of **taxes** may he thrown **on consumption.**

This politician discovers in the Constitution a direct and irresistible **tendency to monarchy.** That one is equally sure it will end in **aristocracy.** Another is puzzled over which of these shapes it will ultimately assume, but sees clearly it must be one or the other.

A fourth is no less confident that the Constitution is so far from having a bias towards either of these dangers that the weight on that side will not be sufficient to keep it upright and firm against its **opposite propensities.**

Another class of adversaries to the Constitution say the **intertwining of legislative, executive, and judiciary** departments contradicts all the ideas of regular government and all the requisite precautions in favor of liberty. While this objection circulates in vague and general expressions, only a few people sanction it.

Two people rarely agree on a specific objection.

In the eyes of one, having the Senate with the president jointly responsible for **appointing to offices** instead of vesting this executive power in the Executive alone, is the vicious part of the Constitution. To another, the exclusion of the House of Representatives, whose numbers alone could provide security against corruption and partiality in the exercise of such a power, is equally obnoxious.

With another, giving the **President** any **power** is always dangerous and an unpardonable violation of the maxims of republican jealousy.

No part of the arrangement, according to some, is more inadmissible than the **trial of impeachments** by the Senate, which alternates between the legislative and executive departments, when this power so clearly belongs to the judiciary.

"We concur fully," reply others, "in the objection to this part of the Constitution, but we can never agree that referring impeachments to the **judiciary** would amend the error. Our principal objection arises from the **extensive powers** already lodged in that department.

Even the zealous patrons of a **council of state** cannot agree on how it should be constituted. One gentleman demands that the council should consist of a small number, appointed by the most numerous branch of the legislature. Another prefers a large number and considers it a fundamental condition that the appointment should be made by the President himself.

Critics Can't Agree

8   Let's look at the situation from a different perspective. Since it can't offend the critics of the proposed federal Constitution, let us assume that their zealousness is matched with sagacity, making them the most discerning and farsighted of the people who think the delegates to the recent convention were not up to the task assigned them and a wiser and better constitution might and should be substituted.

Let us further assume that the country concurs, both in the favorable opinion of their qualifications to judge the issues and in their unfavorable opinion of the convention. And the country forms them into a second convention with full powers and for the express purpose of revising and remolding the work of the first.

If the experiment was seriously tried, although it requires some effort to view it seriously even in fiction, I leave it to you to decide, from the sample of opinions just stated and the enmity they've shown towards their predecessors, whether they would ever depart from the discord and ferment that would mark their own deliberations. Wouldn't the currently proposed Constitution stand as fair a chance of immortality—as Lycurgus gave to Sparta's constitution by making its change depend on his own return from exile and death—if the United States immediately adopted this Constitution and let it continue in force, not until a BETTER but until ANOTHER is agreed upon by this new assembly of lawgivers?

Constitution Better than Articles

9   It is a matter both of wonder and regret that those who raise so many objections against the new Constitution never call to mind the defects of that which is to be exchanged for it. It is

not necessary that the new Constitution is perfect; it is sufficient that the Articles of Confederation are more imperfect.

No man would refuse to exchange brass for silver or gold, because the latter had some alloy in it. No man would refuse to leave a shattered, tottering habitation for a firm, commodious building because the latter had no porch, or because some of the rooms might be a little larger or smaller, or the ceiling a little higher or lower than his fancy would have planned them.

But waiving illustrations of this sort, isn't it clear that the primary objections against the new system lie with tenfold weight against the existing Confederation?

Is an **indefinite power to raise money** dangerous in the hand of the federal government? The present Congress can make requisitions of any amount they please and the States are constitutionally bound to furnish them. It can emit bills of credit as long as it can pay for the paper. It can borrow both abroad and at home as long as a shilling will be lent.

Is an indefinite power to **raise troops** dangerous? The Confederation also gives Congress that power and it has already begun to make use of it.

Is it improper and unsafe to **intermix** the different **powers** of government in the same body of men? Currently Congress, a single body of men, is the sole depository of all the federal powers.

Is it particularly dangerous to give the keys of the **treasury and** command of the **army** into the same hands? The Confederation places them both in the hands of Congress.

Is a **bill of rights** essential to liberty? The Confederation has no bill of rights.

Is there an objection because the new Constitution empowers the Senate with the concurrence of the President to make **treaties** that **are** to be the **laws** of the land? Without any such control the existing Congress can make treaties that it declares and most States recognize as the supreme law of the land.

Is the **importation of slaves** permitted by the new Constitution for 20 years? By the old, it is permitted forever.

Congress Wielding Great, But Not Authorized, Powers

10 I will be told that however dangerous the Confederation's mixture of powers may be in theory, it is rendered harmless because Congress is dependent on the States for the means of carrying them into practice, that however large the mass of power may be, it is in fact a lifeless mass.

Then, say I, the Confederation can be charged with the greater folly of declaring certain powers in the federal government to be absolutely necessary and, at the same time, render them absolutely worthless. And if the Union is to continue with no better government substituted, effective powers must either be granted to, or assumed by, the existing Congress. In either event, the contrast will continue.

But this is not all. An excessive increase in power has already grown out of this lifeless mass. All the dangers from a defective construction of the supreme government of the Union seem to be realized.

It is no longer speculation and hope that the Western territory is a mine of vast wealth to the United States. It won't produce the kind of wealth that could extricate the States from present problems or yield any regular revenue for public expenses for some time to come. But, eventually, under proper management, it will be able to both gradually discharge the domestic public debt and furnish, for a certain period, liberal tributes to the federal treasury. A very large proportion of this fund has been already surrendered by individual States. And we may expect the remaining States will not continue to withhold similar proofs of their equity and generosity.

Therefore, we can calculate that a rich, fertile territory, equal in size to the inhabited area of the United States, will soon become part of the nation. Congress has assumed its administration. It has begun to make it productive. Congress has undertaken to do more, forming new States, erecting temporary governments, appointing officers for them, and prescribing the condition by which the States will be admitted into the Confederacy.

All this has been done, and done without the least constitutional authority. Yet no blame has been whispered; no alarm has been sounded.

A GREAT AND INDEPENDENT fund of revenue is passing into the hands of a SINGLE BODY of men, who can RAISE TROOPS to an INDEFINITE NUMBER, and appropriate money to support them for an INDEFINITE PERIOD OF TIME. Yet there are men who have not only been silent spectators of this, but who advocate for this system while, at the same time, urging against the new system using the objections presented here. Wouldn't they be more consistent to urge the adoption of the new Constitution as no less necessary to guard the Union against future powers and resources of a body constructed like the existing Congress, than to save it from the dangers threatened by the present impotency of that Assembly?

Must Have Powers to Achieve Objectives

11 I don't mean, by anything said here, to throw censure on the measures pursued by Congress. I know they could not have done otherwise. The public interest, the necessity of the case, imposed upon them the task of overlapping their constitutional limits. But is not this fact an alarming proof of the danger resulting from a government that doesn't possess regular powers commensurate to its objectives? A dissolution or usurpation is the dreadful dilemma to which it is continually exposed.

PUBLIUS

Constitutional references:

Article 1, sect 4	85-90	elections, times and places
Article 1, sect 3	42-44	equal representation in Senate
Article 5	540-542	equal representation in Senate
Article 1, sect 2	16-35	unequal representation in House of Representatives
Article 1, sect 8	171-173	taxation
Article 2, sect 2	395-413	President appoints with advice, consent of Senate
Article 1, sect 3	71-72	Senate sole power to try impeachments
Article 1, sect 8	207-212	raise troops
Article 2, sect 2	392-395	President makes treaties with Senate
Article 1, sect 8	238-244	end slave importation in 20 years

Articles of Confederation:

Article 8, Article 9	States' tax quotas
Article 9	raise troops
Article 5	one Congress administers government

Number 39

National vs. Federal Republic

The last paper concluded the introductory observations. We will now proceed to a candid study of the proposed Constitution

Is Proposed Government Republic?

2 The first question is whether the general form and appearance of the proposed government is strictly republican.

Clearly, no other form would be reconcilable with the nature of the American people, with the fundamental principles of the Revolution, or with that honorable purpose—to base our political experiment on the ability for self-government—that animates every ardent advocate of freedom.

Therefore, if the Constitution is discovered to not be of the republican form, its advocates must abandon it because it is no longer defensible.

Erroneously Called "Republics"

3 What are the distinctive characteristics of the republican form of government? We must seek the answer in defined principles. If we looked for the answer by studying the interpretations of political writers as contained in the constitutions of different countries, no satisfactory one would ever be found.

Holland, where none of the supreme authority is derived from the people, is almost universally called a republic. So is Venice, where absolute power over the people is exercised by a small group of hereditary nobles. Poland, a mixture of aristocracy and monarchy in their worst forms, has been dignified with the same name.

The government of England, with only one republican branch combined with an hereditary aristocracy and a monarch, has been, with equal impropriety, frequently placed on the list of republics.

These examples, which are nearly as dissimilar to each other as to a genuine republic, show the extreme inaccuracy with which the term has been used in political discussions.

Republic = *All* Power From People

4 If we look at the principles used to establish different forms of government for a criterion, we may define a republic, or give that name to, a government that derives all its powers directly or indirectly from the people and is administered by persons holding their offices—through election or appointment—at the people's pleasure for a limited period or during good behavior.

It is *essential* that a republican government spring from the great body of society, not from a small proportion or a favored class. Otherwise, a few tyrannical nobles, exercising their oppressions by a delegation of their powers, might call themselves republicans and claim for their government the honorable title of republic.

It is *sufficient* that the persons administering such a government are appointed, either directly or indirectly, by the people and that they hold their appointments by either of the tenures just specified.

Otherwise, every government in the United States and every well-organized or well-executed popular government could be called a republic, degrading the term.

According to the constitution of every State, one or another of the officers of government are only appointed indirectly by the people. In most of them, the chief magistrate [executive] is so appointed. In one, this mode of appointment extends to one of the houses of the legislature.

According to all the constitutions, the tenure of the highest offices is extended to a definite period. And in many instances, the legislative and executive department tenures are a specified period of years. Most of the constitutions, and most respectable opinions on the subject, state that members of the judiciary department retain their offices by the firm tenure of good behavior.

Constitution: Republic Form

5   On comparing the Constitution with the republican form as described here, we immediately see it conforms in the most rigid sense. The House of Representatives, like at least one branch of each State legislature, is elected directly by the great body of the people. The Senate, like the present Congress and the Senate of Maryland, derives its appointment indirectly from the people. The President is indirectly elected by the people, like the example in most of the States. As in the States, even the judges, and all other officers of the Union, will be the choice, though a remote choice, of the people.

The duration of appointments also conforms to the republican standard and the model of State constitutions. The House of Representatives is periodically elected, as in all the States, and for the period of two years, as in South Carolina. The Senate is elected for the period of six years, only one year more than the Mary-

land senate and two more than the senates of New York and Virginia.

The President is to continue in office for the period of four years. In New York and Delaware, the chief magistrate is elected for three years, and in South Carolina for two years. The other States have annual elections. Several States, however, have no constitutional provision for impeachment of the chief magistrate. And in Delaware and Virginia he is not impeachable until out of office. The President of the United States is impeachable at any time during his continuance in office.

The tenure of judges is based on good behavior, as it unquestionably should be.

The tenure of the ministerial offices, generally, will be a subject of legal regulation, conforming to the reason of the case and the example of the State constitutions.

Prohibition of Nobility Titles

6   If further proof is required of the republican complexion of this system, the most decisive might be its absolute prohibition of titles of nobility under both the federal and State governments, and its express guarantee of the republican form.

Convention's Authority, Objective

7   "But it was not sufficient," say the adversaries of the proposed Constitution, "for the convention to adhere to the republican form. They should have preserved, with equal care, the *federal* form, which regards the Union as a *Confederacy* of sovereign States. Instead, they have framed a *national* government, which regards the Union as a *consolidation* of the States.

And they ask, by what authority was this bold and radical innovation undertaken? This objection requires some precise examination.

Analyzing Convention's Work

8 Without looking into whether their distinction between a federal and national government is accurate, their objection should be assessed. We need to:
1. determine the real character of the proposed government,
2. inquire whether the convention was authorized to propose such a government,
3. determine how far duty to their country replaced their lack of regular authority.

Character of Proposed Government

9 *First.* The real character of the government may be determined through studying:

the **foundation** on which the government is to be established,

the **sources** of its ordinary powers,

the **operation** of those powers,

the **extent** of the government's powers, and

the **authority** by which future changes in the government are to be introduced.

Foundation

10 It appears that the Constitution is founded on the assent and ratification of the American people through deputies elected for the special service. This assent and ratification is not to be given by individuals composing one entire nation, but as composing distinct, independent States to which they respectively belong. The States are to assent and ratify, based on the authority of the people. Therefore, ratifying the Constitution will be a *federal,* not a *national,* act.

Ratification: Federal Form

11 As defined by the people objecting to the Constitution, this will be a federal and not a national act. The people act as citizens of independent States, not as citizens of one aggregate nation. This is obvious because the decision isn't made by a *majority* of the people nor by a *majority* of the States.

The States must *unanimously* ratify the Constitution, not by the legislative authority but by the authority of the people themselves. If in this transaction the people were regarded as forming one nation, the will of the majority of all people of the United States would bind the minority, in the same way that the majority in each State must bind the minority. Determining the will of the majority means either a majority of individual votes or a majority of States as evidence of the will of a majority of the people of the United States. Neither of these rules has been adopted.

Each State, in ratifying the Constitution, is considered a sovereign body, independent of all others, and bound only by its own voluntary act. In its **foundation**, then, the new Constitution will be, if established, a *federal*, not a *national*, constitution.

Power Source:
Federal, National Features

12 Next we'll look at the source of the ordinary powers of government. [Do the people (national) or the States (federal) elect/appoint officials?]

The House of Representatives will derive its powers from the American people. The people will be represented in the same proportion and on the same principle as they are in the legislature of each State. In this, the government is *national,* not *federal.*

The Senate, on the other hand, will derive its powers from the States as political, coequal societies. These will be represented on the principle of equality in the Senate, as they are in the existing Congress. In this, the government is *federal,* not *national.*

The executive power will derive from a compound source. The final election of the President is to be made by the States as political units. Their allotted votes are based on a compound ratio, considering each partly as distinct, coequal societies, and partly as unequal members of the same society. The eventual election, again, is made by that branch of the legislature consisting of national representatives but, in this particular act, they are thrown into the form of individual delegations, from so many distinct, coequal political bodies.

As to its **source of powers**, the government appears to be of mixed character, presenting at least as many *federal* as *national* features.

Operation: National Form

13 Adversaries to the proposed Constitution define the difference between a federal and national government, as it relates to the **operation of the government**, as this:

A federal government operates on the political bodies [States] composing the Confederacy. A national government operates on the individual citizens composing the nation.

Following this criteria, the Constitution falls under a *national,* not *federal,* character, but perhaps not as completely as has been believed. In several cases, particularly in the trial of controversies between States, States must be viewed in their collective, political capacities only.

The **operation of the government** on individual citizens in ordinary and the most essential proceedings will designate it, in this relation, a *national* government.

Extent of Powers: Federal Form

14 But if the government is national in the *operation* of its powers, it changes its aspect again when we contemplate the **extent of its powers**.

The concept of a national government involves not only an authority over the individual citizens, but an indefinite supremacy over all persons, things, and issues that can be objects of lawful government.

When people consolidate into one nation, supremacy is completely vested in the national legislature. When communities unite for particular purposes, some supremacy is vested in the united body and some in the local legislatures.

In the former case, all local authorities are subordinate to a national legislature that can control, direct, or abolish local authority at its pleasure.

In the latter, local or municipal authorities form distinct, independent portions of the supremacy. These are no more subject, within their sphere, to the federal authority than the federal authority is subject to them within its own sphere.

In the **extent of its powers**, the proposed government cannot be deemed a national one, since its jurisdiction extends to specific, enumerate objectives only, leaving to the States a residuary and inviolable sovereignty over all other issues.

Controversies relating to the boundary between two jurisdictions will ultimately be decided by a tribunal established under the federal government. But this doesn't change the principle. The decision is to be impartial, according to the rules of the Constitution. The usual, most effective precautions are taken to insure this impartiality. Such a tribunal is clearly essential to prevent an appeal to the sword and a dissolution of the compact. That it will be more safely established under the national, rather than local, governments, is a position few would argue with.

Amending:
Federal, National Features

15 If we evaluate the Constitution in relation to the authority to **amend** it, we find it neither totally *national* nor totally *federal.*

If it was totally national, the supreme, ultimate authority would reside in the *majority* of the people of the Union. This authority at any time, like the majority of every national society, could alter or abolish the established government.

If it were totally federal, on the other hand, the concurrence of every State in the Union would be essential for every amendment that would be binding on all.

The mode provided in the Constitution is not founded on either of these principles. By requiring more than a majority, and particularly in computing the proportion by *States,* not by *citizens*, it departs from the *national* and advances towards the *federal* character. By requiring the concurrence of less than the total number of States, it becomes less *federal* and more of the *national* character.

Neither Strictly National or Federal

16 Therefore, the proposed Constitution is, strictly, neither a national nor federal Constitution, but a composition of both.

Its **foundation** is federal, not national.

Its **source** of ordinary governmental powers is partly federal and partly national.

In the **operation** of these powers, it is national, not federal.

In the **extent** of these powers, it is federal, not national.

And, finally, the authoritative mode of introducing **amendments** is neither wholly federal nor wholly national.

PUBLIUS

Constitutional References:

Article 1, section 2	5-10	House of Representatives elected directly by people, 2-year term
Article 1, section 3	42-44	Senate elected indirectly by people, 6-year term
Article 2, section 1	305-345	President elected indirectly by people, 4-year term
Article 2, section 2	395-408	judges, officers, "remote" choice of people
Article 2, section 4	429-433	President impeachable
Article 3, section 1	438-440	judges tenure during good behavior
Article 4, section 4	518-520	republican form of government in States
Article 1, section 9	265-266	federal prohibition nobility titles
Article 1, section 10	278-279	State prohibition nobility titles
Article 7	565-568	ratification of Constitution
Article 3, section 2	451-457	trials involving more than one State
Article 5	525-542	amendment process
Article 6	548-555	supreme law of the land

Number 40

Was Convention Authorized to Draft Constitution?

[This paper continues the discussion started in Number 39, paragraph 8.]

The *second* point to be examined is whether the convention was authorized to frame and propose this mixed [both national and federal form, as discussed in #39] Constitution.

Convention's Mission Defined

2 In strictness, the convention's powers should be determined through inspecting the commissions given the individual members by their constituents. However, since they all referred to either the September 1786 meeting at Annapolis or the February 1787 congressional meeting, it will be sufficient to reiterate these particular acts.

Annapolis Meeting, Sept. 1786

3 The act from Annapolis recommends the "appointment of commissioners to take into consideration the situation of the United States; to devise *such further provisions* as shall appear to them necessary to render the Constitution of the federal government *adequate to the exigencies of the Union;* and to report such an act for that purpose to the United States in Congress assembled, as when agreed to by them, and afterwards confirmed by the legislature of every State, will effectually provide for the same."

Congress Recommends, Feb. 1787

4 The recommendatory act of Congress is in the following words: "Whereas there is provision in the Articles of Confederation and perpetual Union for making alterations therein, by the assent of Congress of the United States and the legislatures of the several States; and whereas experience has evinced that there are de-fects in the present Confederation; as a means to remedy which, several States, and *particularly the State of New York,* by express instructions to their delegates in Congress, have suggested a convention for the purposes expressed in the following resolution; and such convention appearing to be the most probable means of establishing in these States a *firm national government*:

Resolution to Revise Articles

5 "*Resolved,*—That in the opinion of Congress it is expedient that on the second Monday in May next a convention of delegates, who shall have been appointed by the several States, be held at Philadelphia for the sole and express purpose *of revising the Articles of Confederation,* and reporting to Congress and all the legislatures the *alterations and provisions therein* as shall, when agreed to in Congress and confirmed by the States, render the federal Constitution *adequate to meet the exigencies of government and the preservation of the Union*"

Convention's Objectives/Tasks

6 From these two acts, it appears that:
1. the objective of the convention was to establish *a firm national government,*
2. that this government was to be *adequate for the needs of the government* and the *preservation of the Union,*
3. these goals were to be met through *alterations and provisions in the Articles of Confederation,* as expressed in the act of Congress, or by *such further provision as should appear necessary,* as recommended in the act from Annapolis, and

4. that the alterations and provisions were to be reported to Congress and to the States, in order to be agreed to by the former and confirmed by the latter.

Convention's Charge

7 The authority under which the convention acted can be summarized as follows:

They were to frame a *national government,* adequate to the *exigencies of government* and *of the Union,* and to reduce the Articles of Confederation into a form to accomplish these purposes.

When Goals Conflict: Sacrifice Less Important

8 There are two rules of construction, dictated by plain reason and founded on legal axioms.

First, every part of the expression ought, if possible, have some meaning and made to conspire to some common end.

Secondly, where the several parts can't be combined, the less important should give way to the more important part. The means should be sacrificed to the end, rather than the end to the means.

Change Articles vs. New Constitution

9 Suppose that the specific goals in the mission statement of the convention were irreconcilably at variance with each other, that a "*national . . . [and] adequate government*" could not possibly be accomplished, in the judgment of the convention, by "*alterations* and *provisions* in the *Articles of Confederation.*"

Which part should be embraced and which rejected? Which is more important, which less important? Which end? Which means?

Let those people who can most precisely delineate the delegated powers and the most adamant objectors against the actions of the convention answer these questions. Let them declare whether it was more important for the happiness of the people of America to disregard the Articles of Confederation in order to provide an adequate government and preserve the Union. Or should the adequate government be omitted and the Articles of Confederation preserved.

Let them declare whether the purpose of government reform was to preserve the Articles, themselves originally aimed to establish a government adequate to the national happiness, or whether the Articles, proven insufficient, ought to be sacrificed so an adequate government can be established.

Maybe Goals Are Not Irreconcilable

10 But must we suppose that these goals are absolutely irreconcilable, that no *alterations* or *provisions* in the *Articles of the Confederation* could possibly mold them into a national and adequate government, into a government as has been proposed by the convention?

Alteration vs. Transmutation of Gov't

11 It is presumed that there is no objection to the *title*. A change of title couldn't be deemed an exercise of ungranted power.

Alterations in the body of the instrument are expressly authorized. *New provisions* are also authorized.

Therefore, the convention had the power to change the title, insert new articles, and alter old ones.

Is this power infringed as long as a part of the old Articles remain? Those who say yes should specify the boundary between authorized and usurped innovations. What degree of change falls within the definitions of *alterations and further provisions*, and what amounts to a *transmutation* of the government?

Will it be said that the substance of the Confederation should not have been altered? The States would never have so solemnly appointed a convention nor described its objectives with so much latitude, if some *substantial* reform had not been contemplated.

Will it be said that the **fundamental principles of the Confederation** were not within the purview of the convention and should not have been changed? I ask, what are these principles?

Do they require that, in establishing the Constitution, the States should be regarded as distinct and independent sovereigns? That is how the proposed Constitution regards them.

Must federal representatives be appointed from the legislatures, not from the people of the States? One branch of the new government is to be appointed by these legislatures; under the Confederacy, the delegates to Congress *may all* be appointed immediately by the people and in two States, Connecticut and Rhode Island, are actually so appointed.

Do they require that government power act on States rather than individuals? It has been shown that sometimes the new government will act on the States in their collective characters. In some instances, the existing government acts on individuals, including in cases of capture, piracy, the post office, coins, weights, measures, trade with the Indians, claims under grants of land by different States, and, above all, in the case of trials by courts-martial in the army and navy that may result in the death penalty without the intervention of a jury or even a civil magistrate. In all these cases the powers of the Confederation operate immediately on the persons and interests of individual citizens.

Do these fundamental principles require, specifically, that no tax should be levied without the intermediate agency of the States? The Confederation itself authorizes a direct tax, to a certain extent, on the post office. Congress has construed the power of coinage as a levy.

But putting aside these examples, wasn't it an objective of the convention, and the universal expectation of the people, that the national government would regulate trade so it would be an immediate source of general revenue? Hasn't Congress repeatedly recommended that this measure is consistent with the fundamental principles of the Confederacy? Hasn't every State but one, even New York, complied with the plan of Congress, recognizing the *principle* of the innovation?

Do these principles require that the federal government's powers should be limited and that, beyond this limit, the States should be left in possession of their sovereign and independent jurisdiction? We have seen that in the new government, as in the old, the general powers are limited and the States, in all unenumerated cases, have sovereign, independent jurisdiction.

Constitution Expands Principles

12 The truth is, the important principles of the convention's proposed Constitution are not absolutely new, rather they expand the principles found in the Articles of Confederation. Unfortunately, under the Articles these principles are so feeble and confined as to justify all the charges of inefficiency that have been leveled against it. And the Articles required such a degree of enlargement that it entirely transforms the old system into one that appears new.

Ratification Process Changed

13 In one area, the convention did depart from the tenor of their commission. Instead of reporting a plan requiring the confirmation *of all the States,* they have reported a plan that is to be confirmed and carried into effect by *nine States only.*

It is noteworthy that this is the source of the most plausible objection, but has been the least mentioned in the swarm of writings against the convention. The forbearance can only be the result of an irresistible conviction of the absurdity of subjecting the fate of twelve States to the perverseness or corruption of the thirteenth.

We have had an example of inflexible opposition given by a *majority* of the 1/60 of the American population to a measure approved and called for by the voice of twelve States, comprising 59/60s of the people—an example still fresh in the memory and indignation of every citizen who has felt for the wounded honor and prosperity of his country.

Therefore, since this objection seems to have been waived by those who criticize the powers of the convention, I dismiss it without further observation.

Authority Supplanted by Duty

14 The *third* point to be inquired into is, how far considerations of duty arising out of the case itself could have supplied any defect of regular authority.

Plan Only "Recommended"

15 Up to this point, the convention's work has been rigorously analyzed as if it had the authority to establish a Constitution for the United States. And it has withstood this scrutiny.

Now, it's time to remember that the convention was only authorized to advise and recommend. That is what the States meant and the convention understood. And, accordingly, the convention proposed a Constitution that is nothing more than pieces of paper, unless it is stamped with the approval of the people to whom it is addressed. This puts the subject into an altogether different view and will enable us to properly judge the course taken by the convention.

Convention Delegates: Considerations

16 Let us review the ground on which the convention stood. From the notes of their proceedings, it appears that they were so deeply and unanimously concerned with the crisis within their country that almost with one voice they created the singular and solemn document for correcting the errors of the system that produced this crisis. They were deeply and unanimously convinced that the reform they have proposed was absolutely necessary to accomplish the goals for which the convention was convened.

They knew that the hopes and expectations of the citizens throughout this great empire watched their deliberations with keen anxiety.

Delegates had every reason to believe that contrary sentiments agitated the minds and hearts of every external and internal foe to the liberty and prosperity of the United States

They had seen how quickly a *proposition* for a partial amendment of the Confederacy, made by the State of Virginia, was studied and promoted. They watched the Annapolis convention, with *very few* deputies from a *very few* of the States, *assume liberty* and recommend a great a critical objective, completely foreign to their commission, not only justified by the public opinion, but actually carried into effect by twelve of the thirteen States.

Several times, they had seen Congress assume, not just recommendations, but operative powers, to achieve objectives that, in the public's mind, are infinitely less urgent than those faced by the convention.

Members of the constitutional convention must have realized that whenever great changes are made in established governments, form must give way to substance. Rigid adherence to the form would make the people's transcendent and precious right to "abolish or alter their governments as to them shall seem most likely to effect their safety and happiness"* nearly impossible because people don't spontaneously and universally move in concert towards their objectives. Therefore, it is essential that such changes be instituted by some *informal and unauthorized propositions* made by some patriotic, respectable citizen or number of citizens.

Delegates must have remembered that the States first united against danger threatened by their ancient government because of this assumed privilege—that people could plan for their safety and happiness. Committees and congresses concentrated their efforts, defending their rights. *Conventions* were *elected* in the *States* for establishing the constitutions under which they are now governed. Delegates could not have forgotten that no scruples or zeal for adhering to ordinary forms were seen, except from those who wished to indulge, under masks, their secret enmity towards their goal.

_____
* Declaration of Independence

As they formed this new plan, delegates knew that, once framed, it would be submitted *to the people themselves*. They knew that if the people, the supreme authority, rejected the plan, it would be destroyed forever. Likewise, approval by the people blots out antecedent errors and irregularities.

The delegates might even have realized that once trivial objections were settled, whether they executed the amount of power vested in them or whether they recommended measures not a part of their commission, would not particularly face criticism, particularly if their recommendation met to the national exigencies.

Judging the Delegates

17 Keeping in mind these considerations, if the convention hadn't had the confidence in their country to point out a system they judged capable of securing its happiness, if they had coldly decided to disappoint the country's ardent hopes and sacrificed substance to form, thereby committing the dearest interest of their country to the uncertainties of delay and the hazard of events, let me ask the rational patriot— what judgment should the impartial world, the friends of mankind, every virtuous citizen, pronounce on the conduct and character of this assembly?

Or, if there is a man whose propensity to condemn is not susceptible to control, let me ask what punishment he has in reserve for the twelve States who *usurped power* by sending deputies to the convention, an action no where mentioned in their constitutions, for Congress, who recommended the appointment of this body, equally unknown to the Confederation, and for the State of New York, in particular, which first urged and then complied with this unauthorized interposition?

Source of Advice Unimportant

18 To disarm the objectors of every pretext, let's agree for a moment that the convention was neither authorized by their commission nor justified by circumstances to propose a Constitution for their country. Does it follow that the Constitution ought, for that reason alone, to be rejected?

If, according to some noble precept, it is lawful to accept good advice even from an enemy, shall we set the ignoble example of refusing such advice even when it is offered by our friends?

In all cases, the prudent inquiry shouldn't be *from whom* the advice comes but whether the advice is *good.*

Convention Didn't Exceed Authority

19 We have proved here that the charge against the convention, that it exceeded its power—except its change of the ratification process, a point rarely mentioned by the objectors—has no foundation.

And if they did exceed their powers, they were not only warranted, but required, as the confidential servants of their country, by the circumstances in which they were placed, exercising the liberty they assumed.

And finally, even if they violated both their powers and their obligations in proposing a Constitution, it ought, nevertheless, to be embraced, if it appears to accomplish the views and promote the happiness of the people of America. How far this properly characterizes the Constitution, is the subject under investigation.

PUBLIUS

Articles of Confederation:

Article 13	provision for altering Articles of Confederation
Article 2	States retain sovereignty
Article 5	congressional delegates appointed by State legislatures
Article 9	direct tax: postage

Constitutional reference:

Article 1, Section 3	42-44	Senators elected by State legislatures
Article 7	565-568	ratification process

Number 41

Constitutionally Vested Federal Powers

The Constitution proposed by the convention may be considered from two general points of view.

FIRST: quantity of power it vests in the federal government, including the restraints on the States

SECOND: structure of the government and distribution of this power among its branches.

Federal Power

2 Regarding federal powers, two important questions arise:

1. Are any of the powers transferred to the federal government unnecessary or improper?

2. Are the combined federal powers dangerous to those left to State jurisdictions?

Is Federal Power Too Extensive?

3 Is the federal government's total power greater than should be vested in it? This is the *first* question.

Are Federal Powers Necessary?

4 Everyone aware of the arguments against the extensive powers of the government must have noticed that the people who object to the new Constitution rarely consider whether these powers are necessary to attain a necessary end. Instead they dwell on the inconveniences that must, unavoidably, be blended with political advantages, and the possible abuses that may result from that power or trust.

The American people won't be fooled by this method of handling the subject. It may show the subtlety of the writer. It may open a boundless field for rhetoric and declamation. It may inflame the passions of the unthinking and confirm the prejudice of the misthinking. But cool and candid people will immediately reflect that even the purest of human blessings are part alloy. The choice must always be made, if not of the lesser evil, at least of the GREATER, not the PERFECT, good.

In every political institution, a power to advance the public happiness involves a discretion that may be misapplied and abused. Therefore, whenever power is to be conferred, it must first be decided whether such a power is necessary for the public good.

If the Constitution is ratified, the next point will be to effectually guard against the misuse of power to the public detriment.

Six Categories of Federal Power

5 To form a correct judgment on this subject, we will review the powers conferred on the federal government. As a convenience, they can be reduced into different classes as they relate to the following different issues:

1. Security against foreign danger.

2. Regulate intercourse with foreign nations.

3. Maintain harmony and intercourse in the States.

4. Miscellaneous objects of general utility.

5. Restraint of the States from certain injurious acts.

6. Provisions giving efficacy to these powers.

1. Security Against Foreign Danger

6   The powers within the *first* class are: declaring war and granting letters of marque, providing armies and fleets regulating and calling forth the militia, levying and borrowing money.

Primary Objective of Civil Society

7   Security against foreign danger is one of the primary objectives of civil society. It is an avowed and essential objective of the American Union. Federal councils must be entrusted with the powers required for attaining it.

Declare War

8   Is the power to declare war necessary? No man will answer this question in the negative. It would be superfluous, therefore, to enter into a proof of the affirmative. The existing Confederation established this power.

Military

9   Is the power of raising armies and equipping fleets necessary? This is part of the previous power and involves the power of self-defense.

Power to Raise Armies

10   But was an INDEFINTE POWER of raising TROOPS, as well as providing fleets necessary? Of maintaining both in PEACE as well as in war?

Defense Must Equal Possible Offense

11   These questions have been too thoroughly discussed in another place to extensively discuss them here. The answer, indeed, seems so obvious and conclusive as scarcely to justify such a discussion in any place.

What justifies limiting a defensive force when the force of offense cannot be limited? If a federal Constitution could chain the ambition or limit the exertions of all other nations, then it might prudently chain the discretion of its own government and limit the exertions for its own safety.

Peacetime, Military Prevents War

12   How could a readiness for war in time of peace be safely prohibited, unless we could also prohibit the preparations of every hostile nation?

Security can only be regulated by the means and the danger of attack. It will always be determined by these rules and no others. It is vain to oppose constitutional barriers to the impulse of self-preservation. It is worse than vain because it puts into the Constitution, itself, necessary usurpations of power, every precedent of which is a germ of unnecessary and multiplied repetition.

If one nation constantly maintains a disciplined army, ready to serve ambition or revenge, it forces the peaceful nations within its reach to take corresponding precautions.

The fifteenth century was the unhappy epoch of military establishments in the time of peace. They were introduced by Charles VII of France. All Europe has followed, or been forced to follow, the example. If the other nations hadn't built up their defenses, all of Europe would have long ago worn the chains of a universal monarch. If every nation except France were now to disband its peace establishments, the same event might follow. The veteran legions of Rome were an overmatch for the undisciplined valor of all other nations, rendering her the mistress of the world.

Military Endangers Liberty

13   It is true that the liberties of Rome became the final victim of her military triumphs. And the majority of European liberties, as far as they ever existed, have been the price of her military establishments. Therefore, a standing force is dangerous at the same time that it may be necessary.

On the smallest scale, it has inconveniences. On an extensive scale, its consequences may be fatal. On any scale, it deserves extreme caution.

A wise nation combines all these considerations. And while it doesn't rashly exclude itself from any resource that may become essential to its safety, it will prudently diminish both the necessity and the danger of resorting to a resource that may be unfortunate to its liberties.

Union: Protects against Foreign Army

14 The clearest marks of this prudence are stamped on the proposed Constitution. It secures the Union, which destroys every pretext for a military establishment that could be dangerous. America united, with a handful of troops or without a single soldier, exhibits a more forbidding posture to foreign ambition than America disunited with a hundred thousand veterans ready for combat.

It was mentioned earlier that the lack of this pretext saved the liberties of one nation in Europe. Insulated by geography and impregnable maritime resources, the rulers of Great Britain have never been able, by real or fabricated dangers, to cheat the public into an extensive peacetime military establishment.

The distance of the United States from the powerful nations of the world gives them the same happy security. A dangerous military establishment can never be necessary or plausible, so long as the States continue to be united.

But let it never, for a moment, be forgotten that the States are indebted for this advantage to the Union alone.

The moment of its dissolution will be the date of a new order of things.

The fears of the weaker or ambition of the stronger States, or Confederation, will set the same example in the New World as Charles VII did in the Old World. The same motives that produced universal imitation in the Old World will produce the same here. Instead of taking from our situation the precious advantage that Great Britain has taken from hers, America would become a copy of the European continent. Liberty would be crushed between standing armies and perpetual taxes. The fortunes of a disunited America would be more disastrous than those of Europe. The sources of evil in Europe are confined by geography. No superior powers from other parts of the globe will ally with her rival nations, inflame their mutual animosities, and make them the instruments of foreign ambition, jealousy, and revenge.

However, in America the miseries springing from internal jealousies, contentions, and wars, would form only part of her problem. An additional and plentiful source of evil resides in the unique relationship between Europe and this part of the earth.

Disunion: Disastrous Consequences

15 The consequences of disunion cannot be too strongly or too often stated. Every man who loves peace, every man who loves his country, every man who loves liberty, should always have it before his eyes, so he may cherish an attachment to the Union of America and set an appropriate value on the way of preserving it.

Military Appropriations

16 Next to the establishment of the Union, the best possible precaution against danger from standing armies is limiting the term that revenues may be appropriated for their support. The Constitution has prudently added this precaution.

I won't repeat the observations, which I flatter myself have shown this subject in a just and satisfactory light. But it may be proper to take notice of an argument against this part of the Constitution that draws from the policy and practice of Great Britain.

It is said that continuing an army in that kingdom requires an annual vote of the legislature, where the American Constitution has lengthened this critical period to two years. This is how the comparison is usually stated to the public. But is it a fair comparison? Does the British Constitution restrain the parliamentary discretion to one year? Does the American require two-year Congressional appropriations?

On the contrary, the authors of the fallacy must know that the British Constitution fixes no limit whatever to the discretion of the legislature and that the American limits the legislature to no more than two years.

British vs. U. S. Constitution

17 If the argument from the British example had been honestly stated, it would have been: Although the British Constitution contains no term limit for appropriating supplies to the army establishment, in practice the parliament has limited it to a single year.

In Great Britain, the House of Commons is elected for seven years. A great proportion of the members is elected by a small proportion of the people. The electors are corrupted by the representatives and the representatives are corrupted by the Crown. The representative body has the power to make appropriations to the army for an indefinite term beyond a single year.

Shouldn't we be suspicious about those who pretend that the representatives of the United States, elected FREELY by the WHOLE BODY of the people every second year, cannot be safely entrusted with the discretion over such appropriations, expressly limited to the short period of TWO YEARS?

Union Prevents Multiple Armies

18 A bad cause seldom fails to betray itself. The management of the opposition to the federal government is an unvaried example of this truth. But among all their blunders, none is more striking than the attempt to enlist the support of people who have prudent concerns about a standing army.

This attempt has awakened the public attention to an important subject. It has led to investigations that will terminate in a thorough and universal conviction that the Constitution provides the most effectual guards against danger from that area. It will also lead to the conclusion that nothing short of a Constitution fully adequate to the national defense and the preservation of the Union can save America from having as many standing armies as States, or Confederacies, after the Union splits. The progressive augmentation of armies, if the States disunite, will endanger properties and liberties more than any establishment of armies necessary under a united and efficient government, which will have tolerable property burdens and preserve liberty.

Navy Has Avoided Censure

19 The clear necessity to provide and maintain a navy has protected that part of the Constitution against the censure that has spared few other parts. It must, indeed, be numbered among American's greatest blessings that, since her Union will be the only source of her maritime strength, it will be a principal source of her security against danger from abroad.

In this respect, our situation bears another similarity to the insular advantage of Great Britain. And, happily, the batteries most capable of repelling foreign enterprises on our safety [the navy] are happily such as can never be turned by a perfidious government against our liberties.

New York Seacoast Vulnerable

20 The inhabitants of the Atlantic coastline are deeply interested in this provision for naval protection. Until now, they have slept quietly in their beds, their property has remained safe against the predatory spirit of licentious adventurers, and their maritime towns haven't yet been forced to ransom themselves from the terrors of a conflagration, paying the blackmailing invaders. This good fortune is not the result of the existing government's capacity to protect its citizens. Rather, it has resulted from fugitive and fallacious causes.

Except for Virginia and Maryland, which are peculiarly vulnerable on their eastern frontiers, no State should be more anxious about this subject than New York. Her seacoast is extensive. A very important part of the State is an island. A large navigable river penetrates the State for more than 50 leagues. [A league is about 3 miles.] The great emporium of its commerce, the great reservoir of its wealth, lies every moment at the mercy of events. It could almost be regarded as a potential hostage to the dictates of a foreign enemy or even the rapacious demands of pirates and barbarians.

If a war results from the precarious situation of European affairs and all the unruly passions are let loose on the ocean, it will be truly miraculous if we escape attacks and plundering from Europe and the countries bordering it. In America's present condition, the States most exposed to these calamities have no hope of help from the current phantom national government. If State resources were substantial enough to fortify them against the danger, the object to be protected would be almost totally consumed by the means of protecting it.

Regulating, Calling Forth Militia

21 The power of regulating and calling forth the militia has already been sufficiently justified and explained.

Import Duties Will Decline

22 The power of levying and borrowing money, the financial support of the national defense, properly falls into the same class. This power has already been closely examined and has been clearly shown, I trust, necessary in both the extent and form given it by the Constitution.

I will address one more point to those who believe that the power of taxation should be limited to external taxation, by which they mean taxes on articles imported from other countries. Of course, this will always be a valuable source of revenue. For a long time, in fact, it must be the principal source. And at this moment, it is essential.

But we may form very mistaken ideas on this subject if we do not remember to include in our calculations how the revenue from foreign commerce will vary with both the extent and the kind of imports. And these variations won't correspond with the progress of our population, which is the general measure of the public wants. As long as agriculture continues to be the sole field of labor, importation of manufactured goods will increase as consumers multiply. As soon as domestic manufacturers employ hands not needed for agriculture, imported manufactured goods will decrease as the numbers of people increase. Eventually, imports may primarily be raw materials that will be made into articles for exportation and will, therefore, require encouragement of bounties rather than loaded with discouraging duties. A durable system of government should remember these cycles and be able to accommodate itself to them.

Tax Clause Not Unlimited Power

23 Some, who don't deny the necessity of the power of taxation, have based their fierce attack against the Constitution on the language defining this power. They repeatedly contend that the power "to lay and collect taxes, duties, imposts, and excises, to pay the debts, and provide for the common defense and general welfare of the United States," amount to an unlimited license to exercise any and every power that may be alleged to be necessary for the common defense or general welfare.

There is no stronger proof of how far these writers will reach to find objections to the Constitution than their stooping to such a misconstruction.

Broad Interpretation of Clause

24 Had no other enumeration or definition of Congressional powers been found in the Constitution than the general expression just cited, the critics might have found some basis for the objection, although it would have been difficult to find a reason for such an awkward way to describe an authority to legislate in all possible cases. "To raise money for the general welfare" must be an extraordinary phrase if it includes the power to destroy the freedom of the press, the trial by jury, or even regulate the course of descents, or the forms of conveyances.

Illogical Objections

25 But how will the objection be slanted when the issues alluded to in general terms are specifically mentioned immediately following the clause, not even separated by a longer pause than a semicolon?

If different parts of the Constitution are magnified in this way, adding meanings everywhere it is possible, should the pertinent part of a sentence be excluded while keeping all the more doubtful and ambiguous terms?

Why would specific powers be enumerated, if they were meant to be included in the preceding general power? Nothing is more natural than to first use a general phrase and then to explain and qualify it by a recital of particulars. But the idea of enumerating specifics that neither explain nor qualify the general meaning and can have no other effect than to confuse and mislead is absurd. Since we are reduced to the dilemma of charging this absurdity on either the authors of the objection or the authors of the Constitution, we must take the liberty of guessing it didn't originate with the latter.

Constitution Copies Articles

26 The objection here is even more extraordinary because the language in the Constitution appears to be a copy of that in the Articles of Confederation. The objective of forming a Union among the States, as described in article three, are "their common defense, security of their liberties, and mutual and general welfare." The terms of article eight are even more identical: "All charges of war and all other expenses that shall be incurred for the

common defense or general welfare, and allowed by the United States in Congress, shall be defrayed out of a common treasury," etc. A similar language again occurs in article nine.

If we construe either of these articles by the rules objectors have used on the new Constitution, they give existing Congress a power to legislate in all cases whatsoever. But what would have been thought of Congress if it had locked onto these general expressions, disregarding the specifica-

tions that define and limit their meaning, and exercised an unlimited power of providing for the common defense and general welfare?

I ask those who are making the objections whether they would in that case have employed the same reasoning in justification of Congress as they now make use of against the convention. How difficult it is for error to escape its own condemnation!

PUBLIUS

Constitutional references:
Article 1, section 8　204-222　military defense
Article 1, section 8　171-175　taxes; defense
Article 1, section 8　178-182　borrow money, regulate commerce

Number 42

2. Regulate International, Interstate Intercourse

The national government's *second* class of powers are those that regulate the intercourse with foreign nations.

The national government will make treaties, send and receive ambassadors, ministers, and consuls, define and punish piracies and felonies committed on the high seas and against the law of nations, regulate foreign commerce including a power to prohibit, after 1808, the importation of slaves and, until then, lay a duty of ten dollars per head as a discouragement to such importations.

World Must See Us as One Nation

2　It is obvious that the federal government should have this essential class of powers. If we are to be one nation in any respect, it clearly should be in respect to other nations.

Treaties, Ambassadors, Consuls

3　By their nature, the powers to make treaties, and send and receive ambassadors belong to the federal government. Both are in the Articles of Confederation, with two small differences.

The Constitution removes a phrase under which treaties might be substantially frustrated by State regulations.

And the term ambassador, if interpreted strictly, as seems to be required by the Articles of Confederation, includes only the highest rank of public ministers and excludes the lower level officials that the United States will probably prefer where foreign embassies may be necessary. And under no interpretation will the term include consuls. Yet it has been found expedient and become the practice of Congress to employ lower levels of public ministers, and to send and receive consuls.

Foreign Consuls: Crucial Correction

4 When commercial treaties require a mutual appointment of consuls whose duties are connected with commerce, admitting foreign consuls into the United States may fall within the power of making commercial treaties.

When no commercial treaties exist, establishing American consuls in foreign countries may *perhaps* be covered under the authority of article nine of the Confederation to appoint all such civil officers necessary for managing the general affairs of the United States.

But admitting consuls into the United States, where no treaty has stipulated it, seems not to have been provided for in the Articles of Confederation. Correcting this omission is one of the smaller things improved by the constitutional convention. But the tiniest provisions become important when they tend to anticipate and prevent the necessity, or the pretext, for gradual, unobserved usurpations of power.

A list of the cases where Congress has betrayed or been forced into violating its chartered authorities, because of defects in the Articles of Confederation, would surprise people who haven't paid attention to the subject. These corrections make a strong argument in favor of the new Constitution, which has given as much attention to the small provisions as to the more obvious and striking defects of the Articles of Confederation.

Piracies, Felonies on High Seas

5 The power to define and punish piracies and felonies committed on the high seas, and offenses against the law of nations, also belongs to the national government. It is a great improvement on the Articles of Confederation.

The Articles contain no provision in the case of offenses against the law of nations. Consequently, one indiscreet State could embroil the Confederation with foreign nations.

The provision in the Articles of Confederation about piracies and felonies extends no further than the establishment of courts to try these offenses.

The definition of piracies might, without being inconvenient, be left to the law of nations, even though a legislative definition of them is found in most municipal codes.

A definition of felonies on the high seas is evidently required. The term "felony" has many definitions, even in the common law of England. It is given various meanings in English statute law. But neither the common nor statute law of England, or any other nation, should be the standard unless already adopted by legislation in the United States.

Using the term as defined by the codes of several States would be as impractical as using it as defined by England and other nations would be dishonorable and illegitimate. It is not defined precisely the same in any two of the States, and varies in each State with every revision of its criminal laws. For the sake of certainty and uniformity, therefore, the power to define felonies" in this case was absolutely necessary and proper.

Commerce, Federal Jurisdiction

6 The regulation of foreign commerce has been so fully discussed that it needs no additional proofs here of its being properly under federal jurisdiction.

Slave Trade Abolished in 1808

7 It is wished, without a doubt, that the power to prohibit the importation of slaves had not been postponed until 1808, that there was an immediate ban. But it isn't difficult to explain this restriction on the national government and the way the whole clause is expressed.

It should be considered a great point gained in favor of humanity that in 20 years, a traffic that has so long and so loudly been upbraided as barbarism, will be terminated forever within these States. During that period, it will receive considerable discouragement from the federal government. And it may be totally abolished if the few States that continue the unnatural traffic, agree to prohibit it like the majority of the Union. It would be happy for the unfortunate Africans if an equal prospect lay before them of being redeemed from the oppressions of their European brethren!

Arguments Extreme

8   Some opponents have perverted this clause into an objection against the Constitution. One side says it is a criminal toleration of an illicit practice. The other says it's calculated to prevent voluntary and beneficial emigrations from Europe to America. I mention these misconstructions, not as an answer to them, because they deserve none, but to show the manner and spirit of some people opposing the proposed government.

---

3. Provide Harmony, Intercourse Among States

9   The powers included in the *third* class are those providing for the harmony and proper intercourse among the States.

Brief Review of
Third Class of Powers

10 This classification could include the restraints imposed on State authority and certain judicial power. But the former are reserved for a distinct class and the latter will be examined when we discuss the structure and organization of the government.

I will confine myself to a brief review of the remaining powers under this third description. They are: to regulate commerce among the States and the Indian tribes, to coin and regulate the value of money, to punish counterfeiting coins and securities of the United States, to fix the standard of weights and measures, to establish a uniform rule of naturalization and uniform laws of bankruptcy, to prescribe the manner that public acts, records, and judicial proceedings of each State will be proved and the effect they will have in other States, and to establish post offices and post roads.

Regulate Commerce among States

11 Experience has clearly shown the existing Confederacy defective in its power to regulate commerce between the States. To the remarks made in other papers on this subject may be added that, without this supplemental provision, the great and essential power of regulating foreign commerce would have been incomplete and ineffectual.

An important objective of this power was to give relief to the States that import and export through other States and are forced to pay improper contributions levied on them. If the intermediary States were at liberty to regulate trade between States during the passage through their jurisdiction, they would load the articles of import and export with duties that would have to be paid by manufacturers and consumers. Past experience assures us that such a practice would be introduced by future contrivances. Experience and human psychology shows it would nourish unceasing animosities and probably end in serious interruptions of the public tranquillity.

To people without a vested interest in the question, this desire of commercial States to collect indirect taxes from their uncommercial neighbors must appear even more politically inexpedient than it is unfair. Resentment and self-interest would stimulate the injured party to find less convenient channels for their foreign trade. But the mild voice of reason, pleading the cause of a larger and permanent interest, is too drowned by the clamors of an impatient avarice for immediate and immoderate gain.

Supervision of Interstate Commerce

12 The necessity of a superintending authority over the reciprocal trade of confederated States has been illustrated by other examples as well as our own.

In Switzerland, where the union is very slight, each canton [state] must allow merchandise passage through its jurisdiction into other cantons, without additional tolls.

It is a law in the German empire that the princes and states shall not put tolls or customs on bridges, rivers, or passages without the consent of the emperor and the diet [governing body]. It appears from a quotation in an earlier paper that in practice this law, like many others in the German confederacy, has not been followed, producing the mischiefs predicted here.

Among the restraints imposed by the Union of the Netherlands on its members, one is that they shall not establish imposts disadvantageous to their neighbors without the general permission.

Regulate Commerce: Indian Tribes

13 In the proposed Constitution, the regulation of commerce with the Indian tribes is very properly released from two limitations in the Articles of Confederacy, which render the provision obscure and contradictory.

In the Articles, the power to regulate trade is limited to Indians, not members of any State. And it is not supposed to violate or infringe on the legislative right of any State within its own borders.

Which Indians are supposed to be described as members of a State is not yet settled and has been a frequent question of perplexity and contention in the federal councils. And how the trade with Indians, though not members of a State yet residing within its legislative jurisdiction, can be regulated by an external authority without intruding on the internal rights of State legislation, is absolutely incomprehensible.

This is not the only case in which the Articles of Confederation have inconsiderately endeavored to accomplish impossibilities. One is reconciling a partial sovereignty in the Union with complete sovereignty in the States. This subverts a mathematical axiom—by taking away a part, yet letting the whole remain.

Coin Money, Regulate Currency

14 Concerning the power to coin money and regulate its value and the value of foreign coin, by providing for this last case, the Constitution supplies a material omission in the Articles of Confederation. Currently, Congress only regulates the value of coin *struck* by its own authority or the States. It must be obvious that the proposed uniformity in the *value* of the currency might be destroyed if foreign currency was valued differently by the different States.

Punish Counterfeiters

15 The authority to punish counterfeiters of public securities and currency is given to that part of the government responsible for securing the value of both.

Regulate Weights and Measures

16 The regulation of weight and measures is transferred from the Articles of Confederation and is based on similar considerations as the preceding power of regulating coin.

National Naturalization Rule

17 The dissimilarity in the naturalization rules has long been mentioned as a fault in our system. And it has been the reason for intricate and delicate questions.

The fourth Articles of the Confederacy declared "that the *free inhabitants* of each of these States, paupers, vagabonds, and fugitives from justice excepted, shall be entitled to all privileges and immunities of *free citizens* in the several States; and *the people* of each State shall, in every other, enjoy all the privileges of trade and commerce," etc.

The confusing language is remarkable. Why were the terms *free inhabitants* used in one part, *free citizens* in another, and *people* in another? Or what was meant by adding to the phrase "all privileges and immunities of free citizens," "all the privileges of trade and commerce," cannot easily be determined.

However, there seems to be an unavoidable assumption: people defined as *free inhabitants* of one State—but who are not citizens of that State—are entitled, in every other State, to all the privileges of *free citizens*. In other words, they may be entitled to greater privileges than in their home State. Therefore, every State must give citizenship rights to any person who lives in a different State but who, if he lived in the State, would qualify to be a citizen, *and* to anyone whom it allows to become inhabitants within its jurisdiction.

If the term "inhabitants" was defined so that only "citizens" could have the stipulated privileges, the difficulty would only be diminished, not removed. Each State would still retain the very improper power to naturalize aliens in every other state.

For example, let's say that in one State a short-term resident fulfills all criteria for citizenship. In another, greater qualifications are required. An alien, therefore, who legally doesn't have certain rights in the latter, only has to first reside in the former to elude the greater qualifications in the latter. Thus, preposterously, the law of the first State is dominant to the law of the second, within the jurisdiction of the second State.

We have escaped embarrassment on this subject only by good luck. Several States had laws that described some resident aliens as subjects of a different State. They lived under prohibitions inconsistent not only with the rights of citizenship but with the privilege of residence. What would have happened if such persons, by residence or otherwise, had become citizens under the laws of another State, then demanded their rights to both residency and citizenship within the State which prohibited it? Whatever the legal consequences might have been, other consequences would probably have resulted of too serious a nature not to be provided against.

The new Constitution, properly, makes provision against this problem, and all others proceeding from the defect of the Confederation on this subject, by authorizing the general government to establish a uniform rule of naturalization throughout the United States.

Uniform Bankruptcy Laws

18 The power to establish uniform laws of bankruptcy is so intimately connected with the regulation of commerce and will prevent so many frauds, where the people or property may live or be taken into different States, that the expediency of it seems not likely to be drawn into question.

Validity of Public Records

19 The power of prescribing by federal laws the manner that public acts, records, and judicial proceedings of each State will be proved, and the effect they shall have in other States, is clearly a valuable improvement on the clause relating to this subject in the Articles of Confederation. The meaning of the Articles is extremely indeterminate and can have little importance under any likely interpretation.

This Constitutional power may become a very convenient instrument of justice. It will be particularly beneficial on the borders of contiguous States where the effects liable to justice may be suddenly and secretly translated, in any stage of the process, within a foreign jurisdiction.

Post Roads Help Commerce

20 In every view, the power of establishing post-roads must be a harmless power and may, perhaps, by judicious management, produce a great public conveniency. Nothing that tends to facilitate intercourse between the States can be deemed unworthy of public care.

PUBLIUS

Constitutional references:

Ar 2, sect 2	392-399	treaties, appoint ambassadors, consuls
Ar 2, sect 3	424-425	receive ambassadors, ministers
Ar 1, sect 8	180-182	commerce, foreign, interstate, Indians
Ar 1, sect8	201-203	piracies, law of nations
Ar 1, sect 9	238-244	importation of slaves
Ar 1, sect 10	271-295	restraints on State authority
Ar 3, sect 1-3	(didn't mark)	judicial authority
Ar 1, sect 8	187-192	coin, regulate money; weights and measures; counterfeiting
Ar 1, sect 8	183-186	naturalization, bankruptcy
Ar 4, sect 1	482-487	public acts, records proved
Ar 1, sect 8	193	post offices, roads

Number 43

4. Miscellaneous Federal Powers

The *fourth* class of powers includes:

Copyrights, Patents

2 A power "to promote the progress of science and useful arts by securing for limited times to authors and inventors the exclusive right to their writings and discoveries."

3 The usefulness of this power will hardly be questioned. Great Britain's courts have solemnly judged that the copyright of authors is a right of common law.

The right to obtain the useful benefits of their inventions seems, with equal reason, to belong to inventors.

In both cases, the public good fully coincides with the claims of individuals. The States, individually, cannot make effectual provisions in either of these cases. Most States anticipated this decision, passing laws recommended by Congress.

Federal Capital

4 "To exercise exclusive legislation in all cases whatsoever over such district (not exceeding ten miles square) as may, by cession of particular States and the acceptance of Congress, become the seat of the Government of the United States, and to exercise like authority over all places purchased by the consent of the legislature of the State in which the same shall be, for the erection of forts, magazines, arsenals, dockyards, and other needful buildings."

5 The indispensable necessity of complete independence at the seat of government is self-evident. This power is exercised by every legislature in the Union, I might say in the world, simply because of its general supremacy. Without it, the public authority might be demeaned and its proceedings interrupted with impunity. And if the federal government depends on the State where the seat of government is located for protection, that State might have an imputation of awe or influence on the national councils, equally dishonorable to the government and dissatisfactory to the other members of the Confederacy.

This consideration will have more weight as public improvements in the permanent residence of the government gradually accumulate. This would become too great a public trust to be left in the hands of a single State, creating too many obstacles to moving the government, still further limiting its necessary independence.

The size of this federal district is sufficiently restricted to satisfy every jealousy of an opposite nature. The State ceding the land for this use will consent. No doubt, that State will assure the rights and the consent of the citizens of the district in its compact with the federal government. The inhabitants will find sufficient inducements of interest to become willing parties to the cession. They will elect the municipal legislature that is to exercise authority over them. The legislature of the State, representatives of the entire population of the State, and the inhabitants of the ceded part will concur on the cession, and in their adoption of the Constitution. Therefore, every imaginable objection seems to be obviated.

Forts, Arsenals, Etc

6 That the federal government must have authority over forts, military depots, arsenals, dockyards, etc., is evident. The public money spent on such places, and the property and equipment stored there, requires that they should be exempt from the authority of a State. Nor is it proper that the places so important to the security of the entire Union may depend, to any degree, on one State.

Objections are prevented by requiring the concurrence of the States concerned in every such establishment.

Treason: Definition, Punishment

7 "Treason against the United States shall consist only in levying war against them, or in adhering to their enemies, giving them aid and comfort. No person shall be convicted of treason unless on the testimony of two witnesses to the same overt act, or on confession in open court.

"The Congress shall have power to declare the punishment of treason, but no attainder of treason shall work corruption of blood or forfeiture except during the life of the person attainted."

8 Since treason may be committed against the United States, the United States should have the authority to punish it. However, violent factions, the natural offspring of free government, have created new, artificial treasons, and used them as an excuse for malicious vengeance against each other. The convention has, prudently, erected a barrier against this specific danger by inserting a constitutional definition of the crime, fixing the proof necessary for conviction, and restraining Congress from extending the consequences and punishment beyond the guilty person.

Creation of New States

9 "New States may be admitted by the Congress into this Union; but no new State shall be formed or erected within the jurisdiction of any other State; nor any State be formed by the junction of two or more States or parts of States, without the consent of the legislatures of the States concerned as well as of the Congress."

10 The Articles of Confederation have no provision on this important subject. Canada was to be admitted of right, on her joining in the measures of the United States. And other *colonies*, by which were evidently meant the other British colonies, could be admitted at the discretion of nine States.

The eventual establishment of *new States* seems to have been overlooked by the compilers of the Articles. We have seen the inconvenience of this omission and how it has led Congress into an assumption of power. Quite properly, therefore, the new system corrects the defect.

The general precaution, that no new States will be formed without the concurrence of the federal authority and the States concerned, is appropri-

ate to the principles governing such transactions. The specific precaution against the forming new States by partitioning a State without its consent, quiets the jealousy of the larger States, just as that of the smaller States is quieted by a similar precaution, against joining States without their consent.

Congress Regulates U. S. Territory

11 "The Congress shall have the power to dispose of and make all needful rules and regulations respecting the territory or other property belonging to the United States; and nothing in this Constitution shall be so construed as to prejudice any claims of the United States or of any particular State."

12 This very import power is required for reasons similar to the last one. The proviso is proper and probably necessary by jealousies and questions about the Western territory.

Republican Government in States

13 "The United States shall guarantee to every State in this Union a republican form of government, and shall protect each of them against invasions, and on application of the legislature, or of the executive (when the legislature cannot be convened) against domestic violence."

14 In a confederacy founded on republican principles and composed of republican members, the superintending government should clearly possess the authority to defend the system against aristocratic or monarchical innovations. The more intimate the nature of such a union may be, the greater the interest of the members in the political institutions of each other. And the greater the right to insist on the form of government to be *substantially* maintained.

But a right implies a remedy. And where else could the remedy be found than in the Constitution?

Governments of dissimilar principles and forms are less adaptable to a federal coalition than those of a similar nature. "As the confederate republic of Germany," says Montesquieu, "consists of free cities and petty states, subject to different princes, experience shows us that it is more imperfect than that of Holland and Switzerland . . . Greece was undone," he adds, "as soon as the king of Macedon obtained a seat among the Amphictyons." In the latter case, no doubt, the disproportionate force, as well as the monarchical form of the new confederacy, influenced events.

It may be asked why this precaution is needed and whether it may become a pretext for alterations in the State governments without the States themselves agreeing. These questions have answers.

If the federal government's intervention isn't needed, the Constitutional provision will be harmlessly superfluous. But who can say what experiments will be tried by the caprice of particular States, by the ambition of enterprising leaders, or by the intrigues and influence of foreign powers?

As to the second part of the question, if the national government uses this constitutional authority to interpose, it will be, of course, bound to pursue the authority. But the authority extends no further than a *guarantee* of a republican form of government, which assumes a pre-existing government of the form guaranteed. Therefore, as long as the existing republican forms are continued by the States, they are guaranteed by the federal Constitution. Whenever the States may choose to substitute other republican forms, they have the right to do so and to claim the federal guarantee. The only restriction is that they shall not exchange republican for anti-republican Constitution, a restriction that, it is presumed, will hardly be considered a grievance.

States Protected Against Invasion

15 Every part of a society is entitled to protection against invasion. The latitude expressed in the Constitution seems to secure each State, not only against foreign hostility but against ambitious vindictive enterprises of its more powerful neighbors. The history both of ancient and modern confederacies proves that the weaker members of the union should not be indifferent to the policy of this article.

Union Protection: Domestic Violence

16 Protection against domestic violence is also proper. Even among the Swiss cantons that, properly speaking, are not under one government, provision is made for this. That league's history informs us that mutual aid is frequently claimed and given, by both the democratic as well as other cantons.

A recent, well-known event among ourselves has warned us to be prepared for similar emergencies.

17 At first view, it might not seem to square with the republican theory to suppose either that a majority has no right or that a minority will have the force to subvert a government. And, consequently, that federal intervention can never be required except when it would be improper. But theoretic reasoning must be qualified by the lessons of practice. Couldn't a conspiracy, planning violence, be formed by a majority of a State, especially a small State, just as it could happen in a county, or a district within a State? If the State authority should, in the latter case, protect the local officials, then shouldn't the federal authority, in the former, support the State authority?

Besides, certain parts of the State constitutions are so interwoven with the federal Constitution that a violent blow to one cannot avoid wounding the other.

Insurrections in a State will rarely induce a federal interposition, unless the number involved is large compared to the friends of the government. In such cases, it will be better if the violence is repressed by the superintending power than having the majority left to maintain their cause by a bloody and obstinate contest. The existence of a right to interpose will generally prevent the necessity of exerting it.

Strength May Not be on Ethical Side

18 Is it true that force and right are necessarily on the same side in republican government? Might not the minority party possess such a superiority of monetary resources, military talents and experience, or secret aid from foreign powers, to render it a superior military force?

Might not a more compact and advantageous position tip the scale against a superior number that may be in a weaker situation, unable to quickly and effectively respond? Nothing is less realistic than imagining that in actual battles the larger number of citizens assures victory. Cannot a minority of CITIZENS become a majority of PERSONS by adding alien residents, mercenaries, or people in the State without voting rights?

I take no notice of an unhappy species of population abounding in some of the States who, during the calm of regular government, are sunk

below the level of men; but who, in the tempestuous scenes of civil violence, may emerge into the human character, giving a superiority of strength to any party with which they may associate themselves.

Other States Act as Impartial Judges

19 In cases where it may be doubtful on which side justice lies and two violent factions are tearing a State to pieces, what better umpires could be desired than the representatives of States not heated by the local battles? They could act with the impartiality of judges and the affection of friends. It would be wonderful if all free governments enjoyed such a remedy for its infirmities. And if an equally effective project could be established for universal peace!

Less Risk of Nation-Wide Insurrection

20 If it is asked: What is the redress for an insurrection pervading all the States with a superior force but not a constitutional right? The answer must be: Such a case is outside the ability of human remedies and probably would not occur. This is a sufficient recommendation of the federal Constitution: it diminishes the risk of a calamity for which no possible constitution can provide a cure.

Republic: Remedy Abuse in Part

21 Among the advantages of a confederate republic enumerated by Montesquieu, an important one is, "that should a popular insurrection happen in one of the States, the others are able to quell it. Should abuses creep into one part, they are reformed by those that remain sound."

Confederacy Debts Valid

22 "All debts contracted and engagements entered into, before the adoption of this Constitution, shall be as valid against the United States under this Constitution, as under the Confederation."

Recognizing Debts Satisfies Creditors

23 This can be considered a declaratory proposition. Among other reasons, it may have been inserted to satisfy foreign creditors of the United States, who are probably aware of the pretended doctrine—that a change in the political form of civil society has the magical effect of dissolving its moral obligations.

24 One of the lesser criticisms of the Constitution is that the validity of engagements in favor of the United States should have been asserted, as well as those against them. And in the spirit that usually characterizes little critics, the omission has been transformed and magnified into a plot against national rights. The authors of this criticism may be told what many others already know that, by their nature, engagements are reciprocal, an assertion of their validity on one side, necessarily involves a validity on the other side. Since the article is merely declaratory, the establishment of the principle in one case is sufficient for every case. Further, every constitution must limit its precautions to dangers that are not altogether imaginary. And no real danger can exist that the government would DARE, with or without this constitutional declaration, to remit the debts justly due to the public, on the pretext here condemned.

Amending the Constitution

25 "To provide for amendments to be ratified by three fourths of the States, under two exceptions only."

26 Experience will suggest useful alterations. A way to introduce them was required. The way preferred by the convention seems totally proper. It guards equally against an extremely easy amendment process that would make the Constitution too mutable and an extremely difficult process that would preserve the faults discovered within it. Moreover, the federal and the State governments are equally able to originate the amendment of errors, as experience shows them to one side or the other.

The exception in favor of equal suffrage in the Senate was probably meant as a safeguard to the remaining sovereignty of the States, secured by equal representation in one branch of the legislature. The States particularly concerned with that equality probably insisted on it.

The other exception must have been admitted on the same considerations that produced the privilege defended by it.

Ratification by Nine States

27 "The ratification of the Conventions of nine States shall be sufficient for the establishment of this constitution between the States so ratifying the same."

Unanimous Ratification

28 This article speaks for itself. The authority of the people alone could validate the Constitution. To require the unanimous ratification of the thirteen States would have exposed the essential interests of the entire Union to the caprice or corruption of a single State. This would have shown a lack of foresight by the convention that our own experience would have rendered inexcusable.

29 Two delicate questions present themselves: 1. On what principle can the Confederacy, which exists under a solemn compact among the States, be superseded without the unanimous consent of the parties to it? 2. What relationship will exist between the nine or more States ratifying the Constitution and the remaining few who do not become parties to it?

Majority of States Ratify

30 The first question is immediately answered by reiterating that it is absolutely necessary. The great principle of self-preservation, which is both a transcendent law of nature and God, that the safety and happiness of society are the aims of all political institutions, to which all such institutions must be sacrificed.

PERHAPS an answer may also be found without searching beyond the principles of the compact itself. It has been noted that among the defects of the Confederacy is that in many of the States it received no higher sanction than a mere legislative ratification. The principle of reciprocity seems to require that its obligation on the other States should be reduced to the same standard.

A compact between independent sovereigns, founded on ordinary acts of legislative authority, has no higher validity than a league or treaty between the parties. Treaties are only mutual conditions of each other. A breach of any one article in a treaty is a breach of the whole treaty. A breach committed by either party absolves the others, authorizes them, it they want, to pronounce the compact violated and void.

If it should, unhappily, be necessary to appeal to these delicate truths to justify not receiving the consent of particular States to dissolve the federal pact, won't the complaining parties find it difficult to answer the MULTIPLE and IMPORTANT violations pointed out to them? Previously, the ideas presented in this paragraph were played down. The scene has changed and so has the part that the same motives dictate.

Hopeful Relations Will Remain Good

31 The second question is also delicate. And the hope that it is merely hypothetical, that all States will ratify the Constitution, forbids an over-curious discussion of it. It is one of those cases that must be left to provide for itself.

It may be observed in general that although no political relationship can continue to exist between the assenting and dissenting States, yet the moral relationships will remain uncancelled. Claims of justice on both sides will be in force and must be fulfilled. The rights of humanity must always be duly and mutually respected. Hopefully, considerations of a common interest and, above all, the remembrance of the endearing scenes past the anticipation of a speedy triumph over the obstacles to reunion, will urge MODERATION on one side and PRUDENCE on the other.

PUBLIUS

Constitutional references:

Article 1, section 8	194-198	copyrights, patents
Article 5	525-547	amending; Confederacy debts valid
Article 1, section 8	223-232	capital, forts, arsenals
Article 7	565-568	ratifying
Article 3, section 3	472-481	treason
Article 4, section 3	504-517	creation of new States; U.S. territory
Article 4, section 4	518-520	republican government in States
Article 1, section 8	520-524	protection against invasion, domestic violence

Number 44

5. Provisions Restricting State Authority

A *fifth* class of provisions in favor of the federal authority consists of the following restrictions on the authority of the States:

States Shall Not . . .

2 1. "No State shall enter into any treaty, alliance, or confederation; grant letters of marque and reprisal; coin money; emit bills of credit; make anything but gold and silver coin a tender in payment of debts; pass any bill of attainder, ex post facto law, or law impairing the obligation of contracts, or grant any title of nobility."

Treaties, Alliances, Letters of Marque

3 The prohibition against treaties, alliances, and confederations is part of the existing Articles of Union. For reasons that need no explanation, it is copied into the new Constitution.

The prohibition of letters of marque [retaliation through confiscation] is another part of the old system, but is somewhat extended in the new. The Articles of Confederation allowed States to grant letters of marque after a declaration of war. In the Constitution, these licenses must be obtained, both during and before war, from the government of the United States. The advantage of uniformity in foreign policy justifies this change. As does the States' responsibility to the nation, which is itself responsible for the conduct of every State.

States Can't Coin Money

4 The Confederacy gave both the States and the Union the right to coin, with Congress exclusively, regulating its alloy and value. The new provision takes the right to coin money away from the States and is an improvement. The federal authority has regulated the alloy and value of coins. Allowing the States to manufacture coins has created two problems: (1) many expensive mints, and (2) a diversify of shape, size, and weight of coins. The power to coin money was originally given to the federal government to standardize coinage. State mints were created to prevent the inconvenience of transporting gold and silver to the central mint for recoinage. These problems can be solved by having local mints established under the national authority.

No State Bills of Credit

5 Prohibiting bills of credit must give pleasure to every citizen that loves justice and understands the true source of public prosperity. Since the peace, America has sustained the destructive effects of paper money on the confidence so necessary between man and man, in public councils, in industry, and in the republican government. It constitutes an enormous debt against the issuing States that must long remain unsatisfied. Or it will remain an accumulation of guilt that can only be expiated by a voluntary sacrifice on the altar of justice by the State that issued it.

In addition to these persuasive considerations, the reasons that show the necessity of denying States the power to regulate coin, also prove that they should not be allowed to substitute a paper medium for a coin. If every State could regulate the value of its coin, there might be as many different currencies as States, impeding the intercourse among them. Retroactive alterations in its value would injure the citizens of other States, kindling animosities among the States themselves.

The citizens of foreign nations might suffer from the same cause, discrediting and embroiling the Union by the indiscretion of a single State. These mischiefs are just as likely to occur if the States issue paper money, as if they coin gold or silver.

The power to make anything but gold and silver a tender in payments of debts is withdrawn from the States, using the same principle with that of issuing a paper currency.

Bills of Attainder, *Ex Post Facto* Laws

6 Bills of attainder, *ex post facto* laws, and laws impairing the obligation of contracts, are contrary to the first principles of the social compact and every principle of sound legislation. The two former are expressly prohibited by the prefixes to some of the State constitutions, and all are prohibited by the spirit and scope of the State constitutions.

Our experience, nevertheless, has taught us to create additional fences against these dangers. Very properly, therefore, the convention added this constitutional bulwark in favor of personal security and private rights. I believe that by doing this, they faithfully reflected the genuine sentiments of their constituents. The sober people of America are weary of fluctuating policy directing public councils. They have been both indignant and remorseful at sudden legislative interferences affecting personal rights that have brought profits to enterprising and influential speculators and snares to the more-industrious and less-informed part of the community.

They have seen, too, that one legislative interference is just the first link of a long chain of repetitions, every subsequent interference comes through the effects of the preceding. They very correctly infer, therefore, that some thorough reform is needed, a reform that will banish speculations on public measures, inspire a general prudence and industry, and give a regular course to the business of society.

The prohibition against titles of nobility is copied from the Articles of Confederation and needs no comment.

Taxes, Troops, Foreign Compacts

7 2. "No State shall, without the consent of Congress, lay any imposts or duties on imports or exports, except what may be absolutely necessary for executing its inspection laws; and the net produce of all duties and imposts, laid by any State on imports or exports, shall be for the use of the Treasury of the United States; and all such laws shall be subject to the revision and control of the Congress.

"No State shall, without the consent of Congress, lay any duty of tonnage, keep troops or ships of war in time of peace, enter into any agreement or compact with another State or with a foreign power, or engage in war, unless actually invaded or in such imminent danger as will not admit of delay."

No State Import, Export Duties

8 The restraint on the States over imports and experts is enforced by all the arguments proving that regulation of trade should be handled by the federal councils. Therefore, further remarks on this are unnecessary, except to say that the restraint's one qualification gives the States reasonable discretion to facilitate their imports and exports, and gives the United States a reasonable check against the abuse of this discretion.

The remaining particulars of this clause fall within reasonings which are either so obvious, or have been so fully developed, that they may be passed over without remark.

---

6. Provisions Giving Efficacy to All the Other Powers

9 The *sixth* and last class consists of the powers and provisions that give efficacy to all the rest. These fall into four categories.

1. Make Necessary, Proper Laws

10 "To make all laws which shall be necessary and proper for carrying into execution the foregoing powers, and all other powers vested by this Constitution in the Government of the United States, or in any department or officer thereof."

Opposition

11 Few parts of the Constitution have been assailed with more intemperance than this. Yet on objective investigation, no part appears more completely invulnerable. Without the *substance* of this power, the whole Constitution would be a dead letter.

Therefore, people who object to it being in the Constitution must mean that the *form* of the provision is improper. But have they considered whether a better form could have been substituted?

Alternatives to Clause

12 There are four other approaches the Constitution might have taken on this subject:

1. They could have copied article two of the existing Confederation, prohibiting the exercise of any power not *expressly* delegated.

2. They might have attempted listing every power included under the general terms "necessary and proper."

3. They could have attempted a negative listing, specifying the powers not falling under the general definition.

4. Or they might have been completely silent on the subject, leaving these necessary and proper powers to interpretation and inference.

Adopting Article 2 of Confederation

["Each State retains its sovereignty, freedom, and independence, and every power, jurisdiction, and right, which is not by this Confederation expressly delegated to the United States in Congress assembled."]

13 If the convention had adopted the Second Article of Confederation, the new Congress would be continually exposed, as its predecessors have been, to two diametrically opposite alternatives:

1. Either the term *"expressly"* is rigorously construed, stripping the federal government of all real authority.

2. Or it is interpreted so widely that it completely destroys the force of the restriction.

It would be easy to show, if necessary, that no important power delegated by the Articles of Confederation has been or can be executed by Congress without returning, more or less, to either the doctrine of *construction* or *implication.*

Since the new Constitution delegates extensive powers, the government administering it would face the dilemma of betraying the public interests by doing nothing or violating the Constitution by exercising powers indispensably necessary and proper, but, at the same time, not *expressly* granted.

List of Necessary, Proper Powers

14 If the convention had attempted to list every power necessary and proper for carrying out their other powers, it would have meant listing every law on every subject to which the Constitution relates. They would have had to also accommodate, not only the existing state of things, but all possible futures changes. For every new application of a general power, the *particular powers*, which are the means of attaining the *objective* of the general power, must vary as the objective changes, or vary while the objective remains the same.

List Powers *Not* Necessary, Proper

15 If they attempted to list every power not necessary or proper to execute the general powers, the task would have been no less unrealistic. And it would have been vulnerable to another objection—every defect in the list would have been the same as granting an authority.

If, to avoid this consequence, they had attempted a partial list of exceptions, then summarized the rest in the general terms of *not necessary or proper,* the list would only have included a few of the powers not included in the general definition. These few excepted powers would probably have been those likely to be assumed or tolerated. And the unnecessary and improper powers not included in the list would be less forcibly excepted than if no partial list had been made.

No "Necessary And Proper" Clause

16 If the Constitution was silent on this point, by unavoidable implication all the powers required to execute the general powers would revert to the government.

No axiom is more clearly established in law, or in reason, that whatever the goal, the means are authorized. And wherever a general power to do a thing is given, every particular power necessary for doing it is included.

Therefore, if the convention had done this, every current objection to the clause would continue to be plausible. And it would create a real problem. It would remove a pretext that may be used on critical occasions to raise doubt about the essential powers of the Union.

If Congress Oversteps Its Authority

17 What are the consequences if the Congress misconstrues this part of the Constitution and exercises powers not warranted by its true meaning? I answer, the same thing will happen as will occur if they misconstrue or enlarge any power vested in them. The same thing that will happen if the general power had been reduced to specifics and any one of these were violated. The same thing, in short, as if the State legislatures violated their respective constitutional authorities.

First, the success of the usurpation will depend on the executive and judiciary departments, which are to expound and interpret the legislative acts. And in the last resort, a remedy will be obtained from the people, who can elect more faithful representatives, who can annul the acts of the usurpers.

The truth is, that this ultimate remedy may work better against the unconstitutional acts of the federal than the State legislatures, simply because every such act of the federal government will be an invasion of the rights of a State. The States will always be ready to note deviations, to sound the alarm to the people, and to exert their local influence to change federal representatives.

There is no such intermediate body between the State legislatures and the people interested in watching their conduct. Violations of the State constitutions are more likely to remain unnoticed and unredressed.

2. Federal Laws Supreme

18 "This Constitution and the laws of the United States which shall be made in pursuance thereof and all treaties made, or which shall be made, under the authority of the United States, shall be the supreme law of the land; and the judges in every State shall be bound thereby, anything in the Constitution or laws of any State to the contrary notwithstanding."

Lack of State Supremacy-Saving Clause

19 The indiscreet zeal of the adversaries to the Constitution has betrayed them into an attack on this part of it. Without it, the Constitution would have been clearly and radically defective. To fully realize this, we only need to imagine what would happen if the supremacy of the State constitutions had been left complete by a saving clause in their favor.

Saving Clause, New Authorities

20 First. Since each State constitution invests in its State legislature absolute sovereignty, any authorities contained in the proposed Constitution that exceed those listed in the Articles of Confederation would be annulled. The new Congress would be reduced to the same impotent condition as its predecessors.

Some States Nullify Constitution

21 Second. Since the constitutions of some States do not even expressly

and fully recognize the existing powers of the Confederacy, an explicit statement of the States' supremacy would, in such States, bring into question every power contained in the proposed Constitution.

State Constitutions: Variety

22 Third. Since the State constitutions differ from each other, a treaty or national law, of equal importance to the States, might interfere with some and not with other constitutions. Consequently, it would be valid in some of the States and have no effect in others.

Authority of Union Subordinate to Parts

23 In the end, the world would have seen, for the first time, a system of government founded on an inversion of the fundamental principles of all government. The authority of the whole Union would have been subordinate to the States. It would have seen a monster in which the head was under the direction of the members.

3. Oath to Support Constitution

24 "The Senators and Representatives before mentioned, and the members of the several State Legislatures, and all executive and judicial officers, both of the United States and of the several States, shall be bound by oath or affirmation, to support this Constitution; but no religious test shall ever be required as a qualification to any office or public trust under the United States."

State Judges, Federal Constitution

25 Some people ask why it was necessary to force the State judicial system to support the federal Constitution. And why it's not necessary that officers of the United States take a similar oath in favor of the State constitutions.

State Officials:
Agents of Federal Constitution

26 Several reasons might explain the difference. I'll give one that is obvious and conclusive. Members of the federal government will not be agents of State constitutions. However, members and officers of the State governments will be essential agents of the federal Constitution.

The election of the President and Senate will depend, in all cases, on the State legislatures, as will the election of the House of Representatives. It will, probably forever, be conducted by the officers and according to the laws of the States.

4. Executive, Judicial Powers

27 Among the provisions for giving efficacy to the federal powers might be added those which belong to the executive and judiciary departments. But since these will be examined in another place, I'll pass over them here.

All Constitutional Federal Powers
Are "Necessary And Proper"

28 We have now reviewed, in detail, all the articles that define the power delegated by the proposed Constitution to the federal government. It brings us to the undeniable conclusion that no part of the power is unnecessary or improper for accomplishing the necessary objectives of the Union.

` The question, therefore, of whether this amount of power shall be granted or not, resolves itself into another question: whether or not a government commensurate to the exigencies of the Union shall be established.

Or, in other words, whether the Union itself shall be preserved.

PUBLIUS

. . . .

Constitutional references:

Article 1, section 10	271-295	restrictions on State authority
Article 1, section 8	233-237	necessary & proper clause
Article 6	548-555	federal laws, Constitution supreme over States
Article 6	556-564	oath to support federal Constitution, no religious test

Number 45

Constitutional Federal Powers Not Dangerous to State Sovereignty

Having shown that none of the powers transferred to the federal government is unnecessary or improper, the next question is whether the whole collection of them will be dangerous to the authority left in the States.

Union Benefits vs. State Powers

2 Rather than focusing on the degree of power absolutely necessary to fulfill the purposes of the federal government, the adversaries of the proposed Constitution have exhausted themselves in a secondary inquiry into the possible consequences to the State governments of the proposed degree of federal power.

But if the Union, as has been shown, is essential to the security of the American people against foreign danger, if it is essential to their security against wars among the different States, if it is essential to guard them against violent and oppressive factions that threaten the blessings of liberty, and against those military establishments that gradually poison its very fountain, and if, in a word, the Union is essential to the happiness of the American people, is it not preposterous to argue against a government, without which the objectives of the Union cannot be attained, by saying it may detract from the importance of the governments of the individual States?

Was the American Revolution fought, the American Confederacy formed, the precious blood of thousands spilt, and the hard-earned substance of millions lavished, not so the people of America can enjoy peace, liberty, and safety, but so individual State governments can enjoy some power, with certain dignities and attributes of sovereignty?

The impious doctrine in the Old World said that people were made for kings, not kings for the people. Is the same doctrine to be revived in the New World in another shape—that the solid happiness of the people is to be sacrificed to a different political institution, the States?

It is too soon for politicians to presume that we'll forget the public good. The real welfare of the people is the supreme objective. Attaining this objective is government's only value.

If the Constitution was against the public happiness, I would say, Reject the plan. If the Union itself was inconsistent with the public happiness, I would say, Abolish the Union.

In a similar manner, whenever the sovereignty of the States is incompatible with the happiness of the people, every good citizen should cry out, Let the former be sacrificed to the latter. The necessary depth of the sacrifice has been shown. The question before us is how far the unsacrificed residue will be endangered.

No Danger from Federal Government

3 Several important subjects discussed in these papers disprove the supposition that the federal government will gradually prove fatal to the State governments. The more I evaluate the subject, the more fully I am persuaded that the large number of State governments is much more likely to disturb the balance than the federal government.

History: Federal Government at Risk

4 All the examples of ancient and modern confederacies show the strong tendency for member states to plunder the general government's authority. And the general governments are ineffectual to defend themselves against encroachments. In most examples, the system was very dissimilar from the one we are considering, weakening any possible inferences that can be made. However, since the States will retain a very extensive portion of active sovereignty under the proposed Constitution, the inferences shouldn't be totally disregarded.

In the Achaean league, the federal government had power similar to the government framed by the convention. The Lycia Confederacy, as far as its principles and form are recorded in history, must have been even more similar. Yet history doesn't tell us that either of them ever degenerated, or even tended to degenerate, into one consolidated government. On the contrary, we know that one of them was ruined because the federal authority couldn't prevent the dissensions and, eventually, the disunion of the subordinate authorities.

These are worthy of our attention because in both cases the external causes pushing the parts together were much more numerous and powerful than in our case. Consequently, less powerful bonds between members were sufficient to bind them to the head and to each other.

Feudal System: Local Bonds

5 In the feudal system, we see a similar propensity exemplified. In spite of the antagonistic relationship between the local sovereigns [barons] and the people in every case, and the sympathy between the general sovereign [monarch] and the people in some cases, local sovereigns usually prevailed during encroachment attempts. If external dangers had not forced internal harmony and subordination and, more importantly, if the people had liked their local sovereigns, today there would be as many independent princes as there were formerly feudatory barons instead of a few great European kingdoms.

Advantages of State Governments

6 The State governments will have several advantages over the Federal government: their immediate dependence on one another, the weight of personal influence each side will possess, the powers vested in them, the predilections and probable support of the people, and the disposition and ability to resist and frustrate the measures of each other.

Federal Officials Owe States for Positions

7 The State governments are essential parts of the federal government. But the federal government is in no way essential to the operation or organization of the State governments.

Without the intervention of the State legislatures, the President of the United States cannot be elected at all. In all cases, they participate in his appointment and, in most cases, determine it. The Senate will be elected absolutely and exclusively by the State legislatures. Even though the people elect the House of Representatives, their decision will be influenced by men whose own influence over the people results in their election into the State legislatures.

Thus, each elected official in the federal government will owe his political existence, more or less, to the

State governments. Consequently, they must feel a dependence more likely to produce a disposition too obsequious than too overbearing towards them.

On the other side, the component parts of the State governments will never be indebted for their appointment to the direct agency of the federal government, and very little, if at all, to the local influence of its members.

More People Work for States

8 Fewer people will be federal employees under the Constitution of the United States than the number employed by the States. Consequently, the former will have less personal influence.

The members of the State legislative, executive, and judiciary departments, State justices of peace, militia officers, and all county and city officers—that is, all State and local officials—will have acquaintances in every class and circle of people. They will exceed in number and influence the total number of people employed in the administration of the federal system.

Compare the number of people in the three great departments of the thirteen States, excluding from the judiciary department the justices of peace, with the number of people in the corresponding departments of the one federal government. Compare the number of militia officers of three million people with the military and marine officers of any permanent federal force within the probable, or even possible area of the entire country, and in this view alone, we may pronounce the advantage of the States to be decisive.

Both the federal and State governments will have collectors of revenue. Since the former will be principally on the seacoast and not very numerous, while those of the latter will be spread over the face of the country and will be very numerous, the States again have the advantage. It is true that the Confederation is to possess, and may exercise, the power to collect internal as well as external taxes throughout the States. But this power will probably not be resorted to, except for supplemental purposes of revenue. States will have the option of supplying their quotas by previous collections of their own. And the eventual collection, under the immediate authority of the Union, will generally be made by the officers appointed by the States.

Indeed, it is extremely probable that in other cases, particularly in the judiciary, the officers of the States will also serve under the authority of the Union.

However, if the federal government appoints separate collectors of internal revenue, the total number would be nothing compared to the multitude of State tax collection officers. Every district with a federal collector would have no less than thirty or forty, or even more, officers of different descriptions, many persons of character and weight, whose influence would lie on the side of the State.

Federal Powers Limited; State Indefinite

9 The Constitution delegates a few, defined powers to the federal government. The remaining State powers are numerous and indefinite.

Federal powers will be principally exercised on external objects, like war, peace, negotiation, and foreign commerce. Taxation will be the primary federal power over foreign commerce.

The State powers extend to everything that, in the ordinary course of affairs, concerns the lives, liberties, property of the people, internal order, improvement, and the prosperity of the State.

War vs. Peacetime Influence

10 The federal government's operations will be most extensive and important in times of war and danger. Those of the State governments, in times of peace and security.

Since times of war will probably be small compared to peacetime, the State governments will enjoy another advantage over the federal government. Indeed, the more adequate the federal national defense, the less frequent the danger that might favor its ascendancy over the governments of the States.

Invigorates Powers in Articles

11 An accurate and candid examination of the new Constitution shows that the change it proposes consists much less in the addition of NEW POWERS to the Union than in the invigoration of its ORIGINAL POWERS.

The regulation of commerce is a new power. But it seems to be an addition that few people oppose and from which no apprehensions are entertained.

The Articles of Confederation already gives Congress the powers relating to war and peace, armies and fleets, treaties and finance—and the other more considerable powers. The proposed change doesn't enlarge these powers, it only substitutes a more effective mode of administering them.

The change relating to taxation may be regarded as the most important. Yet the present Congress has the same authority to REQUIRE from the States indefinite supplies of money for the common defense and general welfare as the future Congress will require from individual citizens. And the citizens will be no more bound than the States themselves have been to pay the quotas respectively taxed on them.

If the States had complied punctually with the Articles of Confederation or if their compliance could have been enforced with as peaceable a means as may be used with success towards a single person, our past experience shows that the State governments would not have lost their constitutional powers and gradually consolidated. To maintain that this would have happened is the same as saying that State governments cannot exist within any system that accomplishes the essential purposes of the Union.

PUBLIUS

Constitutional references:

Article 2, section 1	305-309	States appoint presidential electors
Article 1, section 3	42-44	Senator elected by State legislatures
Article 1, section 2	5-10	people elect Representatives
Article 1, section 8	171-177	taxation
Article 1, section 8	180-182	regulation of commerce
Article 1, section 2	16-27	proportioning taxes

Number 46

Federal vs. State Government Authority

Resuming the subject of the last paper, I will proceed with the inquiry into whether the federal government or the State governments will be more preferred and supported by the people. Although appointed or elected by different modes, both are substantially dependent on the citizens of the United States. I will, here, assume this to be true, and will save the proofs for another place.

The federal and State governments are simply agents and trustees of the people with different powers designed for different purposes. The adversaries of the Constitution seem to have lost sight of the people in their discussions on this subject. And they have viewed the federal and State governments not only as mutual rivals and enemies, but as uncontrolled in their efforts to usurp the authorities of each other.

These gentlemen must be reminded of their error. They must be told that the ultimate authority, whatever its origin, resides in the people alone. Whether either one will be able to enlarge its sphere of jurisdiction at the expense of the other will not depend on which is more ambitious or where it is located.

Truth, no less than decency, requires the assumption that every case depends on the sentiments and sanction of their common constituents.

Attachment of People to States

2   Besides those suggested earlier, many considerations seem to show, beyond a doubt, that the first and most natural attachment of the people will be to their State governments. A greater number of individuals will expect to rise within the administrations of State governments. From this gift will flow a greater number of civil service offices and benefits. All the more domestic and personal interests of the people will be regulated and provided for by the superintending care of the States. The people will be more familiar and conversant about State issues. A greater proportion of the people will have the ties of personal acquaintance of friendship, family and party attachments with State officials, strengthening the popular bias towards the State.

Experience Confirms State Bias

3   Experience confirms this bias. Even though the federal administration, up until now, has been very defective compared to what is hoped for under a better system, during the war and as long as the federal government was solvent, it was as important as it will ever be in the future. At the time, it was also engaged in a series of measures to protect everything that was dear and acquire everything that could be desirable to the people at large. Nevertheless, after the transient enthusiasm for the early Congress, it was invariably found that the attention and attachment of the people turned anew to their own State governments. The federal administration was at no time a popular idol. Opponents to proposed enlargements of the few governmental powers and its importance were usually men who wished to build their political importance on the predispositions of their fellow citizens.

Federal Powers Limited

4 Therefore, if people in the future become more partial to the federal than the State governments, the change can only result from manifest and irresistible proofs of better administration overcoming the people's original tendencies. In that case, the people should not be stopped from placing their confidence where they discover it is most appropriate. But even in that case, the State governments would have little to fear because federal powers are only applicable within a certain sphere where federal power can be advantageously administered.

Resources: Federal vs. States

5 The last points on which I propose to compare the federal and State governments are the disposition and the resources each may possess to resist and frustrate the measures of each other.

States Influence Congress not visa versa

6 As already proven, the federal government will depend more on the State governments than the latter on the former. Both will depend on the people, who are predisposed to be more loyal to the State governments. As far as these causes influence the disposition of each towards the other, the State governments clearly have the advantage.

But there is another distinct and very important reason that the State governments will have the advantage. The predispositions of federal officials will generally be favorable to the States. But State officials will rarely carry into the public councils a bias in favor of the federal government. A local spirit will infallibly prevail more often in members of Congress than a national spirit will prevail in the legislatures of the States.

Everyone knows that many of the errors committed by State legislatures are the result of members being willing to sacrifice the comprehensive, permanent interest of the State to the specific, separate views of the counties or districts in which they reside. If State legislators don't sufficiently enlarge their policy to embrace the collective welfare of their State, how can we imagine that federal legislators will make the aggregate prosperity of the Union, and the dignity and respectability of its government, the objects of their affections and consultations?

For the same reason that the members of the State legislatures will be unlikely to attach themselves to national objectives, members of the federal legislature will be likely to attach themselves too much to local objectives. States will be to national legislators what counties and towns are to State legislators. Too often, measures will be decided, not on their effect on national prosperity and happiness, but on the prejudices, interests, and pursuits of the governments and people of the individual States.

What has been the general characteristic spirit of Congress? Its journal and candid statements of members inform us that members have, too frequently, displayed the character of partisans of their respective States than of impartial guardians of a common interest. If local considerations were improperly sacrificed to the aggrandizement of the federal government once, the great national interests have suffered on a hundred occasions from undue attention to State prejudices, interests, and views.

I do not mean to insinuate that the new federal government will not embrace a more enlarged policy than the existing government may have pursued. Nor am I saying that its views will be as confined as those of the State legislatures. I am only saying that the national government will partake sufficiently in the spirit of both the State and federal governments to be disinclined to invade the rights of the individual States, or the prerogatives of their governments. The motives of State governments, to augment their prerogatives by defalcations from the federal government, will not be overruled by reciprocal predispositions in federal officials.

States can Block Federal Encroachments

7 If the federal government, like the State governments, felt disposed to extend its power beyond the due limits, the States would still have the advantage in the means of defeating such encroachments.

If a State act is unfriendly to the national government but generally popular in that State, and doesn't too grossly violate the oaths of the State officers, it is executed immediately, using State resources. If the federal government opposed the action or sent federal officers to stop it, the federal response would inflame the zeal of all parties on the side of the State, and the evil couldn't be prevented or repaired, if at all, without using methods that must always be resorted to with reluctance and difficulty.

On the other hand, if an unreasonable measure of the federal government is unpopular in some States, which would usually be the case, or even if a reasonable measure is unpopular, which may sometimes happen, the means of opposition to it are powerful and at hand. The anxiety of the people, their repugnance and, perhaps, refusal to cooperate with the officers of the Union, the frowns of the State courts, and the embarrassments created by legislative devices that often would be added on such occasions would expose, in any State, difficulties not to be ignored. They would form, in a large State, very serious impediments. And where the sentiments of several adjoining States happened to be in unison, would present obstructions that the federal government would hardly be willing to encounter.

States Would Fight Federal Usurpations

8 But ambitious encroachments of the federal government on State authority would not excite the opposition of only a single State or only a few States. They would be signals of general alarm. Every government would espouse the common cause. A correspondence would be opened. Plans of resistance would be concerted. One spirit would animate and conduct the whole. In short, the same resistance groups would result from an apprehension of the federal yoke as was produced by the dread of a foreign yoke. And unless the federal government's projected innovations are voluntarily renounced, the same appeal to a trial of force would be made in the one case as was made in the other. But what degree of madness could ever drive the federal government to such an extremity.

In the contest with Great Britain, one part of the empire was employed against the other. The more numerous part invaded the rights of the less numerous part. The attempt was unjust and unwise. But it was not in speculation absolutely chimerical.

But what would be the contest in our hypothetical case? Who would be the parties? A few representatives of the people [i.e., elected federal officials] would be opposed by the people themselves. Or one set of representatives would be contending against thirteen sets of representatives, with the whole body of their common constituents on the side of the latter.

Military Force to Usurp State Power

9 There is only one scenario remaining that would fulfill the prophesy of the State governments' downfall at the hands of the federal. It includes the visionary supposition that the federal government previously accumulates a military force for the projects of ambition.

The reasonings in these papers have been employed to little purpose indeed, if it is necessary now to disprove the reality of this danger. That the people and the States would, for a sufficient period of time, elect an uninterrupted succession of men ready to betray both. Throughout this period, the traitors would uniformly and systematically pursue some fixed plan for the extension of the military establishment. The State governments and the people would silently and patiently behold the gathering storm, continuing to supply the materials, until it was prepared to burst on their own heads.

This series of events must appear to everyone more like the incoherent dreams of a delirious jealousy, or the misjudged exaggerations of a counterfeit zeal, than like the sober apprehensions of genuine patriotism.

However, extravagant as the supposition is, let it be made. Let a regular army, fully equal to the resources of the country, be formed. And let it be entirely devoted to the federal government. Still it could be safely assumed that the State governments, with the people on their side, would be able to repel the danger. According to the best computations, the highest number to which a standing army can be carried in any country does not exceed one-hundreth of the whole number of souls, or one twenty-fifth part of the number able to bear arms. This proportion would not yield, in the United States, an army of more than 25,000 or 30,000 men.

These would be opposed by a militia amounting to near half a million armed citizens with officers chosen form among themselves, fighting for their common liberties, and united and conducted by local governments possessing their affections and confidence.

It may be doubted whether this kind of militia could ever be conquered by such a proportion of regular troops. Those best acquainted with the last successful resistance of this country against the British arms will be most inclined to deny the possibility. Besides the advantage of being armed, which Americans possess unlike the people of almost every other nation, the existence of State governments to which the people are attached and by which the militia officers are appointed, forms a barrier against the enterprises of ambition that is more insurmountable than any which a simple government of any form can admit of.

Despite the military establishments in several kingdoms of Europe, which are as large as the public resources will bear, the governments are afraid to trust the people with arms. And it is not certain that with this aid alone they would not be able to shake off their yokes. But if the people possessed the additional advantages of local governments chosen by themselves, who could collect the national disposition, direct the national force, and appoint officers from the militia, it may be said, with the greatest assurance, that the throne of every tyranny in Europe would be speedily overturned in spite of the legions which surround it.

Let's not insult the free and gallant citizens of America with the suspicion that they would be less able to defend the rights that they actually possess, than the debased subjects of arbitrary power would be to rescue theirs from the hands of their oppressors.

Let's no longer insult the American people with the supposition that they can ever reduce themselves to the necessity of making the experiment, by a blind and tame submission to the long train of insidious measures that must precede and produce it.

People Will Stop Federal Usurpation

10 The current argument may be put into a very concise form that appears conclusive. Either the federal government's construction will render it sufficiently dependent on the people, or it will not.

If it is sufficiently dependent on the people, that dependence will restrain schemes obnoxious to their constituents from forming. Or, if not, it will not possess the confidence of the people and its schemes of usurpation will be easily defeated by the State governments, who will be supported by the people.

Federal Powers Won't Hurt States

11 Summing up the ideas in this and the last paper, they seem to amount to the most convincing evidence that the powers proposed to be lodged in the federal government are as little formidable to those reserved to the individual States, as they are indispensably necessary to accomplish the purposes of the Union. And all the alarms that have been sounded, of a meditated and consequential annihilation of the State governments must, on the most favorable interpretation, be ascribed to the chimerical fears of the authors of them.

PUBLIUS

Number 47

Separation of Legislative, Executive, Judicial Powers

Having reviewed the general form of the proposed government and the power allotted to it, I will now examine the specific structure of this government and the distribution of its total power among its parts.

Critics: Violates Separation Maxim

2　One major objection made by the more respectable adversaries to the Constitution is its supposed violation of the political maxim that the legislative, executive, and judiciary departments should be separate and distinct.

It is said that the structure of the federal government doesn't seem to have this essential precaution in favor of liberty. The powers are distributed and blended in a manner that destroys all symmetry and beauty of form, and exposes some essential parts of the government to the danger of being crushed by the disproportionate power of other parts.

Separation of Powers, Liberty

3　This objection is based on a political truth with the greatest intrinsic value and endorsed by the most enlightened patrons of liberty. The holding of all powers—legislative, executive, and judiciary—in the same hands, whether by one person, a few, or many, and whether hereditary, self-appointed, or elective, is the very definition of tyranny. Therefore, if the federal Constitution combined powers, or mixed powers in a way that tended to lead to a dangerous accumulation, no further arguments would be necessary to inspire a universal rejection.

I believe, however, that it will become clear to everyone that the charge cannot be supported and the maxim it relies on has been totally misunderstood and used incorrectly.

In order to make an informed judgment on this important subject, it is proper to investigate why the preservation of liberty requires that the three great departments of power should be separate and distinct.

Political Scientist, Montesquieu, Recommends Separation of Power

4　The expert always quoted on this subject is the famous Montesquieu. If he didn't discover this invaluable precept in political science, he can be credited, at least, with effectually recommending it to mankind. Let's try to discover his meaning.

Maxim in British Constitution

5　The British Constitution was to Montesquieu what Homer has been to the didactic writers on epic poetry. As poets consider the work of the immortal bard as the perfect model from which the principles and rules of the epic art were drawn, and the standard used to judge all similar works, so has the great political critic, Montesquieu, viewed the Constitution of England as the standard. Or, to use his words, it is the mirror of political liberty. It contains several elementary truths, principles that are part of the British system. So that we make no mistakes interpreting his meaning, let's return to the source from which the maxim was drawn.

Powers Mixed in British Constitution

6　A brief look at the British Constitution reveals that the legislative, executive, and judiciary departments are not totally separate and distinct from each other.

The chief executive is an integral part of the legislative authority. He, alone, makes treaties with foreign sovereigns that have, under certain limitations, the force of legislative acts. All the members of the judiciary department are appointed by him, can be removed by him on petition by the two Houses of Parliament, and become, when he wants to consult them, one of his constitutional councils.

One legislative house also forms a constitutional council to the executive chief, at the same time that it is the sole depository of judicial power in cases of impeachment, and is the supreme court of appeals in all other cases.

The judges, again, are so connected with the legislative branch that they often attend and participate in its deliberations, though they cannot vote.

No One Has *Total* Power of Two Branches

7　From these facts, which guided Montesquieu, it may be inferred that, in saying "There can be no liberty where the legislative and executive powers are united in the same person, or body of magistrates," or, "if the power of judging be not separated from the legislative and executive powers," he didn't mean that the government's branches should have no *partial agency* in, or no *control* over, the acts of each other. His words and examples make his meaning clear: when the *whole* power of one branch is in the same hands as the *whole* power of another branch, the fundamental principles of a free constitution are subverted.

This would have been true in the British constitution if the king, who is the sole executive magistrate, also held the complete legislative power, or the supreme administration of justice; or if the entire legislative body was also the supreme judiciary, or the supreme executive authority. This, however, is not among the vices of that constitution.

The chief executive cannot, himself, make law, though he can veto every law; he cannot personally administer justice, though he appoints those who administer it.

The judges can exercise no executive power, though the executive chooses them. Nor any legislative function, though they may be advised by legislative councils.

The entire legislature can perform no judiciary act, but joint acts of the two houses of the legislature can remove a judge from office, and one house has the judicial power of final appeal. The entire legislature, again, can exercise no executive prerogative, though one house constitutes the supreme executive magistracy, and the other, after an impeachment vote by one third, can try and condemn all the subordinate officers in the executive department.

Liberty Demands "Separation" Maxim

8　Montesquieu's reasons for his maxim further demonstrate his meaning.

"When the legislative and executive powers are united in the same person or body," says he, "there can be no liberty, because apprehensions may arise lest *the same* monarch or senate *enact* tyrannical laws to *execute* them in a tyrannical manner."

And: "Were the power of judging joined with the legislative, the life and liberty of the subject would be exposed to arbitrary control, for *the judge* would then be *the legislator.* Were it joined to the executive power, *the judge* might behave with all the violence of *an oppressor.*"

Some of the reasons are more fully explained in other passages. But, even briefly stated as here, they establish the meaning of this celebrated maxim of this celebrated author.

Separation of Powers: New Hampshire

9 If we look at the State constitutions, we find that, despite the emphatical and, sometimes, unqualified terms in which this axiom is stated, there is not a single example of the departments of power being absolutely separate and distinct.

New Hampshire has the newest constitution. Its framers seemed to be fully aware that it would be impossible and inexpedient to avoid any mixture, whatever, of these departments. It qualifies the doctrine by declaring "that the legislative, executive, and judiciary powers ought to be kept as separate from, and independent of, each other *as the nature of a free government will admit; or as is consistent with that chain of connection that binds the whole fabric of the constitution in one indissoluble bond of unity and amity.*"

Accordingly, her constitution mixes these departments in several ways. The Senate, a part of the legislature, is also a judicial tribunal for impeachment trials. The president, who is the chief executive, is the presiding member of the Senate. His vote is equal to the others and a casting vote in case of a tie. The chief executive is elected, yearly, by the legislature and his council is chosen, yearly, by and from the members of the legislature. Several state officials are also appointed by the legislature. And the executive appoints members of the judiciary.

Massachusetts Constitution

10 The Massachusetts constitution expresses this fundamental article of liberty in more general terms. Its prefix declares "that the legislative department shall never exercise the executive and judicial powers, or either of them; the executive shall never exercise the legislative and judicial powers, or either of them; the judicial shall never exercise the legislative and executive powers, or either of them."

This corresponds precisely with Montesquieu's doctrine, as explained earlier. And not a single point is violated by the proposed Constitution. It prohibits, without going any further, any entire branch from exercising the powers of another branch.

The Massachusetts Constitution has a partial mixture of powers. The chief executive has a qualified negative on the legislative body. The Senate, part of the legislature, is the impeachment court for members of both the executive and judiciary departments. Members of the judiciary are appointed by the executive and removable by the two legislative houses. Lastly, the legislature annually appoints a number of government officials. Since the appointment to offices, particularly executive offices, is in its nature an executive function, the authors of the constitution have, in this last point at least, violated the separation rule established by themselves.

Rhode Island, Connecticut

11 I pass over the constitutions of Rhode Island and Connecticut because they were formed prior to the Revolution, and before the principle under examination came under political attention.

New York Constitution

12 New York's constitution has no declaration on this subject. But it appears very clearly to have been framed with an eye to the danger of improperly blending the different departments. However, it gives the chief executive partial control over the legislature. And it gives a similar control to the judiciary. It even blends the executive and judiciary departments in the exercise of this control. Both the legislative and the executive are involved with the appointment of officers, both executive and judiciary. One house of the legislature and the principal members of the judiciary act as its court for appeals and impeachment trials.

New Jersey Constitution

13 New Jersey's constitution blends the powers of government more than any of the preceding. The legislature appoints the governor, who is the chief executive. He, also, is chancellor and ordinary, or surrogate of the State, is a member of the Supreme Court of Appeal, and is president, with a casting vote, of one of the legislative houses.

The same legislative house acts as executive council of the governor and, with him, constitutes the Court of Appeals.

The members of the judiciary are appointed by the legislature and removable by one house of it on the impeachment of the other.

Pennsylvania Constitution

14 According to the constitution of Pennsylvania, the president, who is head of the executive branch, is annually elected by a vote in which the legislature predominates. With an executive council, he appoints the members of the judiciary and forms an impeachment court for trial of all officers, judiciary as well as executive. The Supreme Court judges and justices of the peace seem also to be removable by the legislature. And the legislature, in certain cases, has the power to pardon, normally an executive power. The members of the executive council are made EX OFFICIO [automatically] justices of peace throughout the State.

Delaware's Constitution

15 In Delaware, the chief executive is annually elected by the legislature. The speakers of the two legislative houses are vice-presidents in the executive branch. The chief executive with six others, three appointed by each legislative house, constitutes the Supreme Court of Appeals. The chief executive joins with the legislature to appoint other judges.

Throughout the States, it appears that members of the legislature may be, at the same time, justices of the peace. In New York, the members of one house are EX OFFICIO justices of the peace, as are the members of the executive council. The principal officers of the executive are appointed by the legislature. And one house of the latter forms a court of impeachment. All officers may be removed by formal legislative petition.

Maryland's Constitution

16 Maryland adopted the separation-of-powers maxim in the most unqualified terms, declaring that the legislative, executive, and judicial powers of government should be forever separate and distinct from each other. Her constitution, however, has the legislature appoint the chief executive. And the executive appoints judges.

Virginia's Constitution

17 The language of Virginia's Constitution is still more pointed on this subject. It declares, "that the legislative, executive, and judiciary departments shall be separate and distinct; so that neither exercise the powers properly belonging to the other; nor shall any person exercise the powers of more than one of them at the same time, except that the justices of county courts shall be eligible to either House of Assembly."

Yet we find not only this clear exception with respect to the members of the lower courts, but the chief executive and his council are appointed by the legislature. Every three years, two members of the latter are removed from office at the pleasure of the legislature. And all principal offices, both executive and judiciary, are appointed by the legislature. Also, in one case, the legislature has the executive prerogative of pardon.

North Carolina's Constitution

18 North Carolina's constitution declares "that the legislative, executive, and supreme judicial powers of government ought to be for ever separate and distinct from each other." Yet the legislature appoints not only the chief executive, but all the principal officers within both the executive and the judiciary.

South Carolina's Constitution

19 The South Carolina constitution makes the chief executive eligible by

the legislature. The latter also appoints the members of the judiciary, including justices of the peace and sheriffs, and all officers, from the executive department to captains in the army and navy of the State.

Georgia's Constitution

20 The constitution of Georgia declares "that the legislative, executive, and judiciary departments shall be separate and distinct, so that neither exercise the powers properly belonging to the other."

But we find that the legislature appoints all members of the executive and it has the executive prerogative of pardon. Even justices of the peace are to be appointed by the legislature.

New Constitution
Doesn't Violate Maxim

21 In citing these cases in which the legislative, executive, and judiciary departments aren't kept totally separate and distinct, I don't want to be seen as an advocate for the way these State governments have been organized. I am fully aware that besides the many excellent principles they exemplify, they carry strong marks of the haste and, still stronger, inexperience under which they were framed. It is obvious that in some of the State constitutions the fundamental principle of separation of powers is violated. Some mix the powers too much. Some actually consolidate the different powers. And none of them provide a way to maintain the separation called for by their constitutions.

I wanted to clearly show that the charge brought against the proposed Constitution, that it violated the sacred maxim of free government, is not warranted by either the true meaning of that maxim by its author or by the way it has been, up until now, understood in America.

· ·

Constitutional references:
Article 1, section 1   1-4   legislative powers
Article 2, section 1   300-304   executive powers
Article 3, section 1   434-437   judicial powers

This interesting subject will be resumed in the next paper.

PUBLIUS

Number 48

Separation of Government's Powers, continued

In the last paper, I showed that the political maxim examined does not require that the legislative, executive, and judiciary branches should be totally unconnected with each other.

Next I will try to show that unless the branches are so interconnected and blended that each has a constitutional control over the others, the degree of separation required by the maxim, as essential to a free government, can never be maintained in practice.

Encroaching Nature of Power

2   Everyone agrees that the powers properly belonging to one branch should not to be directly and completely administered by either of the other branches. Clearly none of them should have, directly or indirectly, a superior authority over the others, in the administration of their respective powers.

Power has an encroaching nature and it should be effectually restrained from passing the limits assigned to it. After theoretically dividing the classes of power into legislative, executive, or judiciary, the next—and most difficult—task is to provide some practical security for each against the invasion of the others. The great problem is: what will this security be?

Written Barriers Inadequate

3   If the boundaries between these branches is in the constitution, can these parchment barriers be trusted to stop the encroaching spirit of power? Most of the State constitutions seem to rely principally on this security. But experience assures us that the efficacy of the provision has been greatly overrated. A more adequate defense is needed so the weaker branches of the government are protected from the more powerful.

Across the nation, the legislative is extending the sphere of its activity, drawing all power into its impetuous vortex.

Danger from Legislative Usurpations

4   The founders of our republic deserve so much credit for the their wisdom that no task is less pleasing than pointing out their errors. However, because we respect the truth, we must mention that they seem to have been completely focused on the danger to liberty from an overgrown, all-grasping hereditary magistrate, supported and fortified by an hereditary legislature. They seem to have forgotten the danger from legislative usurpations, which, by assembling all power in the same hands, must lead to the same tyranny as is threatened by executive usurpations.

Protect Liberty from Legislature

5   When a hereditary monarch holds many of government's powers, the executive branch is correctly seen as the source of danger. It is watched with a scrutiny inspired by a zeal for liberty.

In a democracy, a huge number of people gather to exercise the legislative functions. Because all citizens cannot regularly meet to discuss and make laws, it is continually exposed to the ambitious intrigues of the executive officials. A fear that the executive could use the excuse of an emergency to get a tyrannical toehold is wise.

But in a representative republic, the chief executive is carefully limited in both extent and duration of power. The legislative power is exercised by an assembly with a fearless confidence in its own strength, inspired by their assumed influence over the people. The legislature is sufficiently numerous to feel all the passions that motivate a multitude, yet not so numerous as to be incapable of pursuing its passions by means that reason prescribes. It is against the enterprising ambition of the legislature that the people should focus their scrutiny and take all precautions.

Legislative Limits Imprecise

6   The legislative branch derives a superiority in our governments from other circumstances. Its constitutional powers are extensive with imprecise limits. It can easily mask the encroachments it makes on the other branches, using complicated and indirect measures. Legislative bodies frequently question whether, in operation, a particular measure will, or will not, extend beyond the legislative sphere.

On the other side, executive power is restrained within a narrower compass and is simpler in nature. The judiciary is confined within even more specific landmarks. Usurpation attempts by either of these departments would immediately betray and defeat themselves.

Nor is this all. Since the legislative branch, alone, has the power to impose taxes. And in some constitutions it has full discretion, and in all it is a prevailing influence, over the wages of people who fill the other branches. Therefore, all government officials are dependent on the legislature, facilitating even greater legislative encroachments.

State Legislatures Usurping Power

7   For the truth on this subject, I rely on our own experience. If this experience needs specific proofs, they could multiply without end. I could collect an abundance of vouchers from the records and archives in every State in the Union. But as a more concise and equally satisfactory evidence, I will refer to the example of two States, attested to by two respected authorities.

Virginia Legislature Usurped Powers

8   The first example is Virginia. As we have seen, its constitution expressly says that the three great branches should not be intermixed. Mr. Jefferson is the authority supporting it. Besides his other advantages for observing the operation of Virginia's government, he was governor.

To fully convey the ideas on this subject resulting from his experience, it is necessary to quote a fairly long passage from his very interesting *Notes on the State of Virginia*, page 195:

All the powers of government, legislative, executive, judiciary, revert to the legislative body. The concentrating these in the same hands is precisely the definition of despotic government. It will be no alleviation that these powers will be exercised by a plurality of hands, and not by a single one. One hundred and seventy-three despots would surely be as oppressive as one. Let those who doubt it turn their eyes on the republic of Venice. As little will it avail us that they are chosen by ourselves. An *elective despotism* was not the government we fought for; but one which should not only be founded free principles, but in which the powers of government should be so divided and balanced among several bodies of magistracy as that no one could transcend their legal limits without being effectually checked and restrained by the others. For this reason, the convention that organized the government made the legislative, executive, and judiciary separate and distinct, so that no person should exercise the powers of more than one of them at the same time.

But no barrier was provided between these several powers.

The judiciary and executive branches were left dependent on the legislative for their subsistence in office, and some of them for their continuance in it. If, therefore, the legislature assumes executive and judiciary powers, no opposition is likely to be made; nor, if made, can be effectual; because in that case they may put their proceedings into the form of acts of Assembly, which will render them obligatory on the other branches. They have accordingly, *in many* instances, *decided rights* which should have been left to *judiciary controversy*, and *the direction of the executive, during the whole time of their session, is becoming habitual and familiar.*

Pennsylvania Violated Constitution

9 My other example is Pennsylvania. And the other authority is the Council of Censors, assembled in 1783 and 1784. One duty of the council, as stated by the constitution, was "to inquire whether the constitution had been preserved inviolate in every part; and whether the legislative and executive branches of government had performed their duty as guardians of the people, or assumed to themselves, or exercised, other or greater powers than they are entitled to by the constitution."

To accomplish this task, the council compared the actual legislative and executive activities with the constitutional powers of these branches. From the facts, most of the council, on both sides, agreed that the constitution had been flagrantly violated by the legislature in a variety of important instances.

Laws Passed
Without Public Notification

10 A great number of the laws passed violated, without any good reason, the rule that requires all bills of a public nature to be previously printed for the consideration of the people, even though this is one of the important precautions relied on by the constitution to prevent improper acts of the legislature.

Violated Right of Trial by Jury

11 The constitutional trial by jury has been violated and powers assumed that had not been delegated by the constitution.

Usurped Executive Powers

12 Executive powers have been usurped.

Legislature Interference
with Judiciary

13 The salaries of judges, which the constitution expressly requires to be fixed, have been occasionally varied. And the legislature has frequently heard and judged cases belonging to the judiciary.

Council Journal: More Examples

14 Those who want to read the specifics may consult the journals of the council, which are in print. Some of them may be attributable to specific circumstances connected with the war. But the majority must be considered as the spontaneous shoots of an ill-constituted government.

Executive Violated Constitution

15 It appears, also, that the executive branch has not been innocent of frequent violations of the constitution. Three observations, however, should be made:

1. Most were either immediate necessities because of the war, or recommended by Congress or the commander-in-chief.

2. In most of the other instances, they conformed either to the declared or the known sentiments of the legislature.

3. Pennsylvania's executive branch has more members than the other States, so it's as much like a legislative assembly as an executive council. And a council doesn't feel the same restraint as an individual, who is personally responsible for his acts. Members derive confidence from each other and are influenced by each other so that unauthorized measures would be more easily tried than where the executive branch is administered by a single hand, or by a few hands.

Words, Alone, Don't Block Tyrannical Accumulation of Power

16 The conclusion from these observations is that a simple statement within the Constitution, defining the limits of the branches, is not enough protection against the encroachments that lead to a tyrannical concentration of all the powers of government in the same hands.

PUBLIUS

Constitutional references:

Article 1, section 1	1-4	legislative powers
Article 2, section 1	300-304	executive powers
Article 3, section 1	434-437	judicial powers

Number 49

Jefferson: Constitutional Convention to Correct Power Mixing

The author, Mr. Jefferson, of the *Notes of the State of Virginia*, was quoted in the last paper. He added to that valuable work a draft of a constitution, which had been prepared in order to lay before a convention that had been expected to be called by the legislature in 1783 to establish a constitution for Virginia.

The plan, like everything from that author, marks a turn of thinking—

original, comprehensive, and accurate. It is even more worthy of attention because it equally displays a fervent attachment to republican government and an enlightened warning about the dangerous propensities that must be guarded against.

One precaution he proposes may be his original idea. He relies on it to safeguard the weaker branch of power against the invasions of the stronger.

As it relates to the subject we're discussing, it shouldn't be overlooked.

Constitutional Convention

2   His proposition is "that whenever any two of the three branches of government shall concur in opinion, each by the voices of two thirds of their whole number, that a convention is necessary for altering the constitution, or *correcting breaches of it*, a convention shall be called for the purpose."

Citizens Source of Power; Lend Power by Constitution

3   People are the only legitimate source of power. The constitution, under which the branches of government hold their power, is derived from the people. It seems in line with republican theory to return to the original authority, the people, not only whenever it is necessary to enlarge, diminish, or remodel the powers of the government, but also whenever any of the branches encroach on the constitutional authorities of the others.

When branches have constitutionally defined equal authority and power, clearly none of them can pretend to have an exclusive or superior right to determine the boundaries between their respective powers. How are the encroachments of the stronger to be prevented? Or how are the wrongs of the weaker to be redressed without an appeal to the people themselves. The people gave the government its authority and power through the constitution. They, alone, can declare its true meaning and enforce its observance.

Amendments, not Convention

4   There is certainly great force in this reasoning. The people must have a defined constitutional road available for extraordinary occasions. But there are some insurmountable objections to the proposal to return to the people, in all cases, to keep branches within their constitutional limits.

2 Branches Usurp Authority of Third

5   First, the provision doesn't provide for the case of two branches usurping the authority of the third. If the legislative authority, which has so many ways to influence the motives of the other departments, gains the support of either of the others, or even one-third of its members, the remaining department couldn't be helped by this provision. I won't dwell on this objection, however, because if I did, it might appear that my objection is to the specific details of the principle, rather than the principle itself.

Numbers Strengthen Opinions

6   The next objection comes from the inherent nature of the principle itself. Every appeal to the people would imply the government is defective. Frequent appeals would help deprive the government of the veneration that time bestows on everything and, without which, the wisest and freest government would probably not possess the required stability.

If it is true that all governments rest on popular opinion, isn't it also true that the strength of each individual's opinion and its influence on his conduct depends on the number of people he thinks have the same opinion. Man's reasoning, like man himself, is timid and cautious when left alone, and gains confidence as the number of people agreeing with him grows. When examples supporting an opinion are *ancient* and *numerous*, they have a double effect.

In a nation of philosophers, this consideration could be disregarded.

Enlightened reasoning would produce reverence for laws. But a nation of philosophers can no more expected than the philosophical race of kings wished for by Plato.

In every other nation, rational governments know the advantage of having the prejudices of the community on its side.

Danger of Destructive Passions

7 The danger of disturbing the public tranquillity by arousing public passions is an even more serious objection to frequently referring constitutional questions to a decision by the whole society.

Although the success of our governmental reforms honor the virtue and intelligence of the American people, it must be confessed that the experiments are far too ticklish to be unnecessarily multiplied. Remember that all the existing constitutions were formed in the midst of danger. That situation repressed the passions most unfriendly to order and concord. The people's enthusiastic confidence in their patriotic leaders stifled the ordinary diversity of opinions on great national questions. A universal ardor for new and opposite governmental forms produced a universal resentment and indignation against the ancient government. No party partianship mingled its leaven into the operation that made changes and reformed abises. Future situations do not have any equivalent security against the anticipated danger.

Legislature Most Influential Branch

8 But the greatest objection is that the decisions resulting from a constitutional convention would not fulfill the purpose of maintaining constitutional equilibrium in the government.

We have seen that republican governments tend to aggrandize the legislative at the expense of other branches. Therefore, the executive and judiciary branches would usually make the appeals to the people.

But would each side enjoy equal advantages at a convention? Let's review their different situations.

Fewer people are members of the executive and judiciary branches and they can be personally known to only a small number of people. The judiciary has permanent appointments and judges are too far removed from the people to share their predispositions. Politicians not in the executive are usually jealous of it; the executive administration is always susceptible to negative propaganda, making it unpopular.

On the other hand, legislative members are numerous. They live among the people. Their relatives, friends, and acquaintances include a great proportion of the most influential part of society. The fact that they are in the legislature implies that they have personal influence among the people, that they are seen to be the guardians of the rights and liberties of the people. With these advantages, it hardly seems that the branches seeking the correction would have an equal chance for a favorable outcome.

Congressmen Majority of Delegates

9 But members of Congress would not only successfully plead their cause with the people, they would also probably become judges in the issue. The same influence that got them elected to the legislature would get them a seat in the convention. If not all, at least this would be the case for many, especially the legislative leaders. In short, the convention would be composed chiefly of men who had been, who actually were, or who expected to be, members of the branch whose conduct was arraigned. Consequently, parties to the question would be deciding the question.

Passions would Judge

10 Sometimes appeals would be made under circumstances more favorable to the executive and judicial departments. The legislative usurpations might be too flagrant and sudden to allow a specious spin. A strong party might side with the other branches. The president might be a particular favorite of the people. In such a situation, the public might be less swayed by predispositions in favor of the legislative party.

But a convention's decision still could never by expected to turn on the true merits of the question. Inevitably, the decision would reflect the spirit of pre-existing parties or of parties springing out of the question itself. It would be connected with people of distinguished character and extensive influence in the community. It would be pronounced by the very men who had been agents in, or opponents of, the measures to which the decision would relate.

The *passions*, therefore, not the *reason*, of the public would sit in judgment. But public reason, alone, should control and regulate government. Passions should be controlled and regulated by the government.

Words, Convention Can't Enforce

11 We found in the last paper that mere declarations in the written Constitution are not sufficient to keep the branches within their legal rights. From the arguments in this paper, it appears that occasional appeals to the people would not be a proper or effective measure for that purpose.

I will not examine whether other provisions in the Virginia constitution might be adequate. Some are unquestionably founded on sound political principles, and all are framed with singular ingenuity and precision.

PUBLIUS

Number 50

Periodic Conventions to Correct Constitutional Infractions

It might be argued, perhaps, that instead of *occasional* appeals to the people, which are susceptible to the objections urged against them, fixed *periodic* appeals are the proper and adequate means of *preventing and correcting infractions of the Constitution.*

Scheduled Conventions Ineffective

2 I am examining remedies that *enforce* the Constitution, by keeping the branches of power within their bounds, without considering them as provisions for *altering* it.

First, scheduled periodic conventions appear no more desirable than conventions held when problems emerge. If the periods between conventions are short, problems needing review and correction will be in recent memory. Therefore, the same circumstances will exist that tend to slant and pervert the result with occasional appeals.

If the periods between conventions are distant from each other, the same argument applies to all recent measures. Others will receive a dispassionate review depending on their remoteness. However, inconveniences counterbalance this advantage.

First, excesses caused by current motives will be very feebly restrained by the possibility of public censure in the distant future. Can it be imagined that a legislature, with a hundred or two hundred members, eagerly bent to achieve an unconstitutional objective, would be stopped because their conduct might be censored in ten, fifteen, or twenty years?

Second, the mischievous effects of their abuses would often be completed before the remedy could be applied.

And lastly, if not completed, they would be of long standing, taken deep root, and not easily corrected.

Pennsylvania: Branch Encroachment

3   Revising the constitution, to correct recent breaches of it, as well as for other purposes, has actually been tried in one of the States. When the Council of Censors met in Pennsylvania in 1783 and 1784, one of their objectives was to inquire, "whether the constitution had been violated, and whether the legislative and executive branches had encroached on each other."

This important experiment in politics merits attention for several reasons. Because it was a single experiment made under specific circumstances, some examples may be thought not absolutely conclusive. But as applied to this discussion, it involves some facts that present a complete and satisfactory illustration of my reasoning.

Party Activists/Council Leaders

4   *First.* From the names of the gentlemen composing the council, it appears that some of its most active and leading members had also been leading activists in the parties that pre-existed in the State.

Some Reviewed Own Work

5   *Second.* It appears that the same active and leading members of the council had been active, influential members of the legislative and executive branches during the period reviewed. They had supported or opposed the very measures brought before the council for the constitutional test.

Two members had been vice president of the Senate. Several others were members of the executive council within the seven preceding years. One had been speaker and, several others, distinguished members of the legislature during the same period.

Passions, Not *Reasoning*, Ruled Debates

6   *Third.* The recorded minutes of the proceedings clearly show the effect of all these circumstances on the temper of their deliberations. Throughout the council, it was split into two fixed and violent parties. They acknowledged and lamented the fact. But even if they hadn't, an examination of their proceedings exhibits an equally satisfactory proof. No matter how unimportant or unconnected the issues, invariably the same men stood on opposite sides of them. Every unbiased observer may infer, without any danger of making a mistake and without judging either party or any individuals that, unfortunately, *passion*, not *reason*, presided over their decisions.

When men exercise their reason coolly and freely on a variety of distinct questions, inevitably they have different opinions on some of them.

When they are governed by a common passion, their opinions, if they can be called that, will be the same.

Constitutional Misinterpretations

7 *Fourth*. It is at least problematical that in several instances this body misconstrued the limits prescribed for the legislative and executive branches, instead of reducing and limiting them within their constitutional places.

No Effect on Legislature's Behavior

8 *Fifth*. I have never seen the council's constitutional decisions, whether they were right or wrong, influence the practices of the legislature. It even appears, if I'm not mistaken, that in one case the current legislature denied the opinions of the council and actually prevailed in the contest.

Problems Exist, Council No Cure

9 A study of the council, therefore, proves both the existence of the disease and, by its example, the inefficacy of the remedy.

Crisis Doesn't Excuse Liabilities

10 This conclusion cannot be invalidated by alleging that Pennsylvania was at a crisis, and had been in one for a long time, violently heated and distracted by partisan rage. Is it to be presumed that during any future seven-year period it will be free from partisanship? Can we presume that any other State, at any time, will be exempt from it?

Such an event should neither be presumed nor desired, because an extinction of parties necessarily implies either a universal alarm for the public safety or an absolute extinction of liberty.

Excluding Government Officials Wouldn't Solve Council's Problems

11 Excluding from the elected assemblies called to review the preceding administration of the government all the people involved with the government during that period, would not have solved the problem. The important task would probably have fallen to men with inferior capacities who, in other respects, would be little better qualified. Although they might not have been personally concerned in the administration and, therefore, not immediately involved in the measures to be examined, they would probably have been involved with the parties connected with these measures and probably be elected under their sponsorship.

PUBLIUS

Number 51

Separation of Powers: Structural Checks and Balances

What method should we use, then, to maintain the necessary partition of power between the different branches as laid down in the Constitution?

The only answer is: all outside provisions are inadequate. Therefore, the government must be structured, designed, so that the three constitutional branches and their relationships will have the ability to keep each other in their proper places.

Without presuming to undertake a full development of this important idea, I will hazard a few general observations. They may place it in a clearer light.

They may also help us judge the principles and structure of the government planned by the convention.

Perfect Separation: People Appoint All Officials

2   To a certain extent, everyone agrees that a separation of the different powers of government is essential to the preservation of liberty.

As a foundation towards that goal, it is clear that each branch should have a will of its own. Consequently, government should be designed so members of each branch have as little input as possible in the appointment of members of the others.

If this principle [separation of powers] was rigorously adhered to, all appointments to the executive, legislative, and judiciary branches would have to be made from the same fountain of authority, the people, through channels having no communication with one another.

Perhaps such a plan to construct the branches would be less difficult in practice than it appears in contemplation. However, difficulties and additional expense would accompany its execution. Therefore, some deviations from this principle must be allowed.

Judiciary: Specific Qualifications

In the construction of the judiciary, in particular, requiring that the people pick all members might not be very successful.

First, specific qualifications in the members are essential. The most important consideration should be to select the method of choice that best secures these qualifications.

Second, since judges hold permanent tenure, this would soon destroy all sense of dependence on the authority appointing them.

Executive, Judiciary Not Dependent on Legislature for Pay

3   Clearly, the members of each branch should be as little dependent as possible on a different branch for their compensation. Were the executive or the judicial not independent of the legislature on this point, their independence in every other area would be insignificant.

Authority, Motives to Resist Usurpations

4   But the best security against a gradual accumulation of powers in one branch, is giving to the administrators of each branch the necessary constitutional tools and personal motives to resist encroachments.

As in all cases, the provision for defense must be made proportional to the danger of attack. Ambition must be made to counteract ambition. The personal interests of the man must be connected with the constitutional rights of the place.

Government Reflects Human Nature; Angels Don't Need Government

It may be a reflection on human nature that such devices are necessary to control the abuses of government. But what is government itself but the greatest of all reflections on human nature?

If men were angels, no government would be necessary. If angels were to govern men, neither external nor internal controls on government would be necessary.

In framing a government that is to be administered by men over men, the great difficulty lies in this: you must first enable the government to control the governed, and in the next place, force it to control itself.

Dependency on the people is, no doubt, the primary control on the government. But experience has taught mankind that auxiliary precautions are necessary.

Checks and Balances in All Organizations

5   This policy of correcting through opposite and rival interests can be traced throughout the whole system of human affairs, private as well as public. We see it, particularly, in all subordinate distributions of power, where the aim is to divide and arrange the offices in a manner that each may be a check on the other—that the private interest of every individual may be a sentinel over the public rights. These prudent measures are just as important in the distribution of the supreme powers of the state.

Divide Legislative; Fortify Executive

6   But it is not possible to give each branch an equal power of self-defense.

In republican government, the legislative authority necessarily predominates. The remedy for this is to divide the legislature into different houses and make them, by different modes of election and different principles of action, as little connected with each other as the nature of their common functions and their common dependence on the society will allow. It may even be necessary to guard against dangerous encroachments with even further precautions.

Since the weight of the legislative authority requires it should be divided, the weakness of the executive may require, on the other hand, that it should be fortified.

At first view, an absolute negative on the legislature (veto) appears to be the natural defense with which the executive should be armed. But

by itself it might not be completely safe or sufficient. On ordinary occasions, it might not be exerted with the requisite firmness and, on extraordinary occasions, it might be perfidiously abused. Can not a solution to this absolute negative be supplied by some qualified connection between this weaker executive branch and the weaker side of the stronger legislative branch, by which the latter may be led to support the constitutional rights of the former, without being too much detached from the rights of its own branch?

Constitution, Separation of Powers

7   If these observations are based on just principles, as I persuade myself they are, and if they are applied as a criterion to the State constitutions and the federal Constitution, it will be found that, if the federal Constitution doesn't perfectly meet these principles, the State constitutions are infinitely less able to pass such a test.

U. S. Federal System Unique

8   Moreover, two special circumstances apply to the federal system in America, making it a unique situation.

State Governments: Additional Check on Federal Government

9   *First.* In a single republic, all the power surrendered by the people is submitted to the administration of a single government. To guard against usurpations, the government is divided into distinct and separate branches.

In the compound republic of America, the power surrendered by the people is first divided between two distinct governments, state and federal. Then the portion allotted to each is subdivided among distinct and separate branches. Hence the rights of the people are doubly protected. The different governments will control each other, at the same time that each will be controlled by itself.

Oppression from Society

10 *Second.* In a republic, society must not only be protected against the oppression of its rulers, but one part of the society must be guarded against the injustice of the other part.

Different interests necessarily exist in different classes of citizens. If a majority is united by a common interest, the rights of the minority will be insecure. There are only two methods of providing against this evil. One, create a will in the community independent of the majority—that is, of the society itself. Or, two, include into society so many separate descriptions of citizens that it will be either impossible or impractical to form a majority of the people into an unjust alliance.

The first method prevails in all governments possessing a hereditary or self-appointed authority. This is, at best, but a precarious security because a power independent of the society may well espouse the unjust views of the majority, as the rightful interests of the minority, and may possibly be turned against both parties.

The second method will be exemplified in the federal republic of the United States. All authority will be derived from and dependent on the society. The society itself will be broken into so many parts, interests, and classes of citizens that the rights of individuals, or of the minority, will be in little danger from interested combinations of the majority.

In a free government, the security for civil rights must be the same as that for religious rights. In one case, it consists of a multiplicity of interests

and, in the other, a multiplicity of sects. This is presumed to depend on the extent of the country and number of people comprehended under the same government.

To all sincere and serious friends of republican government, this must recommend a proper federal system. It shows that in exact proportion as the Union's territory is formed into more States, an oppressive alliance of a majority will be facilitated. Under the republican forms, it provides the best security for the rights of every class of citizen will be diminished. Consequently the stability and independence of some member of the government, the only other security, must be proportionally increased.

Justice is the final goal of government. It is the goal of civil society. It has always and always will be pursued until it is obtained or until liberty is lost in the pursuit.

In a society structured so that the stronger faction can easily unite and oppress the weaker, anarchy reigns as it does in nature, where the weaker individual is not protected against the violence of the stronger. Yet in nature, the uncertainty of their situation prompts even the stronger individuals to submit to a government that may protect the weak as well as themselves. In society, a similar motive will induce more powerful factions or parties to want a government that will protect all parties, the weaker as well as the more powerful.

Let's suppose the State of Rhode Island was separated from the Confederacy and left to itself. Can it be doubted that the repeated oppressions of factious majorities would cause such insecurity of rights under the popular form of government within such narrow limits that some power altogether independent of the people would soon be called for by the voice of the very factions whose misrule had provided the necessity of it.

The extended republic of the United States will embrace a great variety of interests, parties, and sects. A coalition of a majority of the whole society could seldom happen on any other principles than justice and the general good. While there is less danger to a minority from the will of a majority party, there must be less pre-text, also, to provide for the security of the minority by introducing into the government a will not dependent on the majority or, in other words, a will independent of the society itself.

Despite some opinions to the contrary, it is no less certain than it is important that the larger the society, provided it lies within a practical sphere, the more capable it will be of self-government. And happily for the *republican cause,* the practical sphere may be carried to a very great extent by a judicious modification and mixture of the *federal principle.*

PUBLIUS

Constitutional references:

Article 1, section 1	1-4	two legislative houses
Article 1, section 2	5-7	electing Representatives
Article 1, section 3	42-44	electing Senators
Article 1, section 2	40-41	Representatives impeach
Article 1, section 3	71-72	Senate tries impeachment
Article 1, section 5	95-97	each house judges elections
Article 1, section 5	102-105	each house, own rules
Article 1, section 6	125-131	hold no other government jobs
Article 1, section 7	138-170	Presidential veto, President signs bills

---

Number 52

House of Representatives:
Candidates, Elections, Term in Office

From the more general inquires pursued in the last four papers, I pass on to a more specific examination of the several parts of the government. I will begin with the House of Representatives.

Qualifications of Electors, Elected

2 The first study of this part of the government relates to the qualifications of the voters and Representatives.

The voters are to be the same as the electors of the largest house of the State legislatures.

The right of suffrage is justly defined as a fundamental article of republic government. It was incumbent on the convention, therefore, to define and establish this right in the Constitution. To allow Congress to occasionally regulate it would be improper for the reason just mentioned. To submit it to the discretion of the State legislatures would be improper for the same reason. Additionally, it would make the branch of the federal government that should be dependent on the people alone, too dependent on the State governments.

However, if the convention had established one uniform rule instead of allowing different qualifications in the different States, it would have been as dissatisfactory to some of the States as difficult for the convention. Therefore, the convention's provision appears to be the best option.

Every State will find it satisfactory because it conforms to the standard already established, or which may be established, by the State itself. It will be safe to the United States because, even though it is fixed by the State governments, it is not alterable by the State governments and it cannot be feared that the people of the States will alter this part of their constitutions in such a manner as to abridge the rights secured to them by the federal Constitution.

Candidate for Representative

3 The qualifications of Representatives are less carefully defined by the State constitutions. And it is easier to make them uniform. Therefore, they are defined in the proposed Constitution.

A Representative of the United States must be 25 years old, must have been a citizen of the United States for seven years, at the time of his election he must be an inhabitant of the State he is to represent, and, during the time of his service, he must hold no other office under the United States.

Under these reasonable limitations, the door into this part of the federal government is open to people of merit of every description, whether native or adoptive, whether young or old, and without regard to poverty or wealth, or to any particular religious faith.

Representatives' Term in Office

4 The second discussion about the representatives is their term in office. Two questions must be considered: first, whether biennial elections will, in this case, be safe; secondly, whether they are necessary or useful.

Frequent Elections: Depend on Voters

5 It is essential to liberty that the government has a common interest with the people. It is particularly essential that the House of Representatives has an immediate dependence on, and an intimate sympathy with, the people. Frequent elections are unquestionably the only policy that effectually secures this dependence and sympathy.

But how frequently is absolutely necessary for this purpose doesn't seem susceptible to any precise calculation and must depend on a variety of circumstances. Let us consult experience, the guide that should always be followed whenever it can be found.

Elections in Great Britain

6 Representation, as a substitute for a meeting of all the citizens in person, was imperfectly known to ancient politics. We expect instructive examples in more modern times. And even here, to avoid vague research, we will confine ourselves to the few examples that are best known and bear the greatest analogy to our specific case.

The first is the House of Commons in Great Britain. The history of this branch of the English Constitution, before the Magna Charta, is too obscure to yield instruction. Its very existence is a question among political historians.

The earliest available records prove that parliaments were to *sit* every year, not that they were to be *elected* every year. And even these annual sessions were left so much at the discretion of the monarch that, under various pretexts, very long and dangerous intermissions were often contrived by royal ambition. To remedy this grievance, a statute in the reign of Charles II limited the intermissions to three years.

On the accession of William III, when a revolution took place in the government, the subject was still more seriously confronted. It was declared to be among the fundamental rights of the people that parliament should be held *frequently*. By another statute, passed a few years later in the same reign, the term "frequently," which suggested the triennial period settled in the time of Charles II, is precisely defined. A new parliament shall be called within three years after the termination of the former.

It was changed again, early in the present century. Under an alarm for the Hanoverian succession, the time was extended from three to seven years.

From these facts, it appears that Great Britain has decided three years between elections is the shortest period necessary to bind the representatives to their constituents.

If we look at the degree of liberty retained even with elections every seven years and all the other vicious ingredients in the parliamentary constitution, we cannot doubt that a reduction of the period from seven to three years would extend the influence of the people over their representatives far enough to satisfy us that biennial elections, under our federal system, cannot possibly be dangerous to the required dependence of the House of Representatives on their constituents.

Ireland's Elections Rare

7 Until recently, elections in Ireland were regulated entirely by the crown and were seldom repeated, except on the accession of a new prince or some other contingent event.

The parliament that started when George II began his rule continued throughout his whole reign, a period of about thirty-five years. The representatives were dependent on the people only when there was an election to fill vacancies, and in the chance of some event that might produce a general new election. The Irish parliament's ability to maintain their constituents' rights, as far as they might want to, was extremely shackled by the crown's control over the subjects of their deliberation.

If I am not mistaken, these shackles were recently broken. And octennial parliaments have been established. The effect produced by this partial reform must be left to further experience.

From this view of it, Ireland can throw little light on the subject. As far as we can draw any conclusion from it, it must be that if the people of that country, under all these disadvantages, have been able to retain any liberty whatever, the advantage of biennial elections would secure every degree of liberty that depends on a connection between their representatives and the people.

Colonial States: Elections 1-7 Years

8   Let's bring our inquiry closer to home. The example of the States, when British colonies, claims particular attention and is so well known as to require little be said about it.

The principle of representation in at least one house of the legislature was established in all of them. But the election periods were different. They varied from one to seven years. Have we any reason to infer, from the spirit and conduct of the people's representatives prior to the Revolution, that biennial elections would be dangerous to the public liberties?

The spirit displayed at the start of the struggle that vanquished the obstacles to independence is the best proof that sufficient liberty had been everywhere enjoyed to inspire both a sense of its worth and a zeal for its proper enlargement. This remark is as valid for colonies whose elections were the least frequent as those most frequent.

Virginia was the first colony to resist the parliamentary usurpations of Great Britain. It was also the first to espouse, by public act, the resolution of independence. Nevertheless, in Virginia, if I am not misinformed, elections under the former government were every seven years. This example is brought into view not to prove of any particular merit, the priority of these events was probably accidental. And even less an advantage in *septennial* elections. When compared with a greater frequency, they are inadmissible. But as proof, and I think it is very substantial proof, that the liberties of the people can be in no danger from *biennial* elections.

Short Terms

9   The conclusion from these examples will be strengthened by remembering three circumstances.

First, the federal legislature will possess only part of the supreme legislative authority that is vested completely in the British Parliament and, with only a few exceptions, was exercised by the colonial assemblies and the Irish legislature. It is a well-founded maxim that, excluding all other circumstances, the greater the power, the shorter ought to be its duration. And conversely, the smaller the power, the more safely may its duration be protracted.

In the second place, on another occasion, it has been shown that the federal legislature will not only be restrained by its dependence on the people, but it will be, moreover, watched and controlled by several collateral legislatures, which other legislative bodies are not.

Third, no comparison can be made between the ability possessed by the more permanent branches of the federal government to seduce, if they should want to, the House of Representatives from their duty to the people, and the ability of the Senate to influence the popular house of the legislature. Therefore, with less power to abuse, the federal representatives will be less tempted on one side and doubly watched on the other.

PUBLIUS

Constitutional references:

Article 1, Section 2	5-7	representatives' biennial elections
Article 1, Section 2	7-15	qualifications of electors, elected
Article 1, Section 6	125-131	congress members can't hold another office
Article 6	561-564	no religious test

Number 53

Biennial Elections Safe, Promote Quality Representatives

I am here reminded of a current observation, "that where annual elections end, tyranny begins." If it is true, as has often been remarked, that cliches' are generally based in reason, it is no less true that once established, they are often applied to cases to which the reason of them does not extend. For proof, I need look no further than the case before us.

On what reason was this cliché' founded? No man will pretend that a natural connection exists between the sun or the seasons and how long a man's virtue can withstand the temptations of power. Happily for mankind, liberty is not confined to any single point of time. But liberty lies within extremes, affording sufficient latitude for all the variations required by the various situations and circumstances of civil society. If it was found to be expedient, the election of public officials might be, as in some instances it actually has been, daily, weekly, or monthly, as well as annual. If circumstances require a deviation from the rule on one side, why not also on the other side.

Turning our attention to the terms in the largest house of each State legislature, we find a variety of time periods.

In Connecticut and Rhode Island the periods are half-yearly. In the other States, except South Carolina, they are annual. In South Carolina they are biennial, as proposed in the federal government. The difference is four to one, between the longest and shortest periods. Yet it wouldn't be easy to show that Connecticut or Rhode Island is better governed or enjoys more liberty than South Carolina. Or that either the one or the other of these States is distinguished in these respects, and by these causes, from the States whose elections are different from both.

No Constitution: Legislature Can Change Government

2   In searching for the basis of this doctrine, I discovered only one, and it is completely inapplicable to our case.

The important distinction between a Constitution established by the people and unalterable by the government, and a law established by the government and alterable by the government, is well understood in America, but seems to be little understood and less observed in any other country.

Wherever the supreme power of legislation exists, the full power to change the form of the government also exists. Even in Great Britain where the principles of political and civil liberties have been the most discussed and where we hear of the rights of the Constitution, the authority of the Parliament is transcendent and uncontrollable in regard to the Constitution as an object of legislature. Accordingly several times they have actually changed by legislative acts some of the most fundamental articles of the government, specifically, the election period. On the last occasion, they not only introduced septennial to replace triennial elections, but by the same act continued themselves in place four years beyond the term for which the people elected them.

Frequency of elections is the cornerstone of free governments. These dangerous practices produce a very natural alarm among voters. And it has led them to seek some way to secure their liberty against this danger. In countries without a Constitution that controls the government and where one cannot be obtained, the type of constitutional security established in the United States was not attempted. Some other security was sought. And what better security could be found than the length of time as a standard for measuring the danger of changes, fixing the national sentiment, and uniting the patriotic efforts? The simplest, most familiar length of time applicable was a year. Hence, the doctrine has been inculcated by a laudable zeal in order to erect some barrier against the gradual changes of an unlimited government. The approach of tyranny was calculated by how far away from annual elections.

But what is the necessity of applying this measure to a government limited, as our federal government will be, by the authority of a paramount Constitution? Or who will pretend that the liberties of the American people will not be more secure under biennial elections, unalterably fixed by such a Constitution, than those of any other nation where elections were annual, or even more frequent, but subject to alterations by the ordinary power of the government?

Biennial Elections

3   Are biennial elections necessary and useful? Several obvious considerations will show that an affirmative answer is proper.

Legislator Experience Important

4   No man can be a competent legislator if he doesn't have, in addition to upright intentions, a sound judgment and some knowledge of the subjects on which he is to legislate. Some knowledge can be acquired through information within the compass of men in private as well as public life. Another part can only be thoroughly attained by actual experience in the station that requires the use of it. Therefore, in all such cases, the length of service should be somewhat proportional to how much practical knowledge is required to adequately perform the service.

The length of service established for the larger legislative house in most

States is, as we have seen, one year. The question then is: can a congressman acquire any greater proportion of the knowledge required for federal legislation in two years than the knowledge required and acquired in one year for State legislation? The very form of the question suggests its answer.

Large Area, Diversified Laws

5   In a single State, the required knowledge relates to existing laws, which are uniform throughout the State and with which all the citizens are more or less conversant, and to the general affairs of the State, which lie within a small area, are not very diversified and occupy the attention and conversation of every class of people.

The great theatre of the United States presents a very different scene. The laws are far from being uniform, varying in every State. The public affairs of the Union are spread throughout a very extensive region and are extremely diversified by the local affairs connected with them. They are difficult to learn in any other place than the central councils, where the representatives of every part of the empire bring knowledge of them.

The members from each of the States should possess some knowledge of the affairs, and even the laws, of all the States. How can foreign trade be properly regulated by uniform laws without some acquaintance with the commerce, the ports, the usage, and the regulations of the different States? How can the trade between the different States be regulated without some knowledge of their relative situations in these and other respects? How can taxes be judiciously imposed and effectually collected if

they are not knowledgeable to the different laws and local circumstances relating to these objects in the different States? How can uniform regulations for the militia be duly provided without a similar knowledge of the many internal circumstances that distinguish the States from each other?

These are the principal subjects of federal legislation and suggest, most forcibly, the extensive information that the representatives should acquire. The other interior subjects will require a proportionate degree of information.

Difficulties Will Decrease, Knowledge Increase

6   All these difficulties will, by degrees, diminish. The most laborious task will be properly inaugurating the government and the very first formation of a federal code. Improvements on the first drafts will become easier and fewer every year. Past transactions of the government will be a ready and accurate source of information to new members. The affairs of the Union will become more interesting, conversational subjects among the citizens at large. And the increased intercourse among the different States will contribute to the mutual knowledge of their affairs, as it will contribute to a general assimilation of their manners and laws.

But even with all these abatements, the business of federal legislation will continue to so far exceed, both in novelty and difficulty, the legislative business of a single State, as to justify the longer period of service assigned to those who are to transact it.

Foreign Affairs Learned as Legislator

7   A branch of knowledge a federal representative needs to acquire, and which has not been mentioned, is that of foreign affairs.

In regulating our own commerce, he should be acquainted with the treaties between the United States and other nations, and the commercial policies and laws of other nations. He should not be completely ignorant of the law of nations because it, as far as it is a proper object of municipal legislation, is submitted to the federal government.

And although the House of Representatives will not directly participate in foreign negotiations and arrangements, from the necessary connection between the areas of public affairs, the different areas will frequently deserve attention in the ordinary course of legislation and will sometimes demand legislative sanction and cooperation. Some portion of this knowledge may, no doubt, be acquired in a man's private life. But some of it can only be derived from the public sources of information. And all of it will be best acquired by attention to the subject during the period of actual service in the legislature.

Representatives' Distance Traveled

8 There are other considerations of less importance, perhaps, but worthy of notice.

The distance many of the representatives will be forced to travel, with all the necessary arrangements, might become serious objections made by men fit for this service, if limited to a single year than if extended to two years. No argument on this subject can be drawn from the case of the delegates to the existing Congress. They are elected annually, it is true. But their reelection is considered by the legislative assemblies almost as a matter of course. The election of representatives by the people would not be governed by the same principle.

Some Members Will Serve Long Time

9 As happens in all such assemblies, a few of the members will possess superior talents and, by frequent reelections, will become members of long standing. They will be masters of the public business and perhaps willing to avail themselves of those advantages. The greater the proportion of new members and the less the information of the bulk of the members, the more apt they will be to fall into the snares that may be laid for them. This remark is applicable to both the House of Representatives and the Senate.

Annual Elections Too Short to Unseat Irregular Members

10 With the advantage of frequent elections, comes an inconvenience. In a single, large State where elections and legislative sessions are once a year, spurious elections can not be investigated and annulled in time for the decision to have effect. If an election is won, no matter by what unlawful means, the irregular member, who takes his seat is sure of holding it a sufficient time to fulfill his goals. Hence, a very destructive encouragement is given to the use of unlawful means for obtaining irregular returns. If elections for the federal legislature were annual, this practice might be very seriously abused, particularly in the more distant States.

Each house is, as it necessarily must be, the judge of the elections, qualifications, and returns of its members. And whatever improvements may be suggested by experience for simplifying and accelerating the process in disputed cases, a great portion of a year would unavoidably elapse before an illegitimate member could be dispossessed of his seat. The prospect of such an event would do little to check unfair and illicit means of obtaining a seat.

Biennial Elections Safe to Liberty

11 All these considerations taken together give us reason to affirm that biennial elections will be as useful to the affairs of the public as we have seen that they will be safe to the liberty of the people.

PUBLIUS

Constitutional references:

Article 1, section 2   5-7   biennial elections
Article 1, section 5   95-97   each house judge of its own elections, returns, member qualifications

---

Number 54

Number of Representatives, Direct Taxes: Calculated by Same Rule

The next topic on the House of Representatives relates to the appointment of it members by the States, which is determined by the same rule as that of direct taxes.

Representation/Population; Taxes/Wealth

2 No one is arguing that the population of each State should not be the standard for determining each State's proportional representation. Likewise, using the same rule to determine each State's tax obligation will probably not be contested. However, the rule itself, in these two cases, is founded on two different principles.

In the case of representatives, the rule refers to the personal rights of the people, with which it has a natural and universal connection.

In the case of taxes, it refers to the proportion of wealth. It is not a precise measure. In fact, in most cases, it is a very unfit one. Despite the imperfection of the rule as applied to the relative wealth and contributions of the States, it is evidently the least objectionable among the practical rules. Since it recently received the general sanction of America, the convention selected it.

Objection: Counting Slaves In Population

3 Admitting all this, it might be asked: But does it follow from using numbers to measure representation, or slaves combined with free citizens as a ratio of taxation, that slaves should be included in the numerical rule of representation? Slaves are considered property, not persons. Therefore, they should be counted in estimates of taxation, which are founded on property. And they should be excluded from legislative representation, which is determined by a census of persons.

As I understand it, this is the objection stated in its full force. I will state the reasoning, which may be offered on the opposite side with equal candor.

Change Law, Slaves Become Citizens

4 "We subscribe to the doctrine," one of our Southern friends might observe, "that representation relates more closely to persons and taxation more closely to property. We join in applying this distinction to the case of our slaves. But we must deny the fact that slaves are considered as merely property and in no way whatever as persons. The true state of the case is, they have both qualities. Our laws consider them, in some respects, as persons and, in other respects, as property.

"Since the slave is forced to labor, not for himself but for a master, since one master can sell him to another master, since he is subject at all times to be restrained in his liberty and chastised in his body by the capricious will of another—the slave may appear to be degraded from the human rank and classed with those irrational animals which fall under the legal denomination of property.

"On the other hand, by being protected in his life and limbs against the violence of all others, even the master of his labor and his liberty, and in being punishable himself for all violence committed against others—the slave is clearly regarded by the law as a member of society, not as a part of the irrational creation. He is regarded as a moral person, not as a mere article of property.

"The federal Constitution, therefore, is correct when it views the character of our slaves as a mixture of persons and property. This is, in fact, their true character. It is the character bestowed on them by the laws under which they live. And it will not be denied that these are the proper criterion. Non-slave states dispute the inclusion of slaves in the computation of numbers. But the pretext of laws, alone, has transformed Negroes into property. And it is admitted, if the laws restored the rights that have been taken away, the Negroes could no longer be refused an equal share of representation with the other inhabitants.

Condemn Slavery , Yet Call Slaves Property

5 "This question may be looked at in another way. Everyone agrees that just as wealth and taxation are measured by numbers, numbers are the only proper measure of representation. Would the convention have been impartial or consistent, if they had excluded slaves from the list of inhabitants when calculating representation, then inserted them to calculate tariff contributions (taxes)? Could it be reasonably expected that the Southern States would agree to a system that considered their slaves, in some degree, as men when burdens were imposed, but refused to consider them in the same way when advantages were conferred?

"Wouldn't there also be some surprise that the same people who reproach the Southern States for the barbarous policy of considering part of their human brethren as property, should now contend that the government, to which all States are to be parties, should consider this unfortunate race more completely in the unnatural light of property than the very laws they complain about?

Slaves: Computing State Representation

6 "It may be argued, perhaps, that slaves are not included in computing the state representation in any of the States possessing them. They neither vote nor increase the votes of their masters. On what principle, then, should they be taken into the federal computation of representation? By rejecting them completely, the Constitution would follow the very laws looked to as the proper guide.

Constitution Defines # Representatives; States Define Voters

7 "This objection is repelled by a single observation. It is a fundamental principle of the proposed Constitution that the total number of representatives allotted to each State is determined by a federal rule, based on the total number of inhabitants. However, the State, itself, designates which inhabitants may choose the people who will be Representatives. Voter qualifications may not be the same in any two States. In some of the States, the difference is very material.

"In every State, some inhabitants who are deprived of the right to vote by the State constitution, will be included in the census by which the federal Constitution determines the number of representatives. Following this reasoning, the Southern States might argue that the Constitution doesn't require that all States have the same suffrage policy towards their own inhabitants. Consequently, the full number of slaves should have been included in the census of inhabitants, in the same way that other States count inhabitants who do not have all the rights of citizens.

"A rigorous adherence to this principle, however, is waived by the southern States that would gain by it. All that they ask is that equal moderation be shown on the other side. Let the case of the slaves be considered, as it is in truth, a specific one. Let the Constitutional compromise be mutually adopted, regarding slaves as inhabitants debased by servitude below the equal level of free inhabitants, which regards the *slave* as divested of two-fifths of the *man*.

Government Protects Property, People

8 "After all, isn't there a better basis to defend this article of the Constitution. So far, we have assumed that representation relates only to persons and not at all to property.

"But is this valid? Government is established to protect property as well as people. Therefore, both may be considered as represented in the government.

"On this principle, in several States, particularly New York, one branch of government is intended to more especially be the guardian of property and is, accordingly, elected by that part of society most interested in this governmental objective.

"In the federal Constitution, this policy does not prevail. Property rights are committed into the same hands as the personal rights. Therefore, some attention ought to be paid to property when choosing those hands.

Influence of Wealth

9 "For another reason, the votes allotted in the federal legislature to the people of each State ought to bear some proportion to the comparative wealth of the States.

"States, unlike individuals, don't have an influence over each other, influence arising from wealth. The law allows an opulent citizen only a single vote to choose his representative. However, his wealth frequently influences other voters towards his choice. Through this imperceptible channel, the rights of property are conveyed into public representation.

"A State possesses no such influence over other States. The richest State in the Confederacy will probably never influence the choice of a single representative in any other State. Nor will the representatives of the larger, richer States possess any advantage in the federal legislature over the representatives of other States, except the advantage resulting from their superior number. Therefore, if their superior wealth and influence may entitle them to any advantage, it should be secured to them by a superior share of representation.

"In this respect, the new Constitution is materially different from the existing Confederation, as well as from that of the United Netherlands, and other similar confederacies. In each of the latter, federal resolutions take effect only after the states composing the union voluntarily approve them. Hence the states, though possessing an equal vote in the public councils, have an unequal influence, corresponding with the unequal importance of these subsequent, voluntary resolutions.

"Under the proposed Constitution, the federal acts will take effect without the ratification of the individual States. They will depend only on the majority of votes in the federal legislature and, consequently, each vote, whether from a larger or smaller State, or a State more or less wealthy or powerful, will have equal weight and efficacy. In the same manner that individual votes in a State legislature by representatives of unequal counties have precise equality of value and effect, or if there was any difference in the case, it proceeds from the difference in the personal character of the individual representative rather than from any regard to the wealth of the district from which he comes."

Arguments Favor Apportionment Plan

10 An advocate for the Southern interests might employ such reasoning on this subject. And although it may appear to be a little strained in some points yet, on the whole, I must confess that it fully reconciles me to the scale of representation that the convention established.

States' Census Bias: Increase Representation, Decrease Tax

11 In one respect, the establishment of a single measure to calculate representation and taxation will have a very beneficial effect. The accuracy of the Congressional census will necessarily depend to a considerable degree on the disposition, if not on the cooperation, of the States. It is important that the States should feel as little bias as possible to swell or reduce their numbers. If their share of representation alone was governed by this rule, they would have a reason to exaggerate their inhabitants. If it decided their share of taxation alone, the opposite temptation would prevail. By extending the rule to both, the States will have opposite interests, which will control and balance each other, and produce the requisite impartiality.

PUBLIUS

Constitutional reference:

Article 1, section 2   15-35   apportionment of Representatives and direct taxes, census

---

Number 55

Total Number of Members in House of Representatives

The number of members in the House of Representatives is another interesting topic. Indeed, hardly any article in the whole Constitution seems more worthy of attention, judging by the force of arguments by respected people against it.

The charges are:

1. So **small a number** of representatives will be an unsafe depository of the public interests.

2. They won't possess a proper knowledge of **local circumstances** of their numerous constituents.

3. They will be taken from the **upper class** of citizens, who sympathize the least with the feelings of the mass of the people. And they will, most likely, aim at a permanent elevation of the few on the depression of the many.

4. Defective as the number will be in the beginning, it **will become more and more disproportionate** by the increase of the people and the obstacles preventing a correspondent increase of representatives.

Constituent/Legislator Ratios

2   In general, no political problem is less susceptible to a precise solution than the appropriate number for a representative legislature. Among the States, no policy varies as widely, whether we compare their legislatures directly with each other or compare the proportionate number of constituents to each representative.

The smallest State legislature is Delaware's. Its largest branch has 21 representatives. The largest is Massachusetts, which has between three and four hundred members.

Even States nearly equal in population vary considerably. The number of representatives in Pennsylvania is no more than one-fifth of Massachusetts. New York, whose population is to that of South Carolina as six to five, has little more than one-third of the number of representatives.

As great a disparity prevails between Georgia and Delaware or Rhode Island. In Pennsylvania, the representatives bear no greater proportion to their constituents than one for every 4 or 5,000.

In Rhode Island, their proportion is at least one for every thousand.

According to the constitution of Georgia, the proportion may be one to every ten electors, far exceeding the proportion in any of the other States.

Ratio Changes with Population Size

3   Another general comment is that the ratio between the representatives and the people should not be the same in very large and very small populations.

If the number of representatives in Virginia were calculated as in Rhode Island, they would currently amount to between four and five hundred. And twenty years from now, a thousand.

On the other hand, if Pennsylvania's ratio was applied to Delaware, its representative assembly would have seven or eight members.

Nothing can be more misleading than to base political decisions on arithmetical principles. Perhaps sixty or seventy men can be more trusted with a certain amount of power than six or seven. But it doesn't follow that six or seven hundred would be a proportionately better depository. And if we carry on the supposition to 6,000 or 7,000, the whole reasoning should be reversed.

The truth is, in all cases, the number needs to be large enough to secure the benefits of open discussion and guard against making a conspiracy too easy. Yet the number should be kept within a certain limit, to avoid the confusion and intemperance of a multitude. In all very large assemblies, passion never fails to wrest the scepter from reason. Had every Athenian citizen been a Socrates, every Athenian assembly would still have been a mob.

House's Power Limited

4 It is necessary to remember the observations made about biennial elections. The limited powers of the Congress and the control of the State legislatures justify less frequent elections than the public safety might otherwise require.

For the same reasons, the number of representatives can be fewer than if they were the entire legislative branch and were under only the ordinary restraints of other legislative bodies.

Small Number Can't Be Trusted

5 With these general ideas in mind, let's weigh the objections stated against the number of members proposed for the House of Representatives.

It is said, in the first place, that so small a number cannot be safely trusted with so much power.

Size of House will Quickly Grow

6 When the government begins, the number will be 65. A census will be taken within three years. Then the number may increase to one for every 30,000 inhabitants. A new census is to be taken every ten years. Augmentations may continue to be made under the above limitation.

It isn't extravagant to guess that the first census will, at the rate of one for every 30,000 people, increase the number of representatives to at least 100. Estimating Negroes in the three-fifths proportion, the population of the United States will be three million, if it isn't already.

According to the computed rate of increase, after 25 years the number of representatives will be 200. In 50 years, 400. This number, I presume, will end all fears arising from the smallness of the body.

I assume here what I'll show when answering the fourth objection, that the number of representatives will increase from time to time in the manner provided by the Constitution. If this didn't happen, I admit the objection would have very great weight indeed.

Liberty Not Threatened By Number

7 The true question to be decided is whether the smallness of the number, as a temporary regulation, is dangerous to public liberty? Are 65 members for a few years, and 100 or 200 for a few more, a safe depository for a limited, well-guarded power of legislating for the United States?

To answer no, I would have to erase every impression I have about the current characteristics of the American people, the spirit driving the State legislatures, and the principles incorporated within the political character of every class of citizens.

I cannot conceive that the people of America, in their present mood or under any circumstances within the near future, will elect—and every second year reelect—65 or 100 men who want to pursue a scheme of tyranny or treachery. I am unable to conceive, either now or in the immediate future in the United States, any 65 or 100 men capable of running for office with the desire or daring to, within the short space of two years, betray the solemn trust committed to them.

What future circumstances and a larger population may produce requires a prophet, which is not one of my pretensions. But judging from our present circumstances and the probable state of them in the near future, I must state that American liberties will be safe in the number of hands proposed by the federal Constitution.

Small Congress During Revolution

8 From where will the dangers come? Are we afraid of foreign gold? If foreign gold could so easily corrupt our federal rulers, enabling them to ensnare and betray their constituents, how has it happened that we are at this time a free and independent nation?

The congress that led us through the Revolution was smaller than its successors will be. They were not chosen by, nor responsible to, their fellow citizens. Though appointed from year to year and recallable at pleasure, they generally continued for three years and, prior to the ratification of the federal articles, for an even long term. They always held their discussions under the veil of secrecy. They had complete control of our affairs with foreign nations. Through the whole course of the war, they had the fate of their country more in their hands than, it is hoped, will ever be the case with our future representatives. And from the greatness of the prize at stake and eagerness of the party that lost it, it may be supposed that they wouldn't have hesitated to use means other than force.

Yet we know by happy experience that the public trust was not betrayed. Nor has the purity of our public councils, in this area, ever suffered from even the whispers of calumny.

Would President or Senate Corrupt Representatives?

9 Is the danger feared from the other branches of the federal government? How could the President or the Senate or both do it? The benefits of their offices, it is presumed, will not be enough to be used to corrupt Representatives, except if they are already corrupt. Their private fortunes, as they must all be American citizens, cannot possibly be sources of danger. The only way they can corrupt Representatives will be through giving out government appointments. Is this where suspicion arises? Sometimes we are told that this source of corruption will be exhausted by the President, who will subdue the virtue of the Senate. Now the fidelity of the other House is to be the victim.

The improbability of such a mercenary and perfidious conspiracy of the members of government, standing on as different foundations as republican principles will allow and, at the same time, accountable to the society over which they are placed, should, by itself, quiet this apprehension.

Fortunately, however, the Constitution has provided another safeguard. The members of Congress are rendered ineligible to hold any civil offices that were created or the benefits increased during the term of their election. Therefore, no offices can be given to existing members except when vacated by ordinary casualties. And to suppose these would be sufficient to purchase the guardians of the people, selected by the people themselves, is to renounce every rule by which events are forecast and substitute an indiscriminate, unbounded, illogical jealousy.

The sincere friends of liberty, who extravagate this passion, injure their own cause. Since mankind has a degree of depravity that requires circumspection and distrust, there are also qualities in human nature that justify some esteem and confidence. Republican government presupposes the existence of these qualities in a higher degree than any other form. If the pictures drawn by the political jealousy of some people were a faithful portrayal of the human character, the inference is that people are not virtuous enough for self-government. And that nothing less than the chains of despotism can restrain them from destroying and devouring one another.

PUBLIUS

Constitutional references:

Article 1, Section 2	16-35	number of Representatives, census
Article 1, Section 3	61	Senators, 9 years a citizen of United States
Article 2, Section 1	348-351	President must be natural-born citizen
Article 1, Section 6	125-131	Congressman can hold no other United States office while in Congress

---

Number 56

Opposition: Too Few Representatives to Know, Understand Constituents

The second charge against the House of Representatives is that it will be too small to possess knowledge of the interests of its constituents.

Congress: Different Type of Legislature

2 This objection apparently comes from comparing the proposed number of representatives with the great size of the United States, the number of inhabitants who have a diversity of interests, without considering the specific characteristics that will distinguish Congress from other legislative bodies. The best answer is a brief explanation of these characteristics.

Specific Knowledge Necessary

3 It is a sound and important principle that the representative should be acquainted with the interests and circumstances of his constituents. However, this principle extends only to situations and interests related to a representative's authority.

An ignorance of a variety of minute subjects that don't fall within the legislative domain is consistent with every attribute necessary for proper performance of the legislative trust.

To determine how much information is required to exercise a particular authority, we must look at the objects within the scope of that authority.

Commerce, Taxes, Militia

4 The most important areas of federal legislation that seem to require local knowledge are commerce, taxation, and the militia.

Commerce Complex

5 As mentioned before, the proper regulation of commerce requires much information. But as far as this information relates to State laws and situations, a very few informed federal representatives are sufficient.

Union Tax Codes will Borrow From States

6 Taxation will primarily be duties involved in the regulation of commerce, making the preceding remark about commerce applicable.

As it may include internal tax collections, a wider knowledge of the circumstances within the State may be necessary. But won't a very few intelligent men, diffusely elected within the State, possess enough knowledge? Divide the largest State into ten or twelve districts. No local interests will be found with such an exclusive quality that it will not be within the knowledge of the district's representative.

Besides this source of information, the laws of the State, framed by legislators from every part of it, will almost, by themselves, be a sufficient guide.

Every State has, and will continue to make, tax regulations. In many cases, the federal legislature could simply review the different laws and reduce them to a general act. A skillful person, by himself, with all the local codes before him, might compile a taxation law for the whole Union without any aid from oral information. And it can be expected that whenever internal taxes may be necessary, particularly when uniformity throughout the States is required, the simplest objects will be preferred.

To fully understand how much help in this area of federal legislation the State codes will be, we only need to imagine New York, or any State, divided into a number of parts, each with the power of local legislation.

Isn't it evident that the labors of the general legislature would be shortened by the amount of local information, so that the general legislature needs far fewer members to be sufficient?

Another circumstance will give the federal legislature a great advantage. Representatives from each State will not only bring with them a considerable knowledge of its laws and local knowledge of their districts, but will probably have been members of the State legislature, where all the local information and interests of the State are assembled. From the State legislatures, the information can be easily conveyed by a very few hands into the legislature of the United States.

Within States, Militia Discipline Uniform

7 The observations on taxation apply with greater force to the case of the militia. However different the rules of discipline may be in different States, they are the same throughout each particular State, and depend on circumstances that can differ only a little in different parts of the same State.

Need to Acquire Wider Knowledge

8 The attentive reader will notice that the reasoning used to prove that a moderate number of representatives is sufficient, does not contradict what was stressed on another occasion: the representatives should possess extensive information and the time necessary for acquiring it.

Understanding different local laws and circumstances is necessary and difficult, not within a single State, but among different States.

Within each State, laws are the same and interests only a little diversified. Therefore, a few men will have the knowledge required to properly represent them. If the interests and affairs of each individual State were perfectly simple and uniform—a knowledge of them in one part would mean having the knowledge of every other—the whole State could be competently represented by a single member taken from any part of it.

Comparing different States, we find a great dissimilarity in their laws. And a dissimilarity of many circumstances that will be subjects of federal legislation, all of which the federal representatives should have some acquaintance. While representatives from each State bring with them knowledge of their own State, every representative will need to acquire a lot of information about all the other States.

As formerly remarked, in time, the comparative situation of the different States will have an assimilating effect. The effect of time on the internal affairs of the individual States will have the opposite effect.

At present, some of the States are little more than a society of farmers. Few of them have made much progress in the areas of industry that give a variety and complexity to the affairs of a nation. These will be the fruits of a more advanced population and will require, on the part of each State, a full representation. Accordingly, the foresight of the convention has taken care that the population's progress may be accompanied with a proper increase of the representative branch of the government.

Great Britain: Representative Ratio

9 Great Britain presents many political lessons, both of the monetary and exemplary kind, which have been frequently consulted in these papers.

Its experience affirms what we have just said.

The two kingdoms of England and Scotland have at least eight million inhabitants. These eight million have 558 representatives in the House of Commons. Of this number, 364 people elect one ninth, and 5,723 people elect one half.∗

It can't be assumed that the half elected by so few people, representatives who don't even reside among the people at large, can add anything to the security of the people against the government or to the knowledge of their circumstances and interests in the legislative councils. On the contrary. It is well known that they are more frequently the representatives and instruments of the executive magistrate than the guardians and advocates of the popular rights. Therefore, they could be considered as something worse than just a deduction from the real representatives of the nation. We will, however, consider them in this light alone. We will not deduct the considerable number of other representatives who don't reside among their constituents, are very little connected with them, and have very little specific knowledge of their affairs.

With these concessions, 279 people are the only depository of the safety, interest, and happiness of eight million. In other words, there is only one representative to maintain the rights and explain the situation of 28,670 constituents. And the assembly is exposed to the whole force of executive influence and extends its authority to every subject of legislation within a nation whose affairs are in the highest degree diversified and complicated.

∗ Burph's *Political Disquisitions.*

Yet it is very certain that most of the people's freedom has been preserved under these circumstances. Additionally, the legislature's ignorance of the people's circumstances can only partially be blamed for the defects in the British code.

Allowing the British example the weight due it and comparing it with the House of Representatives, it assures us that a representative for every 30,000 inhabitants will be both safe and a competent guardian of the interests entrusted to it.

PUBLIUS

Constitutional references:

Article 1, section 2	16-35	number of Representatives
Article 1, section 8	180-182	commerce
Article 1, section 9	255-259	commerce
Article 1, section 8	171-173	taxation
Article 1, section 9	250-254	taxation
Article 1, section 8	213-222	militia

Number 57

Charge: Representatives from Society's "Upper Class"

The *third* charge against the House of Representative is that members will come from that class of citizens with the least in common with the mass of the people and who would be most likely to aim at an ambitious sacrifice of the many to the aggrandizement of the few.

Elitist House, Republican Government

2 Of all the objections against the federal Constitution, this is perhaps the most extraordinary. While the objection itself is leveled against an imagined oligarchy, the principle strikes at the very root of republican government.

Rulers Who Pursue Common Good

3 The first aim of every political constitution is, or ought to be, to find men for rulers who possess the most wisdom to discern and the most virtue to pursue the common good of the society. Next, it needs the most effective precautions for keeping them virtuous while they continue to hold their public trust.

Republican governments elect rulers. Numerous and various means are relied on to prevent their degeneracy. The most effective is limiting the term in office to maintain a proper responsibility to the people.

Based on Republican Principles

4 Let me ask: What in the Constitution about the House of Representatives violates the principles of republican government or favors the elevation of the few on the ruins of the many?

Let me ask: Is not just the opposite true? Does not the constitution strictly conform to these principles? Is it not scrupulously impartial to the rights and pretensions of every class and description of citizens?

People Will Elect Representatives

5 Who will elect the federal representatives? Not the rich more than the poor. Not the learned more than the ignorant. Not the haughty heirs of distinguished names more than the humble sons of obscurity and unpropitious fortune.

The voters are the people of the United States. They will be the same people who have the right to elect representatives to the State legislatures.

"Class" Won't Disqualify Candidates

6   Who will be elected by popular choice? A citizen whose merit recommends him to the esteem and confidence of his country. No qualification of wealth, birth, religious faith, or civil profession is permitted to fetter the judgment or disappoint the inclination of the people.

Internal Securities

7   The men freely elected by their fellow citizens will face every security that can be devised or desired to assure their fidelity to their constituents.

Good Qualities of Elected Officials

8   First, since they will be honored by being the choice of their fellow citizens, we presume that they will have, to some degree, those qualities entitling them to be elected and which promise a sincere and scrupulous regard to the nature of their engagements.

Gratitude to Voters

9   Second, as they enter public service, they will have at least a temporary affection for their constituents. Every person responds positively when they are honored or favored, or given the esteem and confidence of their fellow citizens. Apart from all considerations of interest, this guarantees some grateful and benevolent returns.

Ingratitude is a common topic of declamation against human nature. And it must be confessed that instances of it are too frequent and flagrant, both in public and private life. But the universal and extreme indignation it inspires proves the energy and prevalence of the contrary sentiment.

Politicians Court Voters' Favor

10   In the third place, the ties that bind the representative to his constituents are strengthened by selfish motives. His pride and vanity attach him to a form of government that favors his pretensions, giving him a share in its honors and distinctions. Whatever the hopes or plans entertained by a few aspiring characters, a large proportion of men derive their advancement from their influence with the people. They would have more to hope from a preservation of the voters' favor, than from governmental innovations subversive to the authority of the people.

Frequent Elections

11   All these securities, however, would be very insufficient without the restraint of frequent elections. Hence, in the fourth place, the House of Representatives is designed to habitually remind members of their dependence on the people.

Before their exercise of power causes them to completely forget how they became elevated to high office, they will be forced to think about the moment when their power will cease, when their exercise of it will be reviewed, and when they must descend to the level from which they were raised—to remain there forever unless they had faithfully discharged their trust, establishing that they truly deserve to be reelected.

Must Live Under Laws They Pass

12   I will add that, as a fifth restraint on the House of Representatives from enacting oppressive measures, they can make no law that will not have its operation on themselves and their friends, as well as on the great mass of the society.

This has always been deemed one of the strongest bonds by which human policy can connect the rulers and the people together. It creates between them the communion of interests and sympathetic sentiments of which few governments have furnished examples, but without which every government degenerates into tyranny.

If it is asked what restrains the House of Representatives from making legal discriminations in favor of themselves and a specific class of society? I answer: the genius of the whole system, the nature of just and constitutional laws, and, above all, the vigilant and manly spirit actuating the people of America—a spirit which nourishes freedom and, in return, is nourished by it.

Laws that Presage Tyranny

13 If this spirit shall ever be so far debased as to tolerate a law not obligatory on the legislature, as well as on the people, the people will be prepared to tolerate anything but liberty.

Representative/Citizen Bonds

14 Such will be the relation between the House of Representatives and their constituents. Duty, gratitude, interest, ambition are the chords by which they will be bound to fidelity and sympathy with the great mass of the people.

It is possible that these may be insufficient to control the caprice and wickedness of man. But are they not all that government will allow and human prudence can devise? Are they not a genuine way that republican government provides for liberty and

happiness? Doesn't every State government rely on identical means to attain these important ends?

What, then, are we to understand by the objection this paper has combated? What should we say to men who profess the most flaming zeal for republican government, yet boldly impeach the fundamental principle of it; who pretend to be champions for the right and the capacity of the people to choose their own rulers, yet maintain they prefer only those who will immediately and infallibly betray the trust committed to them?

Will Only Few Elite People Vote?

15 If someone who hadn't seen how the Constitution defines the way representatives will be chosen read this objection, he would be forced to conclude that only people owning a large amount of property could vote. Or that eligibility was limited to people within particular families or with fortunes. If nothing else, they would think that the method prescribed by the State constitutions was, in some respect or other, very grossly departed from.

As to the two first points, we see how far such a supposition would err. Nor would it, in fact, be less erroneous as to the last. The only difference between the two cases is, that 5,000 or 6,000 citizens will elect each representative of the United States. In the States, 500 or 600 citizens elect representatives. Is this difference sufficient enough to justify an attachment to the State government and an abhorrence to the federal government? If this is the point of the objection, it deserves to be examined.

5,000 vs. 500 Voters

16 Is it supported by *logic*?

No. It could only be true if 5,000

or 6,000 citizens are less capable of choosing a fit representative or can be more easily corrupted by an unfit one than 500 or 600 citizens.

On the contrary, logic assures us that in so great a number a fit representative would most likely be found, so the choice would be less likely to be diverted from him by the intrigues of the ambitious or the bribes of the rich.

17 Is the *consequence* from this doctrine admissible? If we say that 500 or 600 citizens are the total number that can jointly exercise their right of suffrage, then shouldn't we deprive the people of their immediate choice of public servants whenever the administration of the government does not require as many of them as will amount to one for that number of citizens?

Comparing House of Representatives to British House of Commons

18 Is the doctrine warranted by *facts*? In the last paper, it was shown that in the British House of Commons the real proportionate representation is little more than one for every 30,000 inhabitants.

No variety of powerful causes exists here, causes that in Britain favor the pretensions of rank and wealth.

In Britain, no person is eligible as a county representative unless he possesses real estate with the clear value of 600 pound sterling per year. Nor a city or borough representative unless he possesses an estate of half that annual value. The right of suffrage requires that county voters have a freehold estate with the annual value of more than 20 pounds sterling, according to the present rate of money.

In spite of these unfavorable circumstances and some very unequal laws in the British code, it cannot be said that the representatives of the nation have elevated the few on the ruins of the many.

States with Populous Districts

19 But we need not resort to foreign experience on this subject. Our own experience is explicit and decisive.

In New Hampshire, the state senatorial districts are nearly as large as will be necessary for her congressional representatives. Those of Massachusetts are larger than will be necessary and New York, still more so.

In fact, the members of the New York Assembly for the cities and counties of New York and Albany are elected by very nearly as many voters as will be entitled to a representative in Congress, calculating on the number of 65 representatives only. It doesn't make any difference that in these senatorial districts and counties each voter votes for a number of representatives at the same time. If the same voters at the same time are capable of choosing four or five representatives, they cannot be incapable of choosing one.

Pennsylvania is an additional example. Some counties that elect State representatives are almost as large as the districts from which the federal representatives will be elected. Philadelphia is supposed to contain between 50,000 and 60,000 souls. Therefore, it will form nearly two districts for the choice of federal representatives. However, it forms but one county in which every elector votes for each of its representatives in the State legislature. And what appears to speak more directly to our purpose, the whole city actually elects *a single member* for executive council. This is the case in all counties in the State.

Are Representatives Elected By Larger Group Less Worthy?

20 Don't these facts satisfactorily prove the fallacy employed against the House of Representatives? Have we seen the senators of New Hampshire, Massachusetts, and New York, or the executive council of Pennsylvania, or the members of the Assembly in the two last States, show any peculiar disposition to sacrifice the many to the few? Are they in any respect less worthy of their places than the representatives and magistrates elected in other States by very small divisions of the people?

Entire States Elect Governors

21 But there are more powerful examples than any I have yet quoted. One branch of the Connecticut legislature is so constituted that the whole State elects each member. So are the governors of that State, Massachusetts, and New York, and the president of New Hampshire.

I leave every man to decide whether the result of any one of these experiments can be said to countenance a suspicion that a diffusive mode of choosing representatives of the people tends to elevate traitors and undermine pubic liberty.

PUBLIUS

Constitutional references:

Article 1, section 2	8-10	House of Representatives voter qualifications
Article 1, section 2	11-15	qualifications of representative
Article 6	561-564	no religious test

Number 58

Number of Representatives Will Grow With Population Growth

The remaining charge against the House of Representatives that I am going to examine is based on the supposition that the number of members will not be augmented from time to time as population growth may demand.

Fear Unfounded

2 This objection, if it was true, would be significant. The following observations show that, like most objections against the Constitution, it must be the result of a limited view of the subject or a jealousy that discolors and disfigures every object it beholds.

Temporary Number

3 1. When compared with the State constitutions the federal Constitution won't suffer in the security provided for a gradual augmentation of the number of representatives. The number stated in the Constitution is temporary, for only three years.

10-Year Census Will Adjust Number

4 Every successive ten years a census of inhabitants is to be repeated.

The census has two clear objectives. First, to periodically readjust the apportionment of representatives to the number of inhabitants; the single exception is that each State will have at least one representative. Second, to augment the number of representatives at the same periods, with the only limitation that the whole number will not exceed one for every 30,000 inhabitants.

If we review the State constitutions, some contain no determinate regulations on this subject. Others correspond pretty much with the federal Constitution on this point. And the most effectual security in any of them is resolvable into a mere directory provision.

State Legislatures Have Increased

5 2. Experience under the State constitutions shows a gradual increase of representatives, keeping pace with the increase of constituents. And the representatives have seemed as ready to concur in such measures as the citizens have been to call for them.

Large States Enforce House Increase

6 3. There is a peculiarity in the federal Constitution insuring that both the people and their representatives carefully watch the constitutional augmentation of the latter. The peculiarity lies in this: one branch of the legislature represents the citizens, the other represents the States. Consequently, in the House of Representatives, the larger States will have the most weight. The Senate favors the smaller States. From this circumstance, we may infer that the larger States will be strenuous advocates for increasing the number and weight of the House of Representatives, where their influence predominates.

It so happens that the four largest States will have a majority of the votes in the House of Representatives. Therefore, if the representatives or people of the smaller States oppose a reasonable addition of members, a coalition of a very few States will be sufficient to overrule the opposition. This coalition, despite the rivalship and local prejudices which might prevent it on ordinary occasions, would not fail to take place when not merely prompted by common interest but justified by equity and the principles of the Constitution.

Senate Blocking Increase in House

7 Perhaps it will be alleged that the Senate, prompted by similar motives, will block the coalition. And since their concurrence would be indispensable, the just, constitutional views of the other branch might be defeated.

This difficulty has probably created the most serious apprehensions in the jealous friends of a large representation. Fortunately, this difficulty exists only in appearance and vanishes on a close, accurate inspection. The following reflections will, if I'm not mistaken, give conclusive satisfaction on this point.

House Will Prevail in This Situation

8 The two houses will have equal authority on all legislative subjects except originating money bills. However, it cannot be doubted that the House, composed of the greater number of members, when supported by the more powerful States, and speaking the known and determined sense of a majority of the people, will have an advantage in a question depending on the comparative firmness of the two houses.

House Position Bolstered by Constitution

9 This advantage, on the one side, will be increased by the awareness of being supported by right, reason, and the Constitution. And the awareness, on the opposite side, of fighting against the force of all these solemn considerations.

Senate Also Influenced By State Size

10 Farther, in the gradation between the smallest and largest States, there are several States that are most likely to generally be among the smaller but are too close in size and population to the larger to agree to oppose their just and legitimate claims. Hence, it is by no means certain that a majority of votes, even in the Senate, would be unfriendly to proper augmentations in the number of representatives.

Reapportionment: New, Growing States

11 It will not be reaching to add that the Senators from all the new States may be won over to the just views of the House of Representatives, by an expedient too obvious to be overlooked.

For a great length of time, as these States rapidly increase in population, they will be interested in frequent reapportionments of the representatives to the number of inhabitants. Therefore, the large States, prevailing in the House of Representatives, will make the two processes of reapportionments and augmentations mutual conditions of each other. And the Senators from all the fastest growing States will be bound to contend for augmentations because of their States' interest in reapportionment.

Representatives, Alone, Hold the Purse

12 These considerations seem to afford ample security on this subject and ought, alone, to satisfy all the doubts and fears in regard to it. However, if they were all insufficient to subdue the unjust policy of the smaller States or their predominant influence in the councils of the Senate, a constitutional and infallible resource still remains with the larger States, by which they will be able, at all times, to accomplish their just purposes.

The House of Representatives can not only refuse, but they alone can propose, the supplies requisite for the support of government. They, in a word, hold the purse—that powerful instrument by which we behold, in the history of the British Constitution, an infant and humble representative body of the people gradually enlarging the sphere of its activity and importance, and finally reducing, as far as it seems to have wished, all the overgrown prerogatives of the other branches of government.

This power over the purse may, in fact, be regarded as the most complete and effectual weapon any constitution can arm the immediate representatives of the people for obtaining a redress of every grievance and for carrying into effect every just and salutary measure.

Will House Cave to Senate?

13 But will not the House of Representatives be as interested as the Senate in maintaining the government in its proper functions? And will they not, therefore, be unwilling to stake its existence or reputation on the pliancy of the Senate? Or if a trial of firmness between the two branches were hazarded, would not either one be as likely as the other to yield first?

These questions will create no difficulty for people who reflect that, in all cases, the smaller the number and the more permanent and conspicuous the station of men in power, the stronger the interest they will individually feel in whatever concerns the government. Those who represent the dignity of their country in the eyes of other nations will be particularly sensitive to every possibility of public danger or dishonorable stagnation in public affairs.

The British House of Commons triumphed over the other branches of the government whenever the engine of a money bill was employed. Although an absolute inflexibility by those other branches could not have failed to involve every department of the government in general confusion, it has neither been anticipated nor experienced.

The utmost degree of firmness that can be displayed by the federal Senate or President will not be more than equal to a resistance in which they will be supported by constitutional and patriotic principles.

Danger of Large Governing Body

14 In this review of the Constitution of the House of Representatives, I have passed over the circumstances of economy that, in the present state of affairs, might have some effect on a temporary lowering of the number of representatives. This subject would probably have been as rich a theme of declamation against the Constitution as that of the smallness of the number proposed.

I also omit remarks on the possible difficulty, under present circumstances, in engaging in the federal service as large a number of such characters as the people will probably elect.

One observation, however, I must add on this subject because it claims, in my judgment, very serious attention. It is that, in all legislative assemblies, the greater the number of members composing them, the fewer the men who will, in fact, direct their proceedings.

In the first place, the larger an assembly may be, of whatever characters composed, the greater the ascendancy of passion over reason.

In the next place, the larger the number, the greater the proportion of members with limited information and weak capacities.

It is precisely on these personality types that the eloquence of the few is known to act with all their force.

In the ancient republics, where the whole body of people assembled in person, a single orator or an artful statesman generally ruled with as complete sway as if a scepter had been placed in his single hand.

On the same principle, the more multitudinous a representative assembly may become, the more it will take on the infirmities accompanying collective meetings of the people. Ignorance will be the dupe of cunning. Passion the slave of sophistry and declamation.

The people can never err more than in assuming that by multiplying their representatives beyond a certain limit, they strengthen the barrier against the government of a few. Experience will forever admonish them that, on the contrary, *after securing a sufficient number for the purposes of safety, of local information, and of diffusive sympathy with the whole society*, they will defeat their own purpose by every addition to their representatives. The countenance of the government may become more democratic, but the soul that animates it will be more oligarchic. The machine will be enlarged, but the fewer, and often the more secret, will direct its motions.

Super Majorities Lead to Minority Rule

15 It is proper here to mention the suggestions about the number of members needed for legislative business. It has been said that more than a majority should be required for a quorum.

And in particular cases, if not in all, more than a majority of a quorum for a decision.

Some advantages might result from such a precaution. It might be an additional shield against some special interests and another obstacle to hasty and partial measures.

But these considerations are outweighed by the inconveniences in the opposite side.

In all cases where justice or the general good might require new laws or active measures, a quorum of more than a majority would reverse the fundamental principle of free government. The majority would no longer rule. The power would be transferred to the minority.

If this defensive privilege was limited to specific cases, an interested minority might take advantage of it to screen themselves from equitable sacrifices to the general well being or, in emergencies, to extort unreasonable indulgences.

Lastly, it would facilitate and foster a baneful practice subversive to all principles of order and regular government, a practice which leads more directly to public convulsions and the ruin of popular government than any other which has yet been displayed among us—secessions.

PUBLIUS

Constitutional reference:

Article 1, section 2   16-35   number of members in House, census

---

Number 59

Congress Can Regulate Federal Elections

The natural order of subjects leads us to now consider the provision in the Constitution authorizing the national legislature to regulate, in the last resort, the election of its own members.

It is: "The *times, places,* and *manner* of holding elections for Senators and Representatives shall be prescribed in each State by the legislature thereof; but the Congress may at any time by law make or alter *such regulations,* except as to the *places* of choosing Senators."*

This provision has not only been loudly opposed by those who condemn the whole Constitution, but it has been criticized by people with fewer and more moderate objections. One gentleman, who has declared himself the advocate of every other part of the system, has objected to this provision.

Government's Tool to Preserve Itself

2   Despite this, I believe that no other clause in the whole Constitution is more defensible. Its propriety rests on the evidence of this obvious proposition: *every government should contain in itself the means of its own preservation.*

Every logical person will immediately approve the convention's adherence to this rule. He will also disapprove of every deviation from it not dictated by the necessity of including in the Constitution something not compatible with rigid conformity to the rule. Even then, though he may know it is necessary, he will regret the departure from such a fundamental principle, seeing it as an imperfection in the system

that may prove the seed of future weakness and, perhaps, anarchy.

Power to Modify Election Law

3   No one will claim that an election law could have been framed and put in the Constitution that would always be applicable to every probable change in the country's situation. Therefore, a discretionary power over elections must exist somewhere. I presume that everyone will agree that there are only three ways to reasonably modify this power: completely by the national legislature, or completely by the State legislature, or primarily by the States and ultimately by the national. The convention has, with reason, preferred the last way.

First, local administrations will regulate elections for the federal government. In ordinary cases, when no improper views prevail, this may be both more convenient and more satisfactory. But they have reserved to the national legislature a right to intervene whenever extraordinary circumstances make the intervention necessary to its safety.

States Effect on
Federal Government

4   It is absolutely clear that giving State legislatures the exclusive power to regulate national elections would leave the existence of the Union entirely at their mercy. At any moment, they could annihilate it by neglecting to hold an election of persons to administer its affairs.

It's pointless to say that an omission of this kind would probably not happen. Saying something is consti-

---

* Article 1, Section 4, Clause 1

tutionally possible but there is no risk of it happening, is an unanswerable objection. And no one has given a satisfactory reason for incurring that risk.

The extravagant conclusions [e.g. abuses of power by the federal government] of a distempered jealousy can never be dignified with that character. If we assume there will be abuses of power, it is just as fair to assume them on the part of the State governments as on the part of the national government. And it is more logical to trust the Union with the care of its own existence, than to transfer that care to any other hands.

If abuses of power are to be hazarded on one side or on the other, it is more rational to hazard them where the power is naturally placed [i.e. local government], than where it is unnaturally placed [i.e. national government].

Self Preservation of Government

5   Suppose the Constitution empowered the United States to regulate the elections in the States. Would any man hesitate to condemn it, both as an unjustified exchange of power and a premeditated weapon for the destruction of the State governments? The violation of the principle would have required no comment.

To an unbiased observer, the violation will be just as clear in a plan to subjugate the existence of the national government to the pleasure of the States. An impartial view cannot fail to result in a belief that, as far as possible, each should depend on itself for its own preservation.

State Control of Federal Elections

6   An objection to this position may be based on the Constitution, that it exposes the national Senate to the danger that might flow from an exclusive power in the State legislatures to regulate the federal elections.

Some people may claim that, by not appointing Senators, State legislatures could, at any time, give a fatal blow to the Union. They might infer that since the existence of the Senate is dependent on the States for such an essential point, there could be no objection to entrusting them with it in the specific case under consideration.

Additionally, the interest of each State to maintain its representation in the national councils would provide complete security against an abuse of the trust.

Compromise Election Authority

7   Although it sounds good, on examination this argument is not valid. It is certainly true that if the State legislatures refused to appoint Senators, the national government might be destroyed. But it doesn't follow that because the State legislatures appoint Senators, they should have complete control over every aspect of congressional elections. Under some circumstances, the possible harm from the States having the power to regulate all congressional elections could be far more inevitable than with the States appointing Senators, but without a counter-balancing reason for taking the risk.

Wherever the constitutional organization exposes the Union to possible injury from State legislatures, it is an evil. But the convention recognized that it is an evil that couldn't have been avoided without excluding the States, as political units, from a place in the organization of the national government. Thus, the convention recommends that States appoint Senators.

If there had been no inclusion of the States in the national government, it would have been interpreted as a dereliction of the federal principle. And it would have certainly deprived the State governments of the absolute safeguard they will enjoy under this provision.

Although it is wise to include the inconvenience of States appointing Senators to attain a necessary advantage or a greater good, it cannot be inferred from this that it is all right to accumulate an evil where not necessary or when it doesn't fulfill a greater good.

Rotating Elections: Less State Power

8 Also, it is easily seen that the national government runs a much greater risk from the State legislative power over the elections to the House of Representatives, than from their power to appoint Senators.

Senators will be chosen for a period of six years. Their terms will rotate, with a third of them vacated and replenished every two years. And no State is entitled to more than two senators. A quorum of the body is to consist of sixteen members.

A result of these circumstances, a temporary conspiracy by a few States to stop appointing senators could neither annul the existence nor impair the activity of the body. And it is not from a wide-spread, permanent conspiracy of the States that we can have anything to fear.

A wide-spread conspiracy might be the result of sinister plots by leading members of a few State legislatures. To be permanent, it would require a fixed and rooted disaffection in the great body of the people. This will either never happen or, if it does, it will probably happen because of the national government's ineptitude at advancing the people's happiness—and if this happens, no good citizen could desire its continuance.

State Control: Every House Election Could Cause National Crisis

9 But regarding the federal House of Representatives, all members will be elected every two years. If the State legislatures had exclusive power to regulate these elections and if the leaders of a few important States conspired to prevent an election, every election would create a precarious crisis in the national situation that could result in dissolution of the Union.

Public's Interest vs. Rulers' Ambition

10 The observation that the interests of each State, represented in the federal legislature, will be a security against the abuse of a power over federal elections by the State legislatures is somewhat valid.

But people who understand that there is a difference between the people's interest in the public felicity and their local rulers interest in the power and benefits of their offices know this will not provide complete security. The American people may be warmly attached to the federal government at the same time that specific State rulers, stimulated by a natural power rivalry and hopes of personal aggrandizement, and supported by strong factions in their States, may be in a very opposite temper. Examples of these opposite sentiments, between a majority of the people and individuals with the greatest power in the people's councils, can already be seen in some of the States.

Dividing the nation into several separate confederacies would multiply the chances of ambition. It will be a never failing bait to those influential politicians in State administrations capable of preferring their own emolument and advancement to the public welfare.

With such an effective weapon as the exclusive power of regulating national elections, a group of a few men from the most influential States, where the temptation will always be the strongest, might destroy the Union by using the opportunity of some casual dissatisfaction among the people (that they may have themselves excited) to stop choosing members for the House of Representatives.

It should never be forgotten that a firm Union with an efficient government will probably be an increas-ing object of jealousy to more than one nation of Europe. Sometimes enterprises to subvert it will originate through the intrigues of foreign powers and will seldom fail to be patronized and abetted by some of them. Therefore, whenever it can be avoided, its preservation should not be committed to the guardianship of any but people whose situation will uniformly beget an immediate interest in the faithful and vigilant performances of the trust.

PUBLIUS

Constitutional references:

Article 1, section 4	85-90	Congress regulates its own elections, except places
Article 1, section 3	42-45	two Senators per State; elected for six-year term
Article 1, section 3	46-53	one-third of Senate seats vacant every two years
Article 1, section 4	95-97	quorum of Senators
Article 1, section 2	5-7	Representatives elected every two years

---

Number 60

Dangers of Union Regulating Its Own Elections

We have seen that giving uncontrollable power over federal elections to State legislatures would be hazardous. Now let's see the dangers on the other side, giving the Union the ultimate right of regulating its own elections.

This right would never be used to exclude any State from its share in the representation. In this respect, the interest of all would be the security of all.

But it has been alleged that it might be employed to promote the election of some favorite class of men, excluding others by confining the places of election to particular districts, making it impractical for all citizens to participate in the choice. Of all the unbelievable suppositions, this seems to be the most unbelievable.

On one hand, it's impossible to imagine that the violent and extraordinary disposition implied by such conduct could ever find its way into national councils. On the other, it is certain that, if such an improper spirit ever gained admittance into the, it would display itself in a form altogether different and far more decisive.

If Voting Rights Abridged, States Would Revolt

2 The improbability of an attempt can be inferred from a single reflection: that the State governments would lead and direct an immediate revolt.

During turbulent and factious times, it is possible to imagine that a victorious, overbearing majority could deny a particular class of people this fundamental right of freedom—suffrage. However, it is inconceivable and not credible that a deliberate governmental policy to invade so fundamental a privilege, against the wishes of the great mass of the people, wouldn't cause a popular revolution.

Federal Diversity Creates Protection

3 In addition to this general comment, more specific considerations will wipe out all fears on the subject. The national government will be composed of many dissimilar ingredients. Through its various branches, they will form powerful obstacles to a conspiracy to control elections.

The genius, manners, and habits of the people from different parts of the Union are sufficiently diverse to create a significant diversity of representative dispositions towards different ranks and conditions in society. Although working closely together under the same government will promote some gradual assimilation, there are physical as well as moral causes that may, to a greater or less degree, permanently nourish their different propensities and inclinations.

But the most influential circumstance will be the dissimilar modes of constituting the component parts of the government. The House of Representatives will be elected directly by the people. The Senate by the State legislatures. The president by electors who are chosen for that purpose by the people.

There probably wouldn't be a common interest to cement these different branches into a preference for any specific class of electors.

States Must Conspire to Taint Senate

4 As to the Senate, no regulation of "time and manner," the proposed limit of national authority, can influence the choice of Senators. Entire State legislatures can't be influenced by extraneous circumstances of that sort. This consideration, by itself, should satisfy us that the feared discrimination would never be attempted.

What could induce the Senate to concur in a preference in which it would not share? Or what would be the purpose if it could be established in one federal legislative house, the Senate, but couldn't be extended to the House of Representatives? In this case, the composition of the one would counteract that of the other.

And we can never assume the House would embrace the Senate appointments, unless we can also assume the voluntary cooperation of the State legislatures. If we make the latter assumption, that the State legislatures can be corrupted, it then becomes immaterial where the power in the question is placed—whether in their hands or in the Union.

Which Men Would Be Favored?

5 What would be the objective of this capricious partiality in national councils? Would it be exercised to discriminate between the different departments of industry, or between different kinds of property, or between the different amounts of property? Will it lean in favor of the landed interest, or the mercantile interest, or the manufacturing interest?

Or, to speak in the fashionable language of the adversaries to the Constitution, will it court the elevation of the "wealthy and the well-born" to the exclusion and debasement of all the rest of society?

Partiality in Local Councils

6   If partiality is exerted in favor of people in any specific description of industry or property, I presume the competition will be between landed men and merchants. And I don't hesitate to say that it is far less likely that either would predominate in national councils, than in local councils. By inference, an excessive influence by either is much less to be dreaded in national councils than in State or local.

Nationally, Range of Occupations

7   To various degrees, the States are addicted to agriculture and commerce. In most, if not all, agriculture is predominant. However, commerce nearly divides a few States and it has a considerable influence in most of them.

The proportionate influence of each will be carried into the national representation. Nationally, this will represent a greater variety of interests, in more varied proportions than found in any single State. So it will be much less likely to espouse either of them with a clear partiality than the representation of any single State.

Agriculture Prevail
Over Commerce

8   In a country consisting chiefly of cultivators of the land and where the rules of equal representation exist, agricultural interests will usually predominate in the government. As long as this interest prevails in most State legislatures, it must maintain a correspondent superiority in the national Senate, which will usually be a faithful copy of the majorities of the State assemblies. Therefore, it can't be presumed that a sacrifice of farmers to the benefit of merchants will ever be the objective of the federal Senate.

By applying to the Senate a general observation suggested by the country's situation, I am governed by the consideration that the credulous and devout adherents of State power cannot, based on their own principles, suspect that the State legislatures would be warped from their duty by any external influence.

But in reality, the same situation must have the same effect, in the primitive composition at least, on the federal House of Representatives: an improper bias towards the mercantile class is as little to be expected from this quarter as from the other.

Importance of Commerce

9   It may be asked in support of the objection, isn't there a danger of an opposite bias in the national government, that the federal administration would tend to become a monopoly of the landed class?

Since there is little likelihood that such a bias will worry those who would be immediately injured by it, an elaborate answer to this question will be dispensed with. It will be enough to say that first, for reasons noted elsewhere, it is less likely that a strong partiality would prevail in the Union councils than in the State councils.

Second, there would be no temptation to violate the Constitution in favor of the landed class because, in the natural course of things, that class will enjoy as great an influence and power as it could desire.

And third, men who seriously investigate the sources of public prosperity must be thoroughly convinced that commerce is too important to want to inflict on it the deep a wound that would result from the entire exclusion of the men who best understand its interest from their management of business. In regard to revenue alone, the importance of commerce must effectually guard it against the enmity of a body that will continually request its favors by the urgent calls of public necessity.

Fear: Elite Control of Federal Government

10 I will briefly discuss the probability of preference between different kinds of industry and property because, as far as I understand the meaning of the critics, they contemplate a discrimination of another kind. They appear to be trying to alarm us about politicians defined as "the wealthy and the well-born."

It seems that these "wealthy and well-born" politicians will be exalted to an odious preeminence over the rest of their fellow citizens. However, at one time, critics claim their elevation is the natural consequence of having a small representative body. At another time, they say it is the result of depriving the people at large the opportunity of exercising their right of suffrage to choose that body.

Voter, Candidate Qualifications Unalterable

11 But where can the places of election be put in order to create a preference? Are "the wealthy and the well-born," as they are called, confined to specific geographic locations in the States? Have they, by some miraculous instinct or foresight, set apart in each State a common place of residence? Are they only in town or cities? Or are they, on the contrary, scattered over the face of the country as avarice or chance has cast their lot or that of their predecessors? If the latter is the case (as every intelligent man

knows it to be)* is it not evident that the policy of confining the places of election to specific districts would be as subversive to its own aim as it would be exceptionable on every other account?

The truth is, there's no method to secure the feared preference for the rich except by prescribing qualifications of property either for voters or nominees. But this power is not conferred on the national government. Its authority is expressly restricted to the regulation of the *times*, the *places*, the *manner* of elections. The qualifications of persons who may choose or be chosen, as mentioned on other occasions, are defined and fixed in the Constitution and are unalterable by the legislature.

If Rulers Usurp, Won't Citizens Revolt?

12 However, let's assume, for argument's sake, that selfish interests prevail. And at the same time, let's also assume that the national rulers overcame all the scruples arising from a sense of duty or an apprehension at the danger of the experiment. I imagine it still couldn't be carried out without the aid of a military force sufficient to subdue the resistance of the great body of the people. The improbability of getting a force big enough to do this has been discussed and demonstrated in different parts of these papers. But let's concede for a moment that such a force might exist and the national government has it. What would happen?

If the rulers wanted to invade the essential rights of the community and had the means to do it, are we to presume they would amuse themselves

---

* Particularly in the Southern States and in New York.

with the ridiculous task of fabricating election laws to secure preferences for a favorite class of men?

Wouldn't it be more likely that they would do something for their own immediate aggrandizement? Wouldn't they boldly resolve to perpetuate themselves in office by one decisive act of usurpation, rather than trust to precarious expedients which, in spite of all the precautions that might accompany them, might end in the dismissal, disgrace, and ruin of their authors? Wouldn't they fear that citizens, no less tenacious than conscious of their rights, would flock from remote distances in their respective States to the places of election, overthrow their tyrants and substitute men who would be disposed to avenge the violated majesty of the people?

PUBLIUS

Constitutional references:

Article 1, Section 4	85-90	States election control
Article 1, Section 2	5-15	voter/Representative qualifications
Article 1, Section 3	44-45	Senator 6-year term
Article 2, Section 2	305-345	Senate role in presidential elections
Article 1, Section 3	59-63	Senator qualifications

Number 61

Regulation of Federal Congressional Elections

The more candid critics of the election provision in the Constitution, when pressed in argument, sometimes concede that the provision is proper but that it needs one qualification. They say that it should be accompanied with a declaration that all elections should be in the counties where the voters reside. This, they say, is a necessary precaution against an abuse of the power.

A declaration of this nature would be harmless. If it would quiet apprehensions, it might not be undesirable. But it would, in fact, afford little or no additional security against the feared danger. And an impartial, judicious examiner will never consider the lack of it as a serious, still less insurmountable, objection to the plan.

The different views of the subject in the two preceding papers must satisfy all dispassionate, discerning men that if the public liberty should ever be the victim of the ambition of national rulers, the sacrifice can not be blamed on the election provision.

Distance Reduces Voter Turnout

2   If those who are so worried would carefully inspect the State constitutions, they would find almost as much reason for anxiety and alarm from the latitude in respect to elections as the latitude proposed for the national government. Reviewing the State constitutions would go a long way towards removing any unfavorable impressions remaining on the matter.

But a review of them all would be long and tedious. I'll limit myself to the example of New York.

The constitution of New York makes only the following provisions for *locality* of elections. Members of the Assembly shall be elected in the *counties,* and members of the State Senate are elected in the great districts into which the State is divided.

Presently there are four Senate districts, each with two to six counties. Obviously, it would be just as easy for New York to defeat the suffrages of her citizens by confining elections to specific places as for the United States legislature to defeat the suffrages of citizens in the same way.

Suppose the city of Albany was appointed the only place to vote in its county and district. Wouldn't the inhabitants of Albany quickly become the only electors of the members of both the Senate and Assembly for that county and district? Would the electors living in the remote areas of the counties of Albany, Saratoga, Cambridge, etc., or any part of the county of Montgomery, take the trouble to come to Albany to vote for members of the State Assembly or Senate quicker than they would travel to New York City to participate in the choice of members of the federal House of Representatives?

The alarming indifference found in the exercise of the invaluable privilege of voting under the existing laws, which afford every facility to it, furnishes a ready answer to this question. Our experience shows that when the place of election is at an *inconvenient distance* from the voter, the effect on his conduct is the same whether the distance is 20 miles or 20,000 miles. Therefore, objections to the federal power of regulating elections will, in substance, apply with equal force to the same power in the New York con-stitution. And for this reason, it is impossible to find one satisfactory and condemn the other.

A similar comparison of most State constitutions leads to the same conclusion.

"Problem" Ignored in State Constitutions

3   If it is said that the defects in the State constitutions don't excuse those in the proposed federal Constitution, I answer: the State constitutions have never been accused of neglecting to secure liberty yet the complaints thrown at the federal Constitution apply to them also. Therefore, we must presume that these arguments are calculated and trivial accusations used to support a predetermined opposition rather than logical conclusions from a candid search for the truth.

To people who believe that the unpardonable blemish in the federal Constitution is only an innocent omission in the State constitutions, nothing can be said. Or at most, they can only be asked for a reason why State representatives could resist the lust of power, or other sinister motives, better than the federal representatives?

If they can't explain this, they should at least prove to us that it is easier to subvert the liberties of three million people, who have the advantage of local governments to lead their opposition, than 200,000 people who don't have that advantage. Additionally, they should convince us that, to maintain control, a predominant faction in a single State will be less inclined to promote a specific class of electors, than that similar motives would possess representatives of thirteen States, spread over a vast region, with a diversity of local circumstances, prejudices, and interests.

Uniform Elections to House

4 So far my observations have been aimed only at defending the provision based on whether it is theoretically proper, the danger of placing the power elsewhere, and the safety of placing it in the proposed Constitution. But a positive advantage resulting from this authority has not been mentioned, an advantage that could not have been as effectively obtained in any other way.

I allude to a uniform time for the federal House of Representatives' elections. Experience may prove this uniformity important to the public welfare, both as security against perpetuating an unhealthy spirit in the body and as a cure for the diseases of faction.

If each State could choose its own time for elections, there could be as many different periods as there are months in the year. Currently, the local elections in the States vary between March and November. Consequently, there could never be a total dissolution or remaking of the body at one time. If an improper spirit of any kind happened to prevail in the House of Representatives, the spirit would probably infuse itself into the new members as they joined in succession. The mass would be likely to remain nearly the same, gradually assimilating into itself new members. Example produces an influence that few men have enough willpower to resist.

I suspect that tying the time in office with a total dissolution of the body at the end of that time might be less dangerous to liberty than one-third the duration with gradual, successive alterations.

Uniform Senate Elections

5 Uniform election times seem no less required for Senate rotation and for conveniently assembling the legislature at a stated period in each year.

Election Time in Constitution Unnecessary

6 It may be asked why a time couldn't have been fixed in the Constitution? Since the zealous adversaries of the federal Constitution in New York are, in general, no less zealous admirers of our New York State constitution, the question may be asked: why was not an election time fixed in the State constitution?

The best answer is that it is safe for the legislature to decide. If a time had been fixed in the Constitution, once implemented it might have been found less convenient than some other time. The same answer may be given for the federal Constitution. It may be added that since the possible danger of a gradual change is speculative, it would hardly have been advisable to establish, as a fundamental point, something that would deprive States of the convenience of having State and national elections at the same time.

PUBLIUS

Constitutional reference:

Article 1, Section 4　　　　　85-90　　congressional elections

Number 62

Senators: Qualifications, Appointment of, Reasons Necessary

Having examined the structure of the House of Representatives and answered the most relevant objections against it, I enter next on the examination of the Senate.

Senate: Topics to be Discussed

The subjects to be considered are:

I   The qualification of Senators.

II. The appointment of them by the State legislatures.

III. The equality of representation in the Senate.

IV. The reasons a Senate is needed.

     The number of Senators and the term for which they are to be elected.

V.   The powers vested in the Senate.

I. Qualifications of Senators

2   The qualifications of Senators, as distinguished from those of Representatives, consist of a more advanced age and longer period of citizenship.

A Senator must be at least thirty years of age. A Representative, twenty-five. And a Senator must have been a citizen for nine years. Seven years are required for the Representative.

The nature of the senatorial trust requires more information and stability of character and the Senator should have reached a period of life most likely to supply these advantages, making these distinctions proper.

Since they participate in transactions with foreign nations, they should be weaned from predispositions and habits resulting from a foreign birth and education. Nine years is a prudent compromise between total exclusion of adopted citizens, whose merits and talents may claim a share in the public confidence, and an indiscriminate and hasty admission of them, which might create a channel for foreign influence on the national councils.

II. Legislatures Appoint Senators

3   It is also unnecessary to discuss the appointment of senators by the State legislatures. Of all the ways that this branch of government might have been formed, the method in the Constitution is probably the most consistent with public opinion. It has two advantages. It is a select appointment that gives State governments a role in the forming the federal government. It secures the States' authority and links the two systems.

III. Equal Representation in Senate

4   Equal representation in the Senate, apparently a compromise between the opposite demands of the large and small States, also doesn't need much discussion.

When people incorporate into one nation, every district should have a *proportional* share in the government. When independent, sovereign states form a league, the states, however unequal in size, should have an *equal* share in common councils. If these principles are true, in a compound republic, with both national and federal character, the government should contain a mixture of the principles of proportional and equal representation.

But it is superfluous to evaluate, through a theory, a part of the Constitution that everyone agrees is the result, not of theory, but "of a spirit of amity, and the mutual deference and concession that our special political situation rendered indispensable."

The voice and political situation of America call for a common government with the powers necessary to meet its objectives. The smaller States won't agree to a government founded on principles that favor the larger States. The only option for the larger States, then, lies between the proposed government and a government still more objectionable. From the alternatives, prudence advises us to embrace the lesser evil. And instead of fruitlessly worrying about what mischief may ensue, we should think about the advantageous consequences that may make the sacrifice worthwhile.

Equality Protects State Sovereignty

5   In this spirit, allowing each State an equal vote constitutionally recognizes and preserves the part of sovereignty remaining in the independent States. Large States are as anxious as small States to guard against an improper consolidation of the States into one simple republic. Therefore, the equality should be no less acceptable to the large States.

Block against Bad Legislation

6   Equality in the Senate also creates a block against improper legislative acts. No law or resolution will pass without the concurrence, first, of a majority of the people [represented by the House of Rep-

resentatives] and, then, a majority of the States [the Senate].

Sometimes this complicated check on legislation may be injurious as well as beneficial. The defense of the smaller States is more rational if they have any common interests different from those of the large States that would otherwise be exposed to danger. But since the larger States, by their power over the supplies, will always be able to defeat unreasonable exertions of this prerogative of the smaller States and, as the ease and excess of law-making are the diseases to which our governments are most liable, this part of the Constitution may be more convenient in practice than it appears in contemplation.

IV. Number of Members, Term

7   The number of senators and their term in office are considered next. In order to form an accurate judgment on these points, we will look at the purposes of the Senate. To determine these, we need to look at the inconveniences the republic would suffer from not having such an institution.

Differences Thwart Conspiracies

8   *First*. It is a misfortunate part of republican government, although to a lesser degree than in other governments, that the administrators may forget their obligations to their constituents and prove unfaithful to their important trust. Keeping this in mind, a senate as a second house of legislature, distinct from and dividing the power with the first, must always be a beneficial check on the government. It doubles the people's security by requiring the concurrence of two distinct bodies in schemes of usurpation or perfidy. Without it, the ambition or corruption of one would be sufficient.

This precaution is founded on clear principles, well understood in the United States. Further discussion would be superfluous. I will only say that sinister conspiracies become more improbable as the differences between the genius of the two legislative bodies grows. Therefore, making them as different as possible, consistent with due harmony in all proper measures and the genuine principles of republican government, is prudent.

Passions Sway Large Assemblies

9   *Second.* All single, large assemblies have the propensity to yield to the impulse of sudden, violent passions and be seduced by factious leaders into intemperate, pernicious resolutions. Therefore, a Senate is necessary.

Numerous examples on this subject might be cited both from proceedings within the United States, as well as, the history of other nations. But there is no need to prove a position that will not be contradicted. All that need be said is that a body formed to correct this infirmity should be, itself, free from it. Consequently, it should be less numerous. Moreover, it should possess great stability through terms in office of considerable duration.

Familiarity with Objectives, Principles

10   *Third.* Another defect corrected by a Senate involves a lack of familiarity with the objectives and principles of legislation.

Most members of the House of Representatives will be men with jobs in the private sector. They will have a short term in office with no reason to devote their time while in public service to the study of laws, affairs, and comprehensive interests of their country. If the House was the only legislative assembly, it would make a variety of important errors.

It may be proven, on the best grounds, that many of American's present embarrassments can be charged on the blunders of our governments. And they have come from the heads rather than the hearts of most of the authors of them.

Indeed, what are all the repealing, explaining, and amending laws that fill and disgrace our voluminous codes, but so many monuments to a lack of wisdom? Each legislative session discredits the preceding session, showing the value of the aids expected from a well-constituted Senate.

Good Government Leads to People's Happiness

11   A good government implies two things. First, it is faithful to government's objective—the happiness of the people. Second, it has knowledge of how this objective can be best attained.

Some governments are deficient in both these qualities. Most governments are deficient in the first. I do not hesitate to say that in American governments too little attention has been paid to the last. The federal Constitution avoids this error. And what merits special notice, it provides for the last in a way that increases the security for the first.

Frequent Turnover Hampers Success

12   *Fourth.* The changes in public councils arising from a rapid succession of new members, however qualified they may be, highlights the absolute necessity of some stable institution in the government. Every new election in the States changes half the representatives. This turnover creates a change of opinions and, from a change of opinions, a change of legislation. But a continual change, even if it is good legislation, is inconsistent with every rule of prudence and every prospect of success. Private life verifies this observation. And it becomes more just and more important in national transactions.

Frequent Law Changes Harmful

13 A history of the harmful effects of a mutable government would fill a volume. I will hint at a few only, each of which is a source of innumerable others.

Mutable Government Forfeits Respect

14 In the first place, it forfeits the respect and confidence of other nations, and all the advantages connected with national character.

All prudent people know that an individual who frequently changes his plans or carries on his affairs without any plan at all will quickly fall victim to his own unsteadiness and folly. His friendly neighbors may pity him, but all will decline to connect their fortunes with his. And more than a few people will seize the opportunity to make their fortunes out of his.

One nation is to another what one individual is to another, with perhaps one sad distinction. Nations, with fewer benevolent emotions than people, feel fewer restraints from taking undue advantage of the indiscretions of each other. Consequently, every nation whose affairs betray a lack of wisdom and stability may expect every possible loss to the more systematic policy of their wiser neighbors.

But the best instruction on this subject, unfortunately, is conveyed to America by the example of her own situation. She is ridiculed by her enemies. And she is prey to every nation that has an interest in speculating on her fluctuating councils and embarrassed affairs.

Changing Laws Threatens Liberty

15 The domestic effects of a mutable policy are even more calamitous. It poisons the blessings of liberty itself. It won't benefit the people that the laws are made by men of their own choice, if the laws are so voluminous that they cannot be read or so incoherent that they cannot be understood. Or if they are repealed or revised before they are promulgated or undergo such incessant changes that no man who knows what the law is today can guess what it will be tomorrow.

Law is defined to be a rule of action. But how can it be a rule when it is little known and less fixed?

Laws Benefiting Only a Few Citizens

16 Another effect of public instability is the unreasonable advantage it gives the few sagacious, enterprising, and wealthy citizens over the industrious and uninformed mass of people.

Every new regulation concerning commerce or revenue or affecting property value presents a new opportunity to people who watch the change and can foresee its consequences, an opportunity created, not by themselves, but by the toils and cares of the great body of their fellow citizens. When this happens, it may truthfully be said that laws are made for the *few*, not for the *many*.

Discourages Business, Commerce

17 From another point of view, great injury results from an unstable government. Lack of confidence in public councils discourages every useful undertaking where success and profit may depend on the existing laws continuing.

What prudent merchant will jeopardize his fortunes in a new branch of commerce when he doesn't know if his plans may be made unlawful before they can be executed? What farmer or manufacturer will commit himself to a specific cultivation or establishment when he has no assurance that his preparatory labors and investment will not make him a victim to an inconstant government?

In a word, no great improvement or praiseworthy enterprise can be pursued that requires the protection or security of a steady system of national policy.

Mutability Damages Respect, Attachment

18 But the most deplorable effect of all is the reduced attachment and reverence that steals into the hearts of the people towards a political system that is so obviously weak and disappoints so many of their flattering hopes. No government, any more than an individual, will long be respected without being truly respectable. Nor will it be truly respectable without possessing a certain portion of order and stability.

PUBLIUS

Constitutional references:

Article 1, section 3	59-63	qualifications of Senators
Article 1, section 2	11-15	qualifications of Representatives
Article 1, section 3	42-45	number of Senators; 6-year term

Number 63

IV. (con't) Number Senators, 6-Year Term

A fifth aim, continuing to illustrate the usefulness of having a Senate, is the importance of national reputation. As discussed in the previous paper, without a select, stable part of government, the esteem of foreign powers will be forfeited by an unenlightened and variable policy. Additionally, the national councils will not be sensitive to the opinion of the world, which is no less necessary to obtain than its respect and confidence.

Importance of International Opinion

2 The judgement of other nations is important to every government for two reasons:

1. Independent of the merits of any specific plan or measure, it is desirable that other nations see it as coming from a wise and honorable policy.

2. In doubtful cases, particularly when the national councils may be warped by some strong passion or momentary concern, the opinion of the impartial world may be the best guide.

What has America lost because of her poor reputation with foreign nations? And how many errors and follies would she have avoided, if she had first examined whether her policies appeared just and proper to unbiased observers?

Size, Term Effect Responsibility

3 Yet, however important a good national reputation may be, clearly this will never be achieved by a numerous and changing body. It can only be found in an assembly so small that each individual member may share the praise and blame for public measures. Or in an assembly with such a long term in office that the pride and consequence of its members may become part of the reputation and prosperity of the community.

Arguments based on how measures would be viewed by foreign nations, or even by the sister States, probably would have had little affect on the deliberations over grossly unjust laws by the half-yearly representatives of Rhode Island. However, if the concurrence of a second, select and stable legislative body had been necessary, its desire to be nationally respected, alone, would have prevented the calamities under which that misguided people now labor.

Frequent Elections => Responsibility

4   A *sixth* defect is the lack, in some important cases, of a due responsibility in the government to the people, arising from the frequency of elections that in other cases produces this responsibility. This remark will, perhaps, appear not only new, but paradoxical. Nevertheless, when explained, it must be acknowledged as undeniable as it is important.

Long Term Governmental Goals

5   Responsibility must be reasonable and effectual.

To be reasonable, it must be limited to objects within the power of the responsible party.

To be effectual, it must relate to those operations of that power that the constituents can judge.

Governmental legislation can be divided into two general classes: measures affecting its immediate, day-to-

day operations, and a series of connected measures that have a gradual and, perhaps, unobserved operation.

The importance of the latter to the permanent welfare of every country needs no explanation. Yet, clearly, a legislature elected for so short a term that it can provide only one or two links in a chain of measures essential to the general welfare should not be answerable for the final result, just as a steward employed for one year can be responsible for improvements that can't be accomplished in less than six years.

Nor is it possible for the people to estimate the *share* of influence that each annual assembly may have on an outcome produced by a variety of actions over several years. It is hard enough to preserve a feeling of personal responsibility in the members of a *numerous* body for the acts of the body that have an immediate, detached, and obvious operation on their constituents.

Senate: Long Term Objectives

6   The remedy for this defect is an additional legislative body with members having long enough terms to provide for objectives that require constant attention and a train of measures, so they can be effectually answerable for the attainment of those objectives.

Slowness Blocks Bad Legislation

7   Thus far I have considered the circumstances that make a well-constructed Senate necessary to represent the people.

To a people as little blinded by prejudice or corrupted by flattery as those whom I address, I add that sometimes such an institution may be necessary to protect the people from their own temporary errors and delusions.

The cool, deliberate will of the community should ultimately prevail over the objectives of its rulers in all governments and actually will prevail in all free governments. However, sometimes the people are stimulated by some irregular passion or illicit advantage, or misled by the artful misrepresentations of men with self-serving interests. Sometimes the people will call for laws that they themselves will afterwards be the most ready to lament and condemn. In these critical moments, will the interference of a temperate, respectable body of citizens to block the misguided course, suspending the blow planned by the people against themselves, until reason, justice, and truth can regain their authority over the public mind, have a salutary effect?

What bitter anguishes would have the Athenians escaped if their government had contained such a safeguard against the tyranny of their own passions? Popular liberty might have escaped the permanent blame for decreeing, to the same citizens, hemlock on one day and statues on the next.

Size No Protection
from Mass Hysteria

8   It may be suggested that when people are spread over an extensive region they cannot, like the crowded inhabitants of a small district, be infected by violent passions or the danger of conspiring to pursue unjust measures. I'm not denying that this difference is important. On the contrary, in a former paper I endeavored to show that it is one of the principal recommendations of a confederated republic.

At the same time, this advantage doesn't make auxiliary precautions unnecessary. The extended area will exempt Americans from some of the dangers incident to lesser republics. But

it will also expose them to the inconvenience of living for a longer time under the influence of the misrepresentations passed by interested men.

Senates in All Long-Lived Republics

9   Remember, history shows us no long-lived republic without a senate. Sparta, Rome, and Carthage are, in fact, the only examples.

The first two had a senate for life. The constitution of the senate in Carthage is less known. Circumstantial evidence makes it probable that in this area it was the same as the other two. It certainly had some quality that made it an anchor against popular fluctuations; a smaller council, drawn out of the senate, was both appointed for life and filled up vacancies itself.

Although these examples are as unfit for imitations as they are repugnant to the genius of America, when compared with the fleeting, turbulent existence of other ancient republics, they prove the necessity of some institution that will blend stability with liberty. I am aware of the circumstances that distinguish the American government from other popular governments, ancient, as well as, modern. Extreme caution and care is necessary when comparing the one case to the other. But after understanding and acknowledging their differences, their similarities make these examples worthy of our attention.

As we have seen, many of the defects that can only be corrected by a senate are common to a numerous assembly frequently elected by the people and to the people themselves. Some defects are specific to the numerous legislature, requiring the control of a senate. The people can never willfully betray their own interests, but they may be betrayed by their representatives. The danger is greater when the whole legislative trust resides in the hands of one body of men than when the agreement of separate, dissimilar bodies is required in every public act.

Representatives in Ancient Republics

10 The difference most often mentioned between the American and other republics is the principle of representation. This is the pivotal point of the American republic. And it is supposed to have been unknown in the others, or at least to the ancient ones.

Earlier papers show that I neither deny the existence of this difference nor undervalue its importance. I now make the observation that ancient governments were not totally lacking representation. Without a complete discussion, which here would be misplaced, I will refer to a few known facts supporting my position.

Greece: Representative Executives

11 In the most pure democracies of Greece, many executive functions were performed, not by the people themselves, but by officers elected by the people and *representing* the people in their *executive* capacity.

Representation in Athens, Carthage

12 Prior to the reform of Solon, Athens was governed by nine Archons, annually *elected by the people at large.* The degree of their power is obscure.

After that period, we find an assembly, first of four and, later, 600 members annually *elected by the people* and *partially* representing them as legislators. They both made laws and had the exclusive right to propose legislation to the people.

The senate of Carthage, whatever its power or term in office, appears to have been *elected* by the votes of the people. Similar examples might be found in most, if not all, the popular governments of antiquity.

Representatives in Sparta, Rome, Crete

13 Lastly, in Sparta we meet with the Ephori, and in Roman with the Tribunes. These two bodies were small in numbers, but annually *elected by the whole body of the people* and considered the *representatives* of the people, almost in their *plenipotentiary* capacity.

The Cosmi of Crete were also annually *elected by the people* and have been considered by some authors as an institution analogous to those of Sparta and Rome, with this difference only, that representative body of Crete was elected by only a part of the people.

Large Size, United States Advantage

14 From these facts, to which many others may be added, clearly the principle of representation was known to the ancients and included in their political constitutions.

The true distinction between these and the American governments lies *in totally excluding the people, in their collective capacity,* from any share in the *American governments* and not in the *total exclusion of representatives of the people* from the administration of the *ancient governments.*

However, having made this distinction, the United States has a most advantageous superiority. But to insure the full effect of this advantage, we must be careful not to separate it from the other advantage of an extensive territory. No form of republican government could have succeeded within the tiny area occupied by the democracies of Greece.

Senate Becoming Aristocracy

15 To counter all the arguments that are suggested by reason, illustrated by examples, and enforced by our experience, the jealous adversary of the Constitution will probably content himself with repeating his arguments—that a senate not appointed directly by the people and for the term of six years must gradually acquire a dangerous pre-eminence in the government and, eventually, transform into a tyrannical aristocracy.

Abuse of Liberty Endangers Liberty

16 To this, the general reply should be sufficient. Liberty can be endangered by the abuses of liberty, as well as by the abuses of power. There are numerous instances of the former as well as the latter. And the former, rather than the latter, are apparently most to be feared by the United States. But a more specific reply can be given.

Tyranny: Too Many People Involved

17 Before transforming into a tyrannical aristocracy, the Senate must first corrupt itself. Next it must corrupt the State legislatures. It must then corrupt the House of Representatives. And, finally, corrupt the people at large.

The Senate must be corrupted first before it can attempt establishing a tyranny. To do this, it must corrupt the State legislatures; if not corrupted, the State assemblies would periodically send new members to the Senate, regenerating the whole body.

If the House of Representatives wasn't corrupted, the opposition of that coequal legislative branch of the government would inevitably defeat the attempt.

And without corrupting the people themselves, a succession of new representatives would speedily restore all things to their pristine order.

Can any man seriously persuade himself that the proposed Senate can, by any possible means within human abilities, achieve the objectives of lawless ambition through all these obstructions?

Maryland's Senate Alleviates Fears

18 If reason condemns the suspicion, the same sentence is pronounced by experience.

The Maryland constitution furnishes the best example. That senate is elected, as the federal Senate will be, indirectly by the people and for a term of only one year less than the federal Senate. It also has the remarkable prerogative of filling up its own vacancies within the term of its appointment and, at the same time, doesn't have rotating terms as provided for the federal Senate.

The Maryland senate has some other lesser differences that exposes it to objections that do not apply to the federal Senate. Therefore, if the federal Senate really contained the danger so loudly proclaimed, by this time some symptoms of a similar danger should have been seen in the Maryland senate. But no such symptoms have appeared. On the contrary, the suspicions entertained by men who feared the same problems as those expressed over the same part of the federal Constitution, have been gradually extinguished by the passage of time. And the Maryland constitution daily receives, from the beneficial operation of this part of it, a reputation probably not rivaled by any State in the Union.

Britain: House of Commons More Powerful than Aristocracy

19 But if anything could silence the apprehensions on this subject it should be the British example.

The British senate [House of Lords], instead of being elected to a term of six years and being unconfined to particular families or fortunes, is an hereditary assembly of opulent nobles.

The British house of representatives [House of Commons], instead of being elected for two years by the whole body of the people, is elected for seven years and, most members, by a very small proportion of the people.

In Great Britain we should unquestionably see, in full display, the aristocratic usurpations and tyranny that are expected to happen in the United States. Unfortunately for the anti-federal argument, however, the British hereditary assembly has not been able to defend itself against the continual encroachments of the House of Commons. And it no sooner lost the support of the monarch than it was actually crushed by the weight of the popular branch.

People's Representatives Stronger House

20 As far as antiquity can instruct us on this subject, its examples support our reasonings.

In Sparta, the Ephori, the annual representatives of the people, were an overmatch for the senate for life. It encroached on the senate's authority until it drew all power into its own hands.

It is well known that the Tribunes of Rome, the representatives of the people, prevailed in almost every contest with the senate for life and, in the end, gained the most complete triumph over it. This fact is even more remarkable since unanimity was required in every act of the Tribunes, even after their number was augmented by ten. This proves the irresistible force possessed by the branch of a free government that has the people on its side.

To these examples might be added that of Carthage. Polynius says that instead of drawing all power into its vortex, its senate had, at the commencement of the second Punic War, lost almost the whole of its original share of power.

Senate must Gain People's Support

21 The conclusive evidence resulting from these facts shows that the federal Senate will never be able to transform itself, by gradual usurpations, into an independent, aristocratic body.

Additionally, we have sufficient reason to believe that if such a revolution should ever happen from causes that man's foresight cannot guard against, the House of Representatives with the people on their side will at all times be able to bring the Constitution to its primitive form and principles. Against the force of the immediate representatives of the people, nothing will be able to maintain even the constitutional authority of the Senate except a display of enlightened policy and an attachment to the public good that will gain the affections and support of the entire body of the people themselves.

PUBLIUS

Constitutional reference:

Article 1, section 3   42-45   number of Senators, 6-year term

Number 64

President, with Advice and Consent of Senate, Makes Treaties

It is a legitimate, if not a new, observation that enemies of specific persons and measures, seldom confine their censures only to those parts worthy of blame. This can be the only explanation of the motives of people who condemn the entire proposed Constitution and their severe criticism of some of its most innocuous articles.

Senate Must Ratify Treaties

2 Article 2, section two gives power to the President, "*by and with the advice and consent of the Senate, to make treaties,* PROVIDED TWO THIRDS OF THE SENATORS PRESENT CONCUR."

Indirect Election of President, Senate

3 The power to make treaties is important, especially as it relates to war, peace, and commerce. And precautions should be taken to assure that qualified men exercise it, in the manner most conducive to the public good.

The convention has been attentive to both these points. The President is to be chosen by selected electors, deputed by the people for that express purpose. And the State legislatures appoint the senators.

This system has a vast advantage over direct elections by the people where the activity of party zeal, taking advantage of indifference, ignorance, and the hopes and fears of the unwary and uninterested, often places men in office by the votes of a small proportion of the electors.

Most Qualified Men will be Chosen

4 The select assembly that chooses the President and the State legislatures who appoint the senators will gener-ally be composed of the most enlightened and respectable citizens. We may presume that their attention and their votes will be directed to only those men who have become the most distinguished by their abilities and virtue, and in whom the people perceive solid grounds for confidence.

The Constitution pays particular attention to this objective. By excluding men under 35 from the first office and those under 30 from the second, it confines the candidates to men about whom the people have had time to form a judgment. They will probably not be deceived by brilliant appearances of genius and patriotism which, like transient meteors, sometimes mislead as well as dazzle.

If it is true that wise kings will always be served by able ministers, it is fair to argue that an assembly of select electors, to a greater degree than kings, have access to extensive and accurate information about men and characters, so their appointments bear at least equal marks of discretion and discernment.

We can infer that the President and Senators, so chosen, will always be among men who best understand our national interests, whether as related to the States or foreign nations, the men best able to promote those interests, and whose reputation for integrity inspires and merits confidence. The power of making treaties may be safely lodged with such men.

Term, Rotating Elections => Stability

5 Although it is universally known and acknowledged that any business absolutely requires systems, the high importance of them in national affairs hasn't yet become sufficiently impressed on the public mind.

People who want the House of Representatives, composed of members constantly coming and going in quick succession, to make treaties seem to forget that such a body must necessarily be inadequate to the attainment of those objectives requiring steady contemplation in all their relationships and circumstances. This can only be approached and achieved by talents, exact information, and time. Therefore, the convention wisely gave the power of making treaties to able and honest men who remain in office a sufficient time to become thoroughly acquainted with our national concerns, and to form and introduce a system for the management of them.

During their term in office, they can expand their political information, making their accumulated experience more and more beneficial to their country.

The Constitution also has a prudent way to obviate the inconvenience of periodically transferring great affairs entirely to new men. By leaving a lot of the old ones in place, uniformity and order, as well as a constant succession of official information, will be preserved.

Maintains Conformity in Trade

6 Most people will agree that the affairs of trade and navigation should be regulated by a system cautiously formed and steadily pursued. Both our treaties and our laws should correspond with and promote it.

It is important that this conformity be carefully maintained. Those who agree with this position will admit that making concurrence of the Senate necessary both to treaties and laws supports it.

Treaties Drafted Secretly, Quickly

7 Frequently, treaties must be negotiated, of whatever nature, in perfect *secrecy* and require immediate *execution*.

Sometimes the most useful intelligence can be obtained if the persons possessing it can be free from the fear of discovery. This fear operates on people whether they have mercenary or friendly motives. And doubtlessly many people of both descriptions would rely on the secrecy of the President but would not confide in the Senate, let alone the larger House of Representatives.

The convention has done well, therefore, in dividing the power of making treaties so that although the President must, in forming them, act by the advice and consent of the Senate, he can manage the business of intelligence in such a manner as prudence suggests.

President: Quick Reactions

8 People who study the affairs of men must see that there are cycles in them, cycles very irregular in their duration, strength, and direction, and seldom found to run twice exactly in the same manner or measure.

People who preside over national affairs must discern and profit by these cycles. And men with experience at this inform us that there are occasions when days, nay, even when hours, are precious. The loss of a battle, the death of a prince, the removal of a minister, or other intervening circumstances change the posture and aspect of affairs, sometimes turning the most favorable cycle into a course opposite to our wishes.

As in the field, so in the cabinet. There are moments to seize as they pass. And people presiding in either should have the capacity to improve them.

Until now, we have often suffered from the lack of secrecy and speed. The Constitution would have been inexcusably defective if it had paid no attention to those objectives. Preparatory and auxiliary measures require the most secrecy and speed during negotiations but are not otherwise important in a national view, since they tend to facilitate attaining the objectives of the negotiation. For these, the President will be able to provide. And if anything occurs that requires the advice and consent of the Senate, he may at any time convene them.

The Constitution provides treaty negotiations with every advantage that can be derived from talents, information, integrity, and deliberate investigations on the one hand, and from secrecy and dispatch on the other.

Objections Contrived

9 But to this plan, as to most others that have appeared, objections are contrived and urged.

Objection: Treaty has Force of Law

10 Some are displeased with it not because of any errors or defect, but because ratified treaties will have the force of laws, so they should be made only by the legislature.

The gentlemen making this objection don't seem to consider that the judgment of our courts, and the commissions constitutionally given by our governor, are as valid and binding as the laws passed by our legislature. All constitutional acts of power, whether in the executive or judicial branch, have as much legal validity and obligation as if they proceeded from the legislature. Therefore, whatever name is given to the power of making treaties, or however obligatory they may be when made, it is certain that the people may, properly, commit the power to a distinct body from the legislature, the executive, or the judicial.

It doesn't follow that just because the power of making laws is given to the legislature that, therefore, they must have the power to do every other act of sovereignty by which the citizens are bound and affected.

Objection: Treaty Becomes Supreme Law

11 Others, who are content that treaties should be made in the mode proposed, are averse to treaties being the *supreme* laws of the land. They insist, and profess to believe, that treaties, like legislative acts, should be repealable at pleasure.

This idea seems to be new and specific to this country. But new errors, as well as new truths, often appear.

These gentlemen should remember that a treaty is only another name for a contract. And no nation would make any contract with us that would be binding on them *absolutely*, but on us only so long and so far as we may think.

People who make laws may, without doubt, amend or repeal them. It will not be disputed that people who make treaties may alter or cancel them. But let us not forget that two contracting parties make treaties. Consequently, since the consent of both was essential to their formation, so must it ever afterwards be to alter or cancel them.

The proposed Constitution, therefore, hasn't extended the obligation of treaties. They are just as binding and far beyond the lawful reach of legislative acts now as they will be in the future period under any form of government.

Fear: Treaties Bad for Some States

12 However useful jealousy may be in republics, just like bile in the natural body, when it abounds too much in the body politic, the eyes become easily deceived by delusional appearances that the illness throws on surrounding objects. This is probably what causes the fears and apprehensions of some people that the President and Senate may make treaties without an equal eye to the interests of all the States.

Others suspect two thirds of the Senate will oppress the remaining third and ask whether those gentlemen are made sufficiently responsible for their conduct. Whether, if they act corruptly, they can be punished. And if they make disadvantageous treaties, how are we to get rid of those treaties?

Promoting Good of Whole Nation

13 Since all the States are equally represented in the Senate by men who are able and willing to promote the interests of their constituents, they will all have an equal degree of influence, especially while the proper people continue to be carefully appointed and their punctual attendance is demanded.

As the United States assumes a national form and character, the good of the whole will become more and more an object of attention. The government would have to be weak indeed if it forgets that the good of the whole can only be promoted by advancing the good of each of the parts that compose the whole.

Neither the President nor the Senate will have the power to make any treaties by which they and their families and estates will not be equally bound and affected with the rest of the community. And having no private interests distinct from those of the nation, they will be under no temptations to neglect the latter.

Corruption Voids Treaty

14 As to corruption, the case is not imaginable. Anyone who can think it probable that the President and two-thirds of the Senate will ever be capable of such unworthy conduct, must either have been very unfortunate in his intercourse with the world or has a heart very susceptible to such impressions.

The idea is too gross and too invidious to be entertained. But if it should ever happen, the treaty so obtained from us would, like all other fraudulent contracts, be null and void by the law of nations.

Integrity, Fear, Responsibility

15 With respect to their responsibility, it is difficult to conceive how it could be increased. Every possible influence on the human mind, such as honor, oaths, reputations, conscience, love of country, and family affections and attachments, afford security for their fidelity.

In short, since the Constitution has taken the utmost care that they shall be men of talents and integrity, we have reason to believe that the treaties they make will be as advantageous as could be made, all circumstances considered.

And so far as the fear of punishment and disgrace can operate, the motive for good behavior is amply supplied by the article on the subject of impeachments.

PUBLIUS

Constitutional references:

Article 2, section 2	392-395	treaties
Article 1, section 3	71-84	impeachment
Article 2, section 1	305-345	election of President
Article 1, section 3	44	election of Senators
Article 1, section 3	44-45	Senators 6-year term
Article 2, section 1	351-353	minimum age for President
Article 1, section 3	60	minimum age for Senator

Number 65

Senate as Court for Trial of Impeachments

The remaining powers that the Constitution allots only to the Senate are its participation, with the executive, in the appointment to offices and its judicial character as a court for the trial of impeachments.

Since the executive branch is the principle agent in regard to appointments, the provisions relating to it will be discussed in the examination of that branch.

We will, therefore, conclude this topic with a study of the judicial character of the Senate.

Political Passions => Biased Opinions

2   A well-constituted court for the trial of impeachments is a difficult, but important, objective in a totally elected government.

Their jurisdiction extends to offenses proceeding from the misconduct of public men. Or, in other words, from the abuse or violation of some public trust. The offenses may properly be called POLITICAL, since they relate chiefly to injuries done immediately to society itself. For this reason, the prosecution of them will seldom fail to agitate the passions of the whole community, and divide it into parties more or less friendly or hostile to the accused.

In many cases, the division will align with the preexisting factions, enlisting all their animosities, partialities, influence, and interest on one side or on the other. And in such cases, there will always be the greatest danger that the decision will be regulated more by the comparative strength of the parties, than by the real demonstration of innocence or guilt.

Political Reputations

3   The delicacy and magnitude of trust deeply concerns the political reputation and existence of every man engaged in the administration of public affairs.

In a government entirely based on periodic elections, the difficulty of correctly placing trust is quickly understood when we consider that the most conspicuous people in government will often be, from that circumstances, the leaders or the tools of the most cunning or the most numerous faction. Because of this, they can hardly be expected to possess the required neutrality towards those people whose conduct may be the subject of scrutiny.

Senate as Court of Impeachment

4   The constitutional convention, it appears, thought the Senate the most fit depository of this important trust. Those people who can best discern the intrinsic difficulty of the problem will be the least hasty in condemning this decision and most inclined to seriously consider the arguments that have produced it.

House Impeaches, Senate Tries

5   What, it may be asked, is the true spirit of an impeachment court? Isn't it designed as a method of NATIONAL INQUEST into the conduct of public men? If this is its design, who can more properly be the inquisitors for the nation than the representatives of the nation themselves?

It is not disputed that one house of the legislative body should have the power to originate the inquiry or, in other words, prefer the impeachment. Don't the same reasons that indicate this is proper strongly argue that the other house should share the inquiry?

The convention borrowed this model from Great Britain. The House of Commons prefers the impeachment; the House of Lords decides it.

Several State constitutions follow the example. Those States and Great Britain seem to regard the practice of impeachments as a bridle in the hands of the legislative body on the executive servants of the government. Isn't this the true light in which it ought to be regarded?

Senators Act as Independent Judges

6   Where else than in the Senate could be found a tribunal sufficiently dignified or independent? What other body would be likely to feel *confidence enough in its own situation* to preserve, unawed and uninfluenced, the necessary impartiality between an *individual* accused, and the *representatives of the people, his accuser*?

Impeachment Court Should be Large

7   Could we rely on the Supreme Court to fit this description?

It is doubtful that the members of that tribunal would, at all times, be endowed with the great fortitude needed to execute so difficult a task. And they probably wouldn't possess the degree of credibility and authority essential to reconcile the people on those occasions when their decision clashes with an accusation brought by the people's representatives.

A deficiency in fortitude would be fatal to the accused; a deficiency in credibility, would be dangerous to the public tranquility. In both these respects, the problems could only be avoided, if at all, by making the Supreme Court more numerous than consistent with a reasonable attention to economy.

The nature of an impeachment trial requires a numerous court. In common cases, the discretion of courts is limited in favor of personal security. An impeachment trial can never be tied down by strict rules, either in the delineation of the offense by the prosecutors or in the construction of it by the judges. No jury will stand between the judges, who pronounce the sentence of the law and the party who is to receive or suffer it. The awful discretion that a court of impeachments must necessarily have, to doom to honor or infamy the most trusted and distinguished people of the community, forbids committing the responsibility to a small number of persons.

Separate Court for Ordinary Prosecution

8   These considerations, alone, seem sufficient to support the conclusion that the Supreme Court, as a court of impeachments, would have been an improper substitute for the Senate.

Another consideration strengthens this conclusion. It is this: the punishment that may be the consequence of conviction upon impeachment is not the last chastisement of the offender. After being sentenced to perpetual ostracism from the esteem, confidence, honors, and emoluments of his country, he can be prosecuted and punished in the ordinary course of law. Would it be proper that the persons, who had disposed of his fame and his most valuable rights as a citizen in one trial, should, in another trial for the same offense, also be the people to dispose of his life and his fortune?

Wouldn't it be reasonable to fear that an error in the first trial would be the parent of error in the second? That the strong bias of the first decision would probably overrule the influence of any new information that might change the second? Those who know anything about human nature will not hesitate to answer these questions in the affirmative. They understand that, if the same people are judges in both cases, those being prosecuted would, in great measure, be deprived of the double security intended by a double trial.

If the same judges preside in both trials, when the first sentence of nothing more than dismissal from current office and disqualification from future offices is declared, the loss of life and estate would often be virtually included. It may be argued that the intervention of a jury, at the second trial, would obviate the danger. But juries are frequently influenced by the opinions of judges. They are sometimes induced to find special verdicts that refer the main question to the decision of the court. Who would be willing to stake his life and his estate on the verdict of a jury acting under the auspices of judges who had predetermined his guilt?

Chief Justice, Senate Good Compromise

9 Would the plan have been improved by uniting the Supreme Court with the Senate to form the court of impeachment? This union would have had several advantages. But wouldn't they be overbalanced by the significant disadvantage, already stated, arising from the same judges presiding in the double prosecution to which the offender would be liable?

To a certain extent, the benefits of uniting the Supreme Court and the Senate will be obtained from making the chief justice of the Supreme Court the president of the court of impeachment, as proposed in the Constitution. At the same time, the inconveniences of an entire incorporation of the former into the latter will be substantially avoided. This was, perhaps, the prudent compromise.

I restrain form commenting on how increasing the authority of the judiciary by the Supreme Court hearing impeachments trials would provide an additional pretext for clamor against the judiciary.

Court of "Outsiders"

10 Would it have been desirable to have composed the court for the trial of impeachments of persons who are completely distinct from the other departments of the government? There are weighty arguments in favor and against such a plan.

This would increase the complexity of the political machine, not a trivial objection to some people. It would add a new department to the government, the utility of which would, at best, be questionable.

But an objection worthy of attention is this: such a court would either be very expensive or, in practice, subject to a variety of casualties and inconveniences. It must either have permanent officers based at the seat of government and, of course, entitled to fixed and regular stipends, or specific officers of the State governments who would be called upon whenever an impeachment was actually pending. It isn't easy to imagine any third mode materially different that could be rationally proposed.

Since the court, for reasons already given, should be numerous, every man who can compare the extent of the public wants with the means of supplying them will reject the first scheme.

The second will receive only cautious support after the following problems are seriously considered. The difficulty of collecting men dispersed over the whole Union. The injury to an innocent person from delayed decisions on the charges brought against them. The advantage of a delay to a guilty person, with its opportunities for intrigue and corruption. And, in some cases, the detriment to the State from the prolonged inaction of men whose firm and faithful execution of their duty might expose them to the persecution of an intemperate or designing majority in the House of Representatives. Though this latter supposition may seem harsh, and might

rarely happen, it should not be forgotten that the demon of faction will, at certain times, extend his scepter over all numerous bodies of men.

Government Will Never Be Perfect

11 But even if one of the substitutes, or some other, might be thought preferable to this part of the Constitution, it doesn't follow that the entire Constitution should be rejected for this reason. If mankind agreed that there could be no government until every part of it had been adjusted to an exact standard of perfection, society would soon become an anarchy, and the world a desert. Where is the standard of perfection to renounce his *infallible* criterion for the *fallible* criterion of his more *conceited neighbor*?

Adversaries to the Constitution should prove, not merely that particular provisions are not the best that might be imagined, but that the whole plan is bad and pernicious.

PUBLIUS

Constitutional references:

Article 1, section 3	71-84	Senate as court for impeachment trials
Article 1, section 2	40-41	House of Representatives impeaches
Article 3, section 1	434-435	Supreme court

Number 66

Senate as Court of Impeachments

A review of the principal objections against the proposed court for the trial of impeachments will probably remove any unfavorable impression still existing in regard to this matter.

Objection:
Gives Legislature Judicial Power

2 The first objection is that the provision intermingles legislative and judiciary authority in the same body, in violation of the important, well-estab-

lished maxim requiring a separation between the different branches of power.

The true meaning of this maxim has been discussed and ascertained in another place. It has been shown to be entirely compatible with a partial intermixture of those branches for special purposes, but usually keeping them distinct and unconnected.

In some cases, this partial intermixture is not only proper but also necessary to the mutual defense of the members of the government against each other. The executive authority to absolutely or partially negate legislative acts [presidential veto] is considered, by the best minds in political science, an indispensable barrier against the encroachments of the latter upon the former. It can be equally argued that impeachment powers are, as suggested before, an essential check in the hands of the legislature on the encroachments of the executive.

The division of impeachment powers between the two branches of the legislature, assigning to one the right of accusing, to the other the right of judging, avoids the inconvenience of making the same persons both accusers and judges. And it guards against the danger of prosecution from a prevalent factious spirit in either one.

Since the concurrence of two-thirds of the Senate will be required to condemn, the security to the innocent, from this addition circumstance, will be as complete as can be desired.

Senate Acts as Supreme Court in NY

3   The vehemence with which this part of the proposed Constitution is assailed on the principle of separation of power is curious because it is done by men who profess to admire, without exception, New York's constitution. It makes the Senate, together with the chancellor and judges of the Supreme Court, not only a court of impeachments, but also the highest judicatory in the State in all civil and criminal cases. The number of the chancellor and judges in proportion to the number of senators is so inconsiderable that the New York judiciary authority may be honestly said to reside in its Senate.

If the proposed Constitution is accused of departing form the celebrated maxim, so often mentioned but seemingly so little understood, how much more culpable must be the constitution of New York?*

Objection:
Makes Senate Too Powerful

4   A second objection to the Senate as a court of impeachments is that it contributes to an undue accumulation of power in that body, tending to give to the government too aristocratic a countenance.

The Senate will have concurrent authority with the Executive in forming treaties and appointing to offices. The objectors say that if the authority of deciding impeachments is added to the others, it will give a decided predominance to senatorial influence.

It isn't easy to find a precise answer to such an imprecise objection. To what measure or criterion can we appeal to determine what will give the Senate too much, too little, or barely the proper degree of influence? Won't it be safer, as well as simpler, to dismiss such vague, uncertain calculations, to examine each power by itself, and to decide, on general principles, where it may be held with most advantage and least inconvenience?

Treaties, Appointments,
Impeachments

5   If we take this course, it will lead to a more understandable, if not to a more certain result. If I am not mistaken, the disposition of the power to make treaties will appear to be fully justified by considerations stated in a former paper and in others to come.

---

* In the New Jersey constitution, also, the final judiciary authority is in a branch of the legislature. In New Hampshire, Massachusetts, Pennsylvania, and South Carolina, one branch of the legislature is the court for the trial of impeachments.

The expediency of joining the Senate with the Executive in the power of appointing to offices will, I trust, be placed in a satisfactory light in future papers.

And I flatter myself that the observations in my last paper must have gone a ways to proving that it wasn't easy, if practical, to find a more fitting receptacle for the power of determining impeachments, than that which has been chosen. If this is truly the case, the hypothetical dread of the Senate having too great a weight ought to be discarded from our reasoning.

House Stronger Legislative Body

6 But this hypothesis, such as it is, has already been refuted by the remarks about the senators' term in office. It was shown, with historical examples and reasoning, that the part of every republican government with the representatives most directly elected by the people will be, generally, the favorite of the people and a full match, if not an overmatch, for every other part of government.

House Powers Senate Won't Have

7 But independent of this active, operative principle, to secure the equilibrium of the House of Representatives, the Constitution provides it several important counterbalances to the additional authorities conferred on the Senate.

The exclusive privilege of originating money bills will belong to the House of Representatives.

It will possess the sole right of instituting impeachments. Isn't this a complete counterbalance to that of determining them?

It will umpire all Presidential elections in which no one candidate gets a majority of the total number of electors, a case that will sometimes, if not frequently, happen. This constant possibility must be a fruitful source of influence to that body. The more contemplated, the more important this ultimate, though contingent, power—deciding the competitions of the most illustrious citizens of the Union for the first office in it. It is perhaps not rash to predict that as an influence, it will outweigh all the specific Senate attributes.

Critics: Senate Appointments Role

8 A third objection to the Senate as a court of impeachments is drawn from its role in the appointments to office. It is imagined that because it participated in an appointment, it would be too indulgent when judging the office holder's conduct.

This objection would condemn a practice seen in all the State governments, if not in all governments that we know about. By this I mean, making those who hold offices during pleasure dependent on the pleasure of those who appoint them. It could be alleged, with equal plausibility, that the favoritism of the people who make appointments to offices would always be an asylum for the misbehavior of the people appointed to them.

But that idea contradicts the presumption that those who make appointments will feel responsible for the fitness and competency of appointees. And that their interest in the respectable and prosperous administration of affairs will make them want to dismiss from participating in it anyone who has proved, by their conduct, unworthy of the confidence placed in them.

This presumption may not always be supported by facts. But if it is fundamentally sound, it destroys the supposition that the Senate, which will only sanction executive choices, would feel such a bias towards appointees that it would blind them to such extraordinary evidence of guilt that it induces the Representatives of the nation to become his accusers.

Senate Minor Appointments Role

9 If further arguments are necessary to show the improbability of such a bias, they might be found in the nature of the Senate's part in the business of appointments.

The President will nominate and, with the advice and consent of the Senate, appoint. Of course, the Senate will have no part in the choice. They may defeat one choice by the Executive, forcing him to make another, but they cannot choose. The Senate can only ratify or reject the choice of the President.

The Senate may even prefer someone else at the very moment they assent to the one proposed, because there might be no specific grounds to oppose him. Additionally, they couldn't be sure that if they withheld their assent, the subsequent nomination would be their own favorite, or any other person who in their estimation was more meritorious than the one rejected.

Thus, the majority of the Senate would hardly feel any deeper satisfaction towards the appointee than as appearances of merit might inspire and the lack of proof will destroy.

Objection: Senate Ratifies Treaties

10 A fourth objection to the Senate as a court of impeachments derives from its union with the Executive in the power of making treaties. It has been said that this would make the senators their own judges in every case

of a corrupt or perfidious executive of that trust. That is, after they combined with the Executive to betray the interests of the nation in a ruinous treaty, it is asked whether there would be any hope of their suffering the punishment they deserved, when they were to decide themselves on the accusation brought against them for the treachery of which they have been guilty?

False Base of Argument

11 This objection has been circulated with more earnestness and a greater show of reason than any other appearing against this part of the Constitution. Yet I am deceived if it doesn't rest on an erroneous foundation.

Senate, House Exempt from Punishment for Acts Done as Collective Bodies

12 The security in the Constitution against corruption and treachery when forming treaties is in the numbers and characters of those who are to make them.

The JOINT AGENCY of the **President** and two-thirds of the members of the Senate, a body selected by the collective wisdom of the legislatures of the States, is designed to be the pledge for fidelity of the national councils in this matter.

The convention might have, with propriety, included the Executive's punishment for deviating from the Senate's instructions or a lack of integrity in his conduct during the negotiations. They might also have had in view the punishment of a few leading individuals in the Senate, if they prostituted their influence in that body as the mercenary instruments of foreign corruption. But they could not, with more or equal propriety, contemplate impeaching and punishing two-thirds of the Senate consenting to an improper treaty, any more than it could contemplate punishing a majority of the Senate, or any branch of the national legislature, consenting to a pernicious or unconstitutional law—a principle that, I believe, has never been admitted into any government.

How could a majority in the House of Representatives impeach themselves? It is evident that this is no better than two thirds of the Senate putting themselves on trial. Yet why should the majority of the House of Representatives, after sacrificing the interests of the society by an unjust and tyrannical act of legislation, escape with impunity, any more than two thirds of a Senate that sacrifices the same interests in an injurious treaty with a foreign power?

The truth is, in all such cases it is essential to the freedom and the necessary independence of the body' deliberations that the members be exempt form punishment for acts done in a collective capacity. Society's security depends on the care taken to confide the trust in proper hands, make it their interest to execute it with fidelity, and make it as difficult as possible for them to combine in any interest opposite to that of the public good.

Senate Punishes Abusers of Power

13 If the Executive misbehaves by perverting the instructions or contravening the views of the Senate, we need not worry that that body will not be disposed to punish the abuse of their confidence or vindicate their own authority. For this, we can count on their pride, if not their virtue. And as far as it might even involve the corruption of leading Senators, by whose influence the majority may have been lured into measures odious to the community, if corruption can be proved, the psychology of human nature will lead us to conclude that the body will want to divert the public resentment from themselves by sacrificing the authors of their mismanagement and disgrace.

PUBLIUS

Constitutional references:

Article 1, section 2	40-41	House of Representatives impeachs
Article 1, section 3	71-84	Senate tries impeachments
Article 2, section 2	388-391	President cannot pardon for impeachment
Article 2, section 4	429-433	impeachment for treason, bribery, or other high crimes and misdemeanors
Article 2, section 2	392-408	President, with advice and consent of Senate, makes appointments, treaties
Article 2, section 1	327-343	House of Representatives chooses President when no one get majority
Article 1, section 3	44	State legislatures choose Senators
Article 1, section 7	132-133	House of Representatives originates bills for raising revenues

---

Number 67

Deceptive Arguments Against Proposed Executive

The structure of the executive department of the proposed government next claims our attention.

Framing Executive Controversial

2 Hardly any part of the system was more difficult to arrange than this. And, perhaps, none is more vehemently complained about with less candor or criticized with less judgment.

Magnifying President into Monarch

3 On this subject, the writers against the Constitution seem to have taken pains to showcase their talent for misrepresentation. Using the people's aversion to monarchy, they have encouraged all their fears in opposition to the intended President of the United States, claiming that it is not merely an embryo, but the full-grown child, of that detested parent. To establish the imagined relationship, they have even drawn arguments from fiction.

They have magnified the authorities of the chief executive, some less and some more than those of a governor of New York has, into more than royal prerogatives. They claim he will have more dignity and splendor than a British king. He has been shown to us with a crown sparkling on his brow and the imperial purple flowing in his train, on a throne surrounded with minions and mistresses, giving audience to the envoys of foreign potentates, in supercilious pomp and majesty. The image of Asiatic despotism and voluptuousness has scarcely been wanting to crown the exaggerated scene. We are tremble at the terrific images of murdering guards, and blush at the unveiled mysteries of a future palace.

Accurate Description Needed

4 The extravagant attempts to disfigure, even metamorphose, the presidency, make it necessary to look at its real nature and form. We must determine the true appearance, unmask the disingenuity and expose the fallacy of the counterfeit images that have been so insidiously, as well as industriously, propagated.

Deceit to Pervert Public Opinion

5 In doing this, it's difficult to either look with moderation or treat seriously the issues, no less weak than wicked, that have been contrived to pervert public opinion on the subject. They so far exceed the usual unjustified license of party artifice that even people who are generally indulgent of their political adversaries' conduct feel unreserved indignation.

It is impossible not to accuse them of deliberate fraud and deception on the gross pretense of finding a similarity between a king of Great Britain and a magistrate of the character described for the President of the United States. It is even more impossible to withhold the accusation of fraud from the rash, barefaced expedients used in an attempt to make the deception successful.

President and Senate Vacancies

6 In one instance, which I cite as a sample of the general spirit, they have had the nerve to ascribe to the President of the United States a power that the proposed Constitution *expressly* allots to the Executives of the individual States. I mean the power of filling casual vacancies in the Senate.

False Conclusion
Built on False Premise

7   This bold experiment to test the discernment of his countrymen has been tried by a writer who (whatever may be his real merit) has often been applauded his party.*   And he has built a series of observations equally false and unfounded on this false, unfounded suggestion. Let him now be confronted with the evidence and let him, if he is able, justify or extenuate the shameful outrage he has offered to the dictates of truth and to the rule of fair dealing.

Constitution:
Executive Appointments

8   Article 2, section 2, clause 2 empowers the President of the United States "to nominate, and by and with the advice and consent of the Senate, to appoint ambassadors, other public ministers, and consuls, judges of the Supreme Court, and all other *officers* of the United States whose appointments are *not* in the Constitution *otherwise provided for,* and *which shall be established by law.*"

Immediately after this clause, another says: "The President shall have power to fill up all *vacancies*, that may happen *during the recess of the Senate,* by granting commissions which shall *expire at the end of their next session.*"

The pretended Presidential power to fill vacancies in the Senate has been deduced from this last provision. A slight attention to the connection of the clauses and their obvious meaning will satisfy us that the deduction is not even plausible.

President Appoints
Non-Constitutional Officers

9   The first of these two clauses, it is clear, only provides a mode for appointing officers, "whose appointments are *not otherwise provided for* in the Constitution, and which *shall be established by law.*" Of course, it cannot extend to the appointment of senators, whose appointments are *otherwise provide for* in the Constitution,* and who are *established by the Constitution,* and will not require a future establishment by law. This position will hardly be contested.

President Never Appoints Senators

10   It is equally clear that the last of these two clauses cannot be understood to include the power of filling vacancies in the Senate, for the following reasons:

First. The relationship of that clause to the other, which declares the general mode of appointing officers of the United States, shows that it is nothing more than a supplement to the first, establishing an auxiliary appointment method. The President and Senate *jointly* have the power to make appointments. Therefore appointments can only be made while the Senate is in session. However, vacancies might happen *in their recess,* which may need to be filled without delay. The second clause clearly authorizes the President, *singly,* to make temporary appointments "during the recess of the Senate, by granting commissions which shall expire at the end of their next session."

Second. If this clause is a supplement to the one that precedes it, the

---

* See Cato, No. V.   * Article 1, section 3, clause 1 *vacancies* must be construed to relate to the "officers" described in the preceding one. And this, we have seen, excludes members of the Senate.

Third. The time within which the power is to operate, "during the recess of the Senate," and the duration of the appointments, "to the end of the next session," also helps to make the provision clear. Therefore, if it included senators, it would have naturally referred to the time period when State legislatures were in recess for filling temporary vacancies, since they make the permanent appointments, and not to the recess of the national Senate, who have nothing to do with those appointments. And it would have extended the duration in office of the temporary senators to the next session of the State legislature where the vacancies had happened, instead of making it expire at the end of the ensuing session of the national Senate. The circumstances of the body authorized to make the permanent appointments would, of course, govern the modification of a power relating to temporary appointments. And since the national Senate is the only body mentioned in this clause, it must allude to vacancies in offices in which that body has a concurrent appointment agency with the President.

Lastly. Article 1, section 3, clauses 1 and 2 not only obviate all possibility of doubt but destroy the pretext of misconception. The former provides that "the Senate of the United States shall be composed of two Sena-

tors from each State, chosen *by the legislature thereof* for six years." And the latter directs that "if vacancies in that body should happen by resignation or otherwise, *during the recess of the legislature of* ANY STATE, the Executive THEREOF may make temporary appointments until the *next meeting of the legislature,* which shall then fill such vacancies."

The State Executives have the clear, unambiguous power to fill casual vacancies in the Senate by temporary appointments. This not only invalidates the supposition that the clause under examination is intended to confer that power on the President of the United States, but proves that this supposition, since it is not even plausible, must be intended to deceive the people. It is too obvious to be obscured by sophistry, too atrocious to be excused by hypocrisy.

Example Proves Misrepresentations

11 I carefully selected this misrepresentation and place it in a clear and strong light, as an unequivocal proof of the inexcusable cunning practiced to prevent a fair, impartial judgment of the real merits of the Constitution.

Nor have I, even in this flagrant case, made severely critical comments that would not be within the general spirit of these papers. I ask any candid, honest adversary of the proposed government, whether language can furnish severe enough epithets for so shameless an attempt to defraud the citizens of America.

PUBLIUS

Constitutional references:

Article 2, Section 2	395-413	Executive appointment to offices
Article 1, Section 3	44	State legislatures choose Senators
Article 1, Section 3	54-58	Filling Senate vacancies

Number 68

Method of Electing President

The method of appointing the chief Executive of the United States is almost the only part of the system that has escaped without severe censure, or that has received the slightest mark of approval from its opponents. The most plausible critic, to appear in print, has even deigned to admit that the election of the President is pretty well guarded.*

I'll go further and agree that, if the method isn't perfect, it is at least excellent. It clearly unites all the advantages wished for.

Electing Presidential Electors

2   The will of the people should operate in the choice of the person who will hold such an important trust. To achieve this objective, the men who make the decision will be chosen by the people at the appropriate time for this specific purpose, rather than having any pre-established body make the decision.

Small Group,
Higher Qualifications

3   The men electing the President should be capable of analyzing the qualities suitable to the position. They should act under circumstances favorable to deliberation and a judicious combination of the reasons and inducements proper to govern their choice. A small number of persons, selected by their fellow citizens from the general public, will be most likely to possess the information and the discernment required in such complicated investigations.

* Vide *Federal Farmer.*

Electors Vote in Home State

4   There should also be as little opportunity as possible for tumult and discord, a dreaded evil when electing an executive with so important a job in the administration of the government as the President of the United States. But the precautions within the Constitution promise an effectual security against this mischief.

The people will choose *several* men to form an intermediate body of electors. By choosing several, the community is less likely to convulse with extraordinary or violent actions than if only *one* person was elected.

The electors are to assemble and vote in the State in which they are chosen. This detached, divided situation will expose them to much less heat and ferment than might be communicated from them to the people if they were all to be convened at one time in one place.

Foreign Influence,
Presidential Elections

5   Every practical obstacle against cabal, intrigue, and corruption must be erected. These most deadly adversaries of republican government might be expected to approach from more than one quarter, but chiefly from the desire of foreign powers to gain an improper influence in our councils. How better to do this than by raising a creature of their own to the chief executive of the Union?

But the convention has guarded against all danger of this sort with the most provident and judicious attention.

The appointment of the President is not dependent on any pre-existing bodies of men who might be tampered with beforehand to prostitute their votes.

Instead, first the people of America choose electors for the temporary and sole purpose of making the appointment. Any people whose position might be suspected of too great a devotion to the President in office are not eligible for this trust. No Senator, Representative, or other person holding a place of trust or profit under the United States can be an elector. Thus, without corrupting all citizens, the presidential electors will at least enter on the task free from any sinister bias. Their transient existence and detached situation afford a satisfactory expectation that they will remain unbiased. The business of corruption, when it needs to embrace such a large number of people, requires time and means.

Nor would it be easy to suddenly start a corrupt conspiracy. The dispersal of electors over thirteen States is another protection. Between the appointment of electors and their election of the President, it wouldn't be easy for them to combine for motives that might not be corrupt, but might mislead them from their duty.

President Elected by People

6 Another important goal was that the Executive be independent for continuing in office on all but the people themselves. Otherwise he might be tempted to sacrifice his duty to ingratiate himself with people whose favor was necessary to stay in office. This advantage will also be secured by making his re-election dependent on a special body of electors, delegated by society for the single purpose of making the important choice.

Constitution Includes All Safeguards

7 The Constitution combines all these advantages. The people of each State will choose a number of electors, equal to the number of senators and representatives of each State in the national government. The electors will assemble within the State and vote for some fit person as President. Their votes are to be transmitted to the seat of the national government and the person with a majority of the whole number of votes will be the President.

One man might not always receive a majority of the votes and it might be unsafe to permit less than a majority to be conclusive. Therefore, the Constitution provides that, if this happens, the House of Representatives will select the man who in their opinion is best qualified for the office from the candidates with the five highest number of votes.

Election Method Assures Highest Quality

8 This process of election affords a moral certainty that the office of President will never be held by any man who is not eminently endowed with the required qualifications.

Talent for low intrigues and the charms of popularity may alone suffice to elevate a man to the first honors in single State. But it will require other talents and a different kind of merit to establish him in the esteem and confidence of the whole Union, or enough of it to make him a successful candidate for the distinguished office of President of the United States. It will not be too strong to say that the station will probably be filled by men pre-eminent for their ability and virtue.

This will highly recommend the Constitution to people able to estimate the role the executive in every government necessarily has in its good or ill administration. Though we cannot agree in the political heresy of the poet who says:

For forms of government let fools contest—
That which is best administered is best—

yet we may safely pronounce that the true test of a good government is its aptitude and tendency to produce a good administration.

Vice President Chosen Same Way

9   The Vice President is to be chosen in the same manner with the President, with this difference, that the Senate is to do, in respect to the former, what is to be done by the House of Representatives, in respect to the latter.

V-P Senate's President, May Be President

10   The appointment of an extraordinary person as Vice President has been objected to as superfluous, if not mischievous. It has been alleged that it would have been preferable to authorize the Senate to elect out of their own group an officer answering that description.

But two considerations seem to justify the ideas of the convention in this respect. First, to always secure a definite resolution, the Senate's President should have only a casting vote. And to take the Senator of any State from his seat as Senator and make him President of the Senate, would exchange, in regard to his home State, a constant for a contingent vote.

Second, the Vice President may occasionally become a substitute for the President. So, all the reasons recommending the mode of election prescribed for the one apply with great, if not equal, force to the manner of appointing the other.

This objection, as most others, could be made against the constitution of New York. We have a Lieutenant-Governor, chosen by the people at large, who presides in the senate and is the constitutional substitute for the Governor in casualties similar to those that would authorize the Vice President to exercise the authorities and discharge the duties of the President.

PUBLIUS

Constitutional references:
Article 2, Sec 1   305-345   electing President, Vice-President
Article 1, Sec 3   64-66   Vice-President is Senate President; casting vote

---

Number 69

President's Constitutional Authority

I will now discuss the authorities of the Executive branch of the federal government, as defined in the proposed Constitution. This will highlight the unfairness of the representations made about it.

One Person Has Executive Authority
2   First, a single person will hold most of the Executive authority, the President.

This feature doesn't help us determine whether the Executive authority, as defined in the Constitution, is appropriate. If, in this particular, it resembles the king of Great Britain, there is no less resemblance to the Grand Seignior, to the Khan of Tartary, to the Man of the Seven Mountains, or to the governor of New York.

Four-Year Term

3 The President will be elected for *four* years and is re-eligible as often as the people of the United States think him worthy of their confidence.

This is totally dissimilar to a king of Great Britain, who is a *hereditary* monarch, possessing the crown as a patrimony passed down to his heirs forever.

However, there is a close analogy between the President and a New York governor, who is elected for *three* years and is re-eligible without limitation or intermission. Establishing a dangerous influence in a single State would require much less time than establishing a similar influence throughout the United States. Therefore, we must conclude that the permanency of the President's *four*-year term is less dangerous than a *three*-year term for the top official in a single State.

President Liable for Misdeeds

4 The President of the United States can be impeached, tried, and, on conviction of treason, bribery, or other high crimes or misdemeanors, removed from office. Afterwards he would be liable to prosecution and punishment in the ordinary course of law.

The king of Great Britain is sacred and inviolable. He is not accountable to any constitutional tribunal. And a national revolution is the only way he can be punished.

In the delicate and important area of personal responsibility, the President of the United States will stand on no better ground than the governor of New York. And he will have more personal liability than the governors of Massachusetts and Delaware.

President's Qualified Negative: Veto

5 The President of the United States will have the power to return a bill that has passed the two branches of the legislature for reconsideration. The returned bill becomes law if, on reconsideration, it is approved by two thirds of both houses.

The king of Great Britain has an absolute negative on the acts of the two houses of Parliament. Just because that power hasn't been used for a long time doesn't change its existence. In fact, the only reason it hasn't been used is because the king has found a way to substitute influence for authority.

If the monarch used his authority to permanently veto legislation passed by Parliament, there would be some degree of agitation in the nation. Instead, he has learned the art of gaining a majority in one or the other of the two houses of Parliament. Therefore, the qualified negative of the President differs widely from this absolute negative of the British sovereign.

However, it matches the authority of the Council of Revision of New York, of which the governor is a member. In this respect, the power of the President exceeds that of the governor of New York because the President would possess, himself, what the governor shares with the chancellor and judges. But it is precisely the same as the governor of Massachusetts, from whose constitution this article seems to have been copied by the Constitutional Convention.

Commander-in-Chief, Pardons

6 The President is to be the "commander-in-chief of the army and navy of the United States, and of the militia of the several States, when called into the actual service of the United States

"He is to have power to grant reprieves and pardons for offenses against the United States, *except in cases of impeachment;*

"to recommend to the consideration of Congress such measures as he shall judge necessary and expedient;

"he may, on extraordinary occasions, convene both houses of the legislature, or either of them, and, in case of disagreement between them *with respect to the time of adjournment*, to adjourn them to such time as he shall think proper;

"to take care that the laws be faithfully executed;

"and to commission all officers of the United States."

In most of these, the President's power resembles both the king of Great Britain and the governor of New York. The most important differences are these:

First. The President will only occasionally command the nation's militia, only after Congress has called it into the actual service of the Union by legislative provision.

The king of Great Britain and the governor of New York are, at all times, in command of all the militia within their jurisdictions. In this authority, therefore, the power of the President is inferior to that of either the monarch or the governor.

Second. The President is to be commander-in-chief of the army and navy of the United States.

Both the President and the king of Great Britain have the title "commander-in-chief," but the President's authority is far more limited than the king's. It is nothing more than the supreme command and direction of the military and naval forces, as first general and admiral of the Union.

The British king's power extends to the *declaring* of war and the *raising* and *regulating* of fleets and armies—all of which, by the proposed Constitution, falls under legislative authority.

The governor of New York, on the other hand, can only command the militia and navy. But the constitutions of several other States expressly declare their governors to be commander-in-chief, as well of the army as navy. And it may well be a question whether those of New Hampshire and Massachusetts, in particular, do not, in this instance, confer larger powers on their respective governors than could be claimed by a President of the United States.

Third. The power of the President, in respect to pardons, would extend to all cases *except impeachment.*

The governor of New York can pardon even impeachment, except for treason and murder. Isn't the power of the governor, as far as political clout in this area, greater than that of the President? If a group of people plot and conspire against the State government but the plan hasn't matured into actual treason, the conspirators may be screened from punishment through the governor's prerogative of pardoning. For example, if a governor of New York led a conspiracy, until the design ripened into actual hostility, he could insure his accomplices entire impunity.

On the other hand, although the President of the United States can pardon treason when prosecuted in the ordinary course of law, he could not shelter an offender from the effects of impeachment and conviction.

Wouldn't the possibility of impunity for the preliminary steps be a greater temptation to continue a conspiracy led by the governor of New York against the public liberty, than the more limited possibility of an exemption from death and confiscation if the final execution of the plan and actual appeal to arms should miscarry? Would the expectation of a presidential pardon have any influence when the person expecting the exemption realizes that, because of the President's role in the conspiracy, he might be unable to supply the desired impunity? Remember that, by the proposed Constitution, the offense of treason is limited "to levying war upon the United States, and adhering to their enemies, giving them aid and comfort." By the laws of New York, it is confined within similar bounds.

Fourth. The President can only adjourn Congress in the single case of disagreement about the time of adjournment.

The British monarch can adjourn or even dissolve the Parliament.

The governor of New York can also adjourn the State legislature for a limited time, a power that, in certain situations, may be employed to very important purposes.

Senate Must Approve Treaties

7 The President will, with the advice and consent of the Senate, make treaties, provided two-thirds of the senators present concur.

The king of Great Britain is the sole and absolute representative of the nation in all foreign transactions. On his own, he can make treaties of peace, commerce, alliances, and of every other description. It has been insinuated that his authority, in this respect, is not total and that his treaties with foreign powers are subject to the revision and need the ratification of Parliament. But I believe this doctrine was never heard of until it was broached on the present occasion. Every jurist[1] of that kingdom and every other man acquainted with its constitution knows, as an established fact, that the prerogative of making treaties exists completely in the crown. And treaties made by the monarch have complete legal validity, independent of any other sanction.

Sometimes Parliament alters existing laws so that they conform to the stipulations in a new treaty and this may have given birth to the notion that its cooperation was necessary to the obligatory efficacy of the treaty. But this parliamentary interposition proceeds from a different cause—the necessity of adjusting an artificial, intricate system of revenue and commercial laws to the changes resulting from the treaty, and adapting new provisions and precautions to keep the machine from running into disorder. In this respect, therefore, there is no comparison between the limited presidential power and the actual power of the British sovereign. The one can perform alone what the other can do only with the concurrence of a branch of the legislature.

It must be admitted that, in this instance, the power of the federal Executive would exceed that of any State executive. But this arises naturally from the sovereign power relating to treaties. The question of whether gov-

[1] *Vide* Blackstone's *Commentaries*, vol. I. p.257.

ernors have this delicate and important power would only come up if the Confederacy was dissolved.

Greeting Ambassadors, Ministers

8   The President is also to be authorized to receive ambassadors and other public ministers. Although this provision has been a rich theme of declamation, this is more a matter of dignity than of authority. It will have no effect on the administration of the government. And this will be far more convenient than if the legislature, or one of its houses, had to convene every time a foreign minister arrived, even though he was only replacing a departing predecessor.

Appoints Ambassadors, Judges, Etc.

9   The President is to nominate and, *with the advise and consent of the Senate*, appoint ambassadors and other public ministers, judges of the Supreme Court, and, in general, all officers of the United States established by law and whose appointments are not otherwise provided for by the Constitution.

The king of Great Britain is emphatically and truly called the fountain of honors. He not only appoints to all offices, but can create offices. He can confer titles of nobility at pleasure and dispose an immense number of church preferments.

In this area, the power of the President is clearly inferior to that of the British king. Nor is it equal to that of the governor of New York, if we interpret the New York State constitution by the practices used under it. The power of appointment is lodged in a council composed of the governor and four members of the Senate chosen by the Assembly. The governor *claims*, and has frequently *exercised*,

the right of nomination and is *entitled* to a casting vote in the appointment. If he really has the right of nominating, in this respect his authority is equal to that of the President, and he exceeds it with the casting vote.

In the national government, if the Senate is divided, no appointment could be made; in the government of New York, if the council should be divided, the governor can turn the scale and confirm his own nomination.[2]

The New York governor, in private with an appointment council composed of, at most, four—and frequently only two—persons, appoints State officials. We can compare this with the publicity attending a presidential appointment, which needs a Senate confirmation. It would be much easier to influence the small number of people in an appointment council than the considerable number in the national Senate. Therefore, we cannot hesitate to pronounce that the power of the governor of New York to appoint State officers is, in practice, greatly superior to that of the President of the Union.

President: Far Less Power than King

10   Hence it appears that, with the exception of the President's authority in making treaties, it is difficult to determine whether he would possess more or less power than the governor of New York.

---

[2] Candor, however, demands an acknowledgment that I do not think the claim of the governor to a right of nomination is well founded. Yet it is always justifiable to reason from the practice of a government, until its propriety has been constitutionally questioned. And independent of this claim, when we take into view the other considerations, and pursue them through all their consequences, we shall be inclined to draw much the same conclusion.

More unequivocally, there is no rationale for the parallel that some people have attempted to make between him and the king of Great Britain. But to make the contrast still more striking, it may help to throw the principal dissimilarities into a closer group.

President vs. Monarch's Authorities

11 The President of the United States would be elected by the people for *four* years; the King of Great Britain is a perpetual and *hereditary* prince.

The one could face personal punishment and disgrace; the other is sacred and inviolable.

The one would have a *qualified* negative on the acts of the legislative body; the other has an *absolute* negative.

The one would have a right to command the military and naval forces of the nation; the other, in addition to this, possess the authority of *declaring* war, and *raising* and *regulating* fleets by his own authority.

The one would have a concurrent power with a branch of the legislature in the formation of treaties; the other is the *sole possessor* of the power to make treaties.

The one can confer no privileges whatever; the other can make denizens of aliens, noblemen of commoners, can erect corporations with all the rights incident to corporate bodies.

The one can prescribe no rules concerning the commerce or currency of the nation; the other is in several respects the arbiter of commerce, can establish markets and fairs, regulate weights and measures, can lay embargoes for a limited time, can coin money, can authorize or prohibit the circulation of foreign coin. The one has no particle of spiritual jurisdiction; the other is the supreme head and governor of the national church!

What answer shall we give to those who would persuade us that things so dissimilar resemble each other? The same that should be given to people who tell us that a government, with the whole power in the hands of the elective and periodical servants of the people, is an aristocracy, a monarchy, and a despotism.

PUBLIUS

Constitutional references:

Article 2, Section 1	300-301	one person, President, holds executive authority
Article 2, Section 1	301-302	four-year term for President
Article 2, Section 4	429-433	impeachment of President
Article 1, Section 3	82-84	prosecution after removal from office
Article 1, Section 7	138-150	President's veto power
Article 2, Section 2	379-383	President commander-in-chief
Article 2, Section 2	388-391	Presidential pardons
Article 2, Section 2	392-395	President, with Senate, makes treaties
Article 2, Section 2	395-413	President nominates public officials
Article 2, Section 3	414-418	President recommends legislation
Article 2, Section 3	418-424	President adjourns Congress
Article 2, Section 3	424-425	President receives ambassadors, public ministers
Article 2, Section 3	426-427	President executes laws
Article 2, Section 3	427-428	President commissions U. S. military officers
Article 1, Section 8	213-215	Congress calls militia into service
Article 1, Section 8	204-206	Congress declares war

Number 70

One Person Holds Executive Authority

Some people say that a vigorous Executive is inconsistent with the genius of republican government. People who understand and support this type government must hope that there is no foundation for this idea. If it were true, it would condemn their belief in the principles of good government.

The executive branch of government must have the inherent powers to effectively accomplish its prescribed duties. Energy in the executive [powers equal to responsibilities] is a primary characteristic of good government.

It is essential to protect the community against foreign attacks. It is also essential to the steady administration of laws to protect property against irregular and high-handed conspiracies that sometimes interrupt the ordinary course of justice. And it is essential to secure liberty against the enterprises and assaults of ambition, faction, and anarchy.

Every man with even a little knowledge of Roman history knows how often that republic was obliged to take refuge in the absolute power of a single man with the formidable title of Dictator. He used his author-ity against both internal intrigues, when ambitious and tyrannical individuals threatened the existence of all government, and invasions by external enemies who tried to conquer and destroy Rome.

Feeble Executive => Bad Government

2   This topic doesn't need multiple arguments or examples. A feeble executive implies a feeble execution of government. A feeble execution is just another way to say a bad execution. And whatever it may be in theory, in practice a government badly executed must be a bad government.

Safe Republic, Energetic Executive

3   Therefore, assuming that all thinking men agree that an energetic executive is necessary, what are the ingredients that constitute this energy? How can they be combined with the ingredients that constitute safety, in the republican sense? And how well does the proposed Constitution combine an energetic executive with the safety of a republic?

Qualities of Energetic Executive

4   The ingredients that constitute energy in the Executive are: (1) unity, (2) duration, (3) guaranteed compensation, and (4) competent powers.

Qualities of Republican Safety

5   The ingredients that constitute safety, in the republican sense, are: (1) due dependence on the people, (2) due responsibility.

1 Executive; Numerous Legislature

6   The politicians and statesmen who are the most celebrated for sound principles and just views favor a single executive and a numerous legislature.

They consider energy as the most important and necessary quality of the executive branch of government. And this is achieved when one person holds the executive power.

They consider the numerous legislature as best adapted to deliberation and wisdom, and best able to conciliate the people's confidence and secure their privileges and interests.

Benefits of Unified Executive

7   Unity promotes energy. Decision, activity, secrecy, and dispatch will far more often characterize the proceedings of one man than the proceedings of any greater number. And proportionately, as the number increases, these qualities diminish.

Executive Unity Destroyed

8   Unity may be destroyed in two ways: vesting the executive power in two or more people with equal status and authority, or vesting it ostensibly in one man who is subject, in whole or part, to the control and cooperation of others who act as counselors to him.

The two consuls of Rome serve as an example of the first. Of the last, we find examples in the constitution of several States. New York and New Jersey, if I recollect right, are the only States that entrust the executive authority totally to single men.[1]

Both methods of destroying the unity of the executive have supporters, but the numbers of people who want an executive council are more numerous. Although the two types of plurality in the executive are different, both are liable to similar objections and may be examined together.

History: Plural Executives

9   The experiences of other nations give little instruction on this topic. However, as far as it teaches anything, it teaches us not to be captivated by the idea of having a plural executive.

The Achaeans, on experimenting with two Praetors, were forced to abolish one.

Roman history records many mischiefs to the republic from dissensions between the Consuls and the military Tribunes, who were at times substituted for the Consuls.

But history gives us no examples of any particular advantages of a plural executive. That disagreements between consuls were not more frequent or more fatal is astonishing, until we remember the Roman republic's almost constant situation. Circumstances required the prudent policy of dividing the government between the consuls. The aristocrats perpetually struggled with the common people to preserve their ancient authorities and dignities. The consuls, who were generally chosen from the aristocrats, often united to defend the privileges of their class.

In addition to this motive of union, after the military considerably expanded the bounds of the republi-

---

[1] New York has no council except for the single purpose of appointing to offices. New Jersey has a council the governor may consult. But, I think, from the terms of the constitution, their resolutions do not bind him.

can empire, it became the custom of the consuls to divide the administration between themselves by lot. One consul remained at Rome to govern the city and surrounding area. The other took command in the more distant provinces. No doubt this must have prevented collisions and rivalries that might otherwise have embroiled the peace of the republic.

Logic Rejects Plural Executive

10 If we leave the dim light of historical research and use only logic and good sense, we discover more reasons to reject than approve the idea of a plural Executive under any modification whatever.

Plural Executive: Animosity Inevitable

11 Wherever two or more persons are engaged in a common enterprise or pursuit, there is always danger of differences of opinion. If it is a public trust or office, where they are clothed with equal rank and authority, there is a real danger of personal envy and even animosity. Envy and animosity often cause bitter dissensions. These lessen the respectability, weaken the authority, and distract the plans and operations of the people they divide.

If envy and animosity attacked the supreme executives of a country, consisting of more than one person, they might impede or frustrate the most important measures of the government during critical state emergencies. And what is still worse, they might split the community into the most violent and irreconcilable factions, supporting the different individuals who compose the executive.

Envy, Pride Motivate Opposition

12 Men often oppose a thing just because they had no part in planning it, or because people they dislike may have planned it. But if they have been consulted and have disapproved, their opposition becomes, in their estimation, an indispensable duty of self-love. They feel bound in honor and personal infallibility to defeat a plan that is contrary to their sentiments.

Men of upright, benevolent tempers have told too many horror stories of the desperate lengths this disposition is sometimes carried. And men have often had enough followers to sacrifice the great interests of society to their vanity, conceit, and obstinacy.

Perhaps the consequences of the question now before the public may give us sad proofs of the effects of this despicable frailty, or detestable vice, in the human character.

Legislature Designed to Act Slowly

13 The principle of free government requires that the inconveniences just described must be tolerated from the legislature. But it is unnecessary and, therefore, unwise to introduce them into the executive branch. And they can be the most pernicious in the executive.

In the legislature, prompt decisions are more often an evil than a benefit. Although the differences of opinion and party haggling can sometimes obstruct good plans, they often promote deliberation and circumspection, serving to check excesses in the majority. Also, when a resolution is passed, the opposition must end. The resolution is a law and resistance to it is punishable.

But there are no favorable circumstances to mitigate or atone for the disadvantages of dissension in the executive branch. Here they are pure and unmixed. There is no point at which they cease to operate. They embarrass and weaken the execution of the plan or measure to which they relate, from the first step to the conclusion. They constantly counteract the most necessary executive qualities—vigor and expedition—without any counterbalancing good.

During war, when executive energy is the bulwark of national security, everything would be feared from its plurality.

Council Also Weakens Executive

14 It is confessed that these observations principally apply to the first case—that is, a plurality of executives with equal dignity and authority, a scheme that probably has few advocates.

But the same observations apply, not with equal but considerable weight, to a council whose concurrence is constitutionally necessary to the operations of the ostensible executive.

An artful cabal in the council would be able to distract and weaken the whole system of administration.

If no such cabal existed, the mere diversity of views and opinions, alone, would be sufficient to affect the exercise of the executive authority with a spirit of habitual feebleness and tardiness.

Plurality Hides Faults, Responsibility

15 But one of the strongest objections to both types of plural executive is that it tends to conceal faults and destroy responsibility.

There are two types of responsibility: moral and legal. Therefore, irresponsibility leads to censure and to punishment. Censure is the more important, especially in an elective office. A man in public trust will more often act in such a manner that makes him unworthy of being trusted than in such a manner as to make him subject to legal punishment.

But when more than one person holds the position of Executive, detecting who is morally or legally responsible is more difficult. In fact, it often becomes impossible, amidst mutual accusations, to determine who to blame or punish for a pernicious measure or series of pernicious measures. Blame is shifted from one to another with so much dexterity and under such plausible appearances that the public is left in suspense about the real author.

The circumstances leading to any national misfortune are sometimes extremely complicated. If there are a number of actors with different degrees of responsibility, though we clearly see that there has been mismanagement, it may be impractical to pronounce who is truly responsible for the evil.

Can't Determine Individual Responsibility

16 "I was overruled by my council." "The council was so divided in their opinions that it was impossible to obtain any better resolution on the point."

These and similar pretexts are always available, whether true or false. And who will take the trouble or incur the odium of a strict scrutiny into the secret springs of the transaction? If a citizen zealous enough to undertake the unpromising task is found and if there is a collusion between the parties involved, how easy is it to clothe the circumstances with so much ambiguity that it is uncertain what was the precise conduct of any of those parties?

New York's Disastrous Experience

17 The governor of New York is coupled with a council for one duty, appointing to offices. And we have seen the mischiefs described. Scandalous appointments to important offices. Some cases, indeed, have been so flagrant that EVERYONE agrees they are improper. When asked about them, the governor has blamed the members of the council who, on their part, charged it on his nomination.

Meanwhile, the people remain totally at a loss to determine who committed their interests to such manifestly unqualified and improper hands. In tenderness to individuals, I forbear to descend to particulars.

Accountability, Plural Executive

18 These considerations show that the plurality of the Executive tends to deprive the people of the two greatest securities they have for the faithful exercise of any delegated power:

First. The restraints of public opinion lose their effectiveness because of the difficulty of dividing censure among a number of people and the uncertainty on whom it should fall.

Second. The misconduct of people holding the public trust will be difficult to discover with the facility and clearness needed to either effect their removal from office or their punishment, where appropriate.

King Unaccountable, Perpetual Executive

19 In England, the king is the perpetual executive. For the sake of public peace, he is unaccountable for his administration and his person is sacred. Therefore, nothing can be wiser than to annex to the king a constitutional council, who may be responsible to the nation for the advice they give. Without this, there would be no responsibility whatever in the executive branch—an idea inadmissible in a free government.

But the king is not bound by the resolutions of his council, though they are answerable for the advice they give. He is the absolute master of his own conduct in the exercise of this office. He has total discretion to use or disregard the advice given to him.

Council Would Damage U.S. Executive

20 But in a republic, where every executive should be personally responsible for his behavior in office, the reason for the British council not only ceases to apply, but turns against the institution.

In the monarchy of Great Britain, it substitutes for the prohibited responsibility of the chief executive, who serves in some degree as a hostage to the national justice for his good behavior.

In the American republic, it would destroy, or greatly diminish, the interested and necessary responsibility of the Chief Executive himself.

One Executive Safer

21 The idea of a council to the Executive, which is in many State constitutions, has come from the maxim of republican jealousy, which considers power as safer in the hands of a number of men than of a single man. If the maxim is felt to be applicable to this case, I would argue that the advantage on that side would not counterbalance the numerous disadvantages on the opposite side.

But I do not think the rule is at all applicable to the national executive power. I clearly concur with the opinion on this subject with a writer whom the celebrated Junius pronounces to be "deep, solid, and ingenious, that the executive power is more easily confined when it is ONE."[2] It is far safer to have a single object for jealousy and watchfulness of the people. And, in a word, all multiplication of the Executive is more dangerous than friendly to liberty.

Easier for Group to Usurp Power

22 A little thought will satisfy us that the type of security sought for in the multiplication of the EXECUTIVE is unattainable. The number has to be so great that conspiracy is difficult or they become a source of danger rather than security. The united credit and influence of several individuals must be more formidable to liberty than the credit and influence of either of them separately.

Therefore, when power is placed in such a small number of men that their interests and views can be easily combined in a common enterprise by a talented leader, it becomes more liable to abuse and more dangerous when abused, than if it is lodged in the hands of one man who, from the very circumstances of his being alone, will be more narrowly watched and more readily suspected, and who cannot unite so great a mass of influence as when he is associated with others.

The Decemvirs of Rome, whose name denotes their number,[3] were more to be dreaded in their usurpation than any ONE of them would have been.

[2] DeLolme.
[3] Ten.

No one would think of proposing an executive much more numerous than that body. From six to a dozen have been suggested for the number of the council. The largest of these numbers isn't too great for an easy conspiracy. And America would have more to fear from such a conspiracy than from the ambition of any single individual.

A council to an executive, who is himself responsible for what he does, is generally nothing better than a clog on his good intentions, often acts as the instruments and accomplices of his bad deeds, and is almost always a cloak to his faults.

Plural Executive Expensive

23 I refrain from dwelling on the subject of expense. However, it is evident that if the council was numerous enough to fulfill the goal aimed at by instituting it, the salaries of the members who must be drawn from their homes to reside at the seat of government would create an item in the catalogue of public expenditures too serious to be incurred for an objective of equivocal utility.

I will only add that, prior to the appearance of the Constitution, I rarely met with an intelligent man from any State who didn't admit, as the result of experience, that the UNITY of the New York executive is one of the best of the distinguishing features of our State constitution.

PUBLIUS

Constitutional reference:
Article 2, Section 1   300-304   one person has executive power

---

Number 71

Duration: President's Term in Office

The second requirement for energy in Executive authority is duration in office. This has two objectives: the executive's personal firmness in the employment of his constitutional powers and stable system of administration adopted under his auspices.

As to the first, clearly, the longer the duration in office, the greater will be the probability of obtaining so important an advantage.

It is a general principle of human nature that a man is interested in whatever he possesses in proportion to the firmness or precariousness of the tenure by which he holds it. He will be less attached to what he holds by a momentary or uncertain title. And, of course, he will be willing to risk more for the one he firmly holds than for the one he precariously holds.

This remark applies to a political privilege, honor, or trust just as to any article of ordinary property. The inference is that a chief executive who knows he *must* leave his office is apt to have so little interest in it that he won't take the chance of any significant censure or entanglement from the independent use of his powers. He won't act if he might even encounter some transient ill-humors from either a large part of society or a predominant faction in the legislative body.

Instead, if he only *might* leave office unless reelected, and if he wants to be reelected, his wishes, conspiring with his fears, would tend still more powerfully to corrupt his integrity or debase his fortitude.

In either case, feebleness and irresolution become the characteristics of the executive office.

Leaders Ignore Bad Fads

2   Some people regard the servile pliancy of the Executive to a prevailing current, either in the community or the legislature, as its best recommendation. But these people entertain very crude ideas about both the fundamental purpose of government and the true means of promoting public happiness.

The republican principle demands that the will of the community should govern the conduct of those entrusted with management of their affairs. But it does not require absolute compliance to every sudden breeze of passion or every transient impulse aroused within the people by clever men who flatter the community's prejudices to betray their interests.

It is true that the people commonly *intend* the PUBLIC GOOD. This often applies even to their errors. But the people's good sense would despise the adulator who pretends that they always *reason right* about the *means* of promoting it.

They know from experience that they sometime err. The wonder is that they so seldom err, beset as they continually are by the wiles of parasites and sycophants, by the snares of the ambitious, the avaricious, the desperate, by the artifices of men possessing more confidence than they deserve, and of those who seek to possess rather than to deserve it. When the interests of the people are at variance with their inclinations, it is the duty of the people appointed to be the guardians of those interests, to withstand the temporary delusion and give them time and opportunity for more cool, sedate reflection.

Examples might be cited when this type of conduct saved the people from very fatal consequences of their own mistakes, procuring from the people lasting monuments of their gratitude to the leaders who had courage and magnanimity enough to serve them at the peril of their displeasure.

Executive Should Act Independently

3 But even if we insist that the Executive completely comply with the will of the people, we can not properly argue that the legislature comply in the same way.

The legislature may sometimes stand in opposition to the executive. And at other times, the people may be entirely neutral. In either case, it is certainly desirable that the Executive should act on his own opinion with vigor and decision.

Separation of Power Avoids Legislative Dominance

4 The rule that teaches the importance of a partition between the various branches of power teaches us that this partition should be constructed so that each is independent of the other. What is the purpose of separating the executive or the judiciary from the legislative, if the acts of both the executive and the judiciary can be absolutely voided by the legislative? Such a separation would be merely nominal and incapable of producing the ends for which it was established.

Being subordinate to the laws is different from being dependent on the legislative body. The first agrees with and the last violates the fundamental principles of good government. And despite the Constitution, it unites all power in the same hands.

As shown in some earlier papers, the legislative branch tends of absorb every other branch. In a pure republic, this tendency is almost irresistible. The representatives of the people in a popular assembly sometimes seem to believe that they are the people themselves, betraying strong symptoms of impatience and disgust at the least sign of opposition from any other quarter, as if when the executive or the judiciary exercises its rights, it is a breach of legislative privilege and an outrage to the representatives' dignity.

The legislature often seems to want imperial control over the other branches. And since they commonly have the people on their side, they act with a momentum that makes it very difficult for the other branches of the government to maintain the constitutional balance.

Term Effects Executive Independence

5 How can the shortness of the duration in office affect the independence of the Executive on the legislature, unless the one has the power of appointing or displacing the other?

One answer comes from the principle already mentioned—that is, a man is apt to have little interest in a short-lived advantage and little inducement to expose himself to any considerable inconvenience or hazard. Another answer, perhaps more obvious though no more conclusive, results from the legislative body's influence over the people, influence that might be used to prevent the re-election of a man who, by an upright resistance to any sinister project of that body, makes himself the target of its resentment.

Short Term Protects from Ambition

6 Will a term of four years answer the proposed end? If not, should it be a shorter period, recommended because at least it provides a greater security against ambitious designs, rather than a longer period that was, at the same time, too short to inspire the desired firmness and independence of the executive.

4-Year Term Seems Best

7 It cannot be confirmed that four years, or any other limited duration, would completely answer the proposed end. But it would have a material influence on the spirit and character of the government. Between the beginning and termination of such a period, there would be a considerable interval in which the prospect of annihilation would be sufficiently remote not to have an improper effect on the conduct of a man with enough fortitude. He might reasonably promise himself that there was enough time to make the community aware of the propriety of the measures he wished to pursue.

It is probable that as reelection approached, his confidence and his firmness would decline. Yet both would also derive support from the opportunities during his time in office to establish himself in the esteem and good will of his constituents. So he might take a chance, in proportion to how well he had proven his wisdom and integrity, and acquired the respect and attachment of his fellow citizens.

On the other hand, a four-year term contributes to the firmness of the Executive sufficiently to render it a very valuable ingredient in the composition. On the other, it is not enough to justify any alarm for the public liberty.

From its most feeble beginnings, the British House of Commons has used *the mere power of agreeing or disagreeing to the imposition of a new tax* to quickly reduce and confine the prerogatives of the crown [their executive] and privileges of nobility [one house of their legislature] within the limits they conceived compatible with principles of a free government while raising themselves to the rank of a co-equal branch of the legislature. In one instance, they abolished both the royalty and the aristocracy, and overturned all the ancient establishments, in the Church as well as the State. On a recent occasion, it made the monarch tremble at the prospect of an innovation attempted by them.∗

Therefore, what would be feared from an elected executive with a four-year term and with the limited authorities of a President of the United States? What, but that he might be unequal to the task assigned him by the Constitution?

I will only add that if his duration is such as to leave a doubt of his firmness, that doubt is inconsistent with the worry about his encroachments.

PUBLIUS

∗ This refers to Mr. Fox's India bill that was carried in the House of Commons, and rejected in the House of Lords, to the entire satisfaction, as it is said, of the people.

Constitutional reference:
Article 2, Section 1 301-302 President's term

Number 72

Presidential Term Limits

In its largest sense, the administration of government includes all the operations of the body politic, whether legislative or judicial. But in its usual, and perhaps most precise definition, it is limited to executive duties, falling specifically within the province of the executive department.

Government administration is understood to include actually conducting foreign negotiations, preparing financial plans, applying for and disbursing public money in conformity to the general appropriations of the legislature, directing the army and navy, and operations of war and other similar matters. Therefore, the managers of these different matters should be considered assistants or deputies of the chief executive. For this reason, he should appoint them or, at least, nominate and supervise them. This suggests the close connection between the chief executive's term in office and the stability of the system of administration.

To reverse and undo what a predecessor has done is very often considered by a successor as the best proof he can give of his own capacity and worthiness. And when the change is because of an election, the new person is warranted in supposing that the loss of his predecessor resulted from a dislike of his measures. And the less he resembles his predecessor, the more he will recommend himself to the favor of his constituents. These considerations, and the influence of personal confidences and attachments, would likely induce every new President to change the men filling offices.

Together, these causes could not fail to create a disgraceful and ruinous mutability in government administration.

Re-election of Good Administrator

2   With a positive duration of considerable extent [four-year term in office], I connect the circumstance of re-eligibility [no term limit].

The four-year term gives the president the desire and resolution to function well, and it gives the community the time to observe his measures and form an opinion of their merits. Without term limits, the people, when they approve of his conduct, may re-elect him and prolong the utility of his talents and virtues, giving the government the advantage of permanency in a wise system of administration.

Presidential Term Limit Bad Idea

3   Nothing appears more like a good idea at first glance nor more ill-founded on close inspection, than an idea that has some respectable advocates. I'm referring to the idea of continuing the president in office for a certain time, then excluding him from it, either for a limited period or forever.

This exclusion, whether temporary or perpetual, would have nearly the same effects. And these effects, for the most part, would be more pernicious than salutary.

Possible Re-election
Effects Behavior

4   One ill effect would be a reduction of inducements to good behavior. Most men feel much less zeal as they perform a duty when they know that the advantages connected with their

office must be relinquished at a predetermined time, than when they are permitted to entertain a hope of *obtaining*, by *meriting,* a continuance in office.

This will not be disputed as long as we admit that the desire of reward is one of the strongest incentives of human conduct. Or that the best security for fidelity is to make a man's interest coincide with his duty.

The love of fame, the strongest passion of the noblest minds, would prompt a man to plan and undertake extensive and arduous enterprises for the public benefit, requiring considerable time to mature and perfect them, if he could flatter himself that he might be re-elected and, therefore, finish what he had begun. However, the desire for fame would deter him from undertaking the project when he foresaw that he must leave before finishing the work, giving both it and his reputation to a successor who might be unequal or unfriendly to the task. The most to be expected of men in such a situation is the negative merit of doing no harm, instead of the positive merit of doing good.

Effect on Avaricious Office Holder

5   Another ill effect would be the temptation to sordid views, to embezzlement, and, in some instances, to usurpation. An avaricious man filling the office, who knows when he must give up the benefits he enjoys, could not easily resist the temptation to make the best use of the opportunity he enjoyed while it lasted. He might not hesitate to use the most corrupt methods to make the harvest as abundant as it was transitory.

Probably, the same man, with the possibility of re-election before him, might be content with the regular benefits of his situation. He might be unwilling to risk the consequences of abusing his opportunities. His avarice might be a guard on his avarice.

Perhaps the same man might be vain or ambitious, as well as avaricious. And if he expected to prolong his honors by his good conduct, he might hesitate to sacrifice his appetite for them to his appetite for gain. But with the prospect of being forced to leave office, his avarice would probably win over his caution, his vanity, or his ambition.

Effect on Ambitious Office Holder

6   Also, when an ambitious man held his country's highest position of honor, looking toward when he must descend from the exalted eminence forever— and knowing no merit on his part could save him—he would be more violently tempted to find a way to prolong his power at every personal hazard, than if he could possibly be re-elected by doing his duty.

Effect of Living Ex-Presidents

7   Would it promote the peace of the community or the stability of the government to have half a dozen men who had had enough respect to be raised to the seat of the supreme executive, wandering among the people like discontented ghosts, sighing for a place they are destined never more to possess?

Experience Parent of Wisdom

8   A third ill effect would be to deprive the community of the advantage of the experience gained by the chief executive in the exercise of his office. The adage that experience is the parent of wisdom is recognized as truth by the wisest, as well as, the simplest of mankind. Experience is the most desirable and essential quality in the head of a nation. Is it wise to constitutionally ban this desirable, essential quality, declaring that the moment it is acquired, its possessor will be compelled to abandon the station in which it was acquired and to which it is adapted?

This is, in fact, the precise meaning of regulations excluding men from serving their country by the re-election of their fellow-citizens, after having fitted themselves for doing it with greater utility through service.

Effect of Changing During Crisis

9 A fourth ill effect would be banishing men from offices in which, during emergencies, their presence might be of the greatest importance to the public interest or safety. Every nation has, at one period or another, experienced an absolute necessity of the services of particular men in particular situations, perhaps even to preserve its political existence. Therefore, term limits prohibit a nation from making use of its own citizens in the manner best suited to its exigencies and circumstances!

Even if a man weren't essential, it is evident that changing Presidents as a war breaks out or at any similar crisis, even for a man of equal merit, would always be detrimental to the community. It would substitute inexperience for experience. And it would tend to unhinge and set afloat the already settled train of the administration.

Effect of Policy Changes

10 A fifth ill effect would be a constitutional interdiction of stability in administration. By *requiring* a change of President, it would necessitate a mutability of measures. It can't be expected that men will vary and measures remain uniform. The contrary is normal. And we need not worry about too much stability when there is the option of changing.

Nor should we want to prohibit citizens from continuing their confidence where they think it may be safely placed and where, by re-election, they may prevent the fatal inconveniences of fluctuating councils and changing policy.

Partial/Perpetual Term Limits

11 These are some of the disadvantages flowing from term limits, especially perpetual exclusion. But when we consider that partial exclusion always makes readmission of the former office holder a remote and precarious possibility, they apply nearly as fully to both cases.

Advantages of Term Limits

12 What are the advantages of term limits promised to counterbalance these disadvantages? They are (1) greater independence in the executive, and (2) greater security to the people.

The first advantage can only be inferred if the exclusion is permanent. Couldn't he sacrifice his presidential independence to a future objective? Won't he have friends for whom he may sacrifice it? Might he be less willing to take decisive actions that could make personal enemies, when he knows that very soon he not only MAY, but MUST, be exposed to their resentments on an equal, even an inferior, footing?

It isn't easy to determine whether his independence would be more promoted or impaired by such an arrangement.

Term Limits: People's Security

13 As to the second supposed advantage, there is a still greater reason to entertain doubts about it.

If exclusion were perpetual, a man of irregular ambition, of whom there could be apprehension, would, with infinite reluctance, yield to necessity and leave a post forever in which he had acquired a habitual passion for power and pre-eminence. And if he had been fortunate or adroit enough to conciliate the good will of the people, he might induce them to consider a provision calculated to debar them of the right of giving a fresh proof of their attachment to a favorite as very odious and an unjustifiable restraint.

Circumstances may be conceived in which this disgust of the people, seconding the thwarted ambition of such a favorite, might result in greater danger to liberty than could reasonably be dreaded from the possibility of continuing in office by the voluntary votes of the community, exercising a constitutional privilege.

Disadvantages Outweigh Advantages

14 The idea of stopping the people from voting to continue in office men who in the people's opinion had entitled themselves to approbation and confidence has an excess of refinement. And the advantages are at best speculative and equivocal, and are overbalanced by disadvantages far more certain and decisive.

PUBLIUS

Constitutional references:

Article 2, section 2	400-408	President appoints executive officers
Article 2, section1	301-302	President term 4 years

Number 73

Executive Salary; Executive Powers, Veto

The third ingredient to instill vigor in the executive authority is an adequate provision for its support. Without this, the separation of the executive from the legislative branch would be trivial.

If the legislature had discretionary power over the salary and benefits of the Chief Executive, it could make him compliant to their will. They might reduce him by famine or tempt him by largess to their inclinations. These expressions, taken in all the latitude of the terms, would no doubt convey more than is intended.

There are men who could neither be distressed nor won over into sacrificing their duty. But this stern virtue is rare. Generally, power over a man's support is power over his will.

If so plain a truth needed confirmation by facts, examples wouldn't be lacking, even in this country, of the intimidation or seduction of the Executive by the terrors or allurements of the legislative pecuniary arrangements.

Presidential Compensation

2 Therefore, the judicious attention paid to this subject in the proposed Constitution cannot be commended too highly. It provides that "The President of the United States shall, at stated times, receive for his service a com-

pensation *which shall neither be increased nor diminished during the period for which he shall have been elected;* and he *shall not receive within that period any other emolument* from the United States, or any of them."

It is impossible to imagine any provision more suitable than this. On the appointment of a President, the legislature will declare, once and for all, the compensation for his services during the time for which he has been elected. Once done, they will have no power to alter it, either an increase or decrease, until a new service period by a new election starts. They can neither weaken his fortitude by reducing his ability to pay for necessities nor corrupt his integrity by appealing to his avarice. Neither the Union nor any State will be at liberty to give, nor will he be at liberty to receive, any other benefits. He can, of course, have no monetary inducement to renounce or desert the independence intended for him by the Constitution.

Appropriate Presidential Powers

3   The last enumerated requirement for a vigorous, effective executive is appropriate powers. Let us consider those which are proposed to be vested in the President of the United States.

Qualified Negative: Presidential Veto

4   The first to capture our attention is the qualified negative [veto] of the President on the acts or resolutions of the two houses of the legislature. Or, in other words, his power of returning all bills with objections, preventing their becoming laws unless they should afterwards be ratified by two-thirds of each house of the legislature.

Defense against Legislative Plundering

5   The propensity of the legislative branch to intrude on the rights and absorb the powers of the other branches has already been suggested. The insufficiency of a mere parchment delineation of the boundaries has also been remarked on. And the necessity of furnishing each with constitutional armies for its own defense has been inferred and proved.

The propriety of a negative, either absolute or qualified, in the Executive on legislative acts, results from these clear and indubitable principles. Without the one or the other, the Executive would be absolutely unable to defend himself against the plundering of the legislative. He might gradually be stripped of his authority by successive resolutions or annihilated by a single vote. And in one mode or the other, the legislative and executive powers might speedily come to be blended in the same hands.

Even if the legislative body never felt a propensity to invade the rights of the Executive, the rules of just reasoning and theoretic propriety teach us that the one should not be left to the mercy of the other, but should possess a constitutional and effectual power of self-defense.

Veto Defends against Bad Laws

6   But the power in question has a further use. It not only serves as a shield to the Executive, but it furnishes an additional security against improper laws. It establishes a check on the legislative body calculated to guard the community against the effects of faction, precipitancy, or any impulse unfriendly to the public good that might happen to influence a majority of that body.

Critics: Improper Control over Legislature

7 Sometimes, the propriety of a veto has been refuted by the observation that it shouldn't be presumed that a single man would possess more virtue and wisdom than a number of men. And unless this presumption is seriously considered, it would be improper to give the executive any type of control over the legislative body.

Examine Laws Passed in Haste

8 But this observation, when examined, will appear more specious than solid. The veto power isn't proper because of the Executive's superior wisdom or virtue, but because the legislature won't be infallible

The love of power may sometimes betray itself by encroaching on the rights of other members of the government. A faction may sometimes pervert its deliberation. Momentary impressions may sometimes hurry it into measures which itself, on reflection, would condemn.

The primary inducement to conferring the power in question on the Executive is to enable him to defend himself.

The secondary one is to increase the chances in favor of the community against the passing of bad laws through haste, inadvertence, or design. The oftener the measure is brought under examination, the greater the diversified situations of those examining it, the less must be the danger of the errors that flow from a lack of due deliberation or the missteps proceeding from the contagion of some common passion or interest. It is far less probable that culpable views of any kind would infect all parts of the government at the same

moment and in relation to the same object, than that they should, by turns, govern and mislead each of them.

Restraint on Excess Law-making

9 It may be said that the power of preventing bad laws includes that of preventing good ones and may be used for the one purpose as well as to the other. But this objection will have little weight with those who can properly estimate the mischiefs of inconstancy and mutability in laws that form the greatest blemish in the character and genius of our governments. They will consider every institution calculated to restrain the excess of law making and keep the status quo, as much more likely to do good than harm, because it is favorable to greater stability in the system of legislation.

The injury possibly done by defeating a few good laws will be amply compensated by the advantage of preventing a number of bad ones.

Veto Rarely Used against People's Will

10 Nor is this all. In a free government, the superior weight and influence of the legislature, and the hazard to the Executive in a trial of strength with that body, give satisfactory security that the negative would generally be employed with great caution. In the exercise of it, a charge of timidity would more often be charged, than rashness.

A king of Great Britain with all his train of sovereign attributes and all the influence he draws from a thousand sources would, to this day, hesitate to put a negative on the joint resolutions of the two houses of Parliament. He would exert the utmost resources of his influence to strangle a measure disagreeable to him during its progress to the throne to avoid the dilemma of permitting it to take effect or risking the displeasure of the nation by opposing the will of the legislative body.

Nor is it probable that the king would ultimately venture to use his veto except when it was absolutely proper or necessary. All informed men in that kingdom will agree that this remark is truthful. A very long period has elapsed since the negative of the crown has been exercised.

Cautious Use of Veto Power

11 If a magistrate as powerful and well fortified as a British monarch has scruples about using this power, how much greater caution may be reasonably expected in a President of the United States, clothed for the short period of four years with the executive authority of a government wholly and purely republican?

Rare, But Used When Needed

12 Clearly, there would be greater danger of his not using his power when necessary than of his using it too often or too much. Indeed, an argument against its expediency has been drawn from this very source. It has been represented, on this account, as a power odious in appearance, useless in practice. But it doesn't follow that because it might be rarely used, it would never be used.

In the case for which it is chiefly designed, an immediate attack on the constitutional rights of the Executive, or in a case where the public good was clearly and palpably sacrificed, a man of tolerable firmness would avail himself of his constitutional means of defense and listen to the admonitions of duty and responsibility. In the former supposition, his fortitude would be stimulated by his immediate interest in the power of his office. In the lat-

ter, he'd be stimulated by the probability of the support of his constituents who, though they would normally agree with the legislative body in a doubtful case, wouldn't allow their partiality to delude them in a very plain case. I speak now of an executive possessing only a common share of firmness. There are men who, under any circumstances, will have the courage to do their duty at every hazard.

Qualified Veto, Legislature Concurrence

13 But the convention chose a way that will both facilitate the use of the veto and make its effectiveness depend on the decision of a large part of the legislative body. Instead of an absolute negative, it gives the Executive the qualified negative already described. This power would be much more readily exercised than the other. A man who might be afraid to defeat a law by his single VETO, might not hesitate returning it for reconsideration subject to a final rejection only if more than one-third of each house concurs in his objections. He would be encouraged by the knowledge that if his opposition prevailed, it would be supported by a very respectable proportion of the legislative body, whose influence would unite with his in supporting the propriety of his conduct in the public opinion.

A direct, categorical negative appears more harsh and more apt to irritate than the mere suggestion of argumentative objections to be approved or disapproved by those to whom they are addressed. The less it might offend, the more apt it is to be exercised. For this reason, in practice it may be found more effectual. It is hoped that improper views will not often govern so large a proportion as two-thirds of both branches of the legislature at the same time, in spite of the counterbalancing weight of the Executive. At any rate, it is less probable than that such views would taint the resolutions and conduct of a bare majority.

The executive veto will often have a silent, unperceived, though forcible, operation. When men engaged in unjustifiable pursuits know that obstructions may come from a quarter they cannot control, they are often restrained, by the possibility of opposition, from doing what they would eagerly rush into, if no such external impediments were to be feared.

New York's Veto Successful

14 As has been elsewhere remarked, the qualified negative in New York is vested in a council, consisting of the governor with the chancellor and judges of the Supreme Court, or any two of them. It has been used on a variety of occasions and frequently with success. And its utility has become so apparent that people, who while compiling the constitution were violent opponents of it, have become its declared admirers.*

Maintaining Independent Judiciary

15 In another place I have remarked that the convention, when forming this part of the plan, departed from the model of New York State's constitution in favor of that of Massachusetts. Two strong reasons may be imagined for this preference. One is that the judges, who are interpreters of the law, might be improperly biased from having given a previous opinion in their revisionary capacities. The other is that because they are often associated with the Executive, they might be too vested in the political views of that executive, eventually cementing a dangerous combination between the executive and judiciary branches.

It is impossible to keep the judges too separate from every other avocation than that of expounding the laws. It is peculiarly dangerous to place them in a situation where they could be either corrupted or influenced by the Executive.

_____ PUBLIUS

* Mr. Abraham Yate, a warm opponent of the Constitution, is of this number.

Constitutional references:

Article 2, section 1	365-370	executive compensation
Article 1, section 7	135-170	President's veto power

Number 74

Commander-in-Chief, Reprieves, Pardons

The President of the United States is to be "commander-in-chief of the army and navy of the United States, and the militia of the several States *when called into the actual service* of the United States."

The propriety of this provision is so evident and is, at the same time, so consistent with the precedent of the State constitutions in general, little need be said to explain or enforce it. Most of the people who have, in other areas, coupled the chief executive with a council, have concentrated the military authority in him alone.

Of all the cares or concerns of government, the direction of war specifically demands qualities that distinguish the exercise of power by a single hand. The direction of war implies the direction of the common strength. And the power of directing and employing the common strength forms an essential part in the definition of the executive authority.

Reports from Executive Departments

2 "The President may require the opinion, in writing, of the principal officer in each of the executive departments, upon any subject relating to the duties of their respective officers."

I consider this a mere redundancy in the Constitution since the right it provides would result, anyway, from the office.

Reprieves, Pardons

3 He is also to be authorized to grant "reprieves and pardons for offenses against the United States, *except in cases of impeachment.*"

Humanity and good policy dictate that the benign prerogative of pardoning should be as little as possible fettered or embarrassed. Every country's criminal code is so necessarily severe that, without easy access to exceptions in favor of unfortunate guilt, justice would wear a countenance too vicious and cruel.

Feelings of responsibility are stronger as fewer people are involved. Therefore, it may be inferred that a single man would most carefully study the motives that might plead for a mitigation of the rigor of the law, and least apt to yield to considerations calcu-

lated to shelter a proper target of its vengeance. The reflection that the fate of a fellow creature depended on his *sole fiat* would naturally inspire scrupulousness and caution. Equal caution, though of a different kind, would arise from the dread of being accused of weakness or connivance.

On the other hand, since men generally derive confidence from their numbers, a group of men with this power might often encourage each other's inflexibility and might be less attuned to suspicious apprehensions or censure for an injudicious or affected clemency. For these reasons, one man appears to be a more eligible dispenser of the government's mercy than a body of men.

Pardons for Treason

4 The expediency of vesting the power of pardoning in the President has been only contested, if I'm not mistaken, in relation to the crime of treason. It has been urged that this should depend on the assent of one or both houses of the legislature.

There are strong reasons for requiring this concurrence. Since treason is a crime against the society, when the guilt of the offender has been determined, it seems fit to refer the expediency of an act of mercy towards him to the judgment of the legislature. And this ought to be the case, as the supposition of the connivance of the Chief Executive ought not to be entirely excluded.

But there are also strong objections to such a plan. There is no doubt that a single man of prudence and good sense is better fitted, in delicate conjunctures, to balance the motives that may plead for and against a pardon, than any numerous body whatever.

It deserves particular attention that treason will often be connected with seditious acts embracing a large proportion of the community, as recently happened in Massachusetts. In every such case, we might expect to see the people's representatives tainted with the same spirit that had given birth to the offense. And when parties are pretty equally matched, the secret sympathy of friends of the condemned person, working on the good nature and weakness of others, might frequently bestow impunity where the terror of an example was necessary.

On the other hand, when the sedition proceeded from causes that inflamed the resentments of the majority party, they might often be found obstinate and inexorable when policy demands forbearance and clemency. But the principal argument for reposing the power of pardoning in this case to the Chief Executive is this: in seasons of insurrection or rebellion, there are often critical moments when a well-timed offer of pardon to the insurgents or rebels may restore the tranquillity of the nation. And if the time passed with no action, it may never be possible afterwards to recall. The lengthy process of convening the legislature or one of its houses for the purpose of obtaining its sanction to the measure would frequently be the occasion of letting slip the golden opportunity. The loss of a week, a day, an hour, may sometimes be fatal.

If it is suggested that a discretionary power might occasionally be conferred on the President in such a situation, it may be answered in two ways. First, it is questionable whether, in a limited Constitution, the power could be delegated by law. Second, it would generally be unwise to take any step before hand that might hold out the prospect of impunity. A proceeding of this kind, out of the usual course, would be construed into an argument of timidity or of weakness, and would have a tendency to embolden guilt.

PUBLIUS

Constitutional references:

Article 2, section 2	379-383	President serves as commander-in-chief
Article 2, section 2	384-388	executive officers report to President
Article 2, section 2	388-391	Presidential pardons

Number 75

President, with Senate Approval, Makes Treaties

The President will have the power, "by and with consent of the Senate, to make treaties, provided two thirds of the senators present concur."

Although this provision has been vigorously attacked on different grounds, I believe it is one of the most unexceptional parts of the Constitution.

One objection is based on the trite topic of intermixing powers. Some contend the President alone should possess the power to make treaties. Others, the Senate.

Others object to the small number of people who can make a treaty. Some people making this objection believe the House of Representatives should be involved, while others seem to think that nothing more is necessary than to substitute two thirds of *all* the members of the Senate for two thirds of the members *present.*

Since I flatter myself that remarks made in an earlier paper about this must have placed it, to a discerning eye, in a very favorable light, I will only offer a few additional remarks, addressing the objections just stated.

Treaty Roles, Separation Rule

2 As to the mixing of powers, I will rely on the explanations given in other papers of the true meaning of the separation of powers rule. By inference, I assume the union of the Executive with the Senate when forming treaties is no infringement of that rule. I venture to add that because of the nature of treaties, the union is particularly proper.

Although several writers say it is an executive authority, this is evidently an arbitrary classification. If we carefully study how treaties operate, they have more legislative than executive characteristics, though it doesn't seem to fall strictly within the definition of either of them.

The essence of legislative authority is to enact laws or, in other words, to prescribe rules that regulate society. The execution of the laws and employment of the common strength seem to comprise all the function of the executive.

The power to make treaties is plainly not one or the other. It doesn't relate to executing existing laws or to enacting new ones and, still less, to an exertion of the common strength.

Treaties are CONTRACTS with foreign nations that have the force of law, but derive it from the obligations of good faith. They are not rules prescribed by the sovereign to the subjects, but agreements between sovereign and sovereign. Therefore, this power seems to form a distinct category, belonging to neither the legislative nor the executive.

The qualities listed elsewhere as indispensable in the management of foreign negotiations, show that the Executive is the best agent in those transactions. At the same time, the vast importance of the trust and the operation of treaties as laws plead strongly for the participation of the whole or a portion of the legislative body in the office of making them.

Foreign Influence, President Acted Alone

3 However proper or safe it may be to give an hereditary monarch, who is chief executive, the entire power to make treaties, it would be utterly unsafe and improper to entrust that power to an elected chief executive with a four-year term.

It was said earlier, and is unquestionably true, that an hereditary monarch, though often an oppressor of his people, has personally too much stake in the government to be in any material danger of being corrupted by foreign powers.

But for a man raised from private citizen to chief executive, with a moderate or small fortune, and knowing that in the not too distant future he will again be a private citizen, the temptation to sacrifice his duty to his interest would require superlative virtue to withstand. An avaricious man might be tempted to betray the interests of the state to the acquisition of wealth. An ambitious man might make his own aggrandizement, with the aid of a foreign power, the price of his treachery to his constituents. The history of human conduct doesn't warrant the exalted opinion of human virtue required for a nation to commit such delicate and momentous interests, ones concerning its intercourse with the rest of the world, to the sole disposal of an executive like a President of the United States.

Advantages of President's Involvement

4   Entrusting the Senate alone with the power to make treaties would relinquish the benefits of the President's constitutional participation in the conduct of foreign negotiations. The Senate could employ a person in this capacity, but they would have the option of letting it alone. Animosity or cabal might induce the latter rather than the former.

Besides this, the ministerial officer of the Senate could not be expected to receive the same degree of the confidence and respect of foreign powers as the constitutional representatives of the nation and, of course, would not be able to act with an equal degree of influence or efficacy. The Union would lose a considerable advantage in the management of its external concerns. And the people would lose the additional security resulting from the cooperation of the Executive.

Though it would be imprudent to confide in the Executive, alone, so important a trust, it cannot be doubted that his participation would materially add to society's safety.

It must be clear that the joint power, by the President and Senate, to make treaties affords a greater prospect of security than the separate possession of it by either of them. Additionally, anyone who has seriously studied how the President will be elected knows that the office will always be filled by men of such character that, because of their wisdom and integrity, their concurrence in forming treaties will be especially desirable.

House Too Inexperienced, Large

5   The remarks in an earlier paper, and alluded to here, conclusively show that the House of Representatives shouldn't share in the formation of treaties. Because of the fluctuating and, with its future growth, multitudinous composition of the House, we can't expect it to have the qualities essential to properly executing such a trust. Accurate and comprehensive knowledge of foreign politics, a steady and systematic adherence to the same views, a uniform sensibility to national character, decision, *secrecy*, and dispatch are incompatible with the genius of a body so variable and numerous.

The need to have so many different people concur, alone, would be a solid objection. The need for more and longer sessions of the House of Representatives to sanction the progressive stages of a treaty would be so great an inconvenience and expense that it, alone, should condemn the idea.

Two-Thirds Ratification, Minority Rule

6   The last objection is to substitute the proportion of two-thirds of all members of the Senate, to that of two-thirds of the members *present*.

We have discussed that when more than the majority of any body is required to pass resolutions, it tends to impede governmental operations. And it tends to indirectly subject the will of the majority to that of the minority. This important consideration supports our opinion that the convention has gone as far as necessary to secure the advantage of numbers in the formation of treaties as can be reconciled either with the activity of the public councils or with a reasonable regard to the majority will of the community.

If two thirds of the whole number of members were required, in many cases it would be, from the non-attendance of some members, the same as requiring unanimity. The history of every political body using this principle is a history of impotence, perplexity, and disorder. Proofs might be adduced from the examples of the Roman Tribune, the Polish Diet, and the States-General of the Netherlands, if an example at home didn't make foreign precedents unnecessary.

Proposed Senate, Current Congress

7 To require a fixed proportion of the whole Senate would probably not add to the advantages of requiring a proportion of the attending members.

Requiring a specific number to pass every resolution diminishes the reasons for punctual attendance. But making the legal authority of the body dependent on a *proportion* that can vary by the absence or presence of a single member has the contrary effect.

Promoting punctuality tends to keep the body complete. It is likely that Senate resolutions would be decided by as many members in this case as if two thirds of all members were required, with far fewer reasons for delay.

Under the existing Confederation two members *may*, and usually *do*, represent a State. Consequently, Congress, which currently holds *all the powers* of the Union, rarely consists of more people than the proposed Senate. Additionally, members currently vote by States. When only a single member from a State is present, a State vote is lost. This justifies the assumption that the Senate, where members will vote individually, would rarely have fewer active voices than in the existing Congress.

When we include the President of the Senate, we won't hesitate to infer that the people of America would have greater security against an improper use of the power of making treaties under the new Constitution than they now enjoy under the Confederation. And when we go one step further, looking forward to the probable augmentation of the Senate by new States, we will not only be confident there will be enough members to entrust the power, but we will probably conclude that a larger body than the Senate will likely become would not be fit for the proper discharge of the trust.

PUBLIUS

Constitutional references:
Article 2, Section 2   392-395   President, with Senate, makes treaties
Article 1, Section 3   64-66   Senate president votes to break ties

---

Number 76

President Nominates, Senate Approves, Appointments

The President is "to *nominate, and, by and with the advice and consent of the Senate, to appoint ambassadors, other public ministers and consuls, judges of the Supreme Court, and all other officers of the United States whose appointments are not otherwise provided for in the Constitution.* But the Congress may by law vest the appointment of such inferior officers as they think proper in the President alone, or in the courts of law, or in the heads of departments. The President shall have the power to fill up *all vacancies* which may happen *during the recess of the Senate,* by granting commissions which shall *expire* at the end of their next session."

Best Method of Appointing Officers

2   A former paper observed that "the true test of a good government is its aptitude and tendency to produce a good administration." If this is true, the method of appointing the officers of the United States as stated above, when examined, is entitled to special commendation. It isn't easy to think of a better way to promote a judicious choice of men for filling the offices of the Union. And no proof is needed that the character of government administration depends on this point.

Possible Appointment Methods

3   Of course, having the people at large make appointments is impractical. If nothing else, it would leave them little time to do anything else. Therefore, the power of appointment, in ordinary cases, should be modified in one of three ways. It should either be vested in a single man, or a *select* group of a moderate number, or in a single man with the concurrence of such a group.

In the following discussion, when a group or body of men is mentioned, it refers to a select body as just described. The people collectively, from their number and dispersal, cannot be coerced by the spirit of cabal and intrigue, the chief objections to giving the power to a group of men.

One Man Best Judge

4   People who have thought about the subject, or paid attention to observations made in the other papers relating to electing the President, will, I presume, agree there will always be a great probability that he will be a man of abilities, at least respectable. On this premise, I'll put down the rule that one man of discernment can do a better job analyzing the qualities for specific offices than a group of men of equal, or even superior, discernment.

Reasons Group Decision Bad

5   The sole, undivided responsibility of one man will produce a keener sense of duty and regard to reputation. He will feel a stronger obligation and be more interested in carefully investigating the qualities required to fill the offices. And he will impartially prefer the persons who may have the most qualifications.

He will have *fewer* personal attachments to gratify than a group of men who each may have an equal number. So, he will be much less liable to be misled by friendship and affection. A single, well-directed man cannot be distracted and warped by the diversity of views, feelings, and interests that frequently distract and warp the resolution of a collective body.

Nothing agitates the passions of mankind like personal considerations, whether related to ourselves or others, who are to be the objects of our choice or preference. Hence, every time a group of men exercise the power of appointing to offices, we must expect to see a full display of all private and party likes and dislikes, partialities and antipathies, attachments and animosities, which are felt by those who compose the group. The choice made under such circumstances will be the result either of a victory gained by one party over the other or a compromise between the parties. In either case, the intrinsic merit of the candidate will often not be considered.

In the case of a victory of one party over the other, the qualifications best adapted to uniting the party's votes will be more important than the qualifications that fit the person to the job. If a compromise, the coalition will commonly come up with a trade-off: "Give us the man we wish for this office, and you can have the one you wish for that." This will usually be the bargain. Public good will rarely be the primary objective of either party victories or party negotiations.

Nominate vs. No Approval Needed

6   The intelligent people who find fault with this constitutional provision know this is true. They say the President should be solely authorized to make federal government appointments.

But every advantage expected from such an arrangement will be, in substance, derived from the power of *nomination*, as proposed. At the same time, several disadvantages that might accompany the absolute power of appointment will be avoided.

In the act of nomination, his judgment alone will be exercised. Since he will nominate a man who, with the Senate's approval, will fill an office, his responsibility will be as complete as if he was to make the final appointment.

In this respect, there is no difference between nominating and appointing. The same motives will influence a proper discharge of his duty in both cases. No man could be appointed without being nominated, so every man appointed will be, in fact, the President's choice.

Senate Rejections Rare

7   But might not his nomination be overruled? I grant it might, but he will make the next nomination. The person ultimately appointed will be his preference, though perhaps not his first. And his nomination will probably not be overruled very often.

If the Senate preferred a different person, they couldn't be tempted to reject the proposed nomination because they couldn't be sure that the person they wanted would be the second or any subsequent nomination. They couldn't even be certain that a future nomination would be a candidate any more acceptable to them. And since their dissent might cast a stigma on the individual rejected, and might appear to be a reflection on the judgment of the President, their sanction will rarely be refused except when there are special and strong reasons for the refusal.

Senate Restraint on President

8   Then why require the cooperation of the Senate? I answer: the necessity

of their concurrence will have a powerful though, in general, silent operation. It will be an excellent check on presidential favoritism and will tend to prevent the appointment of unfit characters from State prejudice, from family connection, from personal attachment, or from a view to popularity. In addition, it will be an efficacious source of stability in the administration.

Thoughtful Nomination

9 It's easily understood that a man with sole power to dispense offices is governed more by his private inclinations and interests than when he must submit the propriety of his choice to the discussion and determination of an entire house of the legislature. The possibility of rejection is a strong motive to take care when making a nomination. The danger to his own reputation and his political existence from betraying favoritism, or an unbecoming pursuit of popularity, to the scrutiny of a body whose opinion has great weight in forming public opinion, would operate as a barrier to the one and to the other. He would be both ashamed and afraid to bring forward, for the most distinguished or lucrative federal offices, candidates with no other merit than coming from the same State, or being in some way personally allied to him, or possessing the necessary insignificance and pliancy to make them the obsequious instruments of his pleasure.

Executive Influence on Senate

10 From this reasoning some have objected, saying the President's influence through the nomination power may secure the complaisance of the Senate to his views. Assuming that human nature is universally weak is as much an error in political reasoning as assuming universal integrity.

Delegated power implies that mankind has a portion of virtue and honor that may be a reasonable foundation of confidence. And experience justifies the theory. It has existed in the most corrupt periods of the most corrupt governments.

The British House of Commons has long been accused of venality both in Britain and the United States. And it can't be doubted that the charge is, to a considerable extent, well founded. But a large part of the House of Commons always consists of independent, public-spirited men who have influence on the nation's councils. Hence (the present reign not excepted) it often controls the inclination of the monarch, both with regard to men and to measures.

Therefore, the President may occasionally influence some individuals in the Senate. But the supposition that he could purchase the integrity of the whole body is forced and improbable. A man with a realistic view of human nature, neither flattering its virtues nor exaggerating its vices, will be confident in the integrity of the Senate. He knows that it will be impractical for the President to corrupt or seduce a majority of the Senate. And his need for its cooperation in appointments will be a considerable and salutary restraint on the conduct of the President.

Nor is the integrity of the Senate the only reliance. The Constitution provides some important guards against the danger of executive influence on the legislative body: it declares that "no senator or representative shall, during the time *for which he was elected*, be appointed to any civil office under the United States which shall have been created, or the emoluments whereof shall have been increased, during such time; and no person, holding any office under the United States, shall be a member of either house during his continuance in office." PUBLIUS

Constitutional references:
Article 2, Section 2 395-413 President appoints United States officers
Article 1, Section 6 125-131 Senators, Representatives appointment to government offices

---

Number 77

Executive Appoints Administration Officers

One advantage expected from Senate cooperation in appointments is that it will contribute to the stability of the administration of government. The Senate's consent will be necessary to displace as well as appoint. Therefore, a change of the Chief Executive will not be the occasion of such a violent or general a revolution in governmental officers as might be expected if he was the sole disposer of offices. Where a man in any job has proved his fitness for it, a new President will be restrained from attempting a change in favor of a person he wants by fear that the Senate's disapproval might frustrate the attempt, bringing some degree of discredit on himself.

People who believe a steady administration is valuable will prize a provision connecting the official existence of public men with the approval or disapproval of the Senate. It's greater permanency will probably be less subject to inconstancy than any other part of the government.

Balanced Plan

2 It has been suggested that sometimes the union of the Senate and President when making appointments will give the President too much influence over the Senate. And others say it will have an opposite tendency— a strong proof that neither suggestion is true.

No Undue Influence over Senate

3 By stating the first opposition in its proper form, it is easy to refute it. It amounts to this: the President will have an improper *influence over* the Senate because the Senate will have the power of *restraining* him.

This is an absurdity in terms. There is no doubt that if he had the entire power of appointment he could more easily establish a dangerous empire over the Senate than having the mere power of nomination, subject to its control.

Senate Influencing Appointments

4 Let us view the converse of the proposition: "the Senate will influence the Executive."

As I have said several times, the impreciseness of the objection forbids a precise answer. How is this influence to be exerted? In relation to what?

As used here, the power to influence a person implies a power of conferring a benefit on him. How could the Senate confer a benefit on the President by using their right of negative on his nomination? If it is said that they might sometimes gratify him by an acquiescence to a favorite choice when public motive might dictate differently, I answer that the President will be too rarely personally interested in the result to be materially affected by the compliance of the Senate.

The person or group with the POWER to *originate* the disposition of honors and emoluments is more likely to attract than be attracted to the POWER that can merely obstruct them.

If "influencing" the President means *restraining* him, this is precisely what is intended. And it has been shown that the restraint will have a beneficial effect while not destroying any advantage that might come from the uncontrolled agency of the Executive. The right of nomination produces all the good of an appointment and will avoid most of its evils.

Public Evaluates Appointments

5   When comparing the plan for appointing offices in the Constitution with that established by the constitution of New York, a decided preference must be given to the former. In the New York constitution, the power of nomination is unequivocally vested in the Executive.

The Constitution makes it necessary to submit each nomination to the judgment of an entire house of the legislature. Because of this, the appointment process becomes a public issue. And the public can determine what part was performed by the different actors. The blame for a bad nomination will fall on the President singly and absolutely. The censure for rejecting a good one will likely lie entirely at the door of the Senate, aggravated by the consideration of their having counteracted the good intentions of the Executive. If a bad appointment is made, the Executive, for nominating, and the Senate, for approving, will participate in different degrees in the disgrace.

NY Appointments Veiled in Secrecy

6   The reverse of all this characterizes the manner of appointment in New York. The council of appointment consists of three to five people, one of who is the governor. This small body executes their trust shut up in a private apartment, impenetrable to the public eye.

It is known that the governor claims the right of nomination on the strength of some ambiguous expressions in the constitution. But it is not known to what extent or what manner he exercises it or on what occasions he is contradicted or opposed.

Because of the uncertainty of its author, giving no target, the censure of a bad appointment has neither poignancy nor duration. And when a field for cabal and intrigue lies wide open, all responsibility is lost. The most that the public can know is that the governor claims the right of nomination. *Two* out of the small number of *four* men can too often be managed without much difficulty. If some of the members of the council happen to have an uncomplying character, it is frequently possible to get rid of their opposition by regulating meeting times so their attendance is inconvenient. And from whatever cause, a great number of very improper appointments are sometimes made.

Does a governor of New York avail himself of the dominance he must necessarily have in this delicate and important part of the administration? Does he prostitute that advantage by advancing people whose chief merit is their implicit devotion to his will, supporting a despicable and dangerous system of personal influence? These questions, unfortunately for the community, can only be the subjects of speculation and conjecture.

Appointment Counsel

7 Every appointment council, however constituted, will be a conclave in which cabal and intrigue would have their full scope. Without an unwarrantable increased expense, their number cannot be large enough to exclude easy conspiracy.

Each member would have friends and connections to provide for, so mutual gratification would beget a scandalous bartering of votes and bargaining for places. The private attachments of one man might easily be satisfied. But to satisfy the private attachments of a dozen, or of twenty men, a few families might end up holding a monopoly of government offices. This would lead more directly to an aristocracy or an oligarchy than any measure that could be contrived.

If the people composing the council changed frequently, to avoid an accumulation of offices, this would involve the mischiefs of a mutable administration in their full extent. Such a council would be more apt to influence the executive than the Senate because they would be fewer in number and their actions would be less under public inspection. Such a council, as a substitute for the proposed Constitution, would increase ex-

pense, multiply the evils that spring from favoritism and intrigue in the distribution of public honors, decrease stability in the administration of the government, and diminish the security against an undue influence of the Executive. And yet such a council has been warmly contended for as an essential amendment in the proposed Constitution.

House: No Part in Appointments

8 I couldn't properly conclude my observations on the subject of appointments without mentioning an idea with only a few advocates. I mean that of uniting the House of Representatives in the power of making them.

However, I will do little more than mention it, as I can't imagine that it is likely to gain the approval of any considerable part of the community. A body so fluctuating, and at the same time so numerous, can never be deemed proper for the exercise of that power. Its unfitness will be clear to anyone who remembers that in only fifty years it may consist of three or four hundred people. All the advantages of stability, both of the Executive and of the Senate, would be defeated by including the House of Representatives, and infinite delays and embarrassments would happen. The example of most of the States in their local constitutions encourages us to reject the idea.

Other Executive Powers

9 The only remaining powers of the Executive include: giving information to Congress on the state of the Union, recommending to their consideration measures he judges expedient, convening Congress, or either house, on extraordinary occasions, adjourning them when they cannot themselves agree on the time of adjournment, receiving ambassadors and other public ministers, faithfully executing the laws, and commissioning all the officers of the United States.

Convene Congress; Receive Ambassadors

10 Except some trivial objections about the power of convening *either* house of the legislature and receiving ambassadors, no objection has been made to this class of authorities. Nor could there be any. Indeed, it required an insatiable avidity for censure to invent exceptions to the parts that have been excepted.

Regarding the power of convening either house of the legislature, I will only remark that in respect to the Senate, at least, we can quickly discover a good reason for it. Since it has a concurrent power with the Executive in making treaties, it might often be necessary to call it together with a view to this objective when it would be unnecessary and improper to convene the House of Representatives.

As to the reception of ambassadors, what I have said in a former paper will furnish a sufficient answer.

Safety of Executive

11 We have completed a survey of the structure and powers of the executive department. I have endeavored to show that it combines all the requisites to energy, as far as republican principles will permit.

The remaining inquiry is does it also combine the required safeties, in a republican sense—a due dependence on the people, a due responsibility?

The answer has been anticipated in the investigation of its other characteristics and is satisfactorily deduced from these circumstances: The President is elected once in four years by persons immediately chosen by the people for that purpose. He will be at all times liable to impeachment, trial, dismissal from office, incapacity to serve in any other, and forfeiture of life and estate by subsequent prosecution in the common course of law.

But these precautions, great as they are, are not the only ones provided in favor of the public security in the Constitution. In the only instances in which the abuse of executive authority may materially to be feared, the Chief Executive of the United States will, by the Constitution, be subjected to the control of a house of the legislative body. What more could be desired by an enlightened and reasonable people?

PUBLIUS

Constitutional references:

Ar 2, sec 2	395-408	Presidential power to appoint officers of the U. S.
Ar 2, sec 2	409-413	President fills vacancies during Senate recess
Ar 2, sec 3	414-418	state-of-the-Union; President recommends measures
Ar 2, sec 2	392-395	treaties
Ar 2, sec 3	419-424	President convenes, adjourns legislature
Ar 2, sec 3	424-425	President receives ambassadors
Ar 2, sec 3	426-427	President makes sure laws are faithfully executed
Ar 2, sec 3	427-428	President commissions officers of the United States
Ar 2, sec 4	429-433	President impeachable
Ar 1, sec 3	82-84	President liable to punishment according to the law
Ar 2, sec 1	305-312	presidential electors

Number 78

Federal Judiciary: Hold Office during *Good Behavior*

We will now examine the judiciary branch of the proposed government.

Federal Judiciary Necessary

2 After studying the defects in the existing Confederation, the utility and necessity of a federal judicature is clear. Those considerations don't need to be repeated because the propriety of the institution in the abstract is not disputed.

The only questions that have been raised relate to its structure and its extent. Our observations, therefore, will be confined to these points.

Structure of Federal Judiciary

3 The structure of the federal judiciary seems to include:

1. the mode of appointing judges,
2. their tenure in office, and
3. the partition of judiciary authority between different courts and their relationship to each other.

1. Appointing Judges

4 The mode of appointing judges is the same as that of appointing other officers of the Union. This has been so fully discussed in the last two papers that nothing can be said here that wouldn't be useless repetition.

2. Tenure

5 The tenure of judges, the conditions by which they hold their offices, chiefly concern their duration in office, provisions for their support, and precautions for their responsibility.

Duration in Office: Good Behavior

6 According to the Constitution, all judges appointed by the United States will hold their offices *during good behavior.* This conforms to the most approved State constitutions, including New York's.

Adversaries of the Constitution have questioned whether this is proper. This criticism is a symptom of the rage for objections that disorders their imaginations and judgments. The standard of good behavior for judges continuing in office is one of the most valuable modern improvements in government.

In a monarchy, it is an excellent barrier to the despotism of the prince. In a republic, it is no less an excellent barrier to the encroachments and oppressions of the representative body. And it is the best expedient devised, in any government, to secure a steady, upright, and impartial administration of the laws.

Least Threat to Constitutional Rights

7 Anyone who studies the different departments of governmental power must see that, when they are constitutionally separated from each other, the judiciary, from the nature of its functions, will always be the least dangerous to the political rights of the Constitution because it will have the least capacity to annoy and injure them.

The executive not only dispenses honors but holds the community's sword.

The legislature not only commands the purse but prescribes the rules by which the duties and rights of every citizen are to be regulated.

The judiciary, however, has no influence over either the sword or the purse. It directs neither the strength nor wealth of society. It can take no active resolution whatever.

The judiciary may be said to have neither FORCE nor WILL, merely judgment. It even depends on the aid of the executive arm for the efficacy of its judgments.

Permanency in Office: Independence

8 This simple view suggests several important consequences. The judiciary is incontestably the weakest of the three branches of power.[1] It can never successfully attack the other two. And all possible care is required to enable it to defend itself against their attacks.

It also proves that although the courts of justice may be, now and then, responsible for individual oppression, as long as the judiciary remains truly distinct from both the legislature and the executive, they can never endanger the general liberty of the people. I agree that "there is no liberty, if the power of judging is not separated from the legislative and executive powers."[2]

Liberty has nothing to fear from the judiciary alone, but everything to fear from its union with either of the other branches. This union, with its negative effects, would happen if the judiciary were dependent on the other branches, despite a nominal and apparent separation.

Because of its natural feebleness, the judiciary is continually in jeopardy of being overpowered, awed, or influenced by the legislative and executive branches. Nothing contributes so much to its firmness and independence as permanency in office. Therefore, it lastly proves that permanency in office can be regarded as indispensable and, to a great measure, as the citadel of public justice and public security.

Enforce Limited Legislative Authority

9 The complete independence of the courts of justice is particularly essential in a limited Constitution. By a limited Constitution, I mean one that contains certain specific exceptions to the legislative authority.

For example, that it shall pass no bills of attainder, no *ex post facto* laws, etc. Limitations like these can only be preserved in practice through courts of justice with the duty to declare all acts contrary to the manifest tenor of the Constitution void. Without this, all the reservations of specific rights or privileges would amount to nothing.

Power to Void Unconstitutional Laws

10 The courts will have the right to pronounce legislative acts void because they are contrary to the Constitution. Because of this, some people have imagined that this implies that the judiciary power will be superior to the legislative power. It has been argued that the authority to declare the acts of another void must be superior to the one whose acts may be declared void.

Since this is an important doctrine in all the American constitutions, a brief discussion of the ground on which it rests cannot be unacceptable.

Congress: Actions Limited

11 Every act of a delegated authority that is contrary to the meaning of its commission is void. This concept couldn't be based on clearer principles.

---

[1] The celebrated Montesquieu, speaking of them, says: "Of the three powers above mentioned, the judiciary is next to nothing." *Spirit of Laws,* Vol. I, page 186.
[2] *Idem*, page 181.

Therefore, no legislative act contrary to the Constitution can be valid.

Denying this would affirm that the deputy is greater than his principal, the servant is above his masters, the representatives of the people are superior to the people themselves, that man acting by virtue of powers may do, not only what their powers do not authorize, but what they forbid.

Authority:
Constitution vs. Legislature

12 It may be argued that the legislative body is the constitutional judge of its own powers and that the other branches must accept the interpretation it puts on the powers. But this is not a logical conclusion from any provision in the Constitution.

It can't be supposed that the Constitution intends to enable the people's representatives to substitute their *will* for that of their constituents. It is far more rational to suppose that the courts were designed to be an intermediate body between the people and the legislature. Among other things, the courts keep the legislature within the limits assigned to their authority.

Interpretation of the laws is the proper and specific province of the courts. A constitution is, in fact and must be regarded by the judges as, a fundamental law. Therefore, the courts ascertain its meaning, as well as the meaning of specific legislative acts. If the two should happen to have an irreconcilable variance, the one with the superior obligation and validity should, of course, be preferred.

Or, in other words, the Constitution should be preferred over the statute, the intention of the people to the intention of their agents.

People's Constitution Superior to Both

13 This conclusion, in no way, means the judicial is superior to the legislative power. It only supposes that the power of the people is superior to both.

Where the will of the legislature, declared in its statutes, is in opposition to that of the people, as declared in the Constitution, judges should be governed by the latter rather than the former. They should regulate their decision by the fundamental laws rather than those that are not fundamental.

Decide Validity of Contradictory Laws

14 The judicial discretion of determining between two contradictory laws is exemplified by a familiar circumstance. Sometimes two existing statutes clash in whole or in part with each other, and neither contains any repealing clause or expression. When this happens, the courts have the authority and duty to liquidate and fix their meaning and operation.

So far as they can be reconciled with each other, by any fair construction, reason and law conspire to dictate that this should be done. When this is impractical, it becomes necessary to give effect to one and exclude the other.

The prevailing rule in the courts to determine their relative validity is that the more recent shall be preferred to the first. But this rule is not derived form any positive law. It is only a rule of construction from the nature and reason of the thing. It is not enjoined on the courts by legislative provision, but adopted because it is consistent with truth and propriety, to direct their conduct as interpreters of the law. They thought it reasonable that between conflicting acts of an *equal* authority, the last indication of its will should have preference.

Constitution Superior to Laws

15 But when a superior, original authority and a subordinate, derivative authority produce conflicting acts, by their very nature, reason indicates that the converse of that rule as proper to be followed. The prior act of a superior authority should be preferred to the subsequent act of an inferior and subordinate authority.

Accordingly, whenever a particular statute contravenes the Constitution, judicial tribunals will have the duty to adhere to the latter and disregard the former.

Courts Negating Legislative Will

16 The argument that the courts, on the pretence of a repugnancy, may substitute their own pleasure to the constitutional intentions of the legislature carries no weight. This could happen in the case of two contradictory statutes. Or it could during the adjudication of any single statute.

The courts must declare the meaning of the law. And if they were inclined to exercise their WILL instead of JUDGMENT, their pleasure would be substituted for the pleasure of the legislative body. If this observation proves anything, it proves that there should be no judges distinct from the legislature.

Permanent Tenure of Constitutional Guardians

17 If the courts of justice are to be considered the bulwarks of a limited Constitution against encroachments by the legislature, this duty is a strong argument for the permanent tenure of judicial offices. Nothing will contribute to the independent spirit in judges, which is essential to the faithful performance of so arduous a duty, as permanent tenure.

Independent Judges Protect Liberty

18 This independence of the judges is equally required to guard the Constitution and the rights of individuals from the effects of ill humors caused by designing men or the influence of particular conjunctures that sometimes disseminate among the people themselves. Even though they speedily give place to better information and more deliberate reflection, they have a tendency, in the meantime, to occasion dangerous innovations in the government, and serious oppressions of the minor party in the community.

I trust the friends of the proposed Constitution will never agree with its enemies[3] in questioning that fundamental principle of republican government—that the people have the right to alter or abolish the established Constitution whenever they find it inconsistent with their happiness. But it is not to be inferred from this principle that the representatives of the people whenever a momentary inclination, which is incompatible with the provisions in the existing constitution, happens to lay hold of a majority of their constituents would, because of this, be justifiable in a violation of those provisions. And the courts would not be under a greater obligation to connive at infractions in this shape than when they had proceeded wholly from the cabals of the representative body. Until the people have, by some solemn and authoritative act, annulled or changed the established form, it is binding on them collectively, as well as individually. And no presumption, or even knowledge, of their sentiments, can warrant their representatives in a departure from it, prior to such an act.

[3] *Vide* "Protest of the Minority of the Convention of Pennsylvania," Martin's Speech, etc.

It is easy to see that judges need an uncommon amount of fortitude to do their duty as faithful guardians of the Constitution after legislative invasions of it had been instigated by the majority voice of the community.

Restraint on Bad Legislation

19 But it is not only with a view to infraction of the Constitution that the independence of the judges may be an essential safeguard against the effects of occasional ill humors in the society. These sometimes extend no farther than to the injury of the private rights of specific classes of citizens by unjust and partial laws.

Here, also, the permanency of the judicial magistracy is of vast importance in mitigating the severity and confining the operation of such laws. It both moderates the immediate mischiefs of laws that have been passed and it operates as a check on the legislative body in passing them. The legislature, realizing that obstacles to the success of iniquitous intention are to be expected from the scruples of the courts, are in a manner compelled, by the very motives of the injustice they meditate, to qualify their attempts.

This restraint on bad legislation is meant to have more influence on the character of our governments than many people know. The benefits of the integrity and moderation of the judiciary have already been felt in more States than one. And though they may have displeased people whose sinister expectations they have disappointed, they must have commanded the esteem and applause of all virtuous and disinterested people.

Thoughtful men of every description should prize whatever will tend to create or fortify that temper in the courts. No man can be sure that he may not be tomorrow the victim of a spirit of injustice by which he gains today. And every man must now feel that the inevitable tendency of such a spirit is to sap the foundations of public and private confidence and replace it with universal distrust and distress.

Owe Allegiance Only to Constitution

20 Inflexible and uniform adherence to the rights of the Constitution and of individuals, which is indispensable in the courts of justice, can certainly not be expected from judges who hold their offices by a temporary commission.

Appointments made for a certain period, however regulated or by whomsoever made, would be fatal to their necessary independence in some way or other. If the power of making them was committed either to the Executive or legislature, there would be danger of an improper acquiesce to the branch making the appointment.

If it were a joint appointment by both, there would be an unwillingness to hazard the displeasure of either. If the people appointed judges, or if they were appointed by persons chosen by the people for the special purpose, there would be too great a disposition to consult popularity, to justify a reliance that nothing would be consulted but the Constitution and the laws.

Limited Number of Qualified People

21 There is yet another, more important reason for the permanency of the judicial offices that arises from the nature of the qualifications they require.

It's frequently said, properly, that a voluminous code of laws is one of the inconveniences necessarily connected with the advantages of a free government. To avoid arbitrary decisions, the courts should be bound by strict rules and precedents that define and point out their duty in every case that comes before them. Because of the variety of controversies that grow out of the folly and wickedness of mankind, those precedents will swell to a very considerable bulk. Long and laborious study will be needed to acquire a competent knowledge of them. Hence, only a few men in the society will have sufficient skill in the laws to qualify them for the stations of judges.

After people are disqualified for the ordinary depravity of human nature, the number of people who unite the requisite integrity with the requisite knowledge to become judges is still smaller.

These considerations show us that the government has limited choices between people of fit character. A temporary duration in office would naturally discourage such people from quitting a lucrative line of practice to accept a seat on the bench. Temporary tenure would tend to throw the administration of justice into hands less able and less well qualified to conduct it with utility and dignity.

In our present circumstances, and in those in which it is likely to be for a long time to come, the disadvantages of temporary tenure would be greater than they may at first appear. However, it must be confessed that they are far inferior to those that present themselves under the other aspects of the subject.

Good Behavior Important Inclusion

22   On the whole, there is no doubt that the convention acted wisely in copying from the models of those constitutions that have established *good behavior* as the tenure for judges.

Rather than being blamed for including this, their plan would have been inexcusably defective if it didn't include this important feature of good government. The experience of Great Britain illustrates the excellence of the institution.

PUBLIUS

Constitutional references:

Article 2, section 2   395-400   appointment of judges
Article 3, section 1   438-440   judges hold office during good behavior

---

Number 79

Judicial Branch: Independence, Salary, Impeachment

To assure independent judges, after permanency in office [a lifetime appointment], nothing is more important than a fixed provision for their support. The comment made about the President applies equally here. Psychologically, *a power over a man's subsistence amounts to a power over his will.*

The complete separation of the judicial from the legislative power will never happen if judges are dependent on the legislature for occasional pay.

Some State constitutions don't have precise, explicit precautions about paying judges. And the enlightened friends of good government lament this omission.

Some State constitutions declare that *permanent*[1] salaries should be established for judges. But, in practice, the wording has not been precise enough to make legislative evasion impossible. Something more positive and unequivocal is clearly required. Therefore, the Constitution provides that the judges of the United States "shall at *stated times* receive for their services a compensation which shall not be *diminished* during their continuance in office."

Judicial Salary Can't Be Reduced

2 Considering all possible scenarios, this is the best provision that could have been devised. Because of the fluctuations in the value of money and the state of society, the Constitution couldn't state a fixed rate of compensation. An amount that might be extravagant today, could be penurious and inadequate in half a century. Therefore, it was necessary to leave it to the discretion of the legislature to vary the provision in conformity to the variations in circumstances. However, the legislature is restricted from lowering a judge's pay. Because of this, a judge can be sure of the ground on which he stands and not be deterred from his duty by fears that his salary will be diminished.

The clause quoted combines two advantages. The salaries of judicial officers may, from time to time, be altered when necessary, but the salary of a specific judge can never be lower than when he was appointed.

The convention set up the compensation for the President and for judges differently. The President's compensation can neither be increased nor diminished. Judges' compensation can only not be diminished. This difference probably arose from the difference in the terms in office. The President is elected for no more than four years. Therefore, an adequate salary, fixed at the time he enters office, will almost always be adequate until the end of the four years.

Judges, if they behave properly, will be secured in their places for life. It may happen, especially in the early states of the government, that a stipend, which is sufficient at their appointment, will become too small over the time of their service.

Judicial Independence

3 This provision for the support of the judges appears prudent and effective. It may be safely said that, together with the permanent tenure in office, it makes the federal judges more independent than any of the State judges, as detailed in their constitutions.

Judges Can Be Impeached

4 To assure judges will act responsibly, they are liable to be impeached by the House of Representatives and tried by the Senate. If convicted, a judge may be dismissed from office and disqualified for holding any other. This is the only provision that could be made that is consistent with the necessary independence of the judicial character. It is also the only one found in the New York State constitution in respect to our own judges.

Judges Mental Ability

5 There is no provision for removing judges because they are unable to do their job. This has been a subject of complaint. However, intelligent men will realize that such a provision would

---

[1] Vide *Constitution of Massachusetts*, chapter 2, section 1, article 13.

either not be used or it would be more often abused than used properly.

I don't believe that science has found a way to measure the faculties of the mind. If an attempt were made to fix the boundary between mental ability and mental inability, personal and party attachments and enmities would probably be a greater influence than the interests of justice or the public good. The result, except in the case of insanity, would be mostly arbitrary. And insanity, without any formal or express provision in the Constitution, may be safely said to be a virtual disqualification to become a judge.

No Forced Retirement

6   The New York constitution, to avoid investigations that would be vague and dangerous, has selected a specific age as the criterion of inability. No man can be a judge beyond age sixty. I believe that most people disapprove of this provision. There is no office or position that it applies less to than a judge. For men who survive past age sixty, the mental facilities needed to deliberate generally preserve their strength much past that age. And when we also consider how few men outlive their time of intellectual vigor, and how improbable it is that it would be any considerable portion of the bench at any given time, we will be ready to conclude that limitations of this sort have little to recommend them.

In a republic, where fortunes are not affluent and pensions not expedient, dismissing men from offices where they have served their country long and usefully, on which they depend for subsistence, and from which it will be too late to resort to any other occupation for a livelihood, should have a better apology to humanity than is found in the imaginary danger of a superannuated bench.

PUBLIUS

Constitutional references:

Article 3, section 1	438-440	lifetime term in office
Article 3, section 1	440-442	judges' compensation
Article 1, section 2	40-41	House of Representatives impeaches
Article 1, section 3	71-72	Senate tries impeachment
Article 1, section 3	75-84	impeachment trial
Article 2, section 1	365-370	presidential compensation

Number 80

Extent of Federal Judicature

To accurately judge the proper extent of the federal judicature, it is necessary to first consider its proper objectives.

Cases Heard in Federal Court

2   It doesn't seem to be controversial to say that the judicial authority of the Union should extend to several types of cases:

1. Cases that concern the execution of the provisions in the Constitution.

2. Cases that arise out of the laws of the United States passed through the constitutional power of legislation.

3. Cases in which the United States is a party.

4. Cases involving the PEACE of the CONFEDERACY, whether they relate to the

intercourse between the United States and foreign nations or between the States themselves.

5. Cases that originate on the high seas and are of admiralty or maritime jurisdiction;

6. Cases in which the State courts cannot be expected to be impartial and unbiased.

1. Constitutional Provisions

3 The first type seems obvious. There should always be a constitutional method of giving efficacy to constitutional provisions. What, for instance, would be the point of having restrictions on the authority of State legislatures if the Constitution didn't provide a method of enforcing them?

For instance, the States, in the new Constitution, are prohibited from doing a variety of things. Some are incompatible with the interests of the Union. Others are incompatible with the principles of good government.

Taxing imported articles and issuing paper money are examples. No rational man will believe that such prohibitions would be scrupulously obeyed if the federal government didn't have the power to restrain or correct the infractions of them. There must be either a federal power to veto State laws or an authority in the federal courts to overrule any clear violation of the Union's Constitution. I can't think of any other methods. The convention seems to have thought the latter preferable to the former and, I assume, it will be more agreeable to the States.

2. Federal Legislation

4 As to the second type, no argument or comment will make it clearer than it already is. If political axioms exist, the propriety of the government's

judicial power being as extensive as its legislative power would be one.

National laws must be interpreted uniformly. Thirteen independent courts of final jurisdiction over the same cases, arising out of the same laws, is a hydra in government that will produce nothing but contradiction and confusion.

3. Nation vs. States or Citizens

5 Even less needs to be said about the third type. Controversies between the nation and its States or citizens can only be properly referred to the national courts. Any other plan would be contrary to reason, precedent, and decorum.

4. U.S. vs. Foreign Nations, Citizens

6 The fourth type rest on the proposition that the peace of the WHOLE should never depend on a PART. Undoubtedly, the Union will be answerable to foreign powers for the conduct of its States. And the responsibility [liability] for an injury should always be accompanied with the ability to prevent it.

The denial or perversion of justice by the sentences of courts, as well as in any other manner, is classed among the **just causes of war** [Number 3]. Therefore, the federal judiciary should have jurisdiction in all causes concerning the citizens of other countries. This is essential to both the public faith and the public tranquility.

There may seem to be a distinction between treaties and the laws of nations, and mere municipal laws. Treaties and the laws of nations may seem proper for federal jurisdiction and municipal laws for State jurisdiction. It does seem, however, that any unjust sentence against a foreign citizen, where the subject of controversy was wholly relative to the *lex loci*, would be seen as, if not corrected, an aggression on his sovereign, as well as a violation of a treaty stipulation or the general laws of nations.

And an even greater objection to the distinction [federal vs. municipal laws] would result from the immense difficulty, if not impossibility, of a practical discrimination between the cases of one type and those of the other. Such a great proportion of cases in which foreigners are parties involve national questions, it is by far safer and more expedient to refer all cases involving foreign citizens to the national courts.

Between States, Citizens of Different States

7   The power of determining causes between two States, between one State and the citizens of another, and between the citizens of different States, is perhaps just as essential to the peace of the Union as the one just examined.

History gives us a horrid picture of the dissensions and private wars that distracted and desolated Germany prior to the institution of the Imperial Chamber by Maximilian towards the end of the fifteenth century. It informs us, at the same time, of the vast influence of the Imperial Chamber in appeasing the disorders and establishing the tranquillity of the empire. This was a court invested with authority to make the final decision in differences among the members of the Germanic states.

Territorial Disputes

8   Even the imperfect system that has held the States together up until now had a method of deciding territorial disputes between the States un-

der the authority of the federal government. But there are many other sources of bickerings and animosities among the members of the Union, besides conflicting claims of boundary.

We have witnessed some of these already. It will be quickly seen that I allude to the fraudulent laws that have been passed in many of the States. And although the proposed Constitution establishes specific guards against the repetition of those cases, it is legitimate to worry that the same spirit that produced them will assume a new shape, which could not be foreseen nor specifically provided against.

Any practices that tend to disturb the harmony between the States are proper objectives of federal superintendence and control.

Universal Citizenship

9   It is the **foundation of the Union** that "the citizens of each State shall be entitled to all the privileges and immunities of citizens of the several States." And if every government *ought to possess the means of executing its own provisions by its own authority,* it follows that to preserve that equality of privileges and immunities, to which the citizens of the Union are entitled, the national judiciary should preside in all cases in which one State or its citizens are opposed to another State or its citizens.

This fundamental a provision can be effective only in a court free of all evasion and subterfuge, a court with no local attachments, and a court that probably will be impartial between the different States and their citizens because it owes its official existence to the Union. Therefore, it probably won't have any bias unfavorable to the principles on which it is founded.

5. Maritime Jurisdiction

10 There will be little criticism of the fifth type. The most bigoted idolisers of State authority haven't yet denied the national courts jurisdiction of maritime causes. These are so often based on the laws of nations and so often affects the rights of foreigners that they fall within the considerations relating to the public peace. The most important part of them are, under the present Confederation, submitted to federal jurisdiction.

6. When State Courts Can't Be Impartial

11 The reasonableness of having the national courts decide cases in which the State courts cannot be expected to be impartial speaks for itself.

No man should be a judge in his own cause or in any cause in respect to which he has the least interest or bias. This principle was important in designating the federal courts as the proper tribunals for the determination of controversies between different States and their citizens. And it should have the same operation in regard to some cases between citizens of the same State.

Claims to land under grants of different States, founded on adverse pretension of boundary, are of this description. The courts of neither of the granting States could be expected to be unbiased. The laws may have even prejudged the question, tying the courts to decisions in favor to the grants of the State to which they belong. And even where this had not been done, it would be natural that the judges, as men, would feel a strong predilection to the claims of their own government.

Constitution, Federal Judiciary Principles

12 These are the principles that should regulate the construction of the federal judiciary. Now we will test, using these principles, its powers, according to the Constitution.

The federal judiciary is to decide "all cases in law and equity arising under the Constitution, the laws of the United States,

"and treaties made, or which shall be made, under their authority;

"to all cases affecting ambassadors, other public ministers, and consuls;

"to all cases of admiralty and maritime jurisdiction;

"to controversies to which the United States shall be a party;

"to controversies between two or more States; between a State and citizens of another State; between citizens of different States;

"between citizens of the same State claiming lands and grants of different States;

"and between a State or the citizens thereof and foreign states, citizens, and subjects."

This is the entire judicial authority of the Union, as stated in the Constitution. Let us now review it in detail. It extends to:

Constitutional, Federal Law Cases

13 *First.* To all cases in law and equity *arising under the Constitution* and *the laws of the United States.* This corresponds with the two first types of cases, enumerated above and shown to be proper jurisdictions of the United States.

It has been asked what is meant by "cases arising under the Constitution," as distinct from those "arising under the laws of the United States"?

The difference has been already explained. All the restrictions on the authority of the State legislatures furnish examples of it. They are not, for instance, to emit paper money. This interdiction comes from the Constitution and will have no connection with any law of the United States. If paper money, notwithstanding, is emitted, the controversies concerning it would be cases arising under the Constitution and not the laws of the United States, in the ordinary meaning of those terms. This serves as an example.

"Equitable" Jurisdiction

14 It has also been asked why the word "equity" is needed. What equitable causes can grow out of the Constitution and laws of the United States?

There is hardly a subject of litigation between individuals that may not involve *fraud, accident, trust,* or *hardship* that would render the matter an object of equitable rather than of legal jurisdiction as the distinction is known and established in the States. It is the specific province, for instance, of a court of equity to relieve against what are called hard bargains. These contracts may not involve direct fraud or deceit sufficient to invalidate them in a court of law but may take such undue and unconscionable advantage of the necessities or misfortunes of one of the parties that a court of equity would not tolerate them. In such cases, where foreigners are concerned on either side, it would be impossible for the federal judicatories to do justice without an equitable as well as a legal jurisdiction.

Agreements to convey lands claimed under the grants of different States affords another example of the necessity of an equitable jurisdiction in the federal courts. This reasoning may not be as obvious in those States where the formal and technical distinction between LAW and EQUITY is not maintained, as in New York, where it is exemplified every day in practice.

Federal Judicial Authority

15 The judiciary authority of the Union is to extend:

Treaties, Ambassadors

16 *Second.* To treaties made, or which shall be made, under the authority of the United States, and to all cases affecting ambassadors, other public ministers, and consuls. These belong to the fourth class of the enumerated cases, as they have an evident connection with the preservation of the national peace.

Admiralty, Maritime

17 *Third.* To cases of admiralty and maritime jurisdiction. These form, altogether, the fifth of the enumerated classes of causes proper for the jurisdiction of the national courts.

United States a Party

18 *Fourth.* To controversies to which the United States shall be a party. These constitute the third of those classes.

Between States

19 *Fifth.* To controversies between two or more States; between a State and citizens of another State; between citizens of different States. These belong to the fourth of those classes and partake, in some measure, of the nature of the last.

Land Disputes, Citizens of the Same State

20 *Sixth.* To cases between the citizens of the same State, *claiming lands under grants of different States.* These fall within the last class and *are the only instances in which the proposed Constitution directly contemplates the jurisdiction of disputes between the citizens of the same State.*

State, Citizen vs. Foreign Country, Citizen

21 *Seventh.* To cases between a State and the citizens thereof and foreign countries, citizens or subjects. These have been already explained to belong to the fourth of the enumerated classes and have been shown to be, specifically, the proper subject of the national judicature.

Federal Judiciary Conforms to Principles

22 From this review of the specific powers of the federal judiciary, as marked in the Constitution, it appears that they all conform to the principles that should govern the structure of that department and that are necessary to the perfection of the system. If some partial inconveniences should appear to be connected with the incorporation of any of them into the plan, remember that the national legislature will have ample authority to make such *exceptions* and prescribe such regulations as are calculated to obviate or remove these inconveniences. The possibility of specific mischiefs can never be viewed, by a well-informed mind, as a solid objection to a general principle that is calculated to avoid general mischiefs and to obtain general advantages.

PUBLIUS

Constitutional references:

Article 3, section 2	443-457	federal court jurisdiction
Article 4, section 2	488-490	State citizen treated equally in other States
Article 1, section 10	273-274	States can't issue money
Article 1, section 10	280-283	States can't tax imports

Number 81

Authorities of Supreme, Inferior Federal Courts

Let us now return to the division of the judiciary authority between different courts and their relationship to each other.

Supreme Court, Inferior Courts

2 "The judicial power of the United States is" (by the Constitution) "to be vested in one Supreme Court, and in such inferior courts as the Congress may, from time to time, ordain and establish."[1]

[1] Article 3, Section 1.

Supreme Court as Part of Legislature

3 There probably will not be any arguments that there should be one court of supreme and final jurisdiction. The reasons for this have been given in another place. And they are too obvious to need repetition.

One question has been raised: should the supreme court be a distinct body or a branch of the legislature? This involves the same contradiction discussed in several other cases.

The same men who object to the Senate as a court of impeachments, saying it is an improper intermixture of powers, seem to want to give the ultimate decision of all causes, in the whole or in a part, to the legislative body.

Supreme Court as Legislative Body

4   This charge is founded on arguments, or rather suggestions, of this type:

"The authority of the proposed Supreme Court of the United States, which is to be a separate and independent body, will be superior to that of the legislature. The power of interpreting the laws, according to the *spirit* of the Constitution, will enable that court to mold them into any shape it thinks proper. And it will be superior to the legislature because its decisions will not be in any way subject to the revision or correction of the legislative body. This is as unprecedented as it is dangerous.

"In Britain, the judicial power, in the last resort, resides in the House of Lords, a branch of the legislature. And this part of the British Government has been imitated in the State constitutions. The Parliament of Great Britain and the legislatures of the States can at any time rectify, by law, the exceptionable decisions of their respective courts. But the errors and usurpations of the Supreme Court of the United States will be uncontrollable and remediless."

On examination, this will be found made of completely false reasoning on misconceived fact.

Judging Constitutionality of Laws

5   In the first place, not a syllable in the proposed Constitution *directly* empowers the national courts to construe the laws according to the spirit of the Constitution. Nor does it give them any greater latitude in this respect than may be claimed by the courts of every State.

I admit that the Constitution should be the standard of construction for the laws and that wherever there is an evident opposition, the Constitution should take precedence over the laws. But this doctrine is not deducible from anything in the proposed Constitution, but from the general theory of a limited constitution. And, as far as this doctrine is true, it applies to most, if not to all, the State governments.

Therefore, any objection to the federal judicature based on this reason can be made against the local judicatures in general. And it will not help to condemn every constitution that attempts to set bounds to legislative discretion.

Legislators, Judges: Different Talents

6   But perhaps the objection is to the specific organization of the Supreme Court.

The Supreme Court will be composed of a separate body of magistrates. It will not be one of the branches of the legislature as in the government of Great Britain and New York State.

If the authors of the objection insist that the Supreme Court must be part of the legislative branch, they must renounce the meaning that they have worked to give to the celebrated separation of power maxim.

Admittedly, by the interpretation given to the maxim in these papers, it is not violated by vesting the ultimate power of judging in a *part* of the legislative body. This would not be an absolute violation of the rule, but it is so close to violating it that, on this account alone, making the federal judiciary part of the legislative branch is less eligible than the structure in the Constitution.

Even if the legislature was only partly responsible for passing bad laws, we could rarely expect that the same branch would have the disposition to temper and moderate them in the application. The same spirit that made them would probably interpret them.

There would be even less chance that men who had infringed the Constitution in the character of legislators would be disposed to repair the breach when they acted as judges.

Nor is this all. Every argument that recommends the tenure of good behavior for judges argues against placing the judiciary power, in the last resort, in a body composed of men chosen for a limited period. It is absurd to determine causes, first, in inferior courts where judges have permanent standing, then have the final appeal to judges who are temporarily in office.

It is even more absurd to subject the decision of judges, selected for their knowledge of the laws acquired by long and laborious study, to the revision and control of legislators who don't have the same advantage and are deficient in that knowledge. The members of the legislature will rarely be chosen because they have the qualifications of a judge. Because of this, there will be great reason to expect all the ill consequences of defective information.

Since legislatures naturally divide according to party, there is reason to fear that the pestilential breath of faction may poison the fountains of justice. The habit of being continually marshaled on opposite sides will probably stifle the voice both of law and of equity.

Most States: Separate Supreme Court, Legislature

7 These considerations teach us to applaud the wisdom of the States that have committed the judicial court of last appeals, not to a part of the legislature but to distinct, independent bodies of men.

Contrary to the opinions of the men who say that, in this respect, the Constitution is novel and unprecedented, it is a copy of the constitution of New Hampshire, Massachusetts, Pennsylvania, Delaware, Maryland, Virginia, North Carolina, South Carolina, and Georgia. And the preference given to those models is highly to be commended.

Legislature Changing Supreme Court's Ruling

8 Secondly, the future legislature of the United States will be able to overrule objectionable decisions just as the Parliament of Great Britain and the legislatures of the States do. The theory authorizes the revisal of a judicial sentence by a legislative act. It is not forbidden in the proposed Constitution, any more than in either Britain or the States. In both, the impropriety of the thing, on the general principles of law and reason, is the sole obstacle.

A legislature, without exceeding its authority, cannot reverse a determination once made in a specific case. But it can prescribe a new rule for future cases. This is the principle. And it applies in all its consequences, exactly in the same manner and extent, to the State governments, as to the national government now under consideration. Not the least difference can be pointed out in any view of the subject.

Legislature can Impeach Judges

9 Lastly, the danger of judiciary encroachments on the legislative authority has been often mentioned. It is in reality a phantom. Specific misconstructions and contraventions of the will of the legislature may now and then happen. But they can never be so extensive as to amount to an inconvenience or in any way, which can be noticed, affect the order of the political system.

This is inferred from the general nature of the judicial power, from the objects to which it relates, from the manner in which it is exercised, from its comparative weakness, and from its total incapacity to support its usurpations by force.

This conclusion is greatly fortified by the important constitutional check on the judiciary—that one part of the legislative body can impeach judges and the other, try them.

This is alone a complete security. There never can be danger that judges, by a series of deliberate usurpations on the authority of the legislature, would hazard the united resentment of the legislative body while it could punish their presumption by removing them from office.

While this should remove all worries on the subject, it also is a good argument for constituting the Senate as the court for the trial of impeachments.

Inferior Federal Courts

10 Having now examined and, I trust, removed the objections to the independent organization of the Supreme Court, I proceed to consider the propriety of the power of constituting inferior courts,[2] and the re-

lationship between these and the Supreme Court.

Lower Courts, Federal Jurisdiction

11 The power of constituting inferior courts takes away the necessity of going to the Supreme Court in every case of federal jurisdiction. It is intended to enable the national government to institute or *authorize*, in each State or district of the United States, a court competent to determine matters of national jurisdiction within its limits.

State Courts Hearing Federal Cases

12 Couldn't this have been achieved using State courts? This has several answers.

Even if the State courts are competent to handle federal cases, this constitutional power is necessary. Before the State courts could try federal cases, the national legislature would have to give them jurisdiction over causes arising out of the national Constitution. That action, conferring the power of deciding federal cases on the existing State courts, would perhaps fulfill the requirement "to constitute tribunals" as creating new courts with the same power.

But should the Constitution have a more direct and explicit provision in favor of the State courts? In my opinion, there are substantial reasons why it shouldn't.

It's impossible to foresee how much a local spirit may disqualify the local tribunals for the jurisdiction of

---

[2] This power has been absurdly represented as intended to abolish all the county courts in the States, which are commonly called inferior courts. But the expression in the Constitution is, to constitute "tribunals INFERIOR TO THE SUPREME COURT." The provision is evidently designed to enable the institution of local courts, subordinate to the Supreme Court, either in States or larger districts. It is ridiculous to imagine that this means county courts.

national causes. And every man may discover that the structure of some of the State judiciary systems would be improper channels of the judicial authority of the Union.

State judges that hold their offices during pleasure, or from year to year, will not be independent enough to be relied on for an inflexible execution of the national laws. If there was a necessity for confiding the original hearing of causes arising under national laws to them, there would be a correspondent necessity for leaving the door of appeal as wide as possible. The facility or difficulty of appeals should be in proportion to the grounds of confidence in, or distrust of, the subordinate tribunals. And although I am satisfied the appellate jurisdiction, as defined by the Constitution, is proper, I consider everything calculated to give, in practice, an *unrestrained course* to appeals a source of public and private inconvenience.

Federal Court Districts

13 I am not sure, but it may be found highly expedient and useful to divide the United States into four or five or half a dozen districts and institute a federal court in each district in lieu of one in every State. The judges of these courts, with the aid of the State judges, may hold circuits for the trial of causes in the parts of the respective districts. Justice through them may be administered with ease and dispatch. And appeals may be safely circumscribed within a narrow compass.

This plan appears to me the best of any that could be adopted. And in order to do it, it is necessary that the power of constituting inferior courts should exist, as it is in the Constitution.

Inferior Federal Courts Imperative

14 These reasons seem sufficient to satisfy a candid mind that the lack of a power to establish inferior federal courts would have been a great defect in the Constitution.

Let us now examine in what manner the judicial authority is to be distributed between the Supreme and the inferior courts of the Union.

Ambassadors, Consuls, States

15 The Supreme Court will be invested with original jurisdiction only "in cases affecting ambassadors, other public ministers, and consuls, and those in which a STATE shall be a party."

Public ministers of every class are the immediate representatives of their sovereigns. All questions in which they are concerned are directly connected with the public peace. To preserve the public peace and out of respect to the sovereignties they represent, it is both expedient and proper that such questions should be submitted, in the first instance, to the highest judicatory of the nation.

Although consuls are not strictly diplomatic, they are the public agents of the nations to which they belong. So the same observation is in a great measure applicable to them.

In cases with a State as a party, it would ill suit its dignity to be turned over to an inferior tribunal.

Citizens Suing State for Debt

16 Although it may be a digression from the subject of this paper, I will mention here an assumption that has excited alarm on very mistaken grounds.

It has been suggested that an assignment of public securities of one State to the citizens of another would enable the citizen to prosecute the State in the federal courts for the amount of those securities. The following considerations prove that this assumption has no foundation.

Idea Conflicts with State Sovereignty

17 It is inherent in the nature of sovereignty not to be amenable to the suit of an individual *without its consent.* This is the general sense and the general practice of mankind. And the exemption, as one of the attributes of sovereignty, is now enjoyed by the government of every State in the Union. Therefore, unless there is a surrender of this immunity in the Constitution, it will remain with the States.

And the danger intimated must be merely ideal. The circumstances that are necessary to produce an alienation of State sovereignty were discussed when taxation was discussed and need not be repeated here. Remembering the principles discussed there satisfies us that the State governments would not, by adopting the Constitution, be divested of the privilege of paying their own debts in their own way, free from every constraint but that flowing from the obligations of good faith.

The contracts between a nation and individuals are only binding on the conscience of the sovereign and have no pretensions to a compulsive force. They confer no right of action independent of the sovereign will.

What would be the purpose of authorizing suits against States for the debts they owe? How could recoveries be enforced? Clearly, it couldn't be done by waging war against the State. And to ascribe to the federal courts, by mere implication, the ability to destroy a pre-existing right of

the State governments would be altogether forced and unwarrantable.

Supreme Court Hears 2 Types of Cases

18 Let us resume the train of our observations.

We have seen that the original jurisdiction of the Supreme Court would be confined to two classes of causes, and those of a nature that rarely occur.

All other cases of federal jurisdiction would appertain to the inferior tribunals and the Supreme Court would have nothing more than an appellate jurisdiction "with such *exceptions* and under such *regulations* as the Congress shall make."

Appeals Based on Law, Facts

19 In regard to matters of law, the propriety of this appellate jurisdiction has been rarely questioned. But the clamors have been loud against it as applied to matters of fact.

Some well-intentioned men in New York, deriving their notions from the language and forms that apply to New York courts, have been induced to consider it as an implied supersedure of the trial by jury in favor of the civil-law mode of trial that prevails in our courts of admiralty, probate, and chancery. A technical meaning has been affixed to the term "appellate" that, in New York law parlance, is commonly used in reference to appeals in the course of the civil law.

However, I don't believe the same meaning would have been given to it in any part of New England. There an appeal from one jury to another is familiar both in language and practice. It is a matter of course until there have been two verdicts on one side.

The word "appellate," therefore, will not be understood in the same sense in New England as in New York. This shows the impropriety of a technical interpretation derived from the jurisprudence of any one State.

The expression, taken in the abstract, denotes nothing more than the power of one tribunal to review the proceedings of another, either as to the law or fact, or both. The mode of doing it may depend on ancient customs or legislative provision (in a new government it must depend on the latter) and may be with or without the aid of a jury, as may be judged advisable.

Therefore, if the re-examination of a fact once determined by a jury should in any case be admitted under the proposed Constitution, it may be so regulated as to be done by a second jury, either by remanding the cause to the court below for a second trial of the fact or by directing an issue immediately out of the Supreme Court.

Re-examination of Facts Not Imperative

20 But it does not follow that the re-examination of a fact once ascertained by a jury will be permitted in the Supreme Court.

Might not it be said, with the strictest propriety, that when a writ of error is brought from an inferior to a superior court of law in New York, that the latter has jurisdiction of the fact as well as the law? It is true it cannot institute a new inquiry concerning the fact, but it takes jurisdiction of it as it appears on the record and pronounces the law arising on it.[3] This is jurisdiction of both fact and law.

Nor is it even possible to separate them. Although the common-law courts of New York State ascertain

disputed facts by a jury, they unquestionably have jurisdiction of both fact and law. Accordingly, when the former is agreed in the pleadings, they have no recourse to a jury, but proceed at once to judgment. Therefore, on this ground, I contend that the expressions, "appellate jurisdiction, both as to law and fact," do not necessarily imply a re-examination in the Supreme Court of facts decided by juries in the inferior courts.

Appellate Court May Review Facts

21 The following train of ideas could have influenced the convention in relation to this particular provision.

The appellate jurisdiction of the Supreme Court (they may have argued) will extend to causes determinable in different modes, some in the course of the COMMON LAW, others in the course of the CIVIL LAW. In the former, the proper province of the Supreme Court will only be the revision of the law. In the latter, the re-examination of the fact is agreeable to usage and, in some cases (prize causes, for example), might be essential for the preservation of the public peace. It is therefore necessary that the appellate jurisdiction should, in certain cases, extend in the broadest sense to matters of fact.

Cases originally tried by jury cannot be expressly excluded because in some States *all causes* are tried in this mode.[4] Such an exception would preclude the revision of matters of fact when proper as well as when it might be improper.

---

[3] This word is composed of JUS and DICTO, *juris, dictio,* or a speaking or pronouncing of the law.

[4] I hold that the States will have concurrent jurisdiction with the subordinate federal judicatories in many cases of federal cognizance, as will be explained in my next paper.

To avoid all inconveniences, it will be safest to declare, generally, that the Supreme Court will possess appellate jurisdiction both as to law and *fact*, and that this jurisdiction will be subject to such *exceptions* and regulations as the national legislature may prescribe. The government will be able to modify it in such a manner as will best answer the ends of public justice and security.

Trial by Jury Not Abolished

22 Some people have said that this provision *abolishes* trial by jury. This view of the matter, at any rate, shows this is fallacious and untrue. The legislature of the United States would certainly have full power to provide that in appeals to the Supreme Court there should be no re-examination of facts where juries had tried the original causes. This would certainly be an authorized exception. But if, for the reason already suggested, it is thought too extensive, it might be qualified with a limitation to only causes determinable at common law in that mode of trial.

Summary: Judicial Branch

23 The observations made on the authority of the judicial branch are these:

It has been carefully restricted to those causes that are manifestly proper for the cognizance of the national judicature.

In the partition of this authority, a very small portion of original jurisdiction has been preserved to the Supreme Court and the rest consigned to the subordinate tribunals.

The Supreme Court will possess an appellate jurisdiction both as to law and fact in all the cases referred to them, both subject to any *exceptions* and *regulations* that may be thought advisable.

This appellate jurisdiction does, in no case, *abolish* the trial by jury.

And an ordinary degree of prudence and integrity in the national councils will insure us solid advantages from the establishment of the proposed judiciary without exposing us to any of the inconveniences that have been predicted.

PUBLIUS

Constitutional references:

Article 1, Section 8	199-200	Congress establishes inferior courts
Article 3, section 1	434-437	establishes federal courts
Article 3, section 1	438-440	federal judges hold offices during good behavior
Article 3, section 2	443-457	federal court jurisdiction
Article 3, section 2	458-461	Supreme Court original jurisdiction
Article 3, section 2	462-465	Supreme Court appellate jurisdiction
Article 3, section 2	466-471	trial by jury
Article 2, section 4	429-433	judges impeachable
Article 1, section 3	71-72	Senate has sole power to try impeachments

---

Number 82

Federal-State Judiciary

No matter how carefully or wisely a new government is created, there are intricate questions. This is especially true when a constitution is founded on the total or partial incorporation of a number of distinct sovereignties. Only time can mature and perfect so compound a system, clarify the meaning of all the parts, and adjust them into a harmonious and consistent WHOLE.

State Court Jurisdiction

2   Such questions have arisen about the proposed Constitution, and specifically about the judiciary branch. The main question concerns the relationship of the State courts to causes following under federal jurisdiction.

Is the federal jurisdiction to be exclusive? Or will the State courts have a concurrent jurisdiction? If the latter, in what relation will they stand to the national tribunals?

Wise men make these inquiries. And they certainly deserve attention.

Federal Authorities Defined

3   A former paper established the principle that the States will retain all *pre-existing* authorities not exclusively delegated to the federal government. This exclusive delegation exists in three cases:

1) where an exclusive authority is granted, in express terms, to the Union,

2) where a specific authority is granted to the Union and the exercise of a like authority is prohibited to the States,

3) or where an authority is granted to the Union and a similar authority in the States would be utterly incompatible.

Although these principles may not apply with the same force to the judiciary as to the legislative power, I am inclined to think that they apply to each. And under this impression, I will lay it down as a rule that the State Courts will *retain* the jurisdiction they now have, unless it appears to be taken away in one of the three ways.

Concurrent State/Federal Jurisdiction

4   The only thing in the Constitution that confines the causes of federal jurisdiction to the federal courts is contained in this passage: "The JUDICIAL POWER of the United States *shall be vested* in one Supreme Court and in *such* inferior courts as the Congress shall from time to time ordain and establish."

This might be construed in two ways. It could mean that the supreme and subordinate courts of the Union should have, alone, the power of deciding causes to which their authority is to extend. Or it could simply denote that the organs of the national judiciary should be one Supreme Court and as many subordinate courts as Congress appoints. In other words, the United States should exercise its judicial power through one supreme tribunal and a number of inferior ones.

The first excludes, the last includes, the concurrent jurisdiction of the State tribunals. And as the first would alienate State power by implication, the last appears to me the most natural and the most defensible interpretation.

Concurrent Jurisdiction Unless States Specifically Excluded

5   But the doctrine of concurrent jurisdiction applies only to causes in which the State courts have jurisdiction before the Constitution is adopted. It is not equally evident in relation to cases that may grow out of, and are *specific* to, the Constitution because not allowing the State courts jurisdiction in such cases can't be considered an abridgment of a pre-existing authority.

I do not mean to say that the United States, through legislation, may not commit the decision of causes arising from a specific regulation to the federal courts alone, if such a measure seems expedient. But I maintain that the State courts will be divested of no part of their primitive jurisdiction further than may relate to an appeal.

And I believe when States are not expressly excluded by the future acts of the national legislature, they will, of course, take jurisdiction of the causes to which those acts may give birth.

I infer this from the nature of judiciary power and from the general genius of the system. The judiciary power of every government looks beyond its own local or municipal laws. And, in civil cases, it lays hold of all subjects of litigation between parties within its jurisdiction, even if the causes of dispute are relative to the laws of the most distant part of the globe. Those of Japan, not less than of New York, may furnish the objects of legal discussion in our courts.

The State and national governments are kindred systems and parts of ONE WHOLE. It seems conclusive that the State courts have a concurrent jurisdiction in all cases arising under the laws of the Union when not expressly prohibited.

Final Appeal to Supreme Court

6   Here another question arises: what relationship would exist between the national and State courts in cases with concurrent jurisdiction?

I answer that an appeal could be made to the Supreme Court of the United States.

The Constitution, in direct terms, gives an appellate jurisdiction to the Supreme Court in all the cases of federal jurisdiction where it doesn't have original jurisdiction, without confining its operation to the inferior federal courts.

The objects of appeal, not the courts from which it is made, are alone contemplated. From this circumstance and from logic, it extends to the State courts. Either this is the case or the local courts must be excluded from a concurrent jurisdiction in matters of national concern. If this was not true, the judiciary authority of the Union could be eluded at the pleasure of every plaintiff or prosecutor. Neither of these consequences should be involved without clear necessity. The latter would be entirely wrong because it would defeat some of the most important and avowed purposes of the proposed government and would embarrass its measures. Nor do I perceive any foundation for such a supposition.

As mentioned, the national and State systems are to be regarded as ONE WHOLE. The State courts will be natural auxiliaries to the execution of the laws of the Union. And an appeal from State courts will naturally lie in the court that unites and assimilates the principles of national justice and the rules of national decisions—the federal judiciary.

The clear aim of the Constitution is that all the causes of the specified classes shall, for important public reasons, receive their original or final determination in the courts of the Union. If the appellate jurisdiction of the Supreme Court were confined to appeals from the subordinate federal courts instead of allowing their extension to the State courts, it would abridge the latitude of the terms in subversion of the intent, contrary to every sound rule of interpretation.

Appeal to Lower Federal Courts

7 But could an appeal be made from the State courts to the subordinate federal judicatories? This question is more difficult than the former. The following considerations suggest an affirmative answer.

First, the Constitution authorizes the national legislature "to constitute tribunals inferior to the Supreme Court."*

Next, it says, "the JUDICIAL POWER of the United States *shall be vested* in one Supreme Court, and in such infe-

rior courts as Congress shall ordain and establish."

It then enumerates the cases to which this judicial power extends.

Afterwards, it divides the jurisdiction of the Supreme Court into original and appellate but doesn't define the jurisdiction of the subordinate courts. They are only described as "inferior to the Supreme Court" and won't exceed the specified limits of the federal judiciary.

Whether the lower courts' authority is original or appellate or both is not defined. This seems left to the discretion of the legislature. And this being the case, I can see no impediment to the establishment of an appeal from the State courts to the subordinate national tribunals. Many advantages of doing it may be imagined. It would diminish the motives to the multiplication of federal courts and allow arrangements calculated to contract the appellate jurisdiction of the Supreme Court. The State tribunals may then be left with a more entire charge of federal causes, and most appeals, instead of being carried to the Supreme Court, may be made to lie from the State courts to district courts of the Union.

PUBLIUS

---

* Section 8, article 1.

Constitutional references:

Article 3, section 1 434-437 federal judicial power
Article 1, section 8 199-200 legislative power to constitute courts inferior to Supreme Court

Article 3, section 2 443-465 federal court jurisdiction

Number 83

Trial by Jury

An objection based on the lack of constitutional provision for the trial by jury in civil cases has met with great success in New York, and perhaps several other States. The disingenuousness of this objection has been repeatedly exposed, but it is still used in all the conversations and writings of the opponents of the Constitution.

The proposed Constitution says nothing about *civil causes.* Opponents claim this means that trial by jury is being abolished. And their rhetoric is artfully calculated to create the idea that this pretended abolition is complete and universal. That it extends not only to all civil but even *criminal causes.*

To argue the latter, however, is as vain and fruitless as to attempt the serious proof of the *existence of matter*, or to prove any proposition that, by its own internal evidence, force belief when expressed in language adapted to convey its meaning.

Silence Doesn't Imply Prohibition

2 Regarding civil causes, subtleties almost too contemptible to refute have been used to support the conclusion that a thing that is only *not provided for* is entirely *abolished.*

Every man of discernment understands the wide difference between *silence* and *abolition.*

The inventors of this fallacy have tried to support it by perverting the true meaning of *legal maxims* of law inful to explore their arguments.

Legal Maxim Cited

3 They base their arguments on maxims of this nature: "A specifica-tion of particulars is an exclusion of generals;" or "The expression of one thing is the exclusion of another."

Therefore, say they, since the Constitution has established the trial by jury in criminal cases and is silent in respect to civil cases, this silence is an implied prohibition of trial by jury in civil cases.

Interpretation of Laws: Common Sense

4 The rules of legal interpretation are rules of *common sense* adopted by the courts in the construction of the laws. Therefore, the true interpretation of its application is whether it conforms to the source from which it is derived.

Let me ask, is it common-sense to assume that a provision that says criminal causes must be tried by juries negates the legislature's right to authorize or permit trial by jury in other causes?

Is it natural to suppose that a command to do one thing is a prohibition against another, when there was a previous power to do it and it is not incompatible with the thing commanded to be done? If such a supposition is unnatural and unreasonable, it cannot be rational to maintain that an injunction of the trial by jury in certain cases is an interdiction of it in others.

Create Courts => Determine Trial Mode

5 A power to constitute courts is a power to prescribe the mode of trial. Consequently, if the Constitution said nothing about juries, the legislature could either adopt trial by jury or not.

This discretion in regard to criminal causes is abridged by the express injunction within the Constitution of trial by jury in those cases. But there is silence on the subject of civil causes.

The obligation to try all criminal causes by jury excludes the obligation of employing the same mode in civil causes. But it does not abridge *the power* of the legislature to exercise that mode if thought proper. Therefore, to pretend that the national legislature would not be free to submit all federal civil causes to juries is a pretense destitute of all just foundation.

Maxim Used Incorrectly

6 We must conclude that trial by jury in civil cases would not be abolished. And using the maxims in this way is contrary to reason and common sense, and therefore not admissible.

Even if the precise technical meaning of these maxims were consistent with how they are being used in this case, which it is not, they would not be applicable to a constitution of government. In a constitution, the natural and obvious meaning of its provisions, apart from technical rules, is the true criterion of construction.

e.g. Restricts Legislative Authority

7 The maxims have been misused. I will show their proper use and true meaning by examples.

The Constitution declares that the power of Congress, or, in other words, of the *national legislature,* shall extend to certain enumerated cases. This list of specific authorities clearly excludes a general legislative authority, because an affirmative grant of special powers would be absurd and useless, if a general authority was intended.

Federal Judicial Authority Limited

8 Similarly, the Constitution lists the specific cases within federal jurisdiction. The federal courts cannot extend their jurisdiction beyond these precise limits. The objects of their jurisdiction are enumerated. This specification would be pointless if it did not exclude all ideas of more extensive authority.

Examples Illustrated Maxims

9 These examples illustrate the maxims and show how they should be used. But so there may be no misunderstanding, I will add one more case, to demonstrate the proper use of these maxims and how they have been abused.

Another Example

10 Suppose that, by New York law, a married woman was incapable of conveying her estate, and that the legislature, considering this an evil, enacts a law that says she can dispose of her property by deed executed in the presence of a magistrate. In this case, the specification excludes all other modes of conveyance because the woman had no previous power to alienate her property and the specification determines the specific mode that she is to use.

But let us further suppose that a subsequent part of the same act says that no woman should dispose of any estate of a **specific value** without the consent of three of her nearest relatives, signified by their signing the deed. Could it be inferred from this regulation that a married woman could not get the approval of her relations when conveying property of inferior value? The position is too absurd to merit a refutation. Yet this is precisely the position of those who contend that trial by juries in civil cases is abolished because it is expressly provided for in criminal cases.

Civil Causes: State Jurisdiction

11 Clearly, the Constitution doesn't abolish trial by jury.

It is equally true that for civil causes between individuals, in which the public is likely to be interested, trial by jury will remain precisely in the same situation as it is placed by the State constitutions. It will not be altered or influenced by the adoption of the Constitution.

This assertion is based in the fact that the national judiciary will have no cognizance of them. They will continue to be heard in the State courts, in the manner that the State constitutions and laws prescribe.

All land causes, except those involving claims under the grants of different States, and all other controversies between the citizens of the same State, unless they involve positive violations of the Constitution by acts of the State legislatures, will belong exclusively to the jurisdiction of the State tribunals.

Additionally, admiralty causes and almost all causes of equity jurisdiction are determined under our own government without the intervention of a jury.

We infer from these facts that the institution, as it presently exists, cannot be affected to any great extent by the proposed change in our system of government.

Trial by Jury Valuable

12 The friends and adversaries of the Constitution, if they agree in nothing else, concur in the value they set on the trial by jury. Or if there is any difference between them, it is this: friends of the Constitution regard it as a valu-

able safeguard to liberty, adversaries of the Constitution represent it as the very palladium of free government.

For my own part, the more I study trial by jury, the more reasons I have to hold it in high estimation. It would be superfluous to examine how much it deserves to be esteemed useful or essential in a representative republic. Or how much more merit it has as a defense against the oppression of a hereditary monarch than as a barrier to the tyranny of magistrates in a popular government. Discussions of this kind are more curious than beneficial, since everyone is satisfied that the institution is useful and friendly towards liberty.

But I must admit that I cannot readily see the inseparable connection between the existence of liberty and the trial by jury in civil cases.

Arbitrary impeachments, arbitrary methods of prosecuting pretended offenses, and arbitrary punishments on arbitrary convictions, have always appeared to me to be the great engines of judicial despotism. And these all relate to criminal proceedings. Therefore, trial by jury in criminal cases, aided by the *habeas-corpus* act, is important. And both of these are provided for, in the most ample manner, in the Constitution.

Safeguard Against Oppressive Taxes

13 It's been said that trial by jury is a safeguard against an oppressive taxation. This observation deserves to be studied.

Tax Collection

14 Clearly, trial by jury can have no influence on the legislature in regard to the *amount* of taxes to be laid, to the *objects* on which they are to be imposed, or to the *rule* by which they are to be apportioned.

It's only influence, therefore, must be on the mode of collection and the conduct of the officers entrusted with the execution of the revenue laws.

Recover Taxes: Jury Inappropriate

15 As to the mode of tax collection in New York, under our constitution, the trial by jury is in most cases out of use. The taxes are usually levied by the more summary proceeding of distress and sale, as in cases of rent. And everyone agrees that this is essential to the efficacy of the revenue laws.

The delay of a trial to recover the taxes imposed on individuals would neither suit the needs of the public nor promote the convenience of the citizens. It would often cost more than the original sum of the tax to be levied.

Officers' Conduct Criminal Offense

16 As to the conduct of the revenue officers, the provision in favor of trial by jury in criminal cases will give the security aimed at.

Willful abuses of a public authority, to the oppression of the subject, and every type of official extortion are offenses against the government. The persons who commit them may be indicted and punished according to the facts of the case.

Corrupting Officers of the Court

17 The excellence of the trial by jury in civil cases appears to depend on circumstances other than the preservation of liberty. Security against corruption is the strongest argument in its favor.

Since there is more time and opportunities to tamper with judges than with a jury summoned for one trial, perhaps a judge could more easily be corrupted than a jury. The force of this argument is, however, diminished by others.

The sheriff summons ordinary juries. The clerks of courts nominate special juries. Both are standing officers and, acting individually, they might be more accessible to corruption than the judges, who are a collective body. Those officers could select jurors who would serve the purpose of the party as well as a corrupted bench.

In the next place, it may be fair to suppose that there would be less difficulty in corrupting some of the jurors, which are randomly taken from the public mass, than in gaining men [judges] who had been chosen by the government for their probity and good character.

Despite these considerations, trial by jury is still a valuable check on corruption. It greatly multiplies the blocks to its success.

As matters now stand, it would be necessary to corrupt both court and jury. When the jury has been clearly wrong, the court will generally grant a new trial. In most cases, it would be useless to practice on the jury unless the court could be likewise gained. Here then is a double security.

This complicated agency tends to preserve the purity of both institutions. By increasing the obstacles to successful corruption, it discourages attempts to seduce the integrity of either. The temptations for judges must be much fewer when the cooperation of a jury is necessary, than if they exclusively determined all causes.

Constitutional Definition Difficult

18 Despite my doubts as to whether trial by jury in civil cases is essential to liberty, I admit that in most cases, under proper regulations, it is an excellent method of determining questions of property. Because of this alone it would be entitled to a constitutional provision if it were possible to define the limits within which it should be used.

However, in all cases, there is great difficulty in this. And men not blinded by enthusiasm must realize that in a federal government—a composition of societies whose ideas and institutions materially vary from each other—that difficulty increases. As I study the subject, I become more convinced that there were real obstacles that, we have been informed, prevented the insertion of a provision on this subject in the Constitution.

Judiciary in State Constitutions

19 Within the States, the use of the jury trial varies widely. And this difference is not generally understood. An explanation of the differences is necessary before we make a judgment about the omission being complained about.

The New York judicial system most resembles Great Britain's. New York has courts of common law, courts of probates (analogous in some ways to the spiritual courts in England), a court of admiralty, and a court of chancery. The trial by jury prevails only in the courts of common law and there are some exceptions. In all the others, a single judge presides and proceeds, following either cannon or civil law, without the aid of a jury.[1]

In New Jersey, a court of chancery is like New York's. But it has neither courts of admiralty nor of probates, in the sense of the New York courts. The New Jersey courts of common law have the jurisdiction in cases that in New York are determined in the courts of admiralty and of probates. And, of course, the jury trial is more extensive in New Jersey than in New York.

In Pennsylvania this is perhaps still more the case, for there is no court of chancery in that State, and its common-law courts have equity jurisdiction. It has a court of admiralty, but none of probates, at least like New York's.

Delaware, in this area, imitated Pennsylvania.

Maryland is more like New York, as is Virginia, except that the latter has a plurality of chancellors.

North Carolina is most like Pennsylvania, South Carolina like Virginia.

I believe, however, that in some of the States that have separate courts of admiralty, the cases have jury trials.

Georgia has only common-law courts. An appeal, of course, lies from the verdict of one jury to another, called a special jury, which has a specific mode of appointment.

In Connecticut, they have no distinct courts of chancery or admiralty. And their courts of probates have no jurisdiction of causes. Their common-law courts have admiralty and, to a certain extent, equity jurisdiction. In cases of importance, their General Assembly is the only court of chancery. In Connecticut, therefore, the trial by jury extends in *practice* further than in any other State yet mentioned.

The situation in Rhode Island is, I believe, pretty much the same as Connecticut. Massachusetts and New Hampshire, in regard to the blending of law, equity, and admiralty jurisdictions, are in a similar predicament. In the four Eastern States, trial by jury

---

[1] It has been erroneously insinuated that the Court of Chancery generally tries disputed facts by a jury. The truth is, juries in that court are rare and are not necessary except where the validity of a devise of land comes into question.

not only stands on a broader foundation than in the other States, but it is attended with a peculiarity unknown, in its full extent, to any of them. There is an appeal *of course* from one jury to another, until there have been two verdicts out of three on one side.

State Standard Couldn't Be Used

20 This summary shows there is significant diversity in the institution of trial by jury in civil cases in the States. From this fact these obvious reflections flow:

First, the convention couldn't make a general rule that corresponded with the circumstances of all the States.

And secondly, there would have been as many or more problems if the system of any one State had been made the standard, as by omitting a provision altogether and leaving the matter, as has been done, to legislative regulation.

Federal Judiciary New Institution

21 Suggestions for supplying the omission have illustrated the problem rather than corrected it.

The minority of Pennsylvania proposed this mode of expression: "Trial by jury shall be as heretofore." This, I maintain, would be senseless and worthless.

All general provisions in the Constitution refer to the United States, in their united or collective capacity. Although trial by jury with various limitations is known in each State individually, in the United States, *as such*, it is at this time altogether unknown, because the present federal government has no judiciary power whatever. Consequently, there is no proper antecedent or previous establishment to which the term *heretofore* could relate. It would have no precise meaning and be inoperative from its uncertainty.

Federal Cases Tried by Geography

22 On the one hand, this provision would not fulfil the intent of the people proposing it. On the other, if I properly understand their intent, it would be in itself inexpedient.

I presume that they mean that cases in the federal courts should be tried by jury if, in the State where the courts sat, that mode of trial would apply in a similar case in the State courts. That is to say, admiralty causes should be tried in Connecticut by a jury, in New York without one.

The capricious operation of so dissimilar a method of trial in the same cases, under the same government, is of itself sufficient to indispose every sound judgment towards it. Whether the case should be tried with or without a jury would depend, in many cases, on the accidental situation of the court and parties.

Technical Knowledge Important

23 But this is not, in my estimation, the greatest objection. I strongly believe that trial by jury is not appropriate for all cases. This is particularly true in cases that concern the public peace with foreign nations—that is, in most cases where the question turns wholly on the laws of nations.

Of this nature, among others, are all prize causes. Juries cannot be assumed competent to investigations that require a thorough knowledge of the laws and usages of nations. And they will sometimes be under the influence of impressions that will not allow them to pay sufficient attention to the considerations of public policy that should guide their inquires. There would be the danger that the rights of other nations might be infringed by their decisions, giving reasons for reprisal and war.

Although the proper province of juries is to determine matters of fact, in most cases, legal consequences are complicated with fact in such a manner as to render a separation impractical.

Treaties Often Specify Trial Types

24 Also, treaties with European powers often state the method of determining prize causes.

By treaty, in Great Britain they are determined in the last resort before the king himself, in his privy council, where the fact as well as the law undergoes a re-examination.

This alone demonstrates the impolicy of inserting a fundamental provision in the Constitution that would make the State systems a standard for the national government in the article under consideration. And it shows the danger of encumbering the government with any constitutional provisions that are not indisputably proper.

Separating Equity, Law Jurisdictions

25 My convictions are equally strong that great advantages result from the separation of the equity from the law jurisdiction. The causes that belong to the former would be improperly committed to juries.

The great and primary use of a court of equity is to give relief *in extraordinary cases*, which are *exceptions*[2] to general rules. To unite the jurisdiction of such cases with the ordinary jurisdiction would unsettle the general rules and subject every case that arises to a *special* determination. A separation of the one from the other has the opposite effect, rendering one

---

[2] It is true that the principles by which that relief is governed are now reduced to a regular system. But it is no less true that they are usually applicable to SPECIAL circumstances that form exceptions to general rules.

a sentinel over the other and keeping each within the expedient limits.

Besides this, the circumstances surrounding equity cases are often so intricate that they are incompatible with the genius of trials by jury. They often require long, deliberate, and critical investigation. It would be impractical to call men from their jobs and oblige them to decide the case before they could return to them.

The simplicity and expedition that distinguishes trial by jury requires that the matter to be decided should be reduced to some single and obvious point. While the litigations usual in chancery frequently include a long train of minute and independent particulars.

When Combined, Jury Not Used

26 It is true that the separation of the equity from the legal jurisdiction is unique to the English system of jurisprudence. The model has been followed in several of the States.

But it is equally true that the trial by jury has been unknown in every case in which they have been united. And the separation is essential to preserve that institution in its pristine purity.

The nature of a court of equity will readily permit the extension of its jurisdiction to matters of law. But the attempt to extend the jurisdiction of the courts of law to matters of equity will probably not only be unproductive of the advantages derived from courts of chancery, as established in New York, but will tend gradually to change the nature of the courts of law and to undermine the trial by jury, by introducing questions too complicated for a decision in that mode.

Pennsylvania Suggestion Rejected

27 These are conclusive reasons against incorporating the systems of all the States in the formation of the national judiciary, by using the system proposed by the Pennsylvania minority.

Let's now examine if the Massachusetts proposition will remedy the imagined defect.

Massachusetts Suggests Tiny Change

28 It is in this form: "In civil actions between citizens of different States, every issue of fact, arising in *actions at common law,* may be tried by a jury if the parties, or either of them, request it." **29** This, at best, defines one type of cause. We can infer that either the Massachusetts convention considered it the only class of federal causes proper for trial by jury or that, if they wanted a more extensive provision, they found it impractical to devise one.

If the first, the omission of such a minor regulation can never be considered a material imperfection in the Constitution. If the last, it corroborates the extreme difficulty of the thing.

What cases entitled to jury trial?

30 But this is not all. Let's return to the observations already made about the courts that exist in the States and the different powers exercised by them. No expressions appear more vague and indeterminate than those used to characterize *what* type of causes are entitled to a trial by jury.

In New York, the boundaries between actions at common law and actions of equitable jurisdiction conform to the rules in England. In many of the other States, the boundaries are less precise.

In some of them, every cause is to be tried in a court of common law and, on that basis, every action may be considered as an action at common law to be determined by a jury, if the parties,

or either of them, choose it. Hence the same irregularity and confusion would be introduced by a compliance with this proposition that I have already mentioned as resulting from the regulation proposed by the Pennsylvania minority.

In one State, a cause would be determined by a jury, if the parties, or either of them, requested it. But in another, the same cause must be decided without a jury, because the State judicatories vary as to common-law jurisdiction.

Same Jurisdictions Among States

31 Obviously, therefore, the Massachusetts proposition cannot operate as a general regulation until a uniform plan, with respect to the limits of common-law and equitable jurisdictions, is adopted by all the States. To devise a plan of that kind is an arduous task, requiring much time and reflection. It would be extremely difficult, if not impossible, to suggest any general regulation acceptable to all the States or that would perfectly conform with the State institutions.

Choosing One State System Not Work

32 It may be asked, Why couldn't a reference be made to the constitution of New York, taking that, which I admit is a good one, as a standard for the United States?

I answer that it is not very probable the other States would entertain the same opinion of our institutions as we do ourselves. It is natural to suppose that they are more attached to their own, and that each would struggle for the preference.

If the convention thought of using the plan of one State as a model, we can presume that its adoption would have been made difficult by the predilection of each representative in favor of his own government. And it must be uncertain which State would have been taken as the model. It has been shown that many of them would be improper ones.

And I leave it to conjecture whether New York's or some other State's provision would have been preferred. But even if the convention could have made a judicious selection, there would have been great danger of jealousy and disgust in the other States at the partiality shown to the institutions of one. The enemies of the Constitution would have had a fine pretext for raising a host of local prejudices against it that might have endangered its ratification.

Trial by Jury in All Cases

33 To avoid the embarrassments of defining the cases that trial by jury should embrace, men of enthusiastic tempers sometimes suggest that a provision might have been inserted for establishing it in all cases.

For this, I believe, no precedent is found in any State. And the points stated in discussing the proposition of the minority of Pennsylvania must satisfy every sober mind that the establishment of the trial by jury in *all* cases would have been an unpardonable error in the plan.

Possible Source of Opposition

34 In short, the more it is considered the more arduous will appear the task of fashioning a provision in such a form as not to express too little to answer the purpose or too much to be advisable. Or which might not have opened other sources of opposition to the essential objective of introducing a firm national government.

Conclusions of This Discussion

35 I believe that the different views of the subject in this paper will remove most apprehensions on the point. They have shown the following:

The security of liberty is materially concerned only in the trial by jury in criminal cases, which is provided for in the most ample manner in the Constitution.

Most civil cases, and those of interest to the great body of the community, will use that mode of trial, as established in the State constitutions, untouched and unaffected by the Constitution.

Trial by jury is not abolished[3] by the Constitution.

And there are great, if not insurmountable, difficulties in the way of making any precise and proper provision for it in a Constitution for the United States.

Trial by Jury May Be Over-used

36 The best judges of the matter will be the least anxious for a constitutional establishment of the trial by jury in civil cases. And they will be most ready to admit that the continual changes in society may render a different mode of determining questions of property preferable in many cases in which that mode of trial now prevails.

For my part, I believe that even in New York it might be advantageously extended to some cases to which it does not at present apply and might as advantageously be abridged in others.

---

[3] *Vide* Number 81 in which the supposition of its being abolished by the appellate jurisdiction in matters of fact being vested in the Supreme Court is examined and refuted.

All reasonable men concede that it should not be used in all cases. The examples of innovations that contract its ancient limits, in these States as well as in Great Britain, show that its former extent has been found inconvenient, and give room to suppose that future experience may discover the propriety and utility of other exceptions. I suspect it is impossible, because of its nature, to fix the salutary point at which the operation of the institution should stop. This is a strong argument for leaving the matter to the discretion of the legislature.

Constitution: General Principles

37 This is now clearly understood to be the case in Great Britain. It is equally so in Connecticut.

More encroachments have been made on the trial by jury in New York since the Revolution, though provided for by a positive article of our constitution, than has happened in the same time either in Connecticut or Great Britain. It may be added that these encroachments have generally originated with the men who endeavor to persuade the people they are the warmest defenders of popular liberty but who have rarely suffered constitutional obstacles to arrest them in a favorite career.

The truth is only the general GENIUS of a government can be relied on for permanent effects. Particular provisions, though not altogether useless, have far less virtue and efficacy than commonly ascribed to them. And the want of them will never be, with men of sound discernment, a decisive objection to any plan exhibits the characteristics of a good government.

Criticism Extremely Harsh

38 It certainly sounds both harsh and extraordinary to affirm that there is no security for liberty in a Constitution that expressly establishes the trial by jury in criminal cases, because it does not do it in civil also. It is a notorious fact that Connecticut, which is always regarded as the most popular State in the Union, can boast of no constitutional provision for either.

PUBLIUS

Constitutional reference:

Article 3, section 2	466-471	trial by jury
Article 1, section 9	245-247	habeas-corpus act
article 1, section 3	71-77	Senate tries impeachments

Number 84

Bill of Rights; Capital; Debts due Union; Expenses

In this review of the Constitution, I have endeavored to answer most of the objections that have appeared against it. However, there are few that either did not fall naturally under any specific topic or were forgotten in their proper places. These will now be discussed. But because of the great length of this discussion, I will try to be brief and put all my observations on these miscellaneous points in a single paper.

Bill of Rights

2   The most important of the remaining objections is that the new Constitution contains no **bill of rights**. As I've said several times, some of the State constitutions also have no bill of rights.

New York is one of these. Yet people who oppose the new Constitution, people in New York who profess an unlimited admiration for New York's constitution, are among the most intemperate partisans demanding a bill of rights. To justify their zeal, they allege two things:

1. that although the constitution of New York has no bill of rights attached to it, it contains, in its body, various provisions in favor of specific privileges and rights that, in substance, amount to the same thing; and

2. that the Constitution adopts, in their full extent, the common and statute law of Great Britain, by which many other rights, not expressed in it, are equally secured.

Many Rights within Constitution

3   To the first, I answer that the proposed Constitution, like the New York state constitution, contains a number of such provisions.

Clauses Assuring Rights

4   Besides clauses that relate to the structure of the government, we find the following:

Article 1, section 3, clause 7: "Judgment in cases of impeachment shall not extend further than to removal from office, and disqualification to hold and enjoy any office of honor, trust, or profit under the United States; but the party convicted shall, nevertheless, be liable and subject to indictment, trial, judgment, and punishment according to law."

Section 9, clause 2: "The privilege of the writ of *habeas corpus* shall not be suspended, unless when in cases of rebellion or invasion the public safety may require it."

Clause 3: "No bill of attainder or *ex-post-facto* law shall be passed."

Clause 7: "No title of nobility shall be granted by the United States; and no person holding any office of profit or trust under them, shall, without the consent of the Congress, accept of any present, emolument, office, or title of any kind whatever, from any king, prince, or foreign state."

Article 3, section 2, clause 3: "The trial of all crimes, except in cases of impeachment, shall be by jury; and such trial shall be held in the State where the said crimes shall have been committed; but when not committed within any State, the trial shall be at such place or places as the Congress may by law have directed."

Article 3, section 3: "Treason against the United States shall consist only in levying war against them, or in adhering to their enemies, giving them aid and comfort. No person shall be convicted of treason, unless on the testimony of two witnesses to the same overt act, or on confession in open court."

Article 3, section 3, clause 3: "The Congress shall have power to declare the punishment of treason; but no attainder of treason shall work corruption of blood, or forfeiture, except during the life of the person attainted."

Habeas Corpus, Ex-Post-Facto Laws

5   Are these not, on the whole, of equal importance with any found in the constitution of New York?

The establishment of the writ of *habeas corpus*, the prohibition of *ex-post-facto* laws, and of TITLES OF NOBILITY, *to which we have no corresponding provision in the New York constitution,* are perhaps greater securities to liberty and republicanism than any it contains.

The creation of crimes after the commission of the act or, in other words, punishing men for things that, when they were done, broke no law, and the practice of arbitrary imprisonment, have been, throughout the ages, the favorite and most formidable instruments of tyranny.

The observations of the judicious Blackstone are well worthy of recital: "To bereave a man of life, (says he) or by violence to confiscate his estate, without accusation or trial, would be so gross and notorious an act of despotism, as must at once convey the alarm of tyranny throughout the whole nation; but confinement of the person, by secretly hurrying him to jail, where his sufferings are unknown or forgotten, is a less public, a less striking, and therefore *a more dangerous engine* of arbitrary government."[1]

To remedy this fatal evil, Blackstone emphatically praises the *habeas corpus* act. One place he calls it "the BULWARK of the British Constitution."[2]

Prohibits Titles

6   Nothing need be said to illustrate the importance of the prohibition of titles of nobility. This may truly be called the cornerstone of republican government. As long as titles are excluded, there can never be serious danger that the government will be any other than that of the people.

"Bills of Rights" Limit Government

7   To the second—that is, to the pretended establishment of the common and statute law by the Constitution, I answer, that they are expressly made subject "to such alterations and provisions as the legislature shall from time to time make concerning the same." Therefore, they may, at any moment, be repealed by the ordinary legislative power and, of course, have no constitutional sanction.

The declaration was only used to recognize the ancient law and remove doubts that might have been caused by the Revolution. Consequently, this is not part of a declaration of rights that under our constitutions must be intended as limiting the power of the government itself.

Constitution: People Retain All Power

8   It has been said several times, correctly, that bills of rights are stipu-

---

[1] *Vide* Blackstone's *Commentaries*, vol. 1., p. 136.

[2] *Vide* Blackston's *Commentaries*, vol. Iv., p. 438.

lations between kings and their subjects. Bills of rights abridge prerogatives in favor of privilege, reserving to citizens rights not surrendered to the prince.

Such was MAGNA CHarta, obtained by the barons, sword in hand, from King John. Such were later confirmations of the Magna Charta by succeeding princes. Such was the *Petition of Right* assented to by Charles the First in the beginning of his reign. Such, also, was the Declaration of Rights presented by the Lords and Commons to the Prince of Orange in 1688 and then made into an act of parliament called the Bill of Rights.

Therefore, according to their original meaning, they don't belong in constitutions professedly founded on the power of the people and executed by their immediate representatives and servants. Here, strictly speaking, the people surrender nothing. And since they retain everything, they have no need of specific reservations.

"We, THE PEOPLE of the United States, to secure the blessings of liberty to ourselves and our posterity, do *ordain* and *establish* this Constitution for the United States of America."

This is a better recognition of popular rights than volumes of those aphorisms that make up several of our State bills of rights that would sound much better in a treatise on ethics than in a constitution of government.

Constitution: General Structure

9   But a minute detail of specific rights is even less applicable to a Constitution like the one under consideration, which is merely intended to regulate the general political interests of the nation, than to a constitution that regulates every type of personal and private concern. Therefore, if the loud clamors against the new Constitution, on this point, are well founded, the constitution of New York must be severely condemned. But the truth is that both contain all that, in relation to their objectives, is reasonably to be desired.

Statement of Rights Might Imply a Governmental Power

10   I go further and affirm that a bill of rights, in the sense and to the extent some people want one, is not only unnecessary in the proposed Constitution, but would even be dangerous. It would contain various exceptions to powers not granted. And, on this account, would afford a colorable pretext to claim more powers than were granted. Why declare that things shall not be done when there is no power to do it?

For instance, why say that the liberty of the press shall not be restrained when no power is given to impose restrictions? I will not argue that such a provision would confer a regulating power; but it would furnish, to men disposed to usurp, a plausible pretense for claiming that power. They might argue with some logic that it is absurd to say there is no authority when the Constitution has a provision against the abuse of that authority. And that the provision against restraining the liberty of the press clearly implies that the national government has a power to regulate it.

This may serve as an example of the numerous handles that would be given to the doctrine of constructive powers by the indulgence of an injudicious zeal for bills of rights.

Liberty of the Press

11   On the subject of the liberty of the press, as much as has been said, I cannot help adding a remark or two.

In the first place, there is not a syllable about it in New York's constitution.

In the next, I contend that what has been said about it in other State constitutions amounts to nothing. What signifies a declaration that "the liberty of the press shall be inviolably preserved"? What is the liberty of the press? Who can give it any definition that would not leave the utmost latitude for evasion?

I believe it is impractical. And, from this, I infer that its security, whatever fine declarations are inserted in any constitution regarding it, must completely depend on public opinion and the general spirit of the people and of the government.[3] And this is, after all,

---

[3] To show that there is a power in the Constitution that may affect the liberty of the press, the power of taxation has been used. It is said that duties on publications may be so high as to amount to a prohibition. I don't know by what logic it could be argued that the declaration in the State constitutions, in favor of the freedom of the press, would be a constitutional impediment to the imposition of duties on publications by the State legislatures. It cannot certainly be pretended that any degree of duties, however low, would be an abridgment of the liberty of the press.

Newspapers are taxed in Great Britain and yet it is notorious that the press nowhere enjoys greater liberty than in that country. And if duties of any kind may be laid without a violation of that liberty, it is evident that the extent must depend on legislative discretion, regulated by public opinion. So, general declarations respecting the liberty of the press will give it no greater security than it will have without them. The same invasions of it may be effected under the State constitutions that contain those declarations through the means of taxation, as under the proposed Constitution, which has nothing of the kind. It would be quite as significant to declare that government should be free, that taxes should not be excessive, etc., as that the liberty of the press should not be restrained.

as is intimated on another occasion, where we must look for the only solid basis of all our rights.

Constitution as Bill of Rights

12 In conclusion, there is only one other view of this matter. The truth is, after all the declarations we have heard, that the Constitution is itself, in every rational sense and to every useful purpose, A BILL OF RIGHTS.

The several bills of rights in Great Britain form its constitution and, conversely, the constitution of each State is its bill of rights. And the proposed Constitution, if adopted, will be the bill of rights of the Union.

Does a bill of rights specify the political privileges of the citizens in the structure and administration of the government? This is done in the most ample and precise manner in the new Constitution, which includes various precautions for the public security that are not to be found in any of the State constitutions.

Should a bill of rights also define certain immunities and modes of proceeding in personal and private concerns? This, we have seen, has also been included, in a variety of cases, in the Constitution.

Therefore, referring to what is meant by a bill of rights, it is absurd to allege that it is not to be found in the proposed Constitution. It may be said that it does not go far enough, though it will not be easy to make this point. But it can not, with propriety, be contended that there is no such thing. It certainly must be immaterial what mode is observed as to the order of declaring the rights of citizens, if they are to be found in any part of the instrument that establishes the government. Hence, it is apparent that much of what has been said on this subject rests merely on verbal and nominal distinctions, entirely foreign from the substance of the thing.

Capital too Far from States

13 Another frequent objection has been of this nature: "It is improper (say the objectors) to confer such large powers, as are proposed, on the national government, because the seat of that government must, necessarily, be too remote from many of the States for the citizens to have proper knowledge of the conduct of the representative body."

This argument, if it proves anything, proves there should be no federal government whatever. For the powers that everyone seems to agree should be vested in the Union cannot be safely entrusted to a body that is not under every requisite control.

But satisfactory reasons show that the objection is, in reality, baseless. Most of the arguments relating to distance are entirely imaginary.

How do the people in Montgomery County receive the information they use to judge the conduct of their representatives in the State legislature? Not by personal observation. This is confined to the citizens on the spot. Therefore, they must depend on the information of intelligent men who they trust. And how must these men obtain their information? Evidently from the complexion of public measures, from the public prints, from correspondences with their representatives and with other persons who reside in the state capital.

This doesn't apply only to Montgomery County, but to all the counties that are distant from the seat of government.

Information about National Government

14 Clearly, the same sources of information will be open to the people in relation to the conduct of their representatives in the federal government. And the impediments to prompt communication created by distance will be overbalanced by the effects of the vigilance of the State governments. The executive and legislative bodies of each State will be sentinels over the persons employed in every department of the national administration. It will be in their power to adopt and pursue a regular and effectual system of intelligence. Therefore, they will know the behavior of those who represent their constituents in the national councils and can readily communicate their knowledge to the people. They can be relied on to tell the community of whatever may prejudice its interests from another quarter, if only from the rivalship of power.

We may conclude, with assurance, that the people, through that channel, will be better informed of the conduct of their national representatives than they can be, by any means they now possess, of that of their State representatives.

Capital Citizens Inform Distant Ones

15 It should also be remembered that the citizens who live in or near the capital will, in all questions that affect general liberty and prosperity, have the same interest with those who are at a distance. They will stand ready to sound the alarm when necessary and to point out the actors in any pernicious project.

The public papers will be expeditious messengers of intelligence to the most remote inhabitants of the Union.

Debts due to United States

16 Among the many curious objections against the Constitution, the most extraordinary and the least colorable is the lack of a provision respecting the debts due to the United States.

This has been represented as a tacit relinquishment of those debts and as a wicked contrivance to screen public defaulters. The newspapers have teemed with the most inflammatory railings on this subject. Yet it is clear that the suggestion is entirely void of foundation, the offspring of extreme ignorance or extreme dishonesty. In addition to the remarks I have made on the subject in another place, I will only observe that just as it is a plain dictate of commonsense, so it is also an established doctrine of political law, that "*states neither lose any of their rights, nor are discharged from any of their obligations, by a change in the form of their civil government.*"[4]

Expense of Federal Government

17 The last objection of any consequence, that I presently remember, is expense. However, even if adopting the proposed government meant a considerable increase in expense, it would not be an objection against the Constitution.

Division of Powers Necessary

18 Most citizens of America are, with reason, convinced that Union is the basis of their political happiness. Most men of sense agree that it cannot be preserved under the present system without radical alterations. They agree

---

[4]*Vide* Rutherford's *Institutes,* vol. ii, book II, chap. x., sects, xiv, and xv. *Vide* also Grotius, book 11, chap. ix., sects. Viii. And ix.

that new and extensive power should be granted to the national government. And that these powers require a different organization of the federal government—a single body being an unsafe depositary of such ample authorities.

In conceding all this, the question of expense must be given up. It is impossible, with any degree of safety, to narrow the foundation on which the system is to stand.

In the beginning, the two houses of the legislature will consist of only sixty-five people, the same number as the Congress under the existing Confederation. This number will increase, but this is to keep pace with the progress of the population and resources of the country. Clearly, a smaller number would be unsafe and continuing the present number as the population grows would be a very inadequate representation of the people.

Expense of New Offices

19 From where is the dreaded increase of expense to come? One source mentioned is the multiplication of offices under the new government. Let us examine this a little.

Federal Employees

20 The principal departments of the administration under the present government are the same as those required under the new.

There is now a Secretary of War, a Secretary of Foreign Affairs, a Secretary for Domestic Affairs, a Board of Treasury—consisting of three persons—a Treasurer, assistants, clerks, etc. These officers are indispensable under any system and will suffice under the new as well as the old.

As to ambassadors and other ministers and agents in foreign countries, the proposed Constitution can make no other difference than to render their characters and where they reside more respectable, and their services more useful.

As to persons employed to collect revenues, these will form a very considerable addition to the number of federal officers. But it does not follow that this will increase public expense. It will mostly be an exchange of State for national officers. For instance, in the collection of all duties, the persons employed will be totally of this description. The States, individually, will have no need of any revenue agents for this purpose. What is the difference in the expense to pay customs officers appointed by the State or by the United States? There is no good reason to suppose that either the number or the salaries of the latter will be greater than those of the former.

Federal Judges

21 Where do we look, then, for the additional articles of expense that will swell the account to the enormous size represented to us?

The chief item that occurs to me is the support of the judges of the United States.

I do not add the President because there is now a president of Congress, whose expenses may not be far, if any, short of those that will be incurred by the President of the United States.

The support of the judges will clearly be an extra expense but the extent will depend on the specific plan adopted. But in no reasonable plan can it amount to a sum of material consequence.

Congress Less Expensive

22 Let's see what counterbalances any extra expenses accompanying the establishment of the proposed government.

First, the President will transact much of the business that now keeps Congress sitting through the year. Even the management of foreign negotiations will devolve on him, according to general principles, concerted with the Senate and subject to their final concurrence. Hence, both the Senate and the House of Representatives will need to be in session for only part of the year. We may suppose about a fourth for the latter and a third, or perhaps half, for the former. The extra business of treaties and appointments may make the Senate sessions longer.

From this we infer that, until the House of Representatives is increased greatly beyond its present number, there will be a considerable saving of expense from the difference between the constant session of the present and the temporary session of the future Congress.

Less Burden on State Legislatures

23 But there is another circumstance of great importance in the view of economy. Up until now, the business of the United States has occupied the State legislatures as well as Congress. Congress has made requisitions that the State legislatures have had to fulfill. Therefore, the sessions of State legislatures have been much longer than necessary for the execution of the local business of the States. More than half their time is frequently employed in matters that related to the United States.

There are now more than two thousand members of the State legislatures. And they preformed the same duties that, under the new system, will be done, initially, by sixty-five people.

And, in the future, the number will probably not grow to more than 400 or 500 people.

The Congress under the proposed government will do all the business of the United States themselves, without the intervention of the State legislatures. Henceforth, State legislatures will attend only to the affairs of their specific States, and will not have to sit nearly as long as they have done until now. The shorter sessions of the State legislatures will be a clear gain and will, alone, be a saving equivalent to any additional expense from adopting the new system.

Expenses Balanced by Savings

24 These observations show that the additional expense from the establishment of the proposed Constitution are much fewer than may be imagined. They are counterbalanced by considerable saving. And while it is questionable on which side the scale will preponderate, it is certain that a government less expensive would be incompetent to the purposes of the Union.

PUBLIUS

Constitutional references:
Bill of Rights

Article 1, section 3	78-84	impeachments, limits punishment
Article 1, section 9	245-247	habeas corpus
Article 1, section 9	248-249	no ex-post-facts laws
Article 1, section 9	265-266, 278-279	no titles of nobility
Article 3, section 2	466-467	trial by jury
Article 3, section 3	472-477	2 witnesses to treasonous act
Article 3, section 3	478-481	treason punishment limited to guilt person

Preamable of Constitution

Number 85

In Conclusion, Ratify Now, Amend Later

According to the subjects announced in my first paper, two points appear to remain to be discussed: "the analogy of the proposed government to your own State constitution," and "the additional security that its adoption will give to republican government, to liberty, and to property."

However, these topics have been so fully anticipated and exhausted in these Papers that now I could only repeat, in a more dilated form, what has been said before, which this late date and the time already spent on it, conspire to forbid.

Same "Defects" in NY Constitution

2   The proposed Constitution resembles New York's constitution in many of its imagined defects, as well as the real excellences.

Among the imagined defects are no term limits for the Executive, no executive council, no formal bill of rights, and no provision for the liberty of the press.

These and others discussed in these papers may be charged against the existing constitution of New York as well as the one proposed for the Union. And a man isn't very consistent if he can rail at the latter for imperfections that he easily excuses in the former.

And there is no better proof of the insincerity and affectation of some of the zealous adversaries of the new Constitution, who say they are devoted admirers of the New York state government, than the fury of their attacks on the Constitution for matters to which the New York constitution is equally or more vulnerable.

New Constitutional Securities

3   Adopting the Constitution will provide additional securities to republican government, to liberty, and to property.

Chiefly, preserving the Union will impose restraints on local factions and insurrections, and on the ambition of powerful individuals in single States who may acquire credit and influence enough from leaders and favorites to become the despots of the people.

It will diminish the opportunities for foreign intrigue that would be invited and facilitated by the dissolution of the Confederacy.

It will prevent extensive military establishments that would grow out of wars between the States if disunited.

It will guaranty a republican form of government to each State.

It will absolutely and universally exclude titles of nobility.

And it will guard against the States repeating acts that have undermined the foundations of property and credit, planted mutual distrust in the hearts of all classes of citizens, and caused an almost universal prostration of morals.

Presented Rational Arguments

4   Thus have I, fellow-citizens, executed the task I assigned to myself. With what success, your conduct must determine.

I trust, at least, you will admit that I have not failed in the assurance I gave you about spirit with which my endeavors would be conducted. I have addressed myself purely to your judgments. And I have studiously avoided the harshness that often disgraces political disputes and has been provoked by the language and conduct of the opponents of the Constitution.

The advocates of the new Constitution have been indiscriminately charged with conspiracy against the liberties of the people. This charge is too wanton and malignant not to excite the indignation of every man who feels in his own heart a refutation of the calumny. The perpetual changes rung on the wealthy, the well born, and the great, inspire the disgust of all reasonable men. And the unwarrantable misrepresentations that have kept the truth from the public eye demand the reprobation of all honest men. Because of these circumstances, I may have occasionally used intemperate expressions that I did not intend. I have frequently struggled between sensibility and moderation. If the former sometimes prevailed, my excuse is that it has not been often or much.

Every Man Must Now Decide

5 Let us now pause and ask ourselves whether, in these papers, the Constitution has been satisfactorily vindicated from the aspersions thrown on it. And whether it has been shown worthy of public approval and necessary for the public safety and prosperity.

Every man must answer these questions to himself, according to his conscience and understanding. And he must act according to the genuine, sober dictates of his judgment. This is a duty without dispensation. It is one that he is called on, nay, constrained by all the obligations that form the bands of society, to discharge sincerely and honestly. No partial motive, no particular interest, no pride of opinion, no temporary passion or prejudice, will justify to himself, to his country, or to his posterity, an improper election of the part he is to act. Let him beware of an obstinate adherence to party. Let him reflect that the object on which he is to decide is not a particular interest of the community, but the very existence of the nation. And let him remember that a majority of America has already ratified the plan that he is to approve or reject.

Constitution Best Solution for Us

6 I admit that I am confident of the arguments that recommend the Constitution to your adoption. And I am unable to discern any real force in the opposing arguments. I believe it is the best for our political situation, habits, and opinions, and superior to any the revolution has produced.

Constitution Admittedly Imperfect

7 Concessions on the part of the friends of the new Constitution, that it isn't absolutely perfect, have become a small triumph to its enemies. "Why," say they, "should we adopt an imperfect plan? Why not amend it and make it perfect before it is irrevocably established?"

This may be plausible enough, but it is only plausible. In the first place, these concessions have been greatly exaggerated. They are stated as amounting to an admission that the plan is radically defective and that without material alterations the rights and the interests of the community cannot be safely confided to it. This, as I understand the concessions, is an entire perversion of their meaning. No advocate of the Constitution can be found who will not declare that the system, though it may not be perfect in every part, is, on the whole, a good one. It is the best that the present views and circumstances of the country will permit. And it promises every type of security that a reasonable people can desire.

Group Decisions Never Perfect

8 I answer, next, that it is extremely imprudent to prolong the precarious state of our national affairs and expose the Union to the jeopardy of successive experiments in the chimerical pursuit of a perfect plan.

I never expect to see a perfect work from imperfect man. The deliberations of all groups must necessarily result in a compound of errors and prejudices, as well as good sense and wisdom, of the individuals of whom they are composed. The compact used to embrace thirteen States in a common bond of amity and union, must be a compromise of as many dissimilar interests and inclinations. How can perfection spring from such materials?

New Convention Not Good Idea

9 An excellent pamphlet, recently published in New York City,[1] gives the reasons why a new convention probably couldn't be assembled under circumstances as favorable to producing a good constitution as those in which the late convention met, deliberated, and concluded. I will not repeat the arguments, as I presume the pamphlet has had an extensive circulation. Every friend to his country should certainly read it.

There is, however, one view of amendments that remains to be con-

sidered, a view that has not been publicly discussed. I cannot conclude without discussing it.

Amend After Ratification

10 Clearly, it will be far easier to obtain subsequent than previous amendments to the Constitution. The moment the proposed Constitution is altered it becomes, to the purpose of adoption, a new one, and must be ratified again in each State. Therefore, to establish it throughout the Union, it would require the concurrence of thirteen States.

If, on the contrary, all the States ratify the Constitution, nine States can make alterations at any time. Here, then, the chances are as thirteen to nine[2] in favor of a subsequent amendment over adoption of an entire governmental system.

Issues, States Multiply Difficulty

11 This is not all. Every Constitution for the United States must have a great variety of specifics to accommodate the interests or opinions of thirteen independent States. In any group charged with writing it, we may expect to see different people agreeing on different points. People in the majority on one question may become the minority on a second, and an entirely different group may be the majority on a third.

The specifics of the document must be molded and arranged to satisfy all the parties to the compact. And, hence, the difficulties of obtaining every State's assent multiply. Clearly, the multiplication must be in a ratio to the number of issues and the number of parties.

[1] Entitled "An Address to the People of the State of New York."

[2] It is actually TEN, for though two thirds may propose the measure, three fourths must ratify.

Amendment: One Issue Each

12 But every amendment to the Constitution, if once established, would be a single proposition and could be brought forward singly. Compromise, in relation to any other point—giving or taking—would not be necessary. The will of the required number would decide the issue. And consequently, whenever nine, or rather ten States, wanted an amendment, that amendment must infallibly take place.

Therefore, there is no comparison between the ease of adding an amendment and of establishing a complete Constitution.

National Rulers Must Allow Amendments

13 Opponents argue that amending the Constitution after ratification may be impossible because the people administrating the national government will not want to give up any part of their authority once they have it.

For my part, I believe any amendments that are thought useful, after mature consideration, will apply to the organization of the government, not to the extent of its powers. On this account alone, this observation carries no weight.

And there is little weight in it on another account. The intrinsic difficulty of governing THIRTEEN STATES, independent of assuming an ordinary degree of public spirit and integrity, will, in my opinion, constantly *impose* on the national rulers a spirit of accommodation to the reasonable expectations of their constituents.

But another consideration proves, beyond a doubt, that the observation is wrong. It is this: the national rulers, whenever nine States concur, will have no option on the subject. By the fifth article of the Constitution, the Congress will be *obliged* "on the application of the legislatures of two thirds of the States (currently, nine), to call a convention for proposing amendments, which *shall be valid*, to all intents and purposes, as part of the Constitution, when ratified by the legislatures of three fourths of the States, or by conventions in three fourths thereof."

The words of this article are peremptory. The Congress "*shall* call a convention." Nothing is left to the discretion of Congress. Consequently, all the arguments about the disinclination to a change vanish.

And however difficult it may be to unite two thirds or three fourths of the States in amendments that affect local interests, such a difficulty cannot be feared on points relative to the general liberty or security of the people. We may rely on the State legislatures to erect barriers against the encroachments of the national authority.

Ratification Before Amending

14 If the forgoing argument is a fallacy, then I am deceived by it. It is, in my opinion, one of those rare cases where a political truth can be mathematically tested. Those who see it as I do, however zealous they may be for amendments, must agree it must be ratified first, as the most direct road to their own objective.

Delicate Balance of Creating Constitution

15 The zeal for attempts to amend, prior to the establishment of the Constitution, must abate in every man who is ready to agree to the truth of the following observations of a writer equally solid and ingenious.[3]

"To balance a large state or society (says he), whether monarchical or republican, on general laws, is a work of so great difficulty, that no human genius, however comprehensive, is able, by the mere dint of reason and reflection, to effect it. The judgments of many must unite in the work; EXPERIENCE must guide their labor; TIME must bring it to perfection, and the FEELING of inconveniences must correct the mistakes which they *inevitably* fall into in their first trials and experiments."

These judicious reflections contain a lesson of moderation to all the sincere lovers of the Union. And they should be on guard against hazarding anarchy, civil war, a perpetual alienation of the States from each other, and perhaps the military despotism of a victorious demagogue, while they pursue what they are not likely to obtain but from TIME and EXPERIENCE. I may

lack political fortitude, but I acknowledge that I cannot be as tranquil as people who treat the dangers of continuing in our present situation as imaginary.

A NATION without a NATIONAL GOVERNMENT is, in my view, an awful spectacle. The establishment of a Constitution, in time of profound peace, by the voluntary consent of a whole people, is an EXTRAORDINARY ACCOMPLISHMENT. I look forward to its completion with trembling anxiety. I can think of no reason to let go of the hold we now have on this arduous an enterprise, seven out of the thirteen States having ratified the Constitution, and after having done so much work, start over again. I dread the consequences of new attempts because I know that POWERFUL INDIVIDUALS, in this and in other States, are enemies to a national government in every possible shape.

PUBLIUS

[3] Hume's *Essays*, vol. I, page 128: "The Rise of Arts and Sciences."

Constitutional references:

Article 4, section 4	518-520	republican government in each State
Article 1, section 9	265-266, section 10 278-279	no nobility titles
Article 7	565-568	ratification of Constitution
Article 5	525-540	amending the Constitution

Glossary

abate lessen in degree

abridge diminish, curtail

abrogate abolish formally or officially

abstract theoretical idea; thought not connected with reality

abstruse hard to understand

accede become a party to (by agreement) by associating oneself with others

accession something added

accretion process of growth, enlargement

acquit behave satisfactorily

actuate to move to action

acquiescence comply without protest

acute shrewd discernment, especially of subtle distinctions

address remove a judge by executive order after a petition from the legislature

adduced to bring forward, as in evidence

adept very skilled person

adjudication to settle an issue judicially

admiralty court with jurisdiction over civil/criminal maritime offenses

admonitions caution against a fault, oversight

adulator praises effusively, flatters excessively

advantage benefit arising from course of action

adventitious not inherent; extrinsic

adverse unfavorable; opposed to one's interests

advert call to attention

advocate person who speaks or writes in support of a cause

affect pretend; feign

affectedly frequently

affirm assert positively; declare; confirm

afford furnish; supply

agency means of accomplishing something

agitate emotionally arouse public interest

alacrity cheerful readiness; prompt response

alienation to transfer title to another; diverted from normal function

aliment nourishment

alleviate make easier to endure; to remove or correct

ambiguity doubtfulness; uncertainty

ameliorate make better

amend repair; correct

amity peaceful relationship (as between nations)

amphictyony association of neighboring states in ancient Greece to defend a religious center; developed into league with legislative, judicial functions

analogy similarities

angle corner area; out-of-the-way place

animadversion comment unfavorably, critically

annex attach something

annihilation nonexistence; destroy utterly

antagonistic opposition, antipathy, discord

antecedent preceding; prior; original (first)

anterior earlier, before in time

antipathies natural repugnance; aversion

antiquary studies or collects antiquities

aphorism concise statement of a general truth

appellate authority to review and affirm, reverse, or modify judgment or decision of another tribunal

appellation name, title, designation

appertain to belong as a rightful attribute or part

appointment power of a person or the state to use the property subject to

that power. e.g. government's right to take and use tax money

apportion allocate proportionally

appraise analyze the worth

apprehend anticipate with anxiety or fear

apprised informed

approven proven

arbitrary by whim; convenient, not necessarily rational; characterized by absolute authority

ardent fiercely bright

arraign accuse of wrong, inadequacy, imperfection; find fault

article individual item

artifice trickery; guile; cleverness; ingenuity

ascendant position of dominance, superiority

ascribe attribute

aspect appearance to the eye or mind

asperity severity; harshness

assail to attack vigorously or violently

assiduous constant; working diligently; industrious

assign allocate, attribute

assort classify

asylum place of refuge

attainder (noun) loss of all civil rights upon being sentenced to death or being convicted of treason or a felony

attest correct; accurate; proof; evidence of

augment enlarge

aulic court hall

auspices patronage, sponsorship, kindly guidance, protection

avail value, advantage

avidity intense desire for gain or profit, avarice

avowal to declare frankly, openly

axiom self-evident truth requiring no proof

baffle reduce to ineffectiveness; break the force

bailages bail out

baneful things or people that ruin or spoil

basis foundation

batteries troops of army

bear characteristic, attribute

beget to cause; produce as an effect

belied show to be false; misrepresent; deny the validity; contradict

bid fair seem or appear

bill of credit issued by a state, circulated like money on state's credit

bottoms boat or ship, chiefly of cargo ships

breach infraction or violation, as a law

brook bear; tolerate

bulwark defense wall; protection against external danger

cabals small group of secret plotters, as against a government

calculate make judgment about the future, forecast consequences

calumny slander

candor open, impartial, honest, sincere

cantons small territorial district, especially one of the states of Switzerland

canvass study in detail

capacity legal qualification

capricious lacking predictable pattern, whimsical

captious calculated to confuse, entrap, entangle in argument; raise trivial objections; to stress faults

career (verb) to veer out of control; (noun) the long pursuit of consecutive progressive achievement

casting vote casting voice, vote cast by a presiding officer or judge to break a tie or sometimes to create a tie

casualty accident; victim

cavil captious, trivial, annoying objection

celebrated famous

celerity swiftness; speed

censure strong disapproval, criticize harshly

century Roman voting unit with property being the qualification

cessions ceding; surrender formally; transfer

character good reputation; composite of good moral qualities

chimerical utopian or unrealistic dream or aim; fantastic combination

civil service nonmilitary government administration

circumscribe encircle, restrict; limit; define

circumspect showing caution, consequences

claim demand as a right; assert as a fact

closet private place

code system of laws, rules, regulations

cogent valid; pertinent

cognizance jurisdiction; right and power to hear and decide controvercies; judicial hearing of matter

colorable feigned, factitious; plausible

combat oppose

combination alliance to meet a goal contrary to law or public welfare; conspiracy

commence begin; start

commensurate equal degree, amount

commission authority granted for a particular action or function

compact formal agreement

compendious a summary or abridgment

competent appropriate or suitable to certain position or rank; pertinent to

complacency satisfaction; affability; pleasure

complaisance disposition

to please, ingratiating deportment; compliance

comports agree

comprehend include

concert plan together

conclusive settles or decides a debate

concomitant accompanying; concurrent

concord agreement; harmony; peace; amity

concurrence acting in conjunction

conduce contribute to a result

confide trust

confidential show confidence in, mutual trust, trustworthy

confirm attest to validity

confound fail to discern difference between; mistake one for another; mingle; destroy; corrupt

conjecture opinion formed without enough evidence

connivance cooperate secretly; conspire

consanguinity has the same ancestry

conscious(ness) aware of one's own existence; known to oneself

consequence social importance; appearance of importance; self-importance

considerate given serious consideration, while aware of circumstances and consequences

consonant in accord, "behavior consonant with his character"

constituent component defined by the constitution; has power to frame or alter a political constitution

constitute appoint to office

construct structure

construction construing, interpreting, explaining a declaration or fact

contagion transmission of an idea, emotion (often negative)

contended for argued for; struggled for

contravene deny; oppose; go or act against; violate

contrivance scheme

controverted dispute; deny; argue; debate

contumacy stubborn resistance to authority; refusal to comply

coordinate equal rank, authority with another

copious abundant, plentiful

correspondent similar

countenance toleration; approval; support

counterpoise counterbalance; counteract an opposing force

credulous willing to believe or trust too readily

criminate accuse or charge with crime; incriminate; implying something criminal

culpable meriting condemnation or censure

cupidity excessive desire for

current used as a medium of exchange; circulating as money

---

damp discourage, check, restrain, lack of vitality

debase to lower the quality, character, dignity of

declaim to speak loudly and rhetorically

declaratory declaring what is existing law, legal right

declension deterioration; decline

defalcation failure to meet a promise or expectation

demagogues gains power by arousing people's emotion and prejudices

demesnes estate occupied by and worked exclusively for

denominate give a name to; denote; designate

denomination class or kind of people

denunciation official announcement, formal notice of termination of a treaty

depredations act of preying on, plundering

deputation delegation

derision laughing at what seems ridiculous or contemptible, ridicule, mock

derive receive or obtain from a source

derogate to detract, as from authority; to disparage or belittle

descanted discourse at length

descendible pass from higher to lower place; inheritable

descents sudden attacks

desert deserving of rewards, recompense, or punishment; worthiness

desideratum something desired as essential, sought for or aimed at

despoil strip of possessions, rob, plunder

despotic tyrant, oppressor

desultory lacking in consistency, order; random

detail specific task for person or group

determinate coming to a decision, firmness of purpose

determination settle controversy by judicial decision

devolved pass from one to another, as estate or responsibility; change

devotion disposal or power of disposal; back and call

diet formal public assembly of governing body of realm or confederation

digest compilation of laws, statutes, or decisions systematically arranged

dignities elevated rank, office, station, etc

dilate to describe at length or in detail

dilatory tends to cause delay; tardy

disaffect to make discontented or disloyal

disapprobation condemnation, disapproval

discernment intelligence

discountenance shame, disapprove

disdains treats with contempt; scorn

disembarrass free from embarrassment, impediment, superfluity

disingenuity lacks sincerity; give false appearance of simple frankness

dispassionate calm in judgment; uninfluenced by prejudice, favoritism, partisanship, passions or emotions

dispatch dispose of rapidly or efficiently (as piece of business), execute quickly

dispose of settle; bestow; distribute; apportion; allot

disposition power to settle or control; prevailing tendency, inclination, propensity

disquietude lack of peace; uneasiness, agitation, anxiety

disquisition formal discourse or treatise; systematic inquiry into a subject; elaborate analytical essay or discussion

dominion sovereign authority; realm

draught draft (a document)

due proper, adequate according to excepted norms of what is reasonable, fitting, or necessary

dupes easily deceived or fooled

duty sum paid as tax on import, export, manufacture, or consumption of goods

---

eccentric odd; not having the same center

efface cause to disappear, eliminate completely; to remove from cognizance, consideration, or memory

efficacious effective

elector voter

eligible suitable, preferable

elucidation to make clear

elude avoid; evade

emanation flowing out from a source; consequence, specific products of a particular social milieu or cultural level

embark enlist in an enterprise; vested interest in

embarrass hamper, impede

eminent so outstanding that it is easily noticed

emit issue formally, as paper money

emoluments compensation for employment; recompense; benefit; advantage

emulation contentious rivalry; envy, jealousy

enamor charmed by

encomium high praise

encroach gradually or stealthily trespass on the rights, domain, or property of another

energy effective force; capacity to act or operate effectively, inherent power

enervate lessen vitality or strength; reduce mental or moral vigor; weaken

engagements debts; obligations

engender to cause

enlightened understanding free of ignorance, false beliefs, prejudices

enmity hatred; absence of any friendly spirit

enormous erroneous; outrageous

entail consequence

entertain consider

entrust give to for protection

epidemical prevalent; widespread; rapid spread or increase

epithet characterization

equanimity composure, especially under strain

equitable fair, just, proper

equivocal deliberately ambiguous; questionable; uncertain, doubtful

erroneous having an error; incorrect

eruption disorder; rash

espouse support; adopt as policy

establishment permanent military force

esteem to consider highly; regard

estimate to consider or judge to be of a particular character or nature

event outcome; consequence

evince make evident; manifest

exact demand; require

exceptionable may cause objection; objectionable

excrescence an abnormal or excessive increase

execrable utterly detestable

execration act of cursing or denouncing; objects of curses; detested things

excises internal, indirect tax on commodity within a country

ex officio all people who hold one job or position automatically hold a second position

expedient governed by self-interest, temporarily advantageous, separate from what is just or right

expiate make amends for

expositor person who explains something

ex post facto law adds punishment to act after the fact

extent valuation or assessment made for the purpose of taxation

extirpate eradicate, exterminate

extremity condition of extreme need or danger

fabrics framework, structure

in the face of in opposition to, in defiance of, despite

facility ease of performance; designed or built for a specific purpose; action, process

faction a party or clique (within a government or association) often contentious, self-serving, reckless to the common good

factious form parties or factions in organization and raise dissension, sometimes seditious

faculty powers of the mind; inherent capability of the body; resources

fealty fidelity of a feudal vassal to his lord; loyalty

felicity state of happiness

ferment agitation; excitement; commotion

fetter confine; restrain

fiefs land the vassals use

forbear to bear with, endure; abstain from; be patient or self-controlled

force moral or mental strength, especially manifested as power of effective action

fortunes turns of luck accompanying the progress of a person through life or towards success

frantic mentally deranged; nearly mad

fugitive fleeting; of short duration; likely to deteriorate; not permanent

futurity future prospects

---

genius distinctive inherent characteristic, history

good faith justice trustworthiness

grade rank; class of persons or things

guarantee responsible for the fulfillment of agreement of another; assume suretyship

---

halcyon peaceful; happy; carefree

hazard take a chance that could have a bad outcome

heretofore before this; up until now

hereafter in a future time

hitherto until now

honors title, high public office or rank

humours temperament; mood

husbandman farmer

---

ignominious marked by disgrace or dishonor; deserving contempt

ill hostile; unkindly; unfavorable, adverse

illiberal narrow-minded; bigoted

illicit unlawful

illimitable boundless

imbecility weakness; incapacity; inability

immemorial indefinitely ancient

impatience show disapproval or intolerance

impeachment calling into question or discrediting

imperious dominate, lordly; arrogant

impious lacking proper respect for something usually respected

import convey meaning, information, weight, significance; to bring into

importunate urgent request

importunities urge with excessive persistence

impose deceive, defraud, cheat; to thrust intrusively upon others

imposition deception

imposts tax; duty; generic term for tax

imposture fraud

impracticable lacking common sense in practical matters; impractical

impregnable can resist attack

improvidence didn't prepare for future needs

impunity exemption from punishment or detrimental effects

imputations attribute (something discreditable) to someone or something

inauspicious unfavorable, unfortunate

incitements promote action

incident accompanying condition

incautious injudicious; careless; rash

inconsiderable small, as in value, amount, or size

inconsiderate not well thought out

inconstant likely to change, often without apparent reason; change character, purpose

inculcate impress by repeated admonition

incumbent duty, responsibility, obligation

indefatigable incapable of being tired out

indefinite having no fixed limits

indemnity exempt from incurred penalties or liabilities

indubitable not doubted

induce infer by logic, move by persuasion

indue provide, supply; invest; transfuse

inexpedient not likely to achieve purpose or success

infamy detestable action

infatuate foolish; weaken intellectual powers or deprive of sound judgment; devotion to idea

infidel not a Christian or opposes Christianity; unbeliever in respect to a particular religion

ingenious free from deceit or disguise; innocent

ingenuous cleverness; originality; resourceful

ingraft engraft; to introduce (infective matter) into a host

inimical having disposition of an enemy; hostile; prejudicial tendency

iniquitous grossly unjust act

inordinate exceeding proper limits; not regulated

insensible indifferent

insult attack, assault, unexpected military attack;

treat with insolence or contempt by word or action

insurrection revolt against civil or political authority or against an established government, rebellious

intelligible understandable

intemperate exceeding reasonable limits

interdict any prohibitory act or decree

intermit cause to cease for a time; discontinue, interrupt, suspend

interposition act of interposing; placing between; intervention

intimate make known indirectly, suggested

intrepid resolute fearlessness in meeting dangers or hardships

invade encroach, intrude, infringe

invective vehement denunciation, censure

inveigh protest bitterly, vehemently

inveigling to entice or lure by artful talk

inveterate adamant, persistent

inviolable secure from destruction, infringement, or desecration

irregular haven't satisfied requirements of the group

irregulars soldiers not part of a regular military force

---

janizary loyal or subservient troops, officials, or supporters; Turkish sultan's personal guard

judicature jurisdiction of judge or court

just true; correct

---

kindred similar

---

labored produced through hard work; elaborate; not easy or natural

Lacedaemonia Sparta, ancient Greek city-state

landed class people who own real property (land)

late recent

latent present but not visible

latitude range or variety of action or opinions that is permitted or tolerated

laudable praiseworthy

lay to devise, as a plan

legerdemain sleight of hand; trickery; deception

letters of marque written authority granted by a government to seize the subjects of a foreign state or their goods to retaliate for injuries. Government grants license to a private person to arm a vessel, cruise the sea and plunder the enemy

levies conscription of troops

liable subject or susceptible, likely or apt

licentiousness absence of legal or moral restraints; offensive to accepted standard of conduct

liquidate determine liabilities and apportion assets towards discharging indebtedness. Make clear, plain, unambiguous or less ambiguous.

---

magazine room to keep explosives; military depot for arms, provisions

magistracy collective body exercising governmental powers

magistrate public official entrusted with administration of laws

malignity malicious act

manifest clearly perceived

marque reprisal, retaliation (see *letters of marque*)

mass aggregate, whole

maxim concise saying embodying a general truth

measure legislative bill or enactment

meditate plan; intend

medium intervening or surrounding conditions; means of conveyence

meliorated ameliorate; to improve

mensuration process of measuring

militate (against) have substantial effect; weigh heavily

misconstrue misinterpret the meaning or intention

mission group sent to a foreign country to conduct political or diplomatic negotiations; permanent embassy or legation

moment importance

monitor person who gives advise (as of caution)

monitory serving to warn; admonitory

mulct punish by fire

mutable prone or liable to change, inconstant; being changed in form, quality, or nature

mutual reciprocal; having same relation toward each other

---

nicety exactness of perception, discrimination; precision; accuracy

notorious commonly known

notwithstanding (prep.) in spite of; (adv.) nevertheless; (conj.) although

novelties state or quality of being novel (new kind)

nugatory trifling; worthless

---

obdurate stubbornly persistent in wrongdoing; resistant to persuasion or softening influence

object objective, mission

obnoxious subject to the authority or power of another

obscurity not readily seen

obsequious compliant to will of another; fawning, excessively compliant

obstinacy unreasonable adherence to an opinion

obtain become recognized or established; prevalent or general

obviate anticipate and prevent by effective measures

occasion to cause; bring about

odious hateful

odium intense hatred; discredit some action

officious objectionably aggressive in offering unwanted help or advice

oligarchy despotic power exercised by a privileged, exclusive group

oppose put, place

opprobrium disgrace incurred by shameful conduct, cause of such disgrace

opulent wealthy, rich, richly supplied

oracle expert; person of great authority or wisdom whose opinions are respected

order group of people with common interest, profession, or special privileges

ordinance act of ordering or arranging; rule, policy, practice

ordinary judge of probate in some States

---

pageants role in play; pretense

palladium gives effective protection or security, safeguard

palliate to relieve without curing; try to mitigate the gravity of (an offense) by excuses, apologies, etc.

palpable plainly seen or perceived; obvious

paramount superior to all others (as in power, position, importance)

parlance manner of speaking

paroxysm sudden, violent outburst

parsimony excessive frugality; stinginess

patrimony inherited from one's father or ancestors

partisan supporter of person, cause, etc.

patrician aristocrat

patronize support

peculation embezzlement

peculiar exclusive characteristic

pecuniary of or consisting of money

peremptory leaving no opportunity for denial or refund; dictatorial

perfection quality or state of being finished, complete, whole

perfidy being dishonest, disloyal; act of betrayal

pernicious causing great harm, ruin; highly injurious, destructive; deadly

perpetuate preserve from extinction or oblivion

perplexity entanglement

preponderancy state of having superior weight, influence, importance, or power

perspicuity clearly expressed; lucid

pertinacious holding tenaciously to purpose; opinion stubbornly persistent

perverse turned away from what is right or good; contrary to accepted standard or practice, incorrect

peruse examine for specific points, study

pestilent injuring or endangering society, peace; destructive, annoying

petulance irritation at trifling annoyance

pique mutual animosity; state of strife

pleasure "holding their offices during pleasure" (people's will)

plebeian common person (not an aristocrat)

plenipotentiary conferring full power; invested with full power

plenitude completeness; abundance

plume preen; adorn with plumes

politic shrewd or prudent in practical matters

political concerned with government

polity political organization

populousness heavily populated; crowded with people

portion the share of an individual or group in human fortune or destiny; lot, fate

posse comitatus power of a county, a sheriff may summon help from citizens to preserve public peace or execute laws

positive government formerly laid down or imposed, prescribed by express enactment

precept principle intended as a general rule of action; maxim

precipitate exhibiting lack of due deliberation or care, rash, impetuous

predatory characterized by plunder, robbery, exploitation

predicated based

predilection preference; a partiality

preeminence superior or dominant rank, position, or influence

preferment promotion in office or station; position or office of honor or profit

pregnant abounding in fancy, wit, or resource of mind; fertile

prepossessions predispositions; impression formed beforehand; bias

preside exercise management or control

pretend assert, claim; represent or assert falsely

pretension claim to something, often unwarranted or false; claim recognition of right or privilege

pretermit to let pass without mentioning, omit, leave unpaid; break off, interrupt, suspend

primitive original, primary

privilege fundamental rights considered guaranteed and secured to all persons by modern constitutional governments

probity integrity

prodigy extraordinary accomplishment

projector project what will happen under a theory or plan

promiscuous not restricted to one class of people; random

propitious favorable conditions; auspicious

propositions propose legislation

propriety quality or state of being proper or fitting; suitability

prorogue to adjourn (Parliament); suspend or end legislative session

proscribe condemn or forbid, prohibit

prosecution carry forward to completion; management of occupation or activity

prospect outlook for the future; expectation

prosperity success

prove to ascertain the genuineness of, verify. "acts, records, and proceedings shall be *proved*" U. S. Constitution

provident making provisions for the future; prudent in anticipating conditions or needs

province sphere of authority

provision arrangement made beforehand; legal or formal stipulation

prostitute use for corrupt or unworthy purpose

proviso clause that introduces condition or stipulation (in contract)

prudence judicious in practical affairs; caution

purview scope of authority, responsibility

quadrate conform; make accordant

quarters unspecified sources

quorum number of members required to be present to conduct business

---

radical root; origin; fundamental

railings uttering bitter complaints

raillery good natured ridicule

rapacious extremely greedy

rear care for until maturity

reasonable within the bounds of reason, being in accord with logical thinking

recapitulate summarize

reciprocality given or felt by each toward the other, mutual

recollected recalled to memory

rectitude acts with highest integrity, virtuous; good judgement

redound affecting one's reputation

redress setting right what is wrong; remedy; compensate

refinements subtlety in reasoning; contrivance intended to improve or perfect

refractory difficult to manage; stubborn or disobedient

regard feeling of approval, appreciation, respect based on attractive characteristics

regular characterized by fixed principle or procedure

reiterate say or do again or repeatedly

remarking observing, noticing

remit refrain from enforcing

remonstrate reason or plead in protest, objection, or complaint

render cause to become

repartition distribution

repose rest; to place; to put in person or thing

representation statement made to influence opinion

repugnancy dislike; contradiction or inconsistency between sections of a legal instrument

resistance work to counteract or defeat, striving against, opposing

resulted to (law) reverted to ("the estate will result to him")

retort counter argument based on same logic

retrospective looking back

revolve consider various aspects at length, repeatedly; evaluate

ring the changes to cover a whole range, every possible variation

rule method prescribed for performing a task, function, or operation

---

sacred regarded with reverence

sagacity keen discernment; see what is relevant and significant

sagacious intellectually perceptive; discerning and foresighted judge of men

salutary restorative; corrective; remedial

sanction authoritative permission, approval; punishment or withholding a reward to coerce obedience

sanguinary willing or anxious to shed blood, bloodthirsty;

sanguine cheerfully optimistic; hopeful; confidant

saving clause a clause in an instrument or law exempting something from its operation or providing that the rest of it will stand if part is held invalid

scepter symbol of royal or imperial authority

sedition incitement of discontent or rebellion

against government; conduct tending to treason but without an overt act

select judicious or restrictive when choosing; superior value or excellence

sense significance; sentiment, view, opinion

sensible large enough size, amount, or degree to be clearly perceived

sensibility mental responsiveness; mental acuity

sequel subsequent

seraglio harem; palace of Sultan

set (of men) group with some common trait; mathematical set

signal outstanding; significant; distinctive

signification the meaning of a term

singular extraordinary, exceptional; unique

sinew financial and material resources, supporting force

solecism deviation from the normal or accepted order; something (as theory, situation, act) not logical with known facts; absurd incongruity or incompatibility

solicitude anxious, concerned

sophism fallacious but plausible argument

sovereignty authority of the state

specious seems true but lacking real merit

specter fear-inspiring imaginary vision

stadholder viceroy in province of the Netherlands or chief executive of United Provinces of the Netherlands

stipulate to specify or require in the terms of an agreement

subjoined to add to something said or written; appendix

subscribe approve; give support to

subsist continue in existence

subvert to undermine the principles of; corrupt; overthrow

succours, succors to help; aid

suffice enough, adequate (for)

suffrages opinion in favor of; approval; vote, right to vote

superadd add over and above; superfluous addition

supercede make superfluous or unnecessary

supersedure to replace something with something else

supine manifesting mental, moral lethargy; indifferent to one's duty

supplant to replace (perhaps through force)

supposition assumption

supremacy supreme authority or power

surrogate in some States, judicial officer over probate of wills, settlement of estates; often has power to appoint, supervise guardians of infants, incompetent people

suspended make inactive

sympathy affinity, association, or relationship between persons or things; loyalty

———

tautology needless repetition of an idea in different words

temerity reckless boldness; chutzpa, gall

temper state of mind or feelings

temporize adopt to situation; work out, compromise between parties

tenacious holding fast to something valued

tenets principle, doctrine

tenure conditions that apply to holding something like property or office

tinctured tinged; affected

title sufficient proof or justification; valid reason; ground or right

tone general or prevailing character, quality, or trend of moral, social behavior

tractable easily managed or controlled; malleable

train retinue; staff, etc.

transcendent surpass; excel; go beyond ordinary limits

translate change the form, condition, or nature

transmute undergo change or transformation in form, nature, substance

transpose change relative place or normal order; interchange

tributary person or nation that pays tribute; dependent

trite used so often it's lost its force; stale, vapid

tutelage under a guardian

———

unavailing not effectual; futile

undue improper, inappropriate; excessive

unequivocal not ambiguous; clear

unexceptionable beyond criticism

unpropitious unfavorable

unqualified not modified or limited; complete

untoward unfavorable, unfortunate, not proper, unseemly

usurpation seize power without authority or legal right

utility useful

utopian ideal place; impossibly perfect society

———

vassals persons granted use of land in return for homage and fealty to a lord

venality moral weakness

venial can be forgiven

vent serving as an outlet

vice shortcoming

viceroy person appointed to rule a country or province as the deputy of the sovereign

vicious characterized by vice

vicissitudes difficult change; variation

view objective, aim, purpose

vindicate clear of; afford justification for, defend against opposition

violent tending to distort or misrepresent

virulent violently hostile

visage face; appearance, look; outward show, semblance

visionary utopian fantasy

vitiate impair the quality, make less effective, debase, corrupt, make legally invalid

vivify give life to; animate; enliven

volition act or ability to choose re resolve

votary devout adherent

voucher piece of supporting evidence, proof

———

want lack, deficiency in

weal well-being, prosperity, happiness

whence from which

wholly entirely; totally

[to] wit that is to say

wreak take vengeance, avenge; to bring about (harm), cause, inflict

———

yeoman a class of commoners owning property; in America, a farmer on his own land

Articles of Confederation

Articles of Confederation and perpetual Union between the States of New Hampshire, Massachusetts Bay, Rhode Island and Providence Plantations, Connecticut, New York, New Jersey, Pennsylvania, Delaware, Maryland, Virginia, North Carolina, South Carolina, and Georgia.

Article One

The style of this Confederacy shall be "The United States of America."

Article Two

Each State retains its sovereignty, freedom, and independence, and every power, jurisdiction, and right, which is not by this Confederation expressly delegated to the United States in Congress assembled.

Article Three

The said States hereby severally enter into a firm league of friendship with each other, for their common defence, the security of their liberties, and their mutual and general welfare, binding themselves to assist each other against all force offered to, or attacks made upon them, or any of them, on account of religion, sovereignty, trade, or any other pretence whatever.

Article Four

The better to secure and perpetuate mutual friendship and intercourse among the people of the different States in this Union, the free inhabitants of each of these States, paupers, vagabonds, and fugitives from justice excepted, shall be entitled to all the privileges and immunities of free citizens in the several States, and the people of each State shall have free ingress and regress to and from any other State, and shall enjoy therein all the privileges of trade and commerce, subject to the same duties, impositions, and restrictions as the inhabitants thereof respectively, provided that such restrictions shall not extend so far as to prevent the removal of property imported into any State, to any other State of which the owner is an inhabitant; provided also, that no imposition, duties, or restriction shall be laid by any State, on the property of the United States, or either of them.

In any person guilty of or charged with treason, felony, or other high misdemeanor in any State, shall flee from justice, and be found in any of the United States, he shall, upon demand of the governor or executive power of the State from which he fled, be delivered up and removed to the State having jurisdiction of his offence.

Full faith and credit shall be given in each of these States to the records, acts, and judicial proceedings of the courts and magistrates of every other State.

Article Five

For the more convenient management of the general interests of the United States, delegates shall be annually appointed in such manner as the legislature of each State shall direct, to meet in Congress on the first Monday in November, in every year, with a power reserved to each State to recall its delegates, or any of them, at any time within the year, and to send others in their stead, for the remainder of the year.

No State shall be represented in Congress by less than two, nor by more than seven members; and no person shall be capable of being a delegate for more than three years in any term of six years, nor shall any person, being a delegate, be capable of holding any office under the United States for which he or another for his benefit receives any salary, fees, or emolument of any kind.

Each State shall maintain its own delegates in a meeting of the States, and while they act as members of the committee of the States.

In determining questions in the United States, in Congress assembled, each State shall have one vote.

Freedom of speech and debate in Congress shall not be impeached or questioned in any court or place out of Congress, and the members of Congress shall be protected in their persons form arrests and imprisonments, during the time of their going to or from, and attendance on, Congress, except for treason, felony, or breach of the peace.

Article Six

No State, without the consent of the United States, in congress assembled, shall send any embassy to, or receive any embassy from, or enter into any conference, agreement, alliance, or treaty with, any king, prince, or state; nor shall any person holding any office of profit or trust under the United States, or any of them, accept of any present, emolument, office, or title of any kind whatever from any king, prince, or foreign state; nor shall the United States in Congress assembled, or any of them, grant any title of nobility.

No two or more States shall enter into any treaty, confederation, or alliance whatever between them, without the consent of the United States in Congress assembled, specifying accurately the purposes for which the same is to be entered into, and how long it shall continue.

No State shall lay any imposts or duties, which may interfere with any stipulations in treaties entered into by the United States in Congress assembled, with any king, price, or state, in pursuance of any treaties already proposed by Congress, to the courts of France and Spain.

No vessels of war shall be kept in time of peace by any State, except such number only as shall be deemed necessary by the United States in Congress assembled, for the defence of such State or its trade; nor shall any body of forces be kept up by any State, in time of peace, except such number only as in the judgment of the United States in Congress assembled shall be deemed requisite to garrison the forts necessary for the defence of such State; but every State shall always keep up a well regulated and disciplined militia, sufficiently armed and accoutred, and shall provide and constantly have ready for use, in public stores, a due number of field pieces and tents, and a proper quantity of arms, ammunition, and camp equipage.

No State shall engage in any war without the consent of the United States of Congress assembled, unless such State be actually invaded by enemies, or shall have received certain advice of a resolution being formed by some nation of Indians to invade such State, and the danger is so imminent as not to admit of a delay till the United States in Congress assembled can be consulted; nor shall any State grant commissions to any ships or vessels of war, nor letters of marque or reprisal, except it be after a declaration of war by the United States in Congress assembled, and then only against the kingdom or state, and the subjects thereof, against which war has been so declared, and under such regulations as shall be established by the United States in Congress assembled, unless such State be infested by pirates, in which case vessels of war may be fitted out for that occasion, and kept so long as the danger shall continue, or until the United States in Congress assembled shall determine otherwise.

Article Seven

When land forces are raised by any State for the common defense, all officers of or under the rank of colonel shall be appointed by the legislature of each State respectively, by whom such forces shall be raised, or in such manner as such State shall direct; and all vacancies shall be filled up by the State which first made the appointment.

Article Eight

All charges of war and all other expenses that shall be incurred for the common defence or general welfare, and allowed by the United States in Congress assembled, shall be defrayed out of a common treasury, which shall be supplied by the several States, in proportion to the value of all land within each State, granted to or surveyed for any person, and such land and the buildings and improvements thereon shall be estimated according to such mode as the United States in Congress assembled shall from time to time direct and appoint.

The taxes for paying that proportion shall be laid and levied by the authority and direction of the legislatures of the several States within the time agreed upon by the United States in Congress assembled.

Article Nine

The United States in Congress assembled shall have the sole and exclusive right and power of determining on piece and war, except in the cases mentioned in the sixth article—of sending and receiving ambassadors—entering into treaties and alliances, provided that no treaty of commerce shall be made whereby the legislative power of the respective States shall be restrained from imposing such imposts and duties on foreigners as their own people are subjected to, or from prohibiting the exportation or importation of any species of goods or commodities whatsoever—of establishing rules for deciding, in all cases, what captures on land or water shall be legal, and in what manner prizes taken by land or naval forces in the service of the United States shall be divided or appropriated—of granting letters of marque and reprisal in times of peace—appointing courts for the trial of piracies and felonies committed on the high seas, and establishing courts for receiving and determining finally appeals in all cases of captures, provided that no member of Congress shall be appointed a judge of any of the said courts.

The United States in Congress assembled shall also be the last resort on appeal in all disputes and differences now subsisting or that hereafter may arise between two or more States concerning boundary, jurisdiction, or any other cause whatever; which authority shall always be exercised in the manner following:—Whenever the legislative or executive authority or lawful agent of any State in controversy with another shall present a petition to Congress stating the matter in question and praying for a hearing, notice thereof shall be given by order of Congress to the legislative or executive authority of the other State in controversy, and a day assigned for the appearance of the parties by their lawful agents, who shall then be directed to appoint, by joint consent, commissioners or judges to constitute a court for hearing and determining the matter in question; but if they cannot agree, Congress shall name three persons out of each of the United States, and from the list of such persons each party shall alternately strike out one, the petitioners beginning, until the number shall be reduced to thirteen; and from that number not less than seven nor more than nine names, as Congress shall direct, shall, in the presence of Congress, be drawn out by lot, and the persons whose names shall be so drawn, or any five of them, shall be commissioners or judges, to hear and finally determine the controversy, so always as a major part of the judges who shall hear the cause shall agree in the determination; and if either party shall neglect to attend at the day appointed, without showing reasons, which Congress shall judge sufficient, or, being present, shall refuse to strike, the Congress shall proceed to nominate three persons out of each State, and the Secretary of Congress shall strike in behalf of such party absent or refusing; and the judgment and sentence of the court to be appointed, in the manner before prescribed, shall be final and conclusive; and if any of the parties shall refuse to submit to the authority of such court, or to appear or defend their claim or cause, the court shall nevertheless proceed to pronounce sentence or judgment, which shall in like manner be final and decisive, the judgment or sentence and other proceedings being in either case transmitted to Congress, and lodged among the acts of Congress for the security of the parties concerned: provided that every commissioner, before he sits in judgment, shall take an oath, to be administered by one of the judges of the Supreme or Superior Court of the State where the cause shall he tried, *"well and truly to hear ad determine the matter in question according to the best of his judgment, without favor, affection, or hope of reward,"* provided also that no State shall be deprived territory for the benefit of the United States.

All controversies concerning the private right of soil, claimed under different grants of two or more States, whose jurisdictions as they may respect such lands and the States which passed such grants are adjusted, the said grants or either of them being at the same time claimed to have originated antecedent to such settlement of jurisdiction, shall, on the petition of either party to the Congress of the United States, be finally determined as near as may be in the same manner as is before prescribed for deciding disputes respecting territorial jurisdiction between different States.

The United States in Congress assembled shall also have the sole and exclusive right and power of regulating the alloy and value of coin struck by their own authority, or by that of the respective States—fixing the standard of weights and measures throughout the United States—regulating the trade and *man*aging all affairs with the Indians, not members of any of the States, provided that the legislative right of any State within its own limits be not infringed or violated-establishing and regulating post-offices from one State to another, throughout all the United States, and exacting such postage on the papers passing through the same as may be requisite to defray the expenses of the said office—appointing all officers of the land forces in the service of the United States, excepting regimental officers-appointing all the officers of the naval forces, and commissioning all officers whatever in the service of the United States—making rules for the government and regulation of the said land and naval forces, and directing their operations.

The United States in Congress assembled shall have authority to appoint a committee, to sit in the recess of Congress, to be denominated "A Committee of the States," and to consist of one delegate from each State; to appoint such other committees and civil of officers as 'nay be necessary for managing the general affairs of the United States under their direction; and to appoint one of their number to preside. provided that no person be allowed to serve in the office of president more than one year in any term of three years—to ascertain the necessary sums of money to be raised for

the service of the United States, and to appropriate and apply the same for defraying the public expenses—to borrow money, or emit bills on the credit of the United States, transmitting every half-year to the respective States an account of the sums of money so borrowed or emitted-to build and equip a navy-to agree upon the number of land forces, and to make requisitions from each State for its quota, in proportion to the number of white inhabitants in such State; which requisition shall be binding, and thereupon the legislature of each State shall appoint the regimental officers, raise the men, and clothe, arm, and equip them in a soldier-like manner, at the expense of the United States, and the officers and men so clothed, armed, and equipped shall march to the place appointed, and within the time agreed on by the United States in Congress assembled; but if the United States in Congress assembled shall, on consideration of circumstances, judge proper that any State should not raise men, or should raise a smaller number than its quota, and that any other State should raise a greater number of men than the quota thereof, such extra number shall be raised, officered, clothed, armed, and equipped in the same manner as the quota of such State, unless the legislature of such State shall judge that such extra number cannot be safely spared out of the same, in which case they shall raise, officer, clothe, arm, and equip as many of such extra number as they judge can be safely spared: and the officers and men, so clothed, armed, and equipped shall march to the place appointed, and within the time agreed on, by the United States in Congress assembled.

The United States in Congress assembled shall never engage in a war, nor grant letters of marque and reprisal in time of peace, nor enter into any treaties or alliances, nor coin money, nor regulate the value thereof, nor ascertain the sums and expenses necessary for the defence and welfare of the United States, or any of them, nor emit bills, nor borrow money on the credit of the United States, nor. appropriate money, nor agree upon the number of vessels of war to be built or purchased, or the number of land or sea forces to be raised, nor appoint a commander-in-chief of the army or navy, unless nine States assent to the same; nor shall a question on any other point, except for adjourning from day to day, be determined, unless by the votes of a majority of the United States in Congress assembled.

The Congress of the United States shall have power to adjourn to any time within the year, and to any place within the United States, so that no period of adjournment be for a longer duration than the space of six months, and shall publish the journal of their proceedings monthly, except such parts thereof relating to treaties, alliances, or military operations, as in their judgment require secrecy, and the yeas and nays of the delegates of each State on any question shall be entered on the journal when it is desired by any delegate; and the delegates of a State, or any of them, at his or their request, shall be furnished with a transcript of the said journal, except such parts as are above excepted to lay before the legislatures of the several States.

Article Ten

The Committee of the States, or any nine of them, shall be authorized to execute, in the recess of Congress, such of the powers of Congress as the United States in Congress assembled, by the consent of nine States, shall from time to time think expedient to vest them with: provided that no power be delegated to the said Committee, for the exercise of which, by the Articles of Confederation, the voice of nine States in the Congress of the United States assembled is requisite.

Article Eleven

CANADA, acceding to this Confederation, and joining in the measures of the United States, shall be admitted into and entitled to all the advantages of this Union; but no other colony shall be admitted into the same, unless such admission be agreed to by nine States.

Article Twelve

All bills of credit emitted, moneys borrowed, and debts contracted by or under the authority of Congress before the assembling of the United States in pursuance of the present Confederation, shall be deemed and considered as a charge against the United States, for payment and satisfaction whereof the said United States and the public faith are hereby solemnly pledged.

Article Thirteen

Every State shall abide by the determinations of the United States in Congress assembled on all questions which by this Confederation are submitted to them. And the Articles of this Confederation shall be inviolably observed by every State, and the Union shall be perpetual; nor shall any alteration at any time hereafter be made in any of them, unless such alteration be agreed to in a Congress of the United States, and be afterwards confirmed by the legislatures of every State.

AND WHEREAS it hath pleased the Great Governor of the world to incline the hearts of the legislatures we respectfully represent in Congress to approve of and to authorize to ratify the mid Articles of Confederation and perpetual Union, Know Ye, That we, the undersigned delegates, by virtue of the power and authority to us given for that purpose, do by these presents, in the name and in behalf of our respective constituents, fully and entirely ratify and confirm each and every of the said Articles of Confederation and perpetual Union, and all and singular the matters and things therein contained: and we do further. solemnly plight and engage the faith of our respective constituents that they dial! abide by the determinations of the United States in Congress assembled, on all questions which by the said Confederation are submitted to them. And that the Articles thereof shall be inviolably observed by the States we respectively represent, and the Union shall be perpetual.

George Washington

Bibliography

United States Constitution: 18th and 19th Century Publications
Books

Ames, Herman Vandenburg (1865-1935), *The proposed amendments to the Constitution of the United States during the first century of its history.* Reprint of the 1896 ed. B. Franklin, New York, 1970.

Andrews, Israel Ward (1815-1888), *Manual of the Constitution of the United States.* Wilson, Hinkle & Co., Cincinnati, c1874.

Bayard, James A., Asheton, James, *A brief exposition of the Constitution of the United States: with an appendix . . ., and a copious index.* Hogan & Thompson, Philadelphia, 1845. F.B. Rothman & Co., Littleton, Co., 1992.

Bouvier, John (1787-1851), *A law dictionary,; adapted to the constitution and laws of the United States of America, and of the several states of the American union: with references to the civil and other systems of foreign law.* 15th ed., J. B. Lippincott & Co., Philadelphia, 1883.

Brownson, Orestes A., (1803-1876), *The American Republic: its Constitution, tendencies, and destiny.* College & University Press, New Haven, c1972.

Chipman, Nathaniel (1752-1843), *Principles of government;; a treatise on free institutions, including the Constitution of the United States.* Reprint of the 1833 ed. Da Capo Press, New York, 1970.

Cooper, Thomas (1759-1839), *Two essays: On the foundation of civil government. On the Constitution of the United States.* Press, Reprint of the 1826 ed. Da Capo, New York, 1970.

Curtis, George Ticknor, (1812-1894), *Constitutional history of the United States, from their Declaration of Independence to the close of their Civil War.* Da Capo Press, New York, c1889-96, 1974.

Du Ponceau, Peter Stephen (1760-1844), *A brief view of the Constitution of the United States, addressed to the Law Academy of Philadelphia.* Da Capo Press, New York, c1834, 1974.

Fisher, Sidney George, (1809-1871), *The trial of the Constitution.* Da Capo Press, New York, 1972.

Ford, Paul Leicester (1865-1902), *Essays on the Constitution of the United States, published during its discussion by the people, 1787-1788.* Reprint of the 1892 ed. B. Franklin, New York,

Ford, Paul Leicester (1865-1902), *Pamphlets on the Constitution of the United States; published during its discussion by the people, 1787-1788.* Reprint of the 1888 ed. B. Franklin, New York, 1971.

Hamilton, Alexander, Hamilton, John C., *The works of Alexander Hamilton: comprising his correspondence, and his political and official writings, exclusive of the Federalist, . . .* J. F. Trow, printer, New York, 1850-51.

Harding, Samuel B. (1866-1927), *The contest over the ratification of the Federal Constitution in the State of Massachusetts.* First published in 1896 as v. 2 of the Harvard historical studies. Da Capo Press, New York, 1970.

Jameson, J. Franklin (1859-1937), *Essays in the constitutional history of the United States in the formative period, 1775-1789.* Reprint of the 1889 ed. Da Capo Press, New York, 1970.

Rawle, William (1759-1836), *A view of the Constitution of the United States of America.* Reprint of the 1829 ed. Da Capo Press, New York, 1970.

Scott, E. H., *The Federalist and other constitutional papers.* Scott, Foresman, Chicago, 1894.

Upshur, Abel Parker, (1790-1844), *A brief enquiry into the true nature and character of our Federal Government; being a review of Judge Story's Commentaries on the Constitution of the U. S.* Da Capo Press, New York, 1971.

19th century legal treatises

Andrews, Israel Ward (1815-1888), Homer Morris, *Manual of the Constitution of the United States.* no. 26200-26204. American Book Co., NY, c1900.

Burr, Charles C. (1817-1883), *The history of the Union and of the Constitution; being the substance of three lectures on the colonial, revolutionary, and constitutional periods of American history : with an appendix . . .* 3rd ed. no. 27421-27422. Van Evrie, Horton, New York, 1863.

The Constitution a pro-slavery compact, or, Extracts from the Madison papers, etc. 3rd ed. no. 30699-30701. American Anti-Slavery Society, NY, 1856.

The Federalist; a commentary on the Constitution of the United States: a collection of essays. no. 27220-27228. J. B. Lippincott, Philadelphia, 1864.

The Federalist; a commentary on the Constitution of the United States: a collection of essays. no. 27467-27476. J. B. Lippincott, Philadelphia, 1865.

The Federalist; a commentary on the Constitution of the United States: a collection of essays. no. 30578-30586. J. B. Lippincott, Philadelphia, 1866.

The Federalist; a commentary on the Constitution of the United States: a collection of essays. no. 35871-35879. J. B. Lippincott, Philadelphia, 1868.

The Federalist; a commentary on the Constitution of the United States: a collection of essays. no. 30057-30065. J. B. Lippincott, Philadelphia, 1871.

The Federalist; a commentary on the Constitution of the United States: a collection of essays. no. 30074-30082. J. B. Lippincott, Philadelphia, 1882.

The Federalist, a commentary on the Constitution of the United States, a collection of essays. no. 27198-27206. J. B. Lippincott, Philadelphia, 1885.

Fulton, John (1834-1907) *Free government in England and America; containing the Great Charter, the Petition of Right, the Bill of Rights, the Federal Constitution.* no. 30558-30564. Carleton, New York, 1864.

Hopkins, John Henry (1792-1868), *The American citizen; his rights and duties, according to the spirit of the Constitution of the United States.* no. 1234-1238. Pudney & Russell, New York, 1857.

Jameson, J. Franklin (1859-1937), *Essays in the constitutional history of the United States in the formative period, 1775-1789.* no. 25016-25019. Houghton, Mifflin, Boston, 1889.

Oliver, Benjamin L. (1788-1843), *The rights of an American citizen; with a commentary on state rights, and on the Constitution and policy of the United States.* no. 26751-26755. Marsh, Capen & Lyon; P.H. Nicklin & T. Johnson, Boston, Philadelphia, 1832.

Scott, E. H. *Federalist.* no. 26796-26806. Albert, Scott & Co., Chicago, 1894.

Van Nest, G. Willett (1852-1916), *Impeachable offences under the Constitution of the United States.* no. 41528. s.n., New York ? , 1882.

United States Constitution: 20th Century Publications

Books

Anderson, Thornton, *Creating the Constitution: the Convention of 1787 and the first Congress.* Pennsylvania State University Press, University Park, Pennsylvania, 1993.

Beeman, Richard R., Botein, Stephen, and Carter, Edward Carlos, *Beyond confederation: origins of the Constitution and American national identity.* University of North Carolina Press, Chapel Hill, c1987.

Belz, Herman, Hoffman, Ronald, and Albert, Peter J., *To form a more perfect Union: the critical ideas of the Constitution.* United States Capitol Historical Society by the University Press of Virginia, Charlottesville, 1992.

Bernstein, Richard B., *Are we to be a nation?: the making of the Constitution.* Harvard University Press, Cambridge, Massachusetts, 1987.

Beth, Loren P., *The development of the American Constitution, 1877-1917.* Harper & Row, New York, 1971.

Beyond confederation: origins of the Constitution and American national identity. University of North Carolina Press, Chapel Hill, 1987.

Bibliography of original meaning of the United States Constitution. U.S. Department of Justice, Office of Legal Policy, Federal Justice Research Program, Washington, D. C., 1988.

Bloom, Sol, *The story of the Constitution.* National Archives, Washington, 1986.

Bradford, Melvin E., *Founding Fathers: brief lives of the framers of the United States Constitution.* University Press of Kansas, Lawrence, Kansas, 1994.

Brown, Robert Eldon, *Reinterpretation of the formation of the American Constitution.* Boston University Press, Boston, 1963.

Burdick, Charles Kellogg (1883-1940), *The law of the American Constitution; its origin and development.* G.P. Putman's sons, New York, London, 1922.

Corwin, Edward S., Peltason, J.W., *Corwin & Peltason's understanding the constitution.* 13th ed., Harcourt Brace College Publishers, Fort Worth, 1994.

Crews, Kenneth D., *Edward S. Corwin and the American Constitution: a bibliographical analysis.* Greenwood Press, Westport, Connecticut, 1985.

Currie, David P., *The Constitution in Congress: the Federalist period 1789-1801.* University of Chicago Press, Chicago, 1997.

The debates in the Federal Convention of 1787, which framed the Constitution of the United States of America. Prometheus Books, Buffalo, 1987.

Eidelberg, Paul, *The philosophy of the American Constitution; a reinterpretation of the intentions of the Founding Fathers.* Free Press, New York, 1968.

Farber, Daniel A., *A history of the American constitution.* West Publishing Co., St. Paul, c1990.

Ferguson, E. James, *Confederation, constitution, and early national period, 1781-1815.* AHM Pub. Corp., Northbrook, Illinois, 1975.

Hickok, Eugene W., McDowell, Garl L., Costopoulos, Philip J., and Sandoz, Ellis, *Our peculiar security: the written Constitution and limited government.* Rowman & Littlefield, Lanham, Maryland, c1993.

Hoffmann, Daniel N., *Our elusive Constitution: silences, paradoxes, priorities.* State University of New York Press, New York, 1997.

Janosik, Robert J., *The American Constitution: an annotated bibliography.* Salem Press, Pasadena, California, c1991.

Jensen, Merrill, *The making of the American Constitution.* Van Nostrand, Princeton, 1964. R.E. Krieger Publishing Co., Huntington, New York, 1979.

Johnson, Allen (1870-1931), *Readings in American constitutional history, 1776-1876.* Houghton Mifflin Company, Boston, New York, c1912.

Jones, Robert Francis, *The formation of the Constitution.* Holt, Rinehart and Winston, New York, 1971.

Kaminski, John P., and Leffler, Richard, *Creating the Constitution: a history in documents.* Center for the Study of the American Constitution, University of Wisconsin, Madison, 1991.

Kelly, Alfred Hinsey, *The American Constitution . . .* 6th ed. Norton, NY, 1983.

Kelly, Alfred Hinsey, *Foundations of freedom in the American Constitution.* Books for Libraries Press, Freeport, New York, c1958, 1972.

Ketcham, Ralph, *Framed for posterity: the enduring philosophy of the Constitution.* University Press of Kansas, Lawrence, Kansas, c1993.

Levy, Leonard Williams, *Essays on the making of the Constitution.* Oxford University Press, New York, 1969.

Levy, Leonard Williams, Karst, Kenneth L., and Mahoney, Dennis J, *Encyclopedia of the American Constitution.* Macmillan Pub. Co., New York, 1986.

Levy, Leonard W., and Mahoney, Dennis J., *The Framing and ratification of the Constitution.* Macmillan; Collier Macmillan, New York; London, 1987.

Levy, Leonard Williams, *Seasoned judgments: the American constitution, rights, and history.* Transaction Publishers, New Brunswick, New Jersey, c1995.

Lutz, Donald S. *Colonial origins of the American Constitution: a documentary history.* Liberty Fund, Indianapolis, Indiana, 1998.

Martin, Charles Emanuel, *An introduction to the study of the American Constitution; a study of the formation and development of the American constitutional system and of the ideals upon which it is based, with illustrative materials.* Oxford university press, New York, etc., 1926.

Morison, Samuel Eliot (1887-1976), *Sources and documents illustrating the American Revolution, 1764-1788, and the formation of the Federal Constitution.* 2d ed. Oxford University Press, London, c1965, 1977 printing.

Morris, Richard Brandon, *The forging of the Union, 1781-1789.* Harper & Row, New York, 1987.

A necessary evil?: slavery and the debate over the Constitution. Madison House, Madison, Wisconsin, 1995.

Onuf, Peter S., *The Federal Constitution.* The new American nation, 1775-1820; v. 5. Garland Pub., New York, 1991.

Onuf, Peter S., *Ratifying, amending, and interpreting the Constitution.* The new American nation, 1775-1820 ; v. 6. Garland Pub., New York, 1991.

Paul, Ellen F., Dickman, Howard, *Liberty, property, and the foundations of the American Constitution.* State University of New York Press, Albany, 1989.

Riemer, Neal, *James Madison: creating the American Constitution.* Congressional Quarterly, Washington, D.C., 1986.

Riker, William H., *The strategy of rhetoric: campaigning for the American constitution.* Yale University Press, New Haven, Connecticut, 1996.

Rossiter, Clinton L., *1787: The Grand Convention.* [Macmillan, New York, 1966] reissue W.W. Norton & Co., Inc., 1987.

Rossum, Ralph A., and McDowell, Gary L., *The American founding: politics, statesmanship, and the Constitution.* Kennikat Press, Port Washington, New York, 1981.

Rutland, Robert Allen, *The American solution: origins of the U.S. Constitution.* Library of Congress, Washington, 1987.

Rutland, Robert Allen, *"Well acquainted with books": the founding framers of 1787: with James Madison's list of books for Congress.* Library of Congress, Washington D.C., 1987.

Sanderlin, George William, *A hoop to the barrel: the making of the American Constitution.* Coward, McCann & Geoghegan, New York, 1974.

Schechter, Stephen L., and Bernstein, Richard B., *Roots of the Republic: American founding documents interpreted.* Madison House, Madison, 1990.

Schwartz, Bernard, *From confederation to nation: the American Constitution, 1835-1877.* Johns Hopkins University Press, Baltimore, 1973.

Scott, James Brown (1866-1943), *James Madison's notes of debates in the Federal convention of 1787 and their relation to a more perfect society of nations.* Oxford University Press, American Branch, New York, 1918.

Sellers, M. N. S., *American republicanism: Roman ideology in the United States Constitution.* New York University Press, New York, 1994.

Smith, James Allen (1860-1926), *The spirit of American government: a study of the Constitution : its origin, influence and relation to democracy.* Macmillan, New York, New York, 1907.

Sorenson, Leonard R., *Madison on the "general welfare" of America: his consistent constitutional vision.* Rowman & Littlefield, Lanham, Maryland, 1995.

Statutory requirements for the teaching of United States history and the principles of the United States Constitution. American Bar Foundation, Chicago, 1960.

Stevens, Richard G., *The American Constitution and its provenance.* Rowman & Littlefield Publishers, Lanham, 1997.

Stimson, Frederic Jesup (1855-1943), *The American constitution: the national powers: the rights of the states: the liberties of the people: Lowell Institute lectures delivered at Boston, October-November 1907.* C. Scribner's, New York, 1908.

Supplement to Max Farrand's The records of the Federal Convention of 1787. Yale University Press, New Haven, Connecticut, 1987.

Wade, Martin Joseph, (1861-1931), *The short Constitution ...; being a consideration of the Constitution of the United State, with particular reference to the guaranties of life, liberty, and poperty contained therein, sometimes designated the Bill of rights.* 4th and rev. ed. American Citizen Publishing Co., Cedar Rapids, Iowa, c1921.

Walker, Joseph Burbeen, *Birth of the federal Constitution: a history of the New Hampshire Convention for the investigation, discussion and decision of the federal Constitution and of the Old North meeting-house of Concord, in which it was ratified by the ninth state, and thus rendered operative, at one o'clock p.m., on Saturday, the 21st day of June, 1788.* Cupples & Hurd, Boston, 1888.

Waters, Willard Otis, *Check list of American laws, charters and constitutions of the 17th and 18th centuries in the Huntington library.* Henry E. Huntington Library and Art Gallery, San Marino, California, 1936.

Wheeler, Everett Pepperrell, *Daniel Webster, the expounder of the Constitution.* F.B. Rothman, Littleton, Colorado, 1986.

Wood, Gordon S., *The Confederation and the Constitution: the critical issues.* Little, Brown, Boston, 1973.

Young, Alfred Fabian, *The debate over the Constitution, 1787-1789.* Rand McNally, Chicago, 1965.

Thesis

Hemberger, Suzette, "Creatures of the constitution; the Federalist Constitution and the shaping of American politics." Dissertation thesis (Ph.D)— Princeton University, 1994.

Federalist/Anti-federalist Papers

Books

Bailyn, Bernard, *The Debate on the Constitution: Federalist and antifederalist speeches, articles, and letters during the struggle over ratification, volume 1.* Library of Congress, Washington, D.C., 1993.

Barlow, J. Jackson, Mahoney, Dennis J., and West, John G. *The New Federalist papers.* University Press of America, Lanham, Maryland, 1988.

Boyd, Steven R., *The politics of opposition: antifederalists and the acceptance of the Constitution.* KTO Press, Millwood, New York, c1979.

The constitutional convention debates and the Anti-Federalist papers. New American Library, New York, 1986.

Cooke, Jacob Ernest, *The Federalist, American state papers*. Franklin Library, Franklin Center, Pennsylvania, 1984.

Furtwangler, Albert, *The authority of Publius: a reading of the Federalist papers*. Cornell University Press, Ithaca, New York, 1984.

Grofman, Bernard, and Wittman, Donald, *The Federalist Papers and the new institutionalism*. Agathon Press, New York, 1989.

Kaminski, John P., and Leffler, Richard, *Federalists and antifederalists: the debate over the ratification of the Constitution*. Published for the Center for the Study of the American Constitution by Madison House, Madison, 1989.

Kesler, Charles, *Saving the revolution: the Federalist papers and the American founding*. Free Press, Collier Macmillan, New York, 1987.

Ketcham, Ralph Louis, *The constitutional convention debates and the Anti-Federalist papers*. New American Library, New York, 1986.

Legacy of the Federalist Papers... Harvard Society for Law and Public Policy, Cambridge, Massachusetts, 1997.

Mace, George, *Locke, Hobbes, and the Federalist papers: an essay on the genesis of the American political heritage*. Southern Illinois University Press, Carbondale, 1979.

Main, Jackson Turner, *The antifederalists; critics of the Constitution, 1781-1788*. University of North Carolina Press, Chapel Hill, 1961.

Millican, Edward, *One united people: the Federalist papers and the national idea*. University Press of Kentucky, Lexington, Kentucky, 1990.

Mosteller, Frederick, Wallace, David L. *Applied Bayesian and classical inference: the case of the Federalist papers*. Springer-Verlag, New York, 1984.

Patrick, John J., *James Madison and the Federalist papers*. ERIC Clearinghouse for Social Studies, Social Science Education, Bloomington, Indiana, 1990.

Patrick, John J., *Liberty and order in constitutional government ideas and issues in the federalist papers*. Virginia Jefferson Association, Richmond, 1989.

Patrick, John J., *Teaching the Federalist Papers*. ERIC Clearinghouse for Social Studies, Social Science Education, Bloomington, Indiana, 1988.

Patrick, John J., and Keller, Clair W., *Lessons on the Federalist papers: supplements to high school courses in American history, government, and civics*. Social Studies Development Center, Indiana University, Bloomington, Indiana, 1987.

Pole, J. R., *The American Constitution: for and against: the Federalist and anti-Federalist papers*. Hill and Wang, New York, 1987.

Quinn, Frederick, *The Federalist papers reader and historical documents of our American heritage*. Seven Locks Press, Santa Ana, California, 1997.

Rossiter, Clinton Lawrence, *The Federalist papers*. New American Library, New York, 1961.

Saving the revolution: the Federalist papers and the American founding. Free Press; Collier Macmillan, New York, London, 1987.

Taylor, Quentin P., *The essential Federalist: a new reading of the Federalist papers*. Madison House, Madison, Wisconsin, 1998.

Wilbur, James B., *The Federalist papers: explanation and defense of ideas and issues in the U.S. Constitution: proceedings of the Nineteenth Conference on Value Inquiry, State University College of Arts & Science at Geneseo*. State University College of Arts & Science at Geneseo, Geneseo, 1988.

Index

Great Britain, island helps 8[12]
militia defends 46[9]
militia not threat 29
partisanship strengthens 50[10]
people source of power 37[6]
prosperity 2[12]
protection of 1[5], 62[8-9, 15], 85[1,3]
—against federal usurpation 28[8-end]
public safety, balance with 26[2]
representatives: numerous 37[6]
representatives: small number 55[7-9]
republic promotes 14[12], 37[6]
vs. safety 8[2], 26[2]
specious warnings to incite passions16[3]
separation of powers imperative 9[2-3],
    47[2-3,8], 78[8]
vs. stable government 37[6-7]
term, short 37[6]
trial by jury guards 83[12,17-18]
liberty, endangered 55[7,9], 57[12-13,21],
    61[1,3-4]
by abusing liberty 63[16]
by civil appointments 55[7-8]
by encroaching legislature 48[5]
by executive council 70[22]
by militia 29
by mutable laws 62[15], 63[7]
presidential term limits 72[13]
Locrian, republic 38[2]
Lycia 16[1], confederate republic 9[17]
weak federal authority 45[4]
Lysander 25[10]

———

Mably, Abbe', see *Greek republics*
Macedonia, see *Greek republics*
war with Greece 18[6]
Philip of Macedon 18[9-10,18]
Magna Charta 84[8]
majority
constitution, ratify 39[11]
country's size effects 10[20]
dangers of 10[11-12], 16[4], 51[10],
    71[2], 73[6], 78[18]
—Senate protects against 63[7-9]
overbearing nature 10[1,21], 43[18],
    60[2]
overruled by minority 22[9-11], 75[6]
rule 10[8-12], 22[7-13], 39[15], 58[15]
super majority
—guard against special interests 58[15]
two-thirds majority 22[7-13], 75[6-7]
—easier to corrupt 22[10-13]
majority vs. super majority 22[7-13],
    58[15], 75[6-7]
Maryland
constitution 63[18]

dispute over Vermont 7[4]
economic issues 21[6]
governor 69[4]
judicial system 83[19]
legislature 24[6]; senate 39[5], 63[18]
separation of powers 47[16]
supreme court, State 81[7]
Massachusetts
executive veto 73[15]
governor of 57[21], 69[6]; veto 69[5]
judicial system 81[19], 83[19]
—judges' salary 79[1]
legislative districts 57[19-20]
legislature 24[6]; senate 63[18]
—impeachment court 66[3]
—number of members 55[2]
military, peace time 25[9]
separation of powers 47[10]
Shay's rebellion 6[7,19], 21[4], 25[9]
—sedition 74[4], troops repressed 28[3]
supreme court, State 81[7]
Vermont, dispute over 7[4]
mathematical theorems,compared to
    truths in behavioral sciences 31[1-3]
merchants, in Congress 60[5-9]
military, see *defense*
militia, see *defense*
Milot, Abbe'18[16]
ministers, public 42[1,3], 69[9]
minority
corruption easier 22[10]
—foreign corruption 22[12-13]
detrimental 22[9-11]
faction 10[11]
foreign corruption 22[12-13]
overrule majority 22[9-11], 75[6]
protecting rights of 51[10]
see *faction*
rule 22[7-13], 75[6-7]
State suffrage 22[7-9]
super majority 58[15]
money
bills, House originates 66[7]
coin, regulate 42[10,14]
—States can't issue 44[2], 80[3,13]
counterfeiting 42[15]
government needs 30[2]
paper money 10[22]
turnover increases wealth 12[3]
monopoly, high import duties 35[2]
Montesquieu
confederate republic 9[4-14], 43[14]
separation of powers 47[4-5, 7-8]
morality can't control political injustice 10[12]
morals, political 31[1-3]
multiculturalism 62[2]

impeachment
—mixes legislative, judiciary 66[2-3]
—Senate tries 38[7], 66, 81[3]
individuals, federal power over 38[7],
16[7], 17
—hurt States 45[2], 46[1]
—some additional needed 22[18]
—too much 41[4,23]
judiciary too powerful 38[7], 78[16]
legislation for States, *want* 16[7]
liberty, danger to 38[7], 85[4]
military enforces national laws 27,29[4]
militia, endangers liberty 29
—national government regulates 29
monarchy, tends towards 38[7]
national, not federal form 39[7-end]
"necessary and proper" 33, 44[11-17]
politicians 1[3]
President 38[7], 67; like monarch 67[3]
—election of 68[1]
—veto, improper control of legislature 73[7]
Senate, too powerful 66[4]
—approves executive appointments
66[8]
—aristocracy, evolve into 63[15]
—equal representation 38[7]
—impeachment, tries 38[7], 66, 81[3]
—treaties, ratifies 66[10]
self-government, people not virtuous
enough for 9[2], 55[9]
separation of powers, not enough 38[7,
9-10], 47, 66[2], 75
slaves, counted for apportionment 54[3]
—importation for 20 more years 38[8]
standing army 24[1-2], 25[2], 26
State powers, usurpation of 31[10-11]
no State supremacy clause 44[19-24]
—no States' rights 38[7], 21[2,5]
taxation, national 31, 33; direct 38[7]
—imports only 30[6]
—national legislature usurping States
31[10-11]
treaties, contrived objections 64[9]
—bad for some States 64[12]
—President makes, Senate approves
38[9], 75
—supreme law 64[10-11]
trial by jury, banned (civil cases) 83[1]
Union too big 1[8], 9[4]
veto 73[7]

oppression
by majority of States 16[4]
by society majority 51[10]
by taxation 10[8], 35[1-3,11], 83[13-16]

Ottoman empire 30[3]

pardons, Presidential 69[6], 74[3-4]
vs. governor, New York 69[6]
treason 74[4]

partisan politics 26[10], 37[2]
argument against executive 67
debates: angry, malignant passions 1[5]
democracy, pure, passions worse 10[13]
impeachments 65[2]
in legislatures 81[6]
necessity of 26[10]
opinions, passions always differ 10[6-7]
public good disregarded 10[1]

parties, political 1

passion
effects national councils 63[2]
government formed to control 15[12]
large assemblies swayed 62[9]
leads to war 16[3]
more influence than policy, justice 6[9]
natural 27[4]
political 65[2]
over reasoning 10[1],20[21], 49[6-7, 10],
50[6], 55[3], 58[14],62[9-10], 63[7-9]
within republic 6[9]

patent 43[2-3]

Peloponnesian War with Greece 18[8]

Pennsylvania
Council of Censors 1783 48[9-15],
50[3-11]
executive 47[14]
judicial system 83[19]
legislature, state
—constitution violated 48[9]
—district 57[19-20]
—impeachment court 66[3]
—ratio constituents/legislator 55[2-3]
military, peace time 25[9]
pensions, government employees 79[6]
self-defense 25[9]
separation of powers 48[14]
supreme court, State 81[7]
troops repressed disorder 28[3]
Wyoming, dispute over 7[3]

people
control government 28[5]
decide what is unconstitutional 49[3]
divide against themselves 4[17]
happiness, good government 62[12]
loyalty, State vs. federal 46[1-5]
see *power, people source of*
preserve State/federal balance of
powers 31[12]

Pericles 6[4]

Persian War see *Greek republics*

Petition of Rights 84[8]

philosophical debates 31[1-2]

pardon **69**[3,6], **74**[3-4]
qualifications, age **64**[4]
qualities **64**[4], **68**[8], **75**[4], **76**[4]
—experience **72**[8]
—lawbreaker vs. untrustworthy **70**[15]
—untrustworthy **62**[9]
Representatives, coercing **55**[9]
responsibility **64**[14-15], **69**[4], **71**[1]
Senators, never appoints **67**[10]
state-of-the-union **77**[9]
term 4 years **39**[5], **69**[3], **71-72**, **79**[2]
—vs. judicial term, pay **79**[1-2]
term limits **71**[1], **72**, **85**[2]
—effects behavior **72**[4-6]
treason **74**[4]
treaties **64**, **66**[10-13], **69**[7], **75**, **77**[10]
veto power **51**[6], **69**[5], **73**[4-end]
—New York's successful **73**[14]
press
freedom **41**[24], **84**[10-11], **85**[2]
—State constitutions **84**[11]
influences national discussion **2**[11]
information about government **84**[14]
privacy rights 44[6]
property
ability to acquire **10**[6]
Constitution protects **85**[1,3]
division of, equal **10**[22]
—unequal **10**[6,7,22]
leading cause of faction **10**[7]
government's protection of **54**[8-11]
owners **10**[6-8], **35**[8-9], **60**[5-10]
protection of **54**[8], **85**[1,3]
—in States **54**[8]
rights **10**[6,13], **54**[2-6,8-11]
—originate from people **6**[6]
taxes **21**[6-8,11], **36**[7]
—relationship to **54**[2-3]
value **21**[11]
—decreases with bad government **15**[3]
—laws effecting **62**[16]
as measure of wealth **21**[6,11]
prosperity
bills of credit, prohibition **44**[5]
Constitution will promote **85**[5]
liberty **2**[12]
national, commerce **15**[3], **60**[9]
unity **2**[14]
psychology, see *human nature*
"public good"
politicians and **59**[10], **62**[8], **71**[2]

qualifications, see *President, Senators, Representatives*
national vs. state officials **3**[8]
quotas and requisitions 15[6-12,15]

see *legislation for States*
army enlistment **22**[5-6]
taxes **21**[6-8],**22**[6],**25**[4],**30**[4-7],**36**[10]

ratification 85[5-6], **39**[11], **40**[13], **43**[27-31]
people didn't ratify Articles **22**[19]
reapportionment new, growing States **58**[11]
reasoning vs. passion 49[10], **50**[6], **55**[3], **63**[7-9]
rebellions, revolts
against federal laws by States **16**
use force to control **28**
regulations, laws **62**[1,12-18]
benefiting the few at expense of many **62**[16]
definition, "rule of action" **62**[15-18]
stifling business **62**[17]
religion/religious
civil rights, same security as **51**[10]
debates **31**[2]
inspiring political factions **10**[22]
mysteries **31**[2]
opinions **10**[7]
no religious test for government officials **44**[24], **52**[2]. **57**[6]
sect as political faction **10**[22]
representation 35, 52[5]
distrust of representatives **26**[11]
conflicting State demands **37**[12-13]
representatives, talents needed **35**[6]
Representatives 35[5-11], **52, 57**
(U.S. House of Representatives)
citizens, relationship with **52**[4], **57**[9-10,14]
see *election*
electors (voters) **10**[19], **52**[2]
elite class, from **57**
formerly State legislators **56**[6]
knowledge required **56**
—State issues **36**[3,6], **53**[5], **56**[4-6]
legislation, less knowledge of **62**[10]
live under their own laws **35**[10], **57**[12,13]
militia, knowledge of **53**[5]
number **35**[5-11], **54, 55, 56**
—grow with population **58**
oath to support Constitution **44**[24-26]
occupations of, private sector **35**[5-11], **36**[1-2], **62**[10]
—learned professions, manufacturers, merchants **35**[6,9]
—not lifetime politicians **62**[10]
—property owners **35**[8-9]
qualifications **52**[2], **62**[2]

support of **14**
too large **1**[9]
United Nations
psychology of league of nations **15**
non-compliance by member nations **15**[14]
United States
area will double soon **38**[10]
area (boundaries) defined by peace treaty **14**[6]
culturally united **2**[5]
example for other nations **20**[23]
geographically united **2**[4]
international reputation **63**[1-3]
unique "American" spirit **14**[12]
usurpation; see *abuse of power*
area, small, easier **10**[17-end]
citizen's ability to stop **28**[6-7]
citizen's revolt if rulers usurp **60**[12]
executive powers **48**[12]
federal usurp State authority **17, 33**[7], **44**[17]
by legislature **25**[6], **48**[4-5,10], **49, 50**
—State legislatures, examples **48**[7]
—Pennsylvania **48**[9]
—Senate as block **62**[8]
—Virginia **48**[8]
military expansion **25**[6], **26**[11-13]
militia **29**[12]
people stop **46**[10]
Senate, States must conspire to do **60**[4]
separation of powers blocks **49**
size reduces ruler usurpation **28**[7,9]
by State ruler **28**[6], **85**[3]
States defense against **28, 46**[7-10]
—federal help **21**[4]
by States **16, 33**[5]
trial by jury **48**[11]
written barriers inadequate **48**[3]

Venice
legislative despots **48**[8]
not republic **39**[3]
Vermont: dispute over territory **7**[4]
veto, executive **51**[6], **66**[2], **69**[5], **73**[4-end]
defends against bad laws **73**[5-6, 8-9]
improper control over legislature **73**[7]
Massachusetts **47**[10]
New York's successful **73**[14]
Vice-President: election of **68**[9-10]
Virginia 52[7]
amendment proposed **40**[16]

governor impeachable after term **39**[5]
see ***Jefferson***
legislative usurpation of powers **48**[7-8]
legislature, number of members **55**[3]
—ratio constituents/legislator **55**[2-3]
senate term 4 years **39**[5]
seacoast vulnerable **41**[20]
separation of powers **47**[17]
supreme court, State **81**[7]
voter
apathy **61**[2], **64**[3]
candidate's qualifications **35**[5-11]
federal congressional elections **61**
freedom **10**[18]
New York State elections **61**[2,3,6]
qualifications **35**[8], **52**[2], **54**[7], **57**[5], **60**[11], **64**[3], **68**
rights **60**
—if abridged, States revolt **60**[2]

"Wag the Dog" 25[6]
war to hide personal behavior **6**[4]
war 6
allies **22**[11]
causes of **3**[6-7, 12-15], **8**[1-3], **80**[6]
—commerce **4**[4-9], **6, 7**[5-6]
—Europe controls American rivers **4**[8]
—jealousy **4**[9-10,15]
—"just causes of war" **3**[6-7,12-15], **80**[6]
declare **41**[6,8]
funding **30**[8]
offensive, none **34**[5]
of parchment **7**[9]
passions lead to **6**[9]
peace rare **34**[5]
union provides security from **3**
Washington, D.C. 43[4-5]
too far from States **84**[13-15]
wealth, national 21[6-7,11]
commerce increases **15**[3]
commerce, national **60**[9]
influence of **54**[9]
not related to land, population **21**[6]
unity **2**[14]
weights and measures 42[10,16]
western territorial disputes 7[2-3]
West Indies 11[4-5]
Wolsey, Cardinal **6**[5]
Wyoming
dispute over territory **7**[3]